D1062801

Religion and the People, 800–1700

Published under the auspices of the
Shelby Cullom Davis Center for Historical Studies,
Princeton University

Religion and the People, 800–1700

Edited by
James Obelkevich

The University of North Carolina Press
Chapel Hill

BR735
R44

© 1979 *The University of North Carolina Press*
All rights reserved
Manufactured in the United States of America
ISBN 0-8078-1332-X
Library of Congress Catalog Card Number 78-7847

Library of Congress Cataloging in Publication data

Main entry under title:

Religion and the people, 800–1700.

   "*Written under the auspices of the Shelby Cullom Davis
Center for Historical Studies, Princeton University.*"
   Includes bibliographical references and index.
   *1. Europe—Religious life and customs—Addresses,
essays, lectures. 2. Sociology, Christian—Europe—
Addresses, essays, lectures. I. Geary, Patrick J.,
1948– II. Obelkevich, James. III. Shelby Cullom
Davis Center for Historical Studies.*
BR735.R44   209'.4   78-7847
ISBN 0-8078-1332-X

Contents

Introduction   3
James Obelkevich

1. The Ninth-Century Relic Trade   8
   A Response to Popular Piety?
   Patrick J. Geary

2. Popular Religion and Holy Shrines   20
   Their Influence on the Origins of the German Reformation
   and Their Role in German Cultural Development
   Lionel Rothkrug

3. Cheese and Worms   87
   The Cosmos of a Sixteenth-Century Miller
   Carlo Ginzburg

4. The Catholic Response to Protestantism   168
   Church Activity and Popular Piety in Rouen, 1560–1600
   Philip Benedict

5. The Wonderyear   191
   Reformed Preaching and Iconoclasm in the Netherlands
   Phyllis Mack

6. The Witches of the Cambrésis   221
   The Acculturation of the Rural World
   in the Sixteenth and Seventeenth Centuries
   Robert Muchembled

7. Witch Hunting and the Domino Theory   277
   H. C. Erik Midelfort

Notes   289

Index   327

Religion and the People, 800–1700

Introduction

James Obelkevich

These essays, united by their common theme, are also united by their common link with the Davis Seminar at Princeton University—the research seminar associated with the Princeton History Department and sponsored since 1969 by the Shelby Cullom Davis Center for Historical Studies. The purpose of the seminar is to foster work on some general topic of relatively recent scholarly concern by providing a forum for specialists and others interested in the field. The history of popular religion, a new and promising field of inquiry, was chosen as the theme for 1973–74, and this volume is the result. The essays were among those discussed or written at the seminar that year, and the contributors all participated as Visiting Fellows of the Center, as members of the Princeton History Department, or as visitors from other universities.

The essays in this volume, though novel in their subject matter, are eminently traditional in their limits of time and space. They are concerned with western and central Europe, the heartland of Western Christianity, in the medieval and Reformation periods, which remain the "classic" era in its history. While scholarly interest in the nineteenth century is growing (it attracted the second largest group of papers presented to the seminar), the earlier period continues to pose the central questions of the field, both for ecclesiastical history and for the newer history of religion represented in this volume.

What distinguishes these essays is not only a new subject matter, but, more important, new aims and intellectual concerns. The authors have broken with the related discipline of ecclesiastical history and have abandoned its confines and conventions. The older genre has traditionally been preoccupied with the clergy, with the churches' institutional machinery, and with "pure" theology; it has usually been written "from within" and has often shown traces of denominational bias. While popular religion has not been totally neglected, it has been treated as a marginal affair, too often summed up in the twin clichés, the piety of the masses and their ignorance and superstition. The authors of these essays are writing a different kind of history, with a different problematic, a different set of issues and themes. Not only are they "methodological atheists"; they have moved outside the churches into new territory, following the trail of religion into the wider society and culture. Religion appears in these essays less often in its doctrinal or ecclesiastical purity than with the impurities and accretions of particular social contexts. The authors approach their subject from below as well as from above, and they place it in its *Sitz im Leben*; they throw new light on society as well as on religion. The result, even when the explicit concern is with church and clergy, is not so much ecclesiastical history as a variety of social history—a social and cultural history of religion.

A second feature of the work of these authors is the influence of the social sciences, ranging from classic sociology (including Marx) down to contemporary anthropology. From sociology and anthropology they have gained their understanding of some of the basic terms of their discourse: religion itself, magic, ritual, church, sect, secularization, and syncretism, to name a few. If historians concerned with the nineteenth and twentieth centuries have learned most from sociology, these historians of the earlier period have been influenced mainly by anthropology. Anthropologists' studies of magic and witchcraft, for example, and their general accounts of peasant religion provide direct parallels for historians of these subjects in traditional Europe; Clifford Geertz's recent conception of religion as a "cultural system" has been suggestive to historians of religious "mentalities." Yet they have not converted fully to the new anthropological gospel: they preserve in their own occupational culture a sense of religion's social specificities and functionalities and of its capacity for change. Indeed their findings upset many a facile historical generalization dispensed by "armchair" social science, and it is to be hoped that they will exert some influence in the reverse direction, on the disciplines from which they have learned so much.

What conclusions, then, can be drawn from these essays about the current state of work in the field? The first—which emerged more clearly in the seminar discussions than in the essays themselves—is that the search for an "essence" or definition of popular religion is misguided. If a definition is needed, popular religion is simply the religion—or better, the religious phenomena—of the popular classes. The origins of these phenomena may be high or low: they make a subject for research but do not enter into the definition. More fundamental is the question of what is to count as religion. In practice, a broad definition, taking in magic, superstition, pagan beliefs, and private and group heterodoxies appears to work best. It has the cardinal virtue of encouraging historians to view popular religion as the people themselves view it. Before popular religion can be understood at all, it has to be understood in its own terms, not as a failed version of something else. When judged against the external standard set by the clergy, it is too likely to be regarded as a diminution, debasement, or deformation of a "correct" faith. A broad definition is also justified by the fact that religion, which is universal in human society, can exist without a church. The institutional church therefore makes an unavoidable yet also incomplete and misleading model for the study of popular religious life and is best regarded as one setting for religion among many. The historian, then, should take his popular religion as he finds it: ordinarily it can be seen as an amalgam of "high" and "low" elements—orthodox Christianity, folk Christianity, and paganism.

Nearly all of these essays discuss the problem that is at the heart of the subject: the relationship between the religion of the people and the religion of the clergy and the elite. It is apparent that the relationship could vary enormously, from near identity to outright conflict, and that it varied from period to period, for reasons not fully understood. At one extreme, religion in medieval Europe (and later) is often found to have bridged elite and populace, its symbols and rituals expressing the ethos of an entire society and culture. Religious influence flowed downward from the elite but also upward from the peasant majority. This relatively open situation passed, however, in the sixteenth and seventeenth centuries, as the Reformation and Counter-Reformation gathered force. The militant clergy of both faiths sought to impose on the masses what was essentially an elite pattern of religion, inaugurating an era of one-way religious pressure from the top down—and equally an era of increasing resistance and partial conformity from below. This transition, no less central to the history of popular than to that of elite religion, poses some of the most complex problems in the field.

One of the most fundamental of these problems arises from the fact that when the reformers dismantled medieval Christianity, they transformed the definition of religion itself. Protestant and Catholic alike attacked the popular folklorized Christianity inherited from the Middle Ages; magic, in particular, previously tolerated as an inferior form of religion, was condemned as not religious at all, but as antithetical to true religion.[1] At the same time, they shifted the accent from religion as an attitude—as "faith" or "piety" or "religiousness"—to religion as belief. Christianity in their hands hardened and materialized into articles of belief, its defining act becoming intellectual assent to a creed. By the eighteenth century, the process had gone still further, with "Christianity"

1. See the exchange between Hildred Geertz and Keith Thomas in "An Anthropology of Religion and Magic," *Journal of Interdisciplinary History* 6 (1975): 75–76, 95–97.

and "religion" taking on their modern, reified meanings.[2] Thus the religious gap between the educated elite and the popular classes—apparent everywhere, notably in diverging learned and popular conceptions of witchcraft—widened further with the formulation by the elite of a new and narrow understanding of religion itself. This substantive finding carries with it an important methodological lesson. To apply an elite redefinition of religion to the religious life of the peasants and laboring poor, particularly in the earlier centuries, can only distort what continued to be part of an oral culture, more a matter of feeling and doing and of taking for granted than of abstract subscription to theological doctrines.

A second major problem in the field is that of change, both in the short and in the long term. Popular religion, contrary to the assumption that it is part of an immemorial, immobile culture, does change; religious symbols can lose—and gain—meaning; superstition, too, has its history. Yet if change has been documented, it has not been adequately explained. Much is to be attributed to changes in pressure from above, but these "vertical" links have tended to obscure the "horizontal" links between the religion of the people and their wider conditions of life.

Questions of a more general, even philosophical order are raised by the familiar secularization thesis, regarding the direction of religious change in Western and indeed in world culture. At the theoretical level the notion is much disputed, and there is a growing tendency to dismiss it as antireligious ideology, a mere source of confusion. But when stripped of suggestions of inevitability it retains its power to evoke larger themes and issues, and it may be worthwhile to set down some tentative empirical findings that bear on the question. First, modern research reveals that there never was an "age of faith." In every period the majority resisted as well as accepted elite religion: the discovery of deviant folk beliefs and practices, of lukewarmness verging on indifference, not to mention anticlericalism, has alarmed clerical reformers since the advent of Christianity. The church accomplished great things in western Europe: but it never fully Christianized it. And what is more, its incomplete success was apparent long before the Industrial Revolution and was at least as apparent in parts of the countryside as it was in the towns. Popular irreligion —still to be taken into account by the "sociology of unbelief"—is integral to the history of popular religion. A second observation is that religious activity has markedly risen and fallen in historical periods, with varying phases of "desacralization" and "resacralization"; the notion of a "steady state" of religious need or expression seems difficult to maintain. Third, the trend since the Reformation, though not unilinear, has indeed been toward secularization.

2. Wilfred Cantwell Smith, *The Meaning and End of Religion* (New York, 1962), pp. 37–44, 71–77.

For the moment this "macro" question, on the high plane of Western culture, is more answerable, thanks to the quirks of uneven scholarly development, than are a good many questions of the middle range. Perhaps the most important of these—neglected not only in these essays and in the seminar but also in recent scholarship generally, outside of France —is the question of the pace and process of change in popular religious life between 1650 and 1800: between the major phase of the Reformation and Counter-Reformation and the advent of the modern economic and political revolutions.

The lessons of these essays may be cast in the form of a catechism. What is popular religion? First of all, it is religion. To treat it as ignorance, superstition, debasement, or as compensation or mystification, is to misconceive it. No less than the religion of the elite, it is a realm of the sacred, with its own pattern of symbol, ritual, and morality. At the same time, popular religion is popular: it grows out of the experience of the many, expressing their wider outlook and values and often their ambivalence toward a hegemonic faith. For that reason it is perhaps our best point of entry into the mental world of the poor—the mental world we have lost. Finally, popular religion is not static. If it has no essence, it has a history, to which these essays make their contribution.

The Ninth-Century Relic Trade

A Response to Popular Piety?

Patrick J. Geary

If by "popular piety" is meant a uniquely lay religious tradition separate from that of the clergy, then the obstacles to understanding the popular dimensions of religion in the Carolingian period are such that one must approach the subject with enormous care and leave it, when all that can be said has been said, with equally enormous frustration. The first obstacle is the scarcity of useful documentation. All of the sources are Latin texts written by clerics or members of the high aristocracy—direct evidence from the "people" is entirely lacking. When the witnesses speak of the devotions and practices of the laity, they do so either to present what they wish to find in the laity or to condemn practices, popular in origin, that had developed outside the framework of the official church. In both cases the accounts are usually too polemical to provide accurate information on these phenomena, and, without independent evidence, interpreting them is extremely difficult.

The second problem is the deep gulf between the culture of those literate writers and that of the mass of Europeans. The scattered references to "popular" practices that do exist, which will be examined below, indicate that in the eighth and ninth centuries the gap between the tiny elite participating in the so-called Carolingian renaissance and the masses was enormous. Educated monks and bishops, many of them foreigners from England, Ireland, Italy, or Spain, lived in a world apart from that of most of Europe's population and pursued religious and cultural interests that often were quite alien to those of the people, whom many churchmen understood but little.[1] If official Christianity was ever a "hothouse" phenomenon, this was the age.

The final obstacle is the nature of early medieval religion itself. Across Europe, even in the former Roman areas of the Carolingian Empire, Christianity was qualitatively different from the "popular Christianity" of post-Reformation Europe and indeed even from that of the later Middle Ages. Action was more important than belief, cult and liturgy far more important than confession. In brief, religion both for lay masses and the vast majority of clerics was physical, not intellectual; danced, not believed.

For all of these reasons, exclusively lay religious practice (if there be such a thing) must remain extremely obscure in the Carolingian period. However, if by popular piety we can mean those aspects of this danced religion—such as the cult of saints' relics—that were shared by laity and clerics of all social and cultural strata, then a great deal more can be said. Here, we can examine, through writings of the clerical elite and through their efforts to control and direct mass practices, those commonalities and differences within this popular piety. Although not entirely satisfactory, such an effort is valuable and indeed necessary to understand the roots of later medieval popular movements.

The first documented mass participation of Europeans in religious programs took place in the tenth and eleventh centuries, when the laity, noble and peasant, became involved in monastic reform and the peace of God. Scholars such as Bernard Töpfer[2] and Hartmut Hoffmann[3] have recognized the central role of devotion to saints' relics in changing these movements from merely another series of ecclesiastical reforms into genuinely popular mobilizations. Töpfer in particular, in a brilliant Marxist analysis of the relationship between reform and saints' cults, suggests that the monastic exploitation of popular devotion to relics was the specific means by which clerical elites influenced and mobilized mass support. But such mobilization presupposes popular devotion to saints and their relics. When, one must ask, did Europeans develop this great devotion to saints that could be tapped in the tenth century? Although saints' cults grew slowly from the beginning of Christianity in Gaul and Germany, a crucial stage in this development was the century 740–840, the reigns of the early Carolingians.

In this essay, I shall attempt to outline the process by which Carolingian prelates and kings attempted to control, direct, and encourage the preexisting popular demand for holy men and then to assess the relationship between these elite efforts and popular religion.

Examinations of the cult of relics and the establishment of *patrocinia* in this period, particularly by Friedrich Prinz[4] and Leo Mikoletzky,[5] have established the broad outlines of elite interest in Roman saints. Although transalpine Christians had been interested in the cult of Roman martyrs since at least 397, when Victor of Rouen brought relics of twenty-three martyrs home to that city from Rome,[6] it was the alliance between Pepin the Brief and Pope Stephen II, sealed by Pepin's adoption of Saint Petronilla (held to have been the daughter of Saint Peter) as *auxiliatrix*, that gave the cult of Roman martyrs its major impetus in the North.[7] The second great period of interest in Roman saints was during the reign of Louis the Pious, examined by Mikoletzky, when numerous Roman saints were translated from Rome.[8] Both scholars acknowledge a relationship between these elite interests in saints and some sort of widespread piety, but both are concerned with elite participation in relic cults, Prinz from a political perspective, Mikoletzky from a cultural one. Hence one might argue that the fascination with Roman saints was the result of the interests of a tiny minority of lay and clerical members of the aristocracy and was entirely divorced from the religion of the people.

I would argue rather that the cult of Roman saints was introduced and encouraged in an effort to supplant the cult of other persons across the Frankish empire. In this effort the policies of Pepin, Charles, Louis, and their ecclesiastics were a consistent attempt to control and coopt this sort of popular devotion and to use it to their advantage.

As Heinrich Fichtenau has pointed out, in the eighth and ninth centuries Europeans were inclined to see human beings rather than impersonal forces behind events they could not understand.[9] He cites, for example, the writings of Agobard of Lyons: "In these parts [the Lyonnais]," Agobard complains, "almost everyone, nobles and commoners, city dwellers and rustics, the aged and youth, think that hail and thunder can be caused by human volition."[10] Agobard likewise ridicules the widely held belief that a plague among livestock in the region had been caused by agents of Duke Grimald of Benevento.[11] Just as people were seen as the causes of disasters, so, too, were they the objects of religious devotion. Hence European religious activity focused on saints, but the "holy men" who were the objects of popular devotion were not always the ones chosen by Frankish elites.

The most famous example of a popular holy man in the eighth century is the Gaul Aldebert, whom Boniface persuaded Pope Zacharias to condemn at the Roman synod of 745.[12] Boniface was seldom objective in his accusations against those who opposed his pro-Carolingian political-religious expansionism, but from his testimony Aldebert appears as a classic sort of holy man. He had received, he claimed, a special letter from God as well as miraculous relics by which he could obtain whatever he wished; he could forgive sins without the need of confession; he opposed pilgrimages to the tombs of the apostles and martyrs and refused to dedicate churches in their honor; he founded oratories and set crosses where he pleased and dedicated oratories to himself. Boniface even accuses him of distributing bits of his own hair and nail parings as relics. Aldebert can perhaps be seen more accurately as one of the numerous wandering bishops who opposed the strongly pro-Roman ecclesiastical structure espoused by Boniface and, perhaps, the private penitential-confessional system then being introduced on the Continent by Anglo-Saxon and Irish missionaries. He does seem to have developed a wide following, and one can easily believe that his disciples saved bits of his hair and fingernails as relics.[13] It was precisely to oppose such outlaw holy men that Boniface and Pepin encouraged the cult of Roman saints, who, by their origin, were intimately involved in the Roman-Frankish alliance.

Even when the saints honored were the "right sort" in the eyes of the Carolingians, the forms of devotion shown them were often considered objectionable. Again in the area of *Germania prima*, Boniface discovered that the "people of God" were actively pursuing pre-Christian cult practices transferred to Christian saints. A council held under his direction in 742 decreed that "in accordance with the canons each bishop should take care . . . that the people of God should not do pagan things but should abandon and repudiate all the filthy practices of the gentiles, be it sacrifices to the dead or divination or immolation of sacrificial animals, things which ignorant people do in the pagan way next to churches in the name of the holy martyrs or confessors."[14] Clearly, in this most recently converted area of Europe, conversion had meant simply the substitution of saints for gods.

Such a substitution was not peculiar to the fringes of Christianity. In the same year that his council condemned the pagan practices observed in Germania, Boniface wrote Pope Zacharias to complain of such pagan festivals as the winter solstice and 1 January still being celebrated in Rome. Boniface's complaints led to the condemnation of such practices the following year,[15] although half a century later pagan celebrations were still being held in Rome on saints' days.[16] References to the adaptation of pagan practices to Christian saints' cults suggest that although popular devotion to saints was strong, it was not particularly Christian.

Even when the practices of devotion to recognized saints conformed to "official" standards, Carolingian churchmen found much that was objectionable in them. Charles the Great at the Council of Châlon-sur-Saône in 813 expressed grave concern about the motivations of those from all levels of society who were flocking to such pilgrimage sites as Rome and St. Martin of Tours. Priests and other clerics leading immoral and negligent lives thought that simply by making pilgrimages to such places they would discharge their obligations. Many laymen thought that as long as they frequented these holy places they could continue to sin with impunity. Magnates used the excuse of raising sufficient funds to travel to Rome or Tours as an opportunity to oppress the poor. Finally,

Charles suggested that even paupers traveled to Tours and Rome for no more lofty reason than that they might have better luck begging in such places.[17]

If pilgrims were acting out of base motives, clerics promoting pilgrimages were often seen as no better. In a capitulary of 811, Charles asked his bishops and abbots what was to be done about those "who, as though acting out of love of God and of his saints and martyrs and confessors, transfer bones and relics of saints' bodies from place to place and construct new basilicas and strongly urge whomever they can that they give their belongings to it."[18] Later in the century Bishop Agobard of Lyons expressed similar concern about the motivations of those promoting the cult of Saint Fermin, an early bishop of Uzès. Around 829 a severe infection of unknown origin, symptomized by seizures similar to those of epilepsy and sores like sulphur burns, spread throughout the countryside around Uzès. In terror, people flocked to the shrine of Fermin, bringing offerings in return for hoped-for cures. No cures were effected, and Agobard was particularly critical of the willingness of the clergy who accepted these offerings to keep them to their profit. He suggested that plagues visited on men by God required not simply payment but repentance and that offerings made under such circumstances should be distributed to the poor.[19]

In dealing with these problems of misdirected cults, improper cult practices, and exploitation of popular piety, the early Carolingians followed a course similar to that of other of their reform efforts. From Pepin through Louis they sought not to abolish saints' cults but rather to standardize them, regulate them, and then promote them to their own advantage.

If Pepin was not to allow the cult of Aldebert and his kind, the obvious focus of devotion would be those saints most closely tied to his political-religious program, the Roman martyrs. Thus, as Prinz and, earlier, Holtzelt pointed out, this period marked the beginning of the great influx of Roman martyrs' relics into the North. By providing specifically Roman foci of religious devotion, Pepin was reinforcing, at a truly popular level, the substitution of papal charisma for the sacred Merovingian blood by which he had replaced the old dynasty. Just as Pepin had needed papal approval for his usurpation, however, he needed approval for his appropriation of Roman relics, and it is certain that, as John McCulloh has pointed out, the new policy of Paul I (757–67) to distribute corporeal relics of Roman martyrs was essential to this first phase of the promotion of Roman saints.[20]

The next phase of what might be termed a Carolingian policy toward the cult of relics occurred under Charles the Great. Relatively few translations took place during his reign, but he supported directly and indirectly the cult of Roman saints even while attempting to bring it under ecclesiastical control.

The cult of relics received official support in the 790s in connection with the Franks' reply to Second Nicea's treatment of images. The *Libri Carolini*, the polemical treatise composed as the official answer of the Franks to the "heresy of the Greeks," makes clear the Frankish preference for relics as the proper focus of saints' cults rather than images: "They [the Greeks] place almost all the hope of their credulity in images, but it remains firm that we venerate the saints in their bodies or better in their relics, or even in their clothing, in the ancient tradition of the Fathers."[21] The author of the *Libri* insists further that there could be no equality between relics and images, since relics alone would share in the resurrection at the end of the world. Images might be more or less faithful representations and more or less beautiful, but they could have only a didactic function. Any greater honor or veneration was reserved for relics alone.[22]

At the same time that the Frankish church was reaffirming the importance of relics, it was seeking to control the proliferation of the cults attached to them. Two canons of the Council of Frankfurt dealt specifically with saints' cults: canon xv called for the establishment of oratories within the cloister of monasteries containing saints' bodies, where the monks could pray their office without being disturbed by pilgrims visiting the shrine.[23] The council urged a means by which both pilgrims and monks might carry out their respective religious practices without disturbing each other, but it also directed: "That no new saints be honored or invoked nor memorials to them be erected along roadways, but only those who have been chosen by the authority of their passions or the merit of their lives are to be venerated in the church."[24] This final measure might be seen as the "closing of the frontier" on new saints, whether chosen by the spontaneous attraction exercised by such men as Aldebert or by clerics eager to attract generous pilgrims to a new wonder worker. And this measure came at a time when the demand for acceptable relics was at its height.

The popular desire for contact with holy men had been reinforced by the gradual introduction of the Roman liturgy in the empire and in particular by the increasing practice of including relics of saints in altar stones when dedicating churches.[25] By the end of the ninth century it was assumed that all churches contained or should contain relics. Thus the capitulary of Aix (801–3) mentioned among the aspects of parish life that bishops were to investigate "churches where are found relics."[26] Similarly, a capitulary of ca. 802 ordered that "each priest should build his church with great diligence, and should look after the relics of the saints with the greatest diligence in night vigils and the divine office."[27]

By 813 it was apparently assumed that all parish churches had relics, since the feasts listed by the Council of Mainz to be observed throughout the empire concluded with the "feasts of the martyrs or confessors whose holy bodies rest in each parish."[28] Whether or not this should be taken as a direct reenactment of the canon of the Council of Carthage, understood to order that all altars contain relics,[29] it is apparent that the fathers at Mainz supposed that each parish church had relics of some saint.

If every parish church was to have relics, if saints' relics were to be made the officially supported objects of popular veneration, if monasteries were to contain bodies of saints, where were these relics to come from? Obviously, the finite supply of acceptable relics had to be redistributed, and at times the demand for relics must have outstripped the supply.

The most striking evidence for the shortage of relics by the end of the reign of Charles comes from England, but it is quite probably indicative of conditions on the Continent. In 816 bishops at the Council of Chelsea felt called upon to provide for the possibility that no saints' relics might be available for the consecration of a church: "When a church is built, let it be consecrated by the bishop of its diocese . . . let the Eucharist which is consecrated by the bishop be placed by him along with other relics in a reliquary and let it be deposited in that same church. And if he is unable to find any other relics, nonetheless this alone is surely sufficient because it is the body and blood of our Lord Jesus Christ."[30] The practice of including a bit of the consecrated bread in the altar had been part of the Roman ritual of dedication for some time.[31] Apparently, in the early ninth century, the Eucharist, seen as a relic of Christ, was substituted for other relics because at times none could be found.[32]

This shortage resulted in a rash of unscrupulous and unauthorized translations of relics, as the above-mentioned capitulary of 811 suggests. By 813 the situation had become so acute that it was necessary at the Council of Mainz to forbid unauthorized translations: "Let no one presume to transfer bodies of saints from place to place without the counsel of the prince and or [vel] of the bishops and the holy synod."[33]

By the end of Charles's reign, then, saints' relics were vital in the religious life of the Empire, not just in the great pilgrimage centers but in the most humble parish church. But these relics had to be of officially recognized saints whose written lives and passions assured their orthodoxy. For long-Christianized areas of the Empire, like Aquitaine and Italy, such saints could be found among the early martyrs, hermits, and bishops of the region, such as Fermin at Uzès. In the more recently Christianized areas, however, saints had to be brought in from elsewhere, and again the most obvious source was Rome. In 780, however, Pope Hadrian I discontinued the policy of his predecessors, declining to release relics of Roman martyrs to the North, basing his decision on a mysterious "revelation of terror."[34] Nicole Herrmann-Mascard argues that shifts in papal policy may have been in part due to the Roman populace's disapproval of such donations.[35] McCulloh has seen this change as evidence of the cooling relations between the pope and Charles, who, by 780, had left unkept many of his promises to the pope made in the 770s. In any case, few translations were authorized from Rome over the next forty years.

The 820s, however, saw a significant change in papal-imperial relations. Following the executions of the papal notary Theodore and the nomenclator Leo in 823, the Franks seized the opportunity to intervene in papal affairs as never before. Lothar, coemperor since 817, was able to obtain oaths from Eugenius II that effectively placed the papacy under the tutelage of the emperor.[36] Following closely on this new state of affairs, Frankish churchmen began to extract from the pope some of Rome's most valuable assets—the remains of its martyrs.

The first such translation was that of Saint Sebastian, effected to St. Médard of Soissons by Abbot Hilduin of St. Denis, Louis the Pious's chancellor, in 826.[37] This translation, accomplished only with grudging approval from the Roman clergy, resulted in great popularity for Soissons, which soon became an important pilgrimage site. The success sparked envy among Hilduin's fellow churchmen as they watched the crowds of pilgrims leaving their dioceses to visit Soissons. They were no doubt concerned with their own loss of prestige and, perhaps, revenue. When Odilo of St. Médard wrote a highly fictitious account of this translation a century later, he placed a sermon in the mouth of Ostroldus, the contemporary bishop of Laon. Although a literary set speech, it probably reflects accurately the feelings of many ecclesiastics in Ostroldus's position. Addressing his congregation, Odilo has Ostroldus say: "What do you seek in journeying to Soissons, as though you would find the martyr Sebastian? You know that after his martyrdom he was buried in Rome and there he lies, moved by no one. You have here the church of the venerable Mother of God; frequent it, in it swear your vows and make your contributions. You should not wander to other places to seek external help. All that you ask faithfully through her will be given by the Lord."[38]

Such exhortations fell on deaf ears. The Roman martyrs became immensely popular, attracting crowds of pilgrims wherever they arrived and thus enhancing the prestige of the churches to which they were brought or which received fragments of martyrs' bodies. At St. Benignus of Dijon, for example, the presence of alleged Roman relics was sufficient to cause a mass hysterical reaction among women from throughout the diocese of Langres, even though the relics were clearly bogus.[39]

At Fleury-sur-Loire, when Hilduin presented Abbot Boso with some of the relics of Sebastian, popular enthusiasm was so great that a special wooden structure had to be built outside the cloister so that the relics could be visited by the crowds of lay men and women who came to venerate them.[40] Thus bishops and abbots were drawn into intense competition to acquire famous relics from Rome, and over the next decades at least thirty such translations were recorded.

Most of the *translationes* written to describe these acquisitions are so greatly influenced by hagiographical *topoi* that it is very difficult if not impossible to ascertain the actual means by which the acquisitions took place. It is clear, however, that many ecclesiastics bypassed official channels—which were still often blocked or at least slowed by papal and Roman opposition—and made use of professional relic merchants, who operated what Jean Guiraud has accurately described as a "commerce in contraband."[41]

One of the first and surely the most famous of these merchants was the Roman deacon Deusdona, who contracted with Einhard to steal the relics of Saints Peter and Marcellinus in 827.[42] Deusdona was an expert at his trade, and the picture of his organization and operation is fascinating. He is described as a deacon of the Roman church living near the Basilica of St. Peter in Chains. While it is not probable that he was charged with the ecclesiastical jurisdiction of the third cemetery area of Rome, as has been suggested,[43] he was certainly well acquainted with the catacombs. He evidently had free access to them, no doubt because they had been in ruins for centuries and were for the most part deserted, and he was able to use this familiarity to his profit. He was aided by his two brothers Lunisus, a dealer in southern Italy at whose house relics were secured after being removed from the catacombs, and Theodorus, who traveled with Deusdona to Germany on a second expedition in 830.

The business of supplying relics to the Franks was apparently lucrative. Einhard does not say how much he actually paid for his relics, but the gift of a mule he mentions in his account is clearly only a small part of the price. When another customer entered into a contract with him in 830, he promised that "he would be well paid for it by him."[44] The outfitting of a caravan to cross the Alps with one's wares, as was done in 836, was no small enterprise, and the particulars of the operation were similar to those of later medieval merchant ventures. During the winter months, Deusdona and his associates systematically collected relics from one or another of the Roman cemeteries. Apparently they concentrated on a different area of the city each year. Thus in 826 they provided relics primarily from the via Labicana. In 835 nine of the thirteen relics came from the area of the via Pinciana-Salaria. The following year the associates concentrated on the via Appia, as they did again two years later, when ten of the fourteen relics brought north came from that area.[45] In spring the merchants timed their visits to various monasteries to correspond with the important feast days of their customers. On 2 June 835, the feast of Saints Marcellinus and Peter, Deusdona appeared at Mulinheim with his wares. Two days later he arrived at Fulda on the eve of the feast of Saint Boniface.[46] Just as merchants found in the later Middle Ages, the pilgrims to these celebrations made ideal customers, particularly for the merchandise that Deusdona had to offer. Seeing the glory that the bodies of Marcellinus and Peter had brought to Mulinheim, for example, customers would be eager to acquire relics that would bring fame to their own institutions.

Deusdona operated on a large scale with a considerable organization. Others engaged in smaller but similar operations. Among these was a certain Felix, who dealt in all sorts of relics from various places of origin rather than specializing in Roman relics. For example, he sold Archbishop Otgar of Mainz the body of Saint Severus stolen from Ravenna[47] and the monastery of Fulda a large collection of relics from Rome.[48] In addition, he visited Freising, where he sold the body of Saint Bartholomew to Bishop Erchembert.[49]

This commerce, which was the source of many relics that appeared in the North during the ninth century, was beneficial to all concerned. For the merchant, relics were an excellent article of trade. They were small and easily transported, since even entire bodies of saints centuries old were nothing more than dust and a few bones that could be placed in a small cloth bag. As highly desirable luxury items, they brought an excellent price for very little capital investment. The risks were immaterial except for the danger of the wrath of the local populace at having their patron stolen if one bothered to steal genuine relics and the constant danger that the thief might himself lose the relics to another thief if he were not careful. Perhaps best of all, owing to lack of communication and information as well as to the peculiar nature of the items traded, the fact that the body of a popular saint had already been sold did not prevent one from selling it again to another customer at some future time.[50]

There was considerable political advantage for the pope in allowing the commerce to flourish. It was certainly in his best interest to keep the Frankish ecclesiastics well disposed toward him by not interfering in the relic trade, if indeed he could have done anything to stop it. Furthermore, the popularity of Roman relics in the North could only enhance the prestige of the Roman pontiff. Every martyr's remains that found their way into a Frankish church served to impress upon the Franks the dignity and importance of Rome as a center of Christianity. Moreover, owing again to the peculiar nature of relics, Rome and its pope lost very little in allowing some to be removed or even in giving them away. The fact that Eugenius II had given the body of Saint Sebastian to Hilduin in 826 did not prevent Gregory IV from solemnly translating the body of this same martyr from the catacomb in which it lay to an altar in the Chapel of Gregory the Great in St. Peter's.[51] Finally, the pope himself may have approved Deusdona's smuggling. The *Vita Hludowici Imperatoris* by the so-called Astronomer suggests that the pope approved Einhard's acquisition of Peter and Marcellinus.[52]

The relationship between popular piety, Carolingian politics, and ecclesiastical rivalry in the cult of Roman relics is intimate and complex. From Boniface's mission and indeed long before, relics had been recognized as a wedge with which to separate the masses from paganism and magic. Although specific abuses in the cult had been condemned, the power of relics had been experienced and recognized as something quite different from that of magic. The difference lies in the identification of the relics with the saint whose body they are. Unlike magical charms, relics identified with particular saints were extremely personal and even capricious sources of power effective only for those they chose to aid. Moreover, this choice could change, and the saint could elect to favor different people or communities with his power.

This power was of two kinds. The most obvious was, of course, the ability to perform miracles, and this was the power sought by the thousands of pilgrims who flocked to the tombs of saints. The desire for cures fit well into traditional Christian attitudes toward penance and the increasingly important role of penitential pilgrimages. Had not Christ himself said, "Which is easier to say, thy sins are forgiven thee, or arise and walk?" But this thaumaturgic power was only the tip of their enormous potential. Much more important to the communities that possessed relics was their ability to provide the continual action of divine Providence. Relics brought the special protection of the saint to the community, shielding it from enemies both spiritual and temporal and assuring its prosperity. The presence of an important saint in a monastery or cathedral inspired the laity both rich and poor to give alms. In addition, the miracles performed to heal the sick reminded the unscrupulous that this same power could be used against those seeking to harm a saint's chosen church.

This more general protection and favor could extend beyond the confines of the particular community in which dwelled the saint's body and benefit the larger community of the Frankish kingdom. Thus as the ninth century progressed, many saw the veneration of relics as the best hope for deliverance from the troubles that engulfed the later years of Louis's reign. Paschasius Radbertus, abbot of the Picard monastery of Corbie, suggests: "Nor would I say that it is without reason that miracles of saints long asleep in Christ have recently begun to flash forth. Never before have so many and so great things been done at one time by the relics of saints since the beginning of the world, for everywhere saints in this kingdom and those brought here excite each other to song even as cocks at sunrise."[53]

Finally, the relics of these sacred persons not only brought hope of cures to the poor and of stability to the great, but because they had a historical past, they could bring political and cultural focus to Carolingian policy. Relics not only belonged, in the words of Richard Southern, to "this transitory world [and] eternity,"[54] but also to an unchanging, historical past that could be coopted, integrated into the present, and used to direct men's loyalties to Rome, and thus to Rome's anointed defender. It is no coincidence that the old practice of using relics as oath objects was given particular support by Charles and that the standard form of Frankish oath from the early ninth century on was, "May God and the saints whose relics these are judge me that I speak the truth."[55] By incorporating these physical, tangible links with Rome, the Carolingians sought to solidify, at the popular level, the new spiritual foundations of their empire.

In many essential aspects, the Carolingian effort to give a specifically Roman focus to the cult of holy men in the empire was a failure. European peasant culture demonstrated a remarkable ability to adapt elements of this form of elite religion without sacrificing what would continue to be, in many ways, a separate culture. So-called pagan or rustic forms of individual and group devotion to saints continued throughout the Middle Ages and beyond.[56] The miraculous rather than the penitential aspects of devotion to relics seem to have formed for centuries the basis for popular devotion to local and regional pilgrimage sites. And in spite of the extreme efforts made by Carolingians to procure Roman relics and establish them as cult centers, the great majority of popular saints in the later Middle Ages would be either local saints or saints in some way associated with local traditions: Sebastian never replaced Medardus as the most popular saint in Soissons, and Mary Magdalene (who by the eleventh century was said to have ended her life in Provence) replaced the Roman martyrs whose relics had been brought to Vézelay in the ninth century.

Nevertheless, the confluence of popular devotion, official Christianity, and Roman-Frankish politics did result in the consolidation of the cult of relics in European religion in a more general way. Just as in other areas of Carolingian culture, little new was added to the cult of saints in the eighth and ninth centuries, but the emphasis on corporeal remains, the augmentation of the supply north of the Alps, and the encouragement of devotion to them laid the foundation for their great role in the mass movements of later medieval piety.

Popular Religion and Holy Shrines

Their Influence on the Origins
of the German Reformation and Their Role
in German Cultural Development

Lionel Rothkrug

Discussing German religious life on the eve of the Reformation, Bernd Moeller recently distinguished two general types of popular piety. He contrasts the gentle devotion typical of groups like the Brethren of the Common Life with the ostentatious, sometimes even hysterical spirit displayed in mass pilgrimages to holy shrines.[1] Why did people worship in such different ways? Did particular social groups favor specific forms of devotion? To answer these questions I have established a sample list of 1,036 pilgrimage places founded in Germany before the Reformation.[2] Their distribution in space and time shows above all the profoundly regional character of different types of religious expression. Moreover, the striking correlation between the regional pattern of medieval shrines (see appended map) and the subsequent geography of sixteenth-century German confessional divisions suggests that a region's acceptance or rejection of Reformation teaching proceeded principally out of religious practices that had developed centuries previous to Martin Luther's appearance on the public scene.

If this evidence, along with a considerable body of more conventional documentation, proves the overwhelmingly regional nature of dissimilar forms of folk piety, it also raises the more difficult problem of explaining why divergent types of popular religiosity were peculiar to one area or another. The answers proposed here, perhaps more sweeping than is normally prudent for a historian to write, do have the advantage of appearing to be probable. They are offered in the spirit of opening new avenues of inquiry, and the author would be the first to welcome criticism and to applaud new research—particularly large collections of data processed for computer analysis—that would furnish the evidence necessary to confirm, to modify, or even to deny the conclusions arrived at in this study.

Most of the more general discussion proceeds from the assumption expressed by the French term *mentalité collective*—that certain cultural entities are so fundamental that they appear, albeit in different forms, at all levels of society. The history of pilgrimage and of local shrines can tell a great deal both about popular religious attitudes and about elite culture. Pilgrimage sites show a significant increase in number only after 1300, continue to multiply at a constantly accelerating tempo down to the sixteenth century, and reach a maximum during the Counter-Reformation. Their geographical distribution follows a similar pattern in that it grows increasingly asymmetrical as we approach the Reformation. The regional distinctiveness of popular worship, becoming more pronounced by 1500, suggests that a process of cultural differentiation, beginning in the several regions of the Holy Roman Empire sometime after 1300, continued to develop to the point of hostile confrontation during the Reformation, establishing its final institutionalized forms only after the mid-sixteenth century. If, furthermore, it is true that fundamental popular attitudes reappear in literary and artistic circles, then it follows that intellectual and cultural developments in this period, such as late medieval nominalism, the Renaissance, and subsequently the Baroque, during the Counter-Reformation, also reflect the feelings and outlooks expressed in local forms of folk piety. In this essay I present precisely this view; it rests on the assumption that to identify characteristics that endure for centuries and grow finally to embrace both learned and ignorant alike is to describe some of the essential features of a national culture.

South Germany illustrates graphically those factors which made popular devotion part of intellectual and social history, for it was in this region that the crucial institution of pilgrimage developed more profusely than elsewhere. Part One of this essay begins therefore with a short history of south German pilgrimage; it describes how the local aristocracy imparted to common peregrinating practices the crusading and martial traits expressive of an imperial ideology. The south German nobility also powerfully encouraged associational forms of worship. This corporate piety, the subject of a second subsection, made it increasingly difficult for ordinary and even for some learned people to distinguish sacred qualities traditionally attributed to a church from those they later ascribed, for example, to a confraternity. Popular and learned confusion of ecclesiological and corporate notions, in turn, affected directly the history of thought. I argue, in subsection three, that William of Ockham and Marsilius of Padua, each in his own way, directed their full polemical force against the intrusion of corporate principles into theology and common worship. The concluding section of Part One provides statistical material for the other regions of Germany, extending the analysis presented of the south. The distribution of pilgrimage sites throughout the empire demonstrates the direct correspondence between the structure of local aristocracy and the regional patterns of folk piety.

Part Two discusses how this pluralism of worship affected the evolution of early modern German national culture. It shows a striking contrast between the patriotic and imperial religiosity of the south and the personal, almost private piety in the north—regional differences that even cut across Protestant-Catholic divisions. The first subsection explains how, after about 1470, south German pilgrimage practices developed into a broad stream of rites associated with the famous slogan, "Heiliges Römisches Reich Deutscher Nation." Here I argue that south German humanism and, subsequently, German baroque architecture, express directly the imperial religiosity of ordinary people. The second section treats central and north German devotion, explaining how the absence of a strong aristocracy in many regions permitted women to shape the character of common piety and to prepare the foundations for a lay religion. A concluding section discusses the two German Reformations: north and south. Here the divisions separating Lutheran devotion from the urban traditions of south German–Swiss Protestantism are parallel, I argue, with the broader cultural differences discussed throughout the entire essay.

PART ONE: PILGRIMAGE AND SOCIETY

The Rise of Pilgrimage Piety in the Main–Rhine Valleys and the Lands to the South

The history of pilgrimage to European shrines is related both to crusades and to the institution of indulgences. Pope Urban II (1088–99) granted plenary indulgences on a large scale to members of the First Crusade, an undertaking rooted partially in a long previous tradition of pilgrimage to the Holy Land. After this date pilgrims also could receive unrestricted certificates of divine forgiveness if they journeyed to Palestine. As far as I know, the papacy granted few full remissions of punishment for sin to people visiting shrines located in Europe. Jerusalem alone remained the ultimate site of pilgrimage for more than two centuries after the First Crusade. Although exceptions to this practice grew during the thirteenth century, only in 1300 did the papacy announce formally a fundamental change. During that year, when Boniface VIII celebrated the great year of Jubilee, large numbers of pilgrims for the first time received plenary indulgences for visiting a shrine located in Europe.

Boniface's transference of the center of European devotional pilgrimage from Jerusalem to Rome enhanced the value of the indulgence, which had been growing in importance since the First Crusade. The papacy had worked prodigiously, especially in the thirteenth century, to control and to channel the direction of popular piety. Declaring holy war against the Albigensians (1209) and establishing the Inquisition to eliminate undesired forms of folk religion, Rome also sought to encourage approved expressions of piety by commissioning the newly founded mendicant orders to preach popular support of crusades. When Innocent III convened the fourth Lateran Council in 1215, he inspired the beginning of Europe's most intensive and most elaborately organized crusading effort.

In encouraging popular crusading zeal the papacy helped to impart a new, public dimension to indulgences during the thirteenth century, for broad support for conquest in the Holy Land was part of a wider program to establish ecclesiastical supremacy in secular as well as spiritual affairs. Innocent III elaborated and gave new life to the idea "that the diverse units of the Christian world formed a single *populus Christianus*." After his pontificate, canonists increasingly conceived of the pope as having charge not only of the clerical but also of the whole governmental order. He was "the head of an international society composed of the *ensemble* of Christian kingdoms and cities."[3] In this context the indulgence became a document of citizenship awarded to members of the *communitas*, a far-flung public order. Fighting in holy war or traveling to the greatest shrines were activities that expressed the quintessence of public as well as religious zeal. The plenary indulgence became a certificate of celestial rights granted to patriots and pilgrims who served at least the cause of the *terra* (the holy land), if not yet the *res publica christiana*. Thus, a century of mendicant preaching, as well as the waging of holy war and the promulgation of canonist legislation, had created a situation by Boniface VIII's time in which the piety associated with pilgrimage, crusade, and indulgences proved more powerful and enduring than the papacy's ability to compel or to inspire European sovereigns to engage the Moslem in military combat. The loss in 1291 of the last Christian outpost in Palestine, together with the increasing reluctance of sovereigns and important sections of nobility to participate in future crusades,[4] made the problem of indulgences acute: either Rome must make the Holy Land more accessible to European Christians or she ought more clearly to dissociate the granting of indulgences from crusade and from pilgrimage to Asian shrines.

Driven to the latter alternative, the Holy See acted to reaffirm the indulgence as a source for popular acclaim of papal supremacy in public affairs: henceforth, pilgrimage to Rome itself would enable the faithful to procure special membership in the Christian *communitas*, which, at least for laymen, only a plenary remission could confer. Announcing almost simultaneously (March 1298) a new codification of canon law and seeking throughout his pontificate to organize a European crusade against Islam, Boniface VIII, like his predecessors, sought to marshal the forces of popular piety into closer support of papal monarchy. It is against this background, with hordes of pilgrims streaming into Rome in 1300, the great year of Jubilee, that we must read Boniface's extreme statements of Rome's universalist claims in the famous bulls, *Ausculta Fili* (1301) and *Unam Sanctam* (1302).

Certainly Boniface sought to inject an element of political allegiance into spiritual life. Throughout the thirteenth century the Holy See had frequently used the interdict and excommunication for flagrantly political purposes, and it now posed a novel and in the long run perhaps even more formidable threat to secular authority. Most sovereigns, following the example of Philip the Fair in France, responded by immediately tightening their grip on local ecclesiastical organization. Perhaps contributing also to the confrontation between secular and church authorities was the dwindling stock of specie over which prince and prelate contended in a time of intensified population pressure and on the eve of the first Europe-wide crisis of cereal scarcity.[5] At any rate, the consolidation of secular control over religious institutions at the beginning of the fourteenth century precipitated the disintegration of Europe's ecclesiastical structure into congeries of separate churches. Faced, on the one hand, with the rapid collapse of organizational unity and propelled, on the other, by the thrust of ecumenical crusading piety, European governments and intellectuals struggled to make clear for the first time the difference between universalist claims based on spiritual life and those derived from constitutional principles. Anxious to justify sovereign resistance to Roman pretensions, William of Ockham and Marsilius of Padua emphasized the spiritual bond between popular piety and political allegiance. The two men, each in his own way (Ockham was no Conciliarist), claimed that a general council of the entire church expresses the devotion of the dead as well as the living; subsequently some Conciliarists argued that the faithful represented at the council, both lay and clerical, literally compose the mystical body of Jesus Christ as it extends through time. And since, in their view, popular decision in the distant past established secular authority everywhere, it followed for some theorists in the next generation that government representatives to an ecumenical council carry their countrymen's faith into the general assembly of the church, where delegates from the ensemble of territorial churches unite with their ancestors in the universal body of Christ. But this argument implies that Christianity is limited to the lands represented by officials at that council. For if the Savior's body is made manifest by the assembled delegates expressing their spiritual unity, then people who are not represented at the council cannot become members of the body of Jesus Christ. In this way William of Ockham and Marsilius of Padua not only contributed to making the idea of Christendom synonymous with the concept of Europe,[6] but they also stood at the beginning of a long development that transposed popular fervor for religious unity to a view of Christianity based upon a pattern of political allegiance.

When William of Ockham and Marsilius of Padua said that the bonds uniting the prince with his subjects, being popular in origin, were sanctified through lay participation in spiritual affairs, they encouraged sovereigns to use folk piety as a weapon against the papacy; folk piety could support church territorialization at a time when papal policy sought to establish claims for universal obedience. Although they propounded these theories at the court of Louis of Bavaria, the opportunities for sovereigns to unite political reform with the power of common worship was greater outside of Germany, where such efforts did in fact achieve an added degree of political unity. For, by introducing clerical participation in the new representative assemblies called estates, and above all by joining this right to the conciliar demand for lay participation in an ecumenical church council, western European governments provided a measure of institutional expression for popular piety. The fusion, therefore, of clerical representation in secular government with the conciliar principle of lay participation in church government permitted western sovereigns in some degree to direct common religious ardor to support constitutional movements that openly opposed the concepts of public order embodied in Boniface VIII's new codification of canon law.

In western Europe, then, secular authorities in the early fourteenth century succeeded in countering Rome's bid for popular political allegiance by integrating religious life more closely with territorial identity. In Germany, however, the much less united response of princes to papal pretensions in imperial affairs helped to foster dissension rather than to strengthen political unity. Indeed, the struggle between Louis of Bavaria (1314–47) and Pope John XXII (1316–34), reminiscent of the contest between Boniface VIII and Philip the Fair, intensified the separation between different types of piety developing in the several regions of the empire.

Papal-imperial quarrels only made more apparent the growing cleavage in the development of religious life between north and south Germany. Religious practices in the north—the area extending from the lower Rhine through Westphalia and Saxony to Lübeck—exhibit little of the aristocratic influence that became visible after 1300 in the worship of common people living south of the Main–Rhine valleys. Here in the south were concentrated imperial institutions of every description, lay and ecclesiastical, with a bewildering array of castles, housing a nobility more numerous than anywhere else in Germany. These famous centers of knightly culture, as Herbert Moller shows, produced all of German medieval love poetry, especially the *Minnesang*, appearing between 1170 and 1250. This literary genre was unsuitable for the north, where the Welf party "relied on a few wealthy cities for their power." Love poetry expressed chivalric ideals peculiar to the courts of the Hohenstaufen and neighboring dynasts, who continually recruited "new contingents of knights to man the castles and to secure communications."[7]

Many of these knights came from the north along with the *ministeriales*, who served in military and, perhaps more frequently, in administrative posts, for the emperor, bishops, abbots, and free nobles. Neither villein nor free vassal, neither serf nor free knight, often powerful lords of unfree status, the *ministeriales* were a class of civil servants who by the twelfth and thirteenth centuries had become so large that "they vastly outnumbered the old nobility."[8] Their sheer size, however, hindered upward social movement—a factor contributing, says Moller, to the production of the *Minnesang*, since reduced opportunity for social advancement created a special need among "thousands of knights whose parents or grandparents had been serfs . . . to justify their claims to social superiority."[9] By 1300 most *ministeriales* were emancipated. But their feelings of insecurity remained. And an eagerness to strengthen their newly acquired rights to hereditary nobility impelled them to assume leadership of a popular religious movement, imparting a feudal ethos to ordinary religious practices and transforming the holy shrine into a symbol of a peculiarly corporate form of common worship.

In contrast to the *ministeriales*-dominated countryside, most people living in imperial free cities—numbering some sixty-five on the eve of the Reformation and the vast majority located in the south—rejected aristocratic influence in religious life. The subject is discussed below. For the moment, suffice it to say that at the time of Louis's campaign against John XXII the rural south practiced forms of worship fundamentally different from civic-inspired types of urban devotion. Above all, the purely masculine ceremonies of the hunt, war, and crusade became associated with pilgrimage rites in such a way as to lead country folk to identify aristocratic renown with miraculous deeds performed by angels and saints. In one such traditional story, Christ, nailed to the Cross, makes Himself manifest between the antlers of a stag pursued by Saint Hubert and his hunting dogs; in another, the Mother of God also appears between the antlers of a stag, this time pursued by Duke Peregrin, who, in obedience to the Virgin's spoken command, founds a monastery, Beuron, on the site of the miraculous vision. Beuron later became a holy shrine dedicated to the imperious figure of the heavenly Queen.[10] Literature on the medieval hunt reveals so far eighteen instances of shrines or monasteries being founded allegedly as a result of miraculous happenings connected with hunting, *sixteen of them being located south of the Main*. And the total number was probably far greater.[11]

In Duke Peregrin's time Hubert became the patron saint of the hunt, to whom was offered slaughtered game, especially stags and wild boar, sometimes carried personally to a monastery or a church on the shoulders of the hunter.[12] Moreover, in the same manner that men associated venery with regal and military pursuits, so eleventh- and twelfth-century aristocrats often imputed imperial and warlike roles to Mary. While God was portrayed as an omnipotent Lord holding the cosmos in fee and receiving homage and fealty[13] from all mankind, Mary, seated at His right hand, ruled the universe as Queen and coregent. She held a celestial court of angels and saints.[14] Indeed, Peter Damian declared that nothing was impossible for the Virgin because, receiving all power in heaven and on earth, she appears before God, not as a maid or servant, but as a sovereign.[15] She also made occasional personal appearances as a mailed contender in knightly jousts and tournaments[16] and enjoyed a particularly exalted position in the chivalric *Minnesänger* and *ministerialis* tradition. The south German Dominican student of Meister Eckhard, Heinrich Seuse (1295–1366), said he "served" the heavenly Queen exactly "as a knight in the service of his lady."[17] Indeed, by the fifteenth century some preachers felt the need to prove the Virgin's royal lineage, proclaiming her descent from "forty patriarchs, fourteen queens, and eleven princes."[18] The figure of a scepter-wielding, blue-blooded Virgin, embodying in her person "the highest of human nobility," corresponded in the fifteenth century to the requirement, as in Paderborn, for example, that imperial church canons prove eight generations of noble lineage.[19] The cult of the heavenly Queen thus developed into a powerful ideology that directly inspired literary and artistic pursuits among south German elites in the fifteenth century.

Meanwhile, from about 1290 to 1300, the erstwhile *ministeriales* transferred important elements of imperial and crusading piety to the popular level, inciting the first large-scale Jewish pogroms in Germany. To be sure, crusading armies had from their inception provoked local killings of Jews, and centuries of systematic preaching of holy war had by 1300 intensified hostility toward Jews throughout Europe. But in contrast to the more frequent and more humane practice of expulsion elsewhere, only in regions south of the Main did wide-ranging grass-roots movements annihilate entire populations of Jews. No parallel existed in 1298 to the pogromist ardor of mobs led by Rindfleisch, an obscure Franconian noble, or to the even more fanatical hordes known as Armleders, from the leather patches on their sleeves, who exterminated life in literally hundreds of south German Jewish communities from 1336 to 1339.[20] The triumphs of these armies of *Judenschläger* (Jew killers), who were both urban and rural, were celebrated by special monuments. In the towns, new churches were built. For example, after the Black Death provoked a massacre of Jews in 1349, Charles IV granted the burghers of the imperial city of Nuremberg permission to build a church on the site of the destroyed ghetto, provided that it be dedicated to the heavenly Queen.[21] Similarly, churches were built in honor of the conquering Virgin, later to be known as *Siegerin aller Gottes Schlachten* (Lady Victor of all God's battles), on the ruins of freshly destroyed synagogues and ghettos during the fourteenth and fifteenth centuries in, for example, Eger, Würzburg, Bamberg, Regensburg, Rothenburg, Munich, Heidelberg, Ingolstadt, Cologne, and Amberg.[22]

Whereas in the towns the destruction of Jewish communities was followed by the building of churches, rural folk sometimes founded places of pilgrimage on the sites of the massacres of Jews. Precisely how many of these shrines were established, especially during the first half of the fourteenth century, in Franconia, in the Deggendorf-Straubing region of Lower Bavaria, and on the Franconian border in northeastern Swabia, is not clear. I count at least ten sites and have good reason to suppose a substantially higher number.[23] The shrines were not dedicated to Mary, however, but to Christ himself. The point is noteworthy. For, on the one hand, it helps to show a connection between pogromist fury and a state of mind symbolized in the new feast of Corpus Christi, and, on the other, it illuminates the nobility's role in fostering popular crusading piety. Having its origins in the Beguine communities at Liège, the feast of Corpus Christi, confirmed by the Council of Vienne (1311–12), arose out of a devotional movement among feminine orders and their largely Dominican sponsors. They sought a "more sensuous contact with the humanity of Christ," and by about 1250 their eucharistic devotion proved sufficiently powerful to establish the feast of Corpus Christi in the bishopric of Liège.[24] The growth of a feminine, mendicant drive for more frequent contact with the Host found a parallel around 1250 in a more frequent practice among common people: their use of the Eucharist as a divine instrument to protect men, beasts, and equipment against the workings of evil spirits.[25] And the practice of elevating the Host, an innovation introduced in reformed (especially Cistercian) monasteries in 1210, also became widespread in public worship around 1250.[26] By the end of the century, the two streams of eucharistic devotion, institutional and popular, culminated respectively in the feast and in the processions of Corpus Christi.

The novel public exposure of the Host, making it suddenly visible and more available to entire populations, created anxiety everywhere over its possible desecration, particularly by Jews. The three volumes of *Germania Judaica*, describing briefly the history of each Jewish community in Germany down to 1350, mention literally dozens of instances where an alleged desecration of the Eucharist provoked killings of Jews. The first recorded accusation appears in Paris in 1290.[27] Eight years later Rindfleisch and his supporters set out on their murderous expedition, spurred on by reports that Jews had "stabbed, hammered, and pierced" the Eucharist, and then had thrown the Lord's body into a river, with entire stretches of the stream turning red from His blood.[28] A generation later, during the far more ferocious Armleder movement, rural folk even spoke of waging a war against the enemies of the faith, who had plotted to destroy German Christians. A document written in Lower Bavaria in 1338 declares:

The Jews, who deny the Christian faith, have . . . conspired together in Germany . . . to kill the Christians by means of poison. In many places . . . they have also stolen the consecrated Host, throwing it in a fiery oven, striking it with hammers, and afflicting it with other indignities. Upon taking notice of these events, Sir Hartmann of Degenberg, together with his neighbors from Deggendorf, captured the Jews, burned them, and offered up their possessions for plunder. The same [happenings] also took place in Straubing and in other localities in Bavaria, with the exception of Vienna and Regensburg [where] it was against the will of the authorities.[29]

Rindfleisch in 1298, Hartmann in 1338, and the leaders of the Armleder in 1336 were nobles. Aristocrats also actively promoted popular pilgrimage in the south, and the slaughter of Jews continued to accompany pilgrimage processions, principally in Bavaria, down to the sixteenth century.[30] The Bavarian nobility may have encouraged "crusades" against the Jews: certainly the timing of these events strengthens the suspicion. For in this period John XXII placed the lands of Louis of Bavaria under interdict, and the emperor, like Philip the Fair earlier, sought public support for his campaign against the curia. Among his allies were the imperial *ministeriales*, who gave strong backing to the ideal of a *Sacrum Imperium Romanum*.[31] At the same time, the increasing territorialization of the Bavarian church and the establishment of the estates were associated with a movement among lower nobles, particularly intense around 1300, for emancipation from magnate authority.[32] In these circumstances it seems reasonable to suppose that the clergy and nobility loyal to Louis in his struggle with John XXII—many of the *ministeriales* among them all the more stimulated ideologically by their recent emancipation from baronial households—sought to organize popular support for the emperor by trying to unite aristocracy and folk in a common imperial piety to protect the recently, universally exposed Corpus Christi from the specter of Jewish desecration—an activity offering the additional prospect of confiscating Jewish possessions and canceling debts to Jewish creditors in a period of intense specie scarcity.

The depredations of Rindfleisch and the Armleders coincided with another innovation in popular religion: the new ritual importance given to the horse. Beginning around 1300, peasants brought their horses into visual contact with the Eucharist on the feasts of Saint Leonhard and Saint George, patrons of knightly pursuits in previous centuries.[33] The rite appears to have been a kind of equine communion. For this purpose churches were installed with special doors (on an east-west axis—altars were on a north-south axis). Peasants would ride their smartly decorated animals through the doors into the middle of the church, to have them look either at the exposed Eucharist or at the "windows" of the container housing it.[34] The priests also prepared the horses for their meeting with the Host by blessing them with holy water. The entire ceremony was a variant of the *Umritt*, the most typical form of old Bavarian popular piety, which has been found in approximately two hundred places in its different versions.[35] Indeed, the *Umritt* often constituted a special type of pilgrimage.[36] For example, in the fifteenth century the Upper Bavarian village of Dietramszell (bishopric of Freising) was "distinguished for its horse *Umritte*. Peasants arrived from as far as a four hours' horse ride with specially decorated wagons on the Sunday following the feast of Mary Magdalene. Upon arrival they immediately broke into a sharp trot, driving three times around the [Saint Leonhard's pilgrimage] church amid the chanted prayers of those sitting in the wagons."[37]

A recent *Volkskunde* map of Austrian *Umritte* shows them to be concentrated on the Bavarian border. Describing Bavaria as "an exceedingly *Umritt*-joyful land," the editor names the *Osteritt, Georgritt, Pfingstritt, Fronleichnamsritt, Leonhardiritt, Martiniritt, Stephaniritt, Johanniritt, Blasiusritt* as the chief forms of the ritual.[38] No other territory even approached the intensity and frequency of Bavarian *Umritt* piety, a species of popular devotion that appeared only on a much smaller scale in the north. Certainly no parallel exists elsewhere in the empire for the later development of mass *Umritte* at pilgrimage sites. The Benedictine monastery of Scheyern provides a most dramatic example. Around 1155, Count Konrad I from Dachau donated an alleged fragment from the Holy Cross to the monastery, and the monks then established a shrine. Though authorities differ as to the date when Scheyern became a "true" place of pilgrimage, they all agree that its later pilgrimage renown, beginning after 1550, developed out of a long-uninterrupted medieval

tradition of processions to the local shrine of the Holy Cross. During
Scheyern's period of baroque glory "more than two hundred horsemen"
rode their steeds around the county, circling the entire pilgrimage area,
"from before 5 A.M. to 5 in the evening."³⁹ And even this achievement in
equine ritual grandeur was modest in comparison with 7,055 horsemen
participating in the famous Holy Blood *Umritt*, the *Blutritt*, celebrated
since 1490 on "Bloody Friday" at the shrine housed in the Benedictine
monastery at Weingarten.⁴⁰

Thus the *Umritt* became a major form of Bavarian–south German
pilgrimage practice during the period of *ministeriales* emancipation and
the coincident massacre of Jews after about 1286–1300. But the earliest
Umritte were not invented by emancipated *ministeriales*. In Ottonian
times Saxon emperors, on accession to the throne, embarked on ritual
Umritte of the Empire, receiving everywhere the pledged obedience of
their subjects. Centuries later erstwhile *ministeriales* revived and promoted popular peregrinational variants of the imperial *Umritt*. They did
so in order to induce ordinary people to identify their newly acquired
nobility with ancient imperial traditions which, in this renascent form,
also inspired support for Louis the Bavarian's campaign against Avignon.
These renascent *Umritte* and the killings of Jews together heralded an
enormous development and popularization of pilgrimage, especially to
the heavenly Queen, during the fourteenth and particularly in the fifteenth centuries. And however great or small may have been the degree
of direct aristocratic participation in the murderous expeditions carried
out by Rindfleisch and Armleder bands, solid evidence points to Bavaria
(along with Austria and Bohemia) as the chief center where churches and
shrines dedicated to the Virgin continued for centuries to symbolize the
spirit of pogrom and of crusade. Not only did townsmen in the fourteenth
and fifteenth centuries dedicate churches erected on the ruins of synagogues and ghettos to the heavenly Queen: still more significant are the
mass pilgrimages in the early sixteenth century to the triumphant figure
of the *Schöne Maria* established in Regensburg's recently deserted ghetto.
The appellation *Schöne Maria* was given to the Virgin in response to the
alleged desecration of her name by Jews in synagogue services: but this
new south German image does *not* appear west of the Lech River, old
Bavaria's western boundary!⁴¹

To summarize, in the days of Rindfleisch, townsmen from Bavaria
and south Germany slaughtered Jews in honor of Mary, whereas country
folk massacred them for the sake of Christ. By the turn of the sixteenth
century, however, both urban and rural populations expressed their pogromist ardor in common pilgrimages to the *Schöne Maria*, a militantly
anti-Semitic form of Virgin worship peculiar to Bavaria, Austria, and, to
a lesser extent, Bohemia. To what degree is the ascendancy of a new

nobility connected with this continuous growth for more than two centuries of a largely Bavarian and strikingly bellicose form of peregrinating
devotion? Certainly a presumption of aristocratic influence is raised by
the regional specificity of the *Umritte*: Bavaria is the only region where
Umritte multiplied at a rate comparable to the proliferation of holy
shrines—a phenomenon consistent with the Bavarian pilgrims' marked
preference for reports of miracles associated with the hunt. Equally suggestive is a "list of all those southwest German participants in crusades
who happen to be known by name": members of the *ministeriales* made
up 97 percent of the crusaders recorded in this random sample for the
years 1192–1250![42] The revived and popularized version of the imperial
Umritt, combining crusade, pilgrimage, and pogrom, appeared only in
Bavaria after 1300. All this suggests that the key role in this process was
played by the new nobility.

To prove this crucial relationship, however, requires more evidence.
It falls into two categories: genetic and statistical. Because the first is
explanatory and the second is corroborative, presentation of the one
must precede discussion of the other. Proper description of the genetic
development reveals two dimensions of correlation, social and intellectual; both are subsequently confirmed by the statistical material. The
social correlations, between the structure of nobility and the pattern of
folk piety, show that after about 1280 aristocratic influence intensified
the cult of purgatory and imparted a peculiar type of *genossenschaftlich*
or corporate character to the devotion surrounding holy shrines in south
Germany. As for intellectual history, these unique features of south German devotion throw new light on the writings of William of Ockham
and of Marsilius of Padua, making clear the profound influence popular
religious practices exercised on the evolution of theological doctrine. In
this way the somewhat belated consideration of the actual numbers and
types of holy shrines serves two purposes: in the realm of ideas it helps to
illustrate how particular configurations of pilgrimage sites symbolize de-
finable relations between common piety and learned creeds; in the sphere
of social history it provides dramatic confirmation that a correspondence
exists between patterns of local worship and regional variations in the
structure of nobility.

The Relation of Pilgrimage to the Cult of Purgatory and to the Structure of Popular Piety

Although the south German nobility increasingly participated, after
about 1280, in shaping the character of popular worship, their influence
only strengthened a preexisting, broadly based movement connected with

the rise of the cult of purgatory throughout western Europe. Demographic reasons also contributed to the cult's popularity. The striking increase in mortality in this period, caused by the first Europe-wide cereal scarcity around 1300 and by the massive epidemics a generation later, may well have done much to transform the doctrine of purgatory into a popular cult. Purgatory was welcomed as an escape from the stark alternatives of heaven and hell. For, however grim the prospect of purgatorial fires, it was comforting to know that the sinner's friends and relations, offering sacrifices and prayers for him, could shorten, indeed sometimes entirely eliminate, the term of affliction preparatory to entering paradise. At the same time, a purged soul, upon entering paradise, could intercede most effectively for those who had helped to shorten his purificatory ordeal: his intercession carried the cumulative force of all the prayers he offered up in purgatory for his earthly benefactors. In short, everyone knew that spiritual aid offered for another in the next world contributed to mitigate his own sufferings both on earth and in the hereafter. For this reason people expected rich rewards from indulgences procured for dead friends and relations or from masses sung for their souls or from prayers or pilgrimages made on their behalf.

Spiritual sodalities, corporate bodies of every description, were founded at least partly in order to strengthen and to make more numerous the multiple mutualities uniting living and departed souls in their common endeavor to enter paradise with a minimum of suffering. The Europe-wide pilgrimage expansion, the multiplication of indulgences, the proliferation of saints, and the prodigious rise of confraternities must all be seen as different parts of a single penitential system. It was calculated to enroll the dead in a vast network of reciprocal services, the totality of which constituted both the cult of purgatory and, in its widest theological sense, the "communion of saints," that is, the entire church conceived as "the unity under and in Christ of the faithful on earth, the souls in Purgatory, and the blessed in Heaven."[43] It was in this spirit that a confraternity in Lübeck in 1503 took care to enroll dead souls as members of their brotherhood.[44] In the same manner, local pilgrimage places, such as the one situated near the village of Reilkirch on the right bank of the Mosel, served as centers for brotherhoods founded to encourage visiting pilgrims to enroll deceased friends and relations in order that they, too, could share in the merits earned by the good works and indulgences procured by the confraternal community.[45]

Pilgrimages and confraternities were the major institutions in the cult of purgatory. In the case of brotherhoods, however, it is important to distinguish those officially recognized by the clergy from those that were not. Formal approval required a written agreement with a monastery or a church, in which, among other obligations, the brotherhood undertook to bury deceased members and to care for their souls, as well as to perform some type of "good work," usually a charitable activity. In turn, ecclesiastical recognition conferred on each confraternity member the cherished right to procure indulgences. Without such a contract, guilds and any other lay associations, however pious, could receive no access to the indulgences that always accompanied formal church approval.[46] To be sure, every guild had its patron saint, but the celestial figure performed no penitential service unless the guild or, as was more often the case, members of two or more guilds or professional associations were united in an ecclesiastically approved brotherhood.[47] Although such confraternities frequently also developed around local shrines (like the one at Reilkirch) to accommodate pilgrims, they were in this case not absolutely necessary, for in principle the pilgrimage itself, not the brotherhood attached to it, performed the chief penitential functions. In sum, the two institutions, pilgrimage and confraternity, symbolized a single form of devotion in which groups of people, seeking to establish collective security on earth and in heaven through ritual acts, formed corporate "families" or "artificial kinship groups,"[48] composed of living and dead members, each bound by some local pattern of ritual and confraternal bonds.

The fourteenth century saw a pronounced conceptual intermeshing of this purgatorial vision of artificial kinship groups with principles peculiar to late medieval corporate institutions. Indeed, the one was an ideological expression of the other. This unlikely fusion of penitential and constitutional ideas, though triggered by demographic catastrophes, developed out of a long-established popular movement, and a brief summary of its history is essential. The first "confraternities for the dead" were organized in the early Middle Ages as exclusively clerical fraternities or as lay associations attached to Benedictine monasteries. They were founded, according to Heinrich Fichtenau, "on the model of the old Germanic sworn associations. We find an early example of such a confraternity at the synod of Attigny in 762. Later, there was a vow taken at Tassilo's synod in Dingolfing. This vow constituted a 'confraternity formed by bishops and abbots in Bavaria for the benefit of dead brothers.' ... Such prayer-confraternities soon formed a net which covered the whole Frankish kingdom and stretched even into Spain and England."[49] At this time common people communicated with dead souls most frequently through the veneration of relics. R. W. Southern divides the history of relic worship into two periods, before and after about 1100–1150. Prior to the twelfth century,

relics were the most important feature in the religious landscape.... Every church, every altar, every nobleman, every king, every monastery, had relics sometimes in great quantity. They were instruments of state, of law and order, of

personal well-being. . . . They were the object of huge commerce. . . . Even the
Pope, whatever theoretical claims were made for him, in practice owed most of
his authority to the fact that he was the guardian of the body of St. Peter. This
brought men to Rome and made them listen to the voice of St. Peter mediated
through his representative on earth. . . .

Relics were the main channel through which supernatural power was available for the needs of ordinary life.[50]

Although veneration of relics continued unabated, they ceased to
serve as visible signs of public authority around 1150, about the time,
Southern explains, when the pope rejected the title of "Vicar of St. Peter."
His new claim to be the "Vicar of Christ" signified that the uniqueness
of papal power no longer resided in the presence of Saint Peter's body in
Rome.[51] A precisely analogous development occurred fifty years later
in German pilgrimage practices. Until about 1200, shrines located in the
empire were almost exclusively graves for deceased members of local
ruling families—usually monks, abbots, or bishops—held to be saints.[52]
The buried body, an interred relic, testified to the celestial origins of local
seigneurial rule in the same manner that Peter's entombed presence
in Rome granted authority to the pope. But after the great Investiture
struggle—a conflict concerning the rights accruing to founders of church
establishments—new laws of *Patronat* or advowson, in the twelfth century, permitted the pope to intervene as "Vicar of Christ" in local ecclesiastical appointments. For if the pope's claim to represent Christ rather
than Peter justified Rome's assertion of new authority over lay rulers, so
pontifical abandonment of the traditional powers flowing from Peter's
bones forced aristocrats also to disregard the authenticating power of
relics and to turn instead to legal specialists for aid in finding constitutional grounds to counter the curia's political pretensions. And since
a nobility preoccupied with trying to resolve problems of competing
jurisdiction showed little further interest in fostering pilgrimages to the
tomb of some alleged ancestral saint, people were no longer encouraged
to journey to grave sites, and grave sites slowly ceased to provide the
supreme attraction for most pilgrims.

Popular reaction to the desacralization of the interred relic was two-
fold. On the one hand, common people around 1200 demanded that
relics be uncovered. They wanted to see the sacred bones, ordinarily in
some transparent repository.[53] On the other hand, pilgrims transferred
the quality of holiness from the buried corpse to the place of the pilgrimage itself, often the same site; the image of the protecting saint, not
the sepulcher, became the symbol of devotion.[54] The passionate desire to
make relics visible, a folk aspiration not to be deterred even by the most
determined ecclesiastical resistance,[55] was of a piece with the movement
to substitute first statues and later pictures for buried corpses at pilgrim-

age sites. These images received thaumaturgic powers from the presumed physical presence of the saint or some other celestial patron. Europe entered the age of depicted saints. Aside from its obvious importance for the history of art, the desacralization of graves also contributed power-fully to the dissociation of shrines (and therefore of confraternities) from monastic ties during the thirteenth and especially in the fourteenth and fifteenth centuries. Meanwhile, the widespread eagerness in the early thirteenth century to view the actual relics did not lead at once to a great increase in local pilgrimages, for the popular demand for greater acces-sibility to sacred objects focused above all on the Eucharist. Just as a bone from the physical remains of a saint, in popular belief, *was* in fact the saint himself, so the Eucharist, believed to be the physical and spiri-tual presence of Christ, constituted the ultimate, the most precious, of all relics. Around 1200, therefore, people insisted with a special fervor on beholding the Savior with their own eyes.

The clergy must have responded rapidly to folk pressure, for the first official account of a public elevation of the consecrated Host, about 1195, says explicitly that the ceremony was introduced in response to popular demand.[56] In one instance, officers of a guild introduced an ac-tion at law against a priest who assigned their members places in church from which they could not see the Host.[57] It seems reasonable to suppose that this ground swell of eucharistic piety is related to Innocent III's definition of transubstantiation as a dogma at the Lateran Council of 1215. I discussed earlier how common worship of the Eucharist, often seen as a powerful relic to ward off evil spirits, led directly to the found-ing of the feast and procession of Corpus Christi shortly after 1250—the same time that Saint Thomas Aquinas provided the classic formulation for the doctrine of transubstantiation. And there is no need to relate once more how the enormous popularity of these celebrations helped to pro-voke the massacre of Jews in south Germany and contributed generally to intensify the crusading piety that culminated in the procession of possibly two million pilgrims through Rome in 1300, the great year of Jubilee.[58]

Massive popular pressure for more palpable, at least more ocular, participation in religious rites expressed a fundamental drive among common folk to win entry into the church's penitential system. Most people were excluded from this solace in the early Middle Ages, when the flow of remissions from monasteries was limited to the upper classes. The idea was simple. If one person may pay others to perform his penance and if bishops impose impossibly harsh penalties on the upper classes, it follows that the rich will hire substitute penitents. But the surrogates must be reliable, for "the popular literature of this age, when the doctrine of Purgatory was still unformed, contained stories to prove that he who left his compensation incomplete was forever doomed." Penance was a debt, and "monasteries offered a safer way of paying . . . than any other method of substitution, whether by alms or lay-helpers. Monks could be relied upon to perform their service of substitution forever: they were bound by vows; they were established in perpetuity; their property was safeguarded by appalling anathemas against the disturbers of their peace. No matter how large the debt, it would in the end be paid, and the soul of the sinner would be free."[59]

In monastic life this pre-Hildebrand Benedictine program for "continuous penitential activity for founders and benefactors"[60] gave way in the twelfth and thirteenth centuries not only to the Cistercian zeal for colonization, but also to their important penitential innovations. For the Cistercian system of *conversi*—lay brethren who vowed to follow a simplified monastic regime and to serve exclusively in the monastery's labor force—provided "for the first time in the history of medieval western Christendom . . . a full assurance of salvation to illiterate men."[61] Not everyone could become a *conversus*, however, and alternative ways to salvation were developed for the common man during the thirteenth century. Clerics preaching crusades urged the purchase of indulgences to benefit dead souls.[62] Before 1300 the papacy seems neither to have expressly approved nor disapproved of this practice, but it did ratify the doctrine, first formulated around 1230, that the pope had exclusive jurisdiction over a treasure of merits left by Christ. This was a treasure vast beyond compare: Clement VI proclaimed in 1343 that "one drop of Christ's blood would have sufficed for Redemption of the entire human race."[63] Thus the democratization of penance led to its more intimate association with the dead. Before 1200 indulgences freed recipients from penalties imposed by churchmen, but this was no longer the case when the papacy appealed to a heavenly treasure of merits. For to say that Christ personally releases, with His own blood, a sinner from penitential obligations is to heighten the remission's transcendental value and to extend its applicability to penances enjoined by God—both on earth and in purgatory—an absolution valid after death as well as in life! The inference was inescapable: possession of a plenary indulgence at death meant immediate entry into paradise, a reward curiously reminiscent of the one Urban II promised to crusaders who died in the Holy Land. It is understandable, therefore, that pilgrims entering Rome in 1300 might think their plenary indulgences enabled them to free purgatorial souls for direct entry into paradise. How many used this new and awesome power is unknown. But it is certain that the intensification of relic worship, the shift from sepulcher to image at pilgrimage sites, the ground swell of eucharistic enthusiasm, and the popularization and progressively mortuary character of indulgences were all inseparable components of a single vast movement that sought to democratize Europe's penitential system, finding its ultimate expression around 1300 in a cult of purgatory. Nearly everyone could assure his own salvation, because, like the monks in the Benedictine age, everyone contributed toward the redemption of another. Common laymen now enjoyed a qualified power of remission. Perhaps the intimate connection of all these developments with the popular veneration of depicted saints explains why people everywhere in Germany began to receive Christian names only after around 1300.[64]

But if the thirteenth-century movement for penitential democracy enhanced the spiritual dignity of the common man, it did so only by making more intimate the relations between the living and the dead. This made more important the intercessory powers of saints, and their images and numbers multiplied in direct proportion to the growth of communication between people and the departed souls to whom they rendered penitential assistance. Furthermore, while care for the spiritual welfare of the deceased had always been a largely cooperative enterprise, the new accessibility of indulgences permitted lay confraternities to break away from monasteries, which until about 1200 had been the sole institutions capable of expiating penalties for other people's sins.

Just as confraternities grew more autonomous because laymen could perform penances for others without the services of monks, so the more frequent resort to pilgrimages to procure indulgences tended to connect the shrine more closely to confraternities. In this way the rise of grass-roots penitential peregrination helped to transform both pilgrimage sites and lay brotherhoods into triumphant expressions of soteriological democracy. Ordinary folk used indulgences to benefit the dead in the same manner that rich people employed monks to do penance on their behalf; their shrines and confraternities guaranteed salvation for the poor in the same way that monasteries did for the rich, providing an institutional assurance of the divine favor they expected in exchange for the penitential assistance they had offered to departed souls. In this sense, there was a highly developed and broadly based cult of purgatory in 1300, shortly before cereal crises and epidemics set in motion the harrows of mass mortality throughout Europe.

But, however similar later practices may appear, the disastrous events of the fourteenth century did help to bring about fundamental changes in purgatorial piety. The most important was the shift from the principle of substitution to the principle of collective responsibility, from performing penance for someone else to taking responsibility for the sins or wrongdoings of a neighbor or even a stranger. Collective punishments were, of course, common throughout the Middle Ages. But the use of interdict, amercement, confiscation, and worse against towns, localities, and corporate bodies became more frequent after the late thirteenth century. The reason is clear. A spate of popular uprisings, beginning around 1280, continued to mount in intensity and frequency throughout Europe, culminating finally in the "revolutionary years of 1378–1382," when more than a dozen revolts occurred in Italy, France, England, the Netherlands, and other parts of the Empire. In the absence of permanent security forces, it was extraordinarily easy to start a rebellion, and both the ease and frequency of uprisings, as well as their growing intensity, provoked authorities to impose punishment indiscriminately, with little regard for individual guilt or innocence.[65] Since punishment and its remission were collective in character, applied to guilty and innocent alike, it is understandable that people projected the same principle into the religious sphere. Everyone knew that both God and prince might harry or spare the land without much concern for individual right or wrong. It followed that a practical way of limiting the risk that one person's misbehavior could endanger an entire group was to restrict membership in the group, whether lay or religious. Trading guilds, communal and civic councils, monastic and cathedral chapters, and corporations of every description all presented some form of legally enforceable right of limited liability; the innumerable ritual reciprocities binding these corporate personalities on earth to the departed souls of their erstwhile members and to their patrons in heaven proceeded from a universal desire to establish local exclusiveness under the aegis of divine favor.

Confraternities, to use Gabriel Le Bras's words, were "the religious dimension of the corporation,"[66] a projection of closed-shop principles into the religious realm. Each saint in the multitude that peopled the heavens in the fourteenth and fifteenth centuries was the patron of some exclusive assembly, congregation, or locality on earth:[67] the rise of a saint worship productive of indulgences—which was essential to the transformation of purgatory into a popular cult—provided a spiritual component for the corporate organization of urban and rural life in western and central Europe. But the placing of purgatorial devotion on a corporate basis seriously compromised the democratic principle of allowing all men equal access to indulgences. In practice, a member of a confraternity limited his penitential activities to the narrow sphere of the confraternity itself. Its deceased members were enlisted to intercede for the living, who thereby secured divine approbation for their brotherhood's social or professional distinctiveness; similarly, its patron saint was assumed to accept intercessory petitions only from erstwhile brethren freed from purgatory by the devotional assistance of the confraternity. In this way, the principle of restrictive recruitment became anchored in the very structure of the purgatorial system.

Indeed, in the fourteenth century the confraternity, not the church, may have appeared to ordinary folk as the institution outside of which there was no salvation. For to sever one's corporate ties meant to dissolve all the horizontal and vertical expiatory relationships that bound a member to his fellows, both living and dead, through whom alone he had access to an all-powerful patron saint. Without their aid, eternal perdition seemed inevitable. Thus the widespread adoption of the corporative principle of collective responsibility and its corollary, collective redemption, as a chief tenet of penitential piety made it difficult for men to distinguish religious bonds from communal ones. Every locality, every occupation, established some form of local ritual network uniting living and departed souls in common devotional assistance. No one was excluded, not even knackers and other "dishonorable" people. Indeed, a mere group of peasants traveling on a common pilgrimage to a local shrine formed a temporary brotherhood, whose visible expression was the *Eulogie*—a species of popular substitute for the consecrated Host.[68] This fundamental and mass regroupment of the faithful into multitudes of quasi-autonomous units free from monastic direction not only created a new social pattern for Christian life: it also raised new and perplexing problems for theologians. For example, if a religious character is attributed to a confraternity and if priests officiate in its ceremonies and at its altars, how is it to be distinguished from a church? Such questions had a profound effect on the history of late medieval thought, and the schoolmen and clerics who discussed them throw important additional light on the character of corporate forms of worship.

The Impact of Popular Piety on Late Medieval Intellectual Life

Before 1300 theologians paid so little attention to the idea of the "church" that a distinguished historian of the subject says that the thirteenth century "still belongs to the pre-history of ecclesiology."[69] Only toward the end of the century did schoolmen try to formulate a definition of the church that would conform to the increasing corporate regroupment of popular worship. One of the first to make the attempt, though he did not present a systematic account of the theme, was Godfrey of Fontaines, writing in 1288. Taking exception to Aquinas's view of the church as the *tota congregatio fidelium*,[70] Godfrey argued that the multitude of social bodies, all organized as self-contained hierarchies, constituted an equal number of *corpora mystica*, each dependent on the other: "The church is one because she has a single head. As the Church of Paris has a particular unity because she constitutes a mystical body, that is to say a congregation of individual persons between whom is established a subordination to a single head. . . . So the church universal contains many members . . . the ones dependent on the others and all dependent from the principal member who is the head and the guide: the pope."[71]

Godfrey used the term "mystical body," *corpus mysticum*, in the same sense that Boniface VIII did about a decade later in the famous bull, *Unam Sanctam*, giving it a relatively new meaning. Uniquely Christian, but with no biblical origin, the expression *corpus mysticum* had referred in Carolingian times to the consecrated Host. In contrast, the Pauline term *corpus christi* designated the church or society. Subsequently, as Ernst Kantorowicz explains, people interchanged the expressions. *Corpus mysticum* came to mean the church or society and *corpus christi* (or *corpus verum* or *corpus naturale*) the Host: "The notion *corpus mysticum*, hitherto used to describe the host, was gradually transferred—after 1150—to the Church as the organized body of Christian society united in the sacrament of the Altar. In short, the expression 'mystical body,' which originally had a liturgical or sacramental meaning, took on a connotation of sociological content. It was finally in that relatively new sociological sense that Boniface VIII defined the Church as 'one mystical body the head of which is Christ.'" Kantorowicz calls this case history of a crisscross in meanings "a strange and perplexing development—*un curieux chassé-croisé*."[72] But its significance becomes clear in the light of the history of popular piety. *Corpus mysticum* referred to the Host until popular pressure drove the clergy to remove the Eucharist from its ritual concealment and to exhibit the body of Christ in full public view. The Savior's real presence was no longer mysterious in the sense that His body was hidden and inaccessible to the common laity. Only after the assembled faithful beheld His body could they become one with the *corpus christi*, forming in this manner "the congregation of individual persons or a *corpus mysticum*," which Godfrey of Fontaines defined as a church. And his notion of the union of churches, the hierarchy of corporate mutualities uniting living and departed souls in the single body and head of Christ, corresponds exactly to the concept of *ecclesia* proclaimed in *Unam Sanctam*: "One mystical body whose head is Christ" (*Unum corpus mysticum cuius caput Christus*).

Boniface's definition of the church as a mystical body had a special importance for theologians in 1300 because it was consistent with his institutionalization of the principle of equal access to indulgences in granting millions of plenary remissions to pilgrims in the year of Jubilee. For just as the Eucharist united the faithful in the *body* of Christ when the priest exposed the Host before an assembled congregation, so the authority to grant plenary indulgences—the right, as Vicar of Christ, to confer on the common penitent a power to free someone from purgatory —enabled the pope to use the merits flowing from the Savior's *blood* to join the living and the dead in mutual expiation. A lay community led by a priest was thereby transformed into a *corpus mysticum*, a church united to other churches by virtue of the papal administration of Christ's blood or the treasury of merits. This is the essential background to what Kantorowicz called "the new sociological content" which Boniface injected into his relatively novel definition of the church.

Some learned clerics, alarmed by the rising tide of purgatorial devotion, fought strenuously against the massive intrusion of corporate principles into systematic theology—a struggle made all the more difficult by the new quarrels arising between secular and church authorities during the Avignonese papacy and the Great Schism. For the new emphasis on spiritual collectivism and corporate exclusiveness raised serious theological, ecclesiological, and pastoral problems. The notions of free will, reason, predestination, and their relations to grace and salvation were called into question. But the new piety raised a still more serious theological problem. The parallel proliferation of saints and lay confraternities suggested that the corporations themselves shared in the divine attributes of their celestial patrons. This amalgam of purgatorial and corporate notions had two consequences: it made imperative the task of distinguishing the church from other corporate institutions; and it led theologians to face more directly the general question posed by the disturbing practice of ascribing transcendental qualities to collectivities. In these circumstances it is not surprising that around the mid-thirteenth century, schoolmen began to debate Averroist teachings. The doctrine that the entire human race participates in a single world intellect and the consequent denial of personal immortality, the rejection of freedom of the will and of individual moral responsibility—all were propelled toward the center of learned disputation.

In this setting, Saint Thomas Aquinas composed a treatise against the Averroist school in 1270 (*De Unitate Intellectus contra Averroistas*). Nevertheless, even he adopted the notion of collective personality, when he argued, in his account of original sin, "that all men born from Adam can be considered as *one* man (*possunt considerari ut unus homo*) in so far as they concur in the nature which they have received from the first man—just as in civil affairs all men of a community are reputed, so to say, as one body and the whole community as one man."[73]

As Kantorowicz points out, if it was orthodox for Aquinas to affirm the corporate nature of mankind through "the unity of original sin," it still was heretical for Averroists to establish a collective ideal in the universal intellect.[74]

A generation later, Dante—assigning the Averroist, Siger of Brabant, a place in paradise next to Aquinas—described the difference between human and divine spheres as a contrast between the principles of collective and individual beatitudes. On earth, Dante visualized an age of "intellectual oneness,"[75] brought about by the association of mankind into a universal body corporate under a single ruler. Only the destiny of the soul was individual. Nevertheless, the prominent place of purgatory in the *Divine Comedy* suggests that, even for Dante, the ultimate fate of a departed person continued to be influenced by the corporate, locally organized devotion of the living. Indeed, Dante depicts mankind's pilgrimage through purgatory and wishes to regenerate the human race by reestablishing its original state of intellectual and corporate unity: his vision of collective redemption is strikingly similar to the confraternal notion that salvation can be achieved only through a penitential union of living and departed members. In this connection, Dante even describes a scene from pilgrimages to Rome during the great year of the Jubilee.[76] As Kantorowicz brilliantly observes, Dante presented a moral philosophy and a civic virtue that corresponded structurally to the sacramental system. He constructed a *"corpus mysticum adae quod est humanitas"* as a direct complement to the *"corpus mysticum Christi quod est ecclesia."*[77] The conception of lay society as a *corpus mysticum* (this is the message not the words of Dante) suggests that Dante not only transposed to the philosophical plane the confraternal commingling of lay and sacramental traits, but also wrote an enduring tribute to the popular yearning for all men to be allowed to participate in the church's penitential system. Perhaps this explains why Dante placed both Siger of Brabant and Aquinas, his declared opponent, in paradise. For Siger and his followers had professed to reconcile their teachings with church dogma by asserting the doctrine of double truth, claiming a right to believe as theologians precisely what they denied as philosophers. Dante suggests here that although popular belief in the divine character of plural personalities flagrantly contradicts official dogma, it constitutes a living testimony to the principle that all men, standing equally before God, ought to have equal access to the instruments of salvation. Interpreted in this sense, Dante's evenhanded praise of Siger and Aquinas points to the reasons for late medieval and Renaissance disputes about free will and predestination. The doctrine of free will expresses the notion of a natural right to soteriological self-determination—a notion implicit in the new corporate piety. In contrast, Aquinas stressed the unity of mankind in sin. Whatever his view of free will, one possible inference seems clear: if the equality of all men before God refers exclusively to an equality in sin, then the right of forgiveness remains alone with the Lord.

Although inspired by Aquinas, Dante's solution of the problem of individuation—his distinction between the collective character of human and the individual nature of divine beatitudes—was not entirely faithful to Aquinas. Aquinas's view was that "all men born from Adam can be considered as one man . . . just as in civil affairs all men of a community

are reputed, so to say, as one body"; he drew an analogy between civil
and religious guilt which he refused to extend to the realm of virtue,
where he emphatically distinguished civil from religious merit: "It sometimes happens that someone is a good citizen who has not the quality
according to which someone is also a good man, from which it follows
that the quality according to whether someone is a good man or a good
citizen is not the same."[78] In other words, as far as sin was concerned,
Aquinas made each individual an exact replica of another. He insisted,
furthermore, on man's physical nature and attempted systematically
to make general regulative principles of moral life purely natural phenomena; he thus regarded reproductive and corporate traits as characteristic of the natural and social orders, defining the spiritual sphere as
a domain devoid of collective beings—a realm of pure individuation.
Given the assumption that corporeal beings are composed of matter and
form—in contrast to incorporeal entities like angels, which are pure
form—and that all composite beings have "an exigency for quantity"[79]
as well as a unicity of substantial forms, it follows that moral laws are
functions of the multiplicity of the bodies they regulate. Conversely, since
angels are pure form, each one is by itself an entire species, and its
behavior is indistinguishable from its individuality or ontological uniqueness. For this reason every celestial intelligence is a separate universal.

Aquinas's contrast between the natural order of multiplicability and
the divine realm of individuation rested squarely on the concept of unity
in sin, positing some measure of collective responsibility of all men for
the spiritual and civic faults of their corporate fellows. It was against
the increasing acceptance of this position that William of Ockham and
Marsilius of Padua argued so powerfully, the first from a theological, the
latter from a political and social point of view. While both admitted that
special bonds of loyalty are essential for any group to unite in common
worship, they insisted that these communal ties, being devoid of sacramental significance, justify neither a special status for the clergy nor any
claim that the sacraments constitute the church or any other collectivity.
Ockham's denial of the objective existence of universals, his refusal to
admit that two members of a single species participate in a common
reality, destroyed the notion of collective personality and liberated each
person from spiritual responsibility for the sins of his neighbors. Ockham
rejected not only the extreme realist notion of a *universale in re*, but also
the Thomistic and Augustinian doctrine of a *universale ante rem* (that
members of a single species possess a similar nature insofar as each is a
partial fulfillment of God's idea of the species to which they belong); he
thus confined human knowledge to experience in this world and removed
the concept of the Divine Will from any connection with traits held to be
inherent in mental, natural, or corporate processes. Ockham's defense of

God's omnipotence, therefore, was linked with his concern to deliver men from the supernatural consequences said to flow from other people's trespasses; it was also an expression of his determination to root every person's sense of right and wrong in the individual conscience. For these reasons, Ockham maintained that, however important the sacraments, they neither testify to the existence of a spiritual community nor do they give priests, as distinct from God, the power to condemn or to forgive.

Ockham's refusal to sanctify corporate ties followed from his effort to distinguish systematically between religious values and institutional structures. By emphasizing divine omnipotence so as radically to individualize moral and spiritual responsibility, Ockham said that no one can be guilty for the sins of his fellows, for every single being in the entire human and natural order, utterly contingent on God's will, and therefore incapable of a priori description, is a distinct entity bound to no other by necessary laws or by logical relations. Moral law, Ockham says, derives from no ontological source; it is an obligation arising out of the created free will's duty to will in accordance with right reason's perception, correct or erroneous, of God's commands. In sum, having placed God above all obligation, and having defined moral virtue as behavior conforming to the exigencies of personal conscience, even when invincibly erroneous, Ockham could say that society's institutions, being the product of mere human effort, may be justified or described without reference to supernatural influence.

Because Ockham located moral law in the individual conscience, preserving thereby a self-governing sphere of personal religious values, he said that no action could be moral without virtuous intentions. The ethical quality of an action was inseparable from the character of the will and thought that elicited it. Marsilius proceeded from the opposite position. He separated overt behavior from its intention, distinguishing "transient" or exterior deeds from their "immanent" or interior motives.[80] Religion concerns the interior life; in contrast, external behavior falls entirely within the competence of civil government. And the laws pertaining to one sphere are unrelated to the principles regulating the other. For that reason the evangelical law "ought to be called a doctrine, not a law . . . for taken in its proper sense" law is a coercive rule.[81]

Coercion points to enactment or application of a law, not to its contents, which, says Marsilius, receive the qualities of justice and equity from the collective wisdom and historical experience of the entire community. "The law is an eye composed of many eyes, that is, the considered comprehension of many comprehenders."[82] Thus by restricting moral judgment to the realm of external behavior, and by defining virtue as the product of centuries of human collaboration in "art and reason," Marsilius identifies moral law with historical development. Both he and Ockham regarded society as the result of human effort. But where Ockham supplanted belief in corporate sanctity with a conviction that the principle of divine omnipotence, properly understood, provides the strongest defense for the moral autonomy of a free created being, the *Defensor pacis*, in contrast, replaced the *corpus mysticum* with an evolutionary variant of a *volonté collective*.

The distinction is important. Both Ockham and Marsilius were eager to abolish the influence of corporate notions in church organization and in the direction of religious life, Marsilius even denying that penance performed on earth could affect a soul's destiny in the hereafter.[83] In contrast to Ockham, however, Marsilius avoided most theological issues. Ockham's determination to individualize human responsibility, to emancipate reason and will from ontological and corporate structures, were purposes totally foreign to the *Defensor pacis*—a treatise that to this day remains partially misunderstood. Unwilling to discredit the doctrine of collective responsibility in all its aspects, Marsilius sought to project corporate ideals into a historical dimension, both by rejecting their expiatory properties and by retaining their redemptive features in a secularized form. Above all, he emphasized the fideistic, perhaps Averroist-inspired division between a private sphere of revealed theology and a public realm of moral precepts. The distinction, arrived at by declaring the ethical value of overt acts to be independent of the propriety of their intentions, permitted Marsilius to portray the moral character of a community as the product of a long common history. This attempt to root virtue in historical evolution underscores the corporate thrust of his argument. For such a view presupposes that historical continuity proceeds out of the future fulfillment of past purposes, as revealed in the laws, customs, and institutions of a particular polity. In short, it is by exalting the collective and evolutionary character of human law, conceived to be independent of divine justice, that Marsilius presented in a secularized form the familiar confraternal mutuality between living and departed souls: previous generations enter into a common past with the living to the measure that a body politic continues to fulfill the purposes of its forebears. He created in this way a place for civic virtue in a vision of communal immortality: it was as if Augustine's idea of the incommensurate nature of the divine and historical spheres had been referred somehow to the perennial incompatibility between the private and public realms.

Ockham's and Marsilius's writings, formulating respectively a theology and a kind of political sociology, both attacked the ideas that penance and punishment could be vicarious or that sin and forgiveness might be imputed. In this respect they throw much light on the role of popular devotion in the development of late medieval theology. Indeed, the whole scholastic debate about free will and predestination, as well as erudite arguments about the place of experience in epistemological explanation, are directly connected with developments central to the history of common lay piety. The fundamental issue on both the learned and the folk level was that neither philosophy nor popular perception could deny that to share the guilt and partake in the forgiveness granted to others —devotional attitudes typical of indulgences and of supplications and penances performed for other persons, living and dead—is to separate moral judgment from private experience and to attribute extrapersonal traits to vice and virtue. To punish or to forgive one person for another's faults or merits is to place sin outside of personal memory and to transform vice and virtue into figures similar to those in a morality play, personifying qualities whose carnal form conflicts with more inward notions of private conscience.

Moreover, opportunities for manipulation were enormous. The dominant classes could project moral principles as objectivized traits into the sphere of public ritual and ceremony in order to direct human behavior without reference to personal recollection. And it is no accident that realist and quasi-realist theologians discussed man as a species, not as an individual, allowing them to assign to the concept of knowledge a role in the learned sphere precisely parallel to the popular perception of morality in the context of corporate devotion: both proceeded out of an objective existence rather than from personal experience. Such theologians organized the sundry groupings of knowledge, natural and supernatural, corporeal and incorporeal, into an orderly variety: an ontological whole that attributed moral value to its derivative concepts in the same manner that a collectivity imputed innocence or guilt to different categories of its members. Reason served to unite metaphysical constructions with corporate institutions, classifying knowledge homologously with ecclesiastical and community organization, propounding thereby the view that justice—defined as "to each his own"—is best revealed through epistemological demonstration. In this sense, the medieval platitude that "truth is justice" was accurate, at least in the spirit of Leibnitz's principle of "the best of all possible worlds."

It is Ockham's enormous merit to have destroyed the philosophical grounds either for imputing moral responsibility to others or for deriving definitions of justice from a priori propositions. The entire thrust of Ockham's epistemology denied all logical and emotional grounds for divorcing personal experience from general moral precepts. He said that "nothing can be known naturally in itself unless it is known intuitively," that is, from experience. Knowledge proceeds either from sense perception or from introspection. It is an immediate apprehension of things or of internal dispositions so evident that the intellect may instantly confirm or deny their existence. Neither moral nor "natural" judgment may exist independent of experience, because natural intuition, flowing directly from human experience, forms the bases for wider influences that, when taken in their entirety, shape the total structure of our cognition.[84] Moreover, Ockham's experiential epistemology caused him to subordinate reason to will. For when he tied moral criteria both to motive and to overt deeds—precluding thereby the attribution of vice and virtue to plural personalities—he made external behavior stand toward motive as reason to intuition: the rectitude of the one and the validity of the other depended respectively upon proper volition and immediate apprehension. Outward acts and the process of reasoning subserve will and intuition because these irrational faculties, totally contingent on divine command, cause justice and truth to reside in man's personal relations to an omnipotent Creator.

We have seen how Marsilius, critical of epistemological notions, was no less critical of concepts of reason that permitted theologians to create all-purpose syntagmae, applicable indifferently to pure learning, political organization, and the pastoral care of souls. Therefore, like Ockham, Marsilius also excluded reason from a role in divine affairs, subordinating it to the will. But his voluntaristic notions are radically different from those of Ockham. Declaring the moral quality of overt or "transient" behavior to be unrelated to the intentions of the actors and conceiving the totality of worthy deeds performed over time to constitute the moral structure of the community, Marsilius described the will as a collective process, whereby the ideals of public service—being by definition independent of private thoughts—are transmitted from one generation to another. He transformed the confraternal notion of a perpetual mutuality between living and departed souls into a vision of corporate or civic immortality free of all expiatory obligation: an urban ideal that was destined to have a long life. Even at the end of the sixteenth century, for example, Richard Hooker defined the moral structure of a corporation as the totality of worthy deeds that unite the living and dead members of a community in an immortal body: "Wherefore as any man's deed past is good as long as himself continueth, so the act of a public society of men done five hundred years since, standeth as theirs who presently are of the same societies, because corporations are immortal: we were then alive in our predecessors, and they in their successors do live still."[85]

From the point of view of the history of thought, the chief importance of Marsilius's contribution is that he freed the concept of corporation from its purgatorial context. In his view, the living and the dead find a solidarity in *time*—as opposed to seeking a union through some form of penitential mutuality—making it possible to perceive political relations and cultural developments in a historical perspective. More important for our purposes, however, is a parallel development in late medieval folk piety, when people had conflicting notions about the place of the dead in time. For example, if someone performed a penance to procure a plenary indulgence on behalf of a soul in purgatory, the fact that he could expect a reciprocal intercessory favor only subsequently might lead him to think that the dead are located in a future state rather than in the past. His choice between future and past—which had enormous consequences for the content of his piety—depended a great deal on where he lived and on the character of his relations to aristocracy, to patricians, and to guild organizations. In the next section I discuss how these circumstances helped to shape different attitudes toward the holy shrine.

The Structure of Nobility and the Pattern of Popular Piety

Whether religious sentiments encourage a person to look backward or forward in time is largely decided by what Heiko Oberman describes as the difference between *confessional* and *pastoral* theology. Augustine is a representative of the former: by concentrating on past sins, he intensifies his consciousness of God's aid in previous ordeals, creating a state of mind in which the sinner recognizes his inability to avoid subsequent backsliding without continued support from divine grace. Memory transforms past wrongs into present experience, and the effect of thankful recollection is to unite gratitude for previous grace to future prayer. *Pastoral* piety, however, is much different. A priest cannot expect a largely uninitiated audience to "look backward in gratitude" like Augustine. Instead, he exhorts his flock to "look forward in hope" and to think about what they, not God, are able to accomplish. Moreover, Oberman continues, the predominance of this missionary, forward-looking piety in the early Middle Ages often made theology "appear naively Pelagian."[86] But the Pelagian attitude inherent in missionary or pastoral exhortation was not in theological conflict with the confessional insistence on the individual's total dependence on God's grace, says Oberman: the difference is only one of emphases, corresponding to different levels of understanding prevailing among different categories of the faithful. In one sense, the point is well taken, especially from the perspective of present-day ecumenical movements, but to discuss the issue from an exclusively doctrinal point of view obscures the popular dimensions of the problem. For pilgrimage was the purest possible expression of a devotion "looking forward in hope." Together with brotherhoods, indulgences, and the intercessory functions of saints, the pilgrimage shrine was not only the very embodiment of the doctrine of free will, but stood at the center of a system fostering an anticipatory, truly pastless form of penance—one that impaired the common man's ability to identify his own life with a wider temporal process.

Pilgrimage also formed a kind of lay analogue to the monastic ideal of *contemptus mundi*. This is the reason why classic accounts of famous shrines often explain that miracles are more likely to occur in distant places among strangers; they try to persuade the reader that the pilgrim's hopes may grow according to the distance, the perils, and the hardships of his journey.[87] For the viator's sacred trek found an exact parallel in the monk's contemplative and ascetic exercises in the sense that each measured his nearness to salvation according to the degree of his peculiar form of remoteness from worldly preoccupations. Thus death in Jerusalem, both the most distant and the holiest of all sites, guaranteed the pilgrim immediate entry into paradise.[88] Of course, only the prosperous could afford such lengthy expeditions. But travel to local shrines also contributed, though for different reasons, to promote this form of religious sentiment, which made human aspirations appear significant only in proportion to their social irrelevance. In this way it weakened ordinary people's perception of community continuity and undermined their sense of the autonomy of human experience.

Not all pilgrimages were the same, however, and the pastless character of religious sentiment varied widely in intensity from region to region. The reasons for these variations were profoundly social, and they are perhaps best approached by describing more closely differences between urban and rural piety. In the cities, assembled burghers made periodic public pledges, and related ceremonies were held for ritual protection; these required the presence of large numbers of townsmen, whose vows expressed a promissory faithfulness uniting the living and departed members of the community in the common continuity of civic endeavor. In contrast, if a rural shrine were to convey a sense of continuity, it proceeded more from the holy place than from the people who visited it. Here the patron saint performed wonders on demand, so to speak, without suggesting that participation in local traditions, however important, was a condition essential to receiving his celestial favor. Indeed, no emotion could be more alien to pilgrimage piety, for the sacredness of the journey, *even to local sites*, lay precisely in the relative isolation of the holy place.[89] It is true that many urban residents also participated in late medieval pilgrimages. But these were largely long-distance journeys, undertaken by established citizens. Such excursions were not destructive of civic piety. Rather, they expressed a need to escape occasionally from the constraints of convention-ridden social structures, to seek relief in the spontaneous and often intense interpersonal relations that were possible, as Victor Turner explains, in the essentially structureless community of pilgrims.[90] The fundamental difference between urban devotion and that of the local shrine lies in the townsmen's sense of the autonomy and continuity of human affairs, their feeling that immortality involves carrying forward the cumulative achievements of countless generations of forebears.

The contrast between town and country, however, does not explain the vast differences among rural forms of worship. For peasant pastless piety appears dominant in some regions and virtually absent from others. The reasons for this lie in the history and character of local aristocracies. Because nobility was granted as the direct issue of a previous greatness or fame, at least in principle, its legitimacy rested upon past grandeur. And members of individual seigneurial houses also often continued to enjoy the reputation of *vicarius sancti* even after the great thirteenth-century movement away from pilgrimage to tombs, sites of interred relics. But the additional dignity of representing a saint did not permit an aristocrat to share his glory with the community. The common man could develop no sense of community continuity from narrations of ancestral seigneurial renown—accounts invariably containing references to miracles or to other forms of divine participation in family fame—when the nobility purged these tales of local ritual content by refusing to pilgrimage to local sites and instead sought miracles in distant places. For, in contrast with urban patricians, the rural aristocracy took their past with them, so to speak, when they traveled to far-off shrines. The former fled tradition; the latter were its personification. And they carried away the only material from which common people could fabricate some place for themselves, however modest, in the local sagas of ancestral prowess.

It was above all in south Germany, particularly in the area of present-day Bavaria, that aristocrats encouraged local pilgrimages, yet simultaneously refused to visit neighborhood shrines. This weakened men's sense of relation with previous community achievement and led rural folk to dissociate the dead from the past and to locate them in a state of purgatorial symbiosis with the living. For this reason, people could neither exclude the dead from their daily lives nor emancipate them from obligations binding them in the present. Thus only in Bavaria and immediately surrounding regions did souls in purgatory, the *Armeseelen*, appear on earth in the grotesque form of toads—condemned to find salvation by undertaking long pilgrimages.[91] *Armeseelen* sometimes held special masses, usually late at night; these were priests, who, having neglected their duties in life, were now obliged to fulfill them under unusually difficult circumstances.[92] The variety of apparitions is bewildering, but the population seemed always ready to come to the assistance of *Armeseelen* with specially prepared food and other types of aid appropriate to the needs of the particular soul.[93] *Armeseelen* frequently made personal visits to erstwhile relatives, friends, or neighbors, to plead with them to undertake a pilgrimage on their behalf.[94] Most revealing, however, is the way that the doctrinal vision of the "community of saints" was interpreted by common people as the *Ringburgschaftsgedanken* of a closed circle of reciprocal, expiatory sureties uniting the living and the dead. When someone received charitable aid, common people said that the poor recipient also vouchsafed a gift on the giver, insofar as "*poor people are the bodily representation of Armeseelen, souls in purgatory, who are here to bear witness for the good works of their fellows.*"[95] A view so pathetically solicitous of portraying the poor as instruments of divine justice against the rich and powerful rendered it difficult for the common man to find a meaningful distinction between living and departed members of his community.

This attitude becomes still more apparent when other aspects of ordinary people's relations with the dead are considered. While no information as yet exists about the behavior of Protestant and Catholic crowds with respect to the desecration of dead bodies in Germany, Natalie Zemon Davis observes that in France, "desecration of corpses . . . is primarily an action of Catholic crowds in the sixteenth century."[96] Moreover, despite the paucity of studies on German popular attitudes toward death, in contrast to the many high-quality French treatises on the subject,[97] considerable evidence does show that in late medieval south Germany—in Bavaria, the Upper Palatinate, Franconia, and in parts of Swabia, particularly the regions outside the Duchy of Württemburg— relations between the living and the dead were profoundly different from those in north Germany. In south Germany country folk wished not only to be buried among their "own," but they wanted also to have their bones (often elaborately painted and decorated) stacked up alongside those of their neighbors and ancestors amid ossuary frescoes of purgatory and the Last Judgment.[98] Indeed, late medieval German ossuaries were located "above all in the south and southeast," and these were the only regions where they attained artistic significance.[99] Particularly numerous in Upper and Lower Bavaria and the Upper Palatinate, ossuaries seem also to have been favored locations for prayers.[100] And most suggestive of all are the results of recent research on the Dance of Death (*Der Totentanz*). In south Germany it was a popular belief that the *Armeseelen* actually danced and performed purgatorial rites in graveyards. Elsewhere in Europe, in France, for example, where such macabre visions appear to have been unknown, men understood the Dance of Death only in an allegorical sense—a notion that returned from France via the Netherlands to western and to northern Germany.[101] It is also significant that in the south, cemeteries were often fortified, that the dead were said to participate in the defense of the community,[102] and that there was a flowering of late medieval sepulchral architecture[103] in Bavaria. All these points confirm the archival findings of south German village historians.

Karl Bader explains that the village sense for living in community with the dead (*dieses Miteinander von Lebenden und Toten*)

comes up again and again . . . in documentary testimony, along with the corresponding need of a village to bury its dead in its own church, in the protective space of the village and churchyard cemetery. This [practice] goes back to the time of the *Eigenkirchenrecht* [the principle of feudal investment of clergy]: *the true cemetery is the place where the church founders lay buried.* Thus the drive of village brotherhoods in the high and late Middle Ages to acquire their own church proceeded from the explicitly emphasized first and more fundamental wish to bury the dead in their own cemetery and not in a foreign one.[104]

Of course, very small villages often could not afford to build, staff, and maintain a church. Perhaps this circumstance explains why many pilgrimage places were adjacent to popular burial grounds.[105] And pilgrimage places were so dense in old Bavaria that many were less than two hours' walking distance and very few were more than a half day's travel from the points of departure. Medieval Bavaria and the areas immediately surrounding it constituted the only regions in the entire Holy Roman Empire in which rural pilgrimage sites formed scores of clusters or tiny constellations varying from about twelve to approximately twenty-five shrines, each group forming a small panoply of celestial protection; each also provided a sufficiently wide choice of holy figures—saints, Mary, and Christ—to satisfy the requirements of different expiatory obligations.[106] Just as townsmen built cathedrals in "an attempt to reproduce the structure of the universe"—not in the sense of a symbol, but of an actual "model" or true representation[107]—so south German rural folk portrayed their cosmic, or rather their purgatorial vision in mosaics of churchyard cemeteries, ossuaries, and holy shrines.

Hundreds of Bavarian and south German shrines not only provided a spectacle unique in the German religious landscape; they also testify to the power of aristocratic influence in the development of this extreme and deeply rooted form of pastless piety. We have already discussed the probability that aristocratic encouragement of popular *Umritte* and massacres of Jews around 1300 were related both to the multiplication of shrines and to the development of an imperial ideology among the newly emancipated south German *ministeriales*. Although the *ministeriales* acquired a free status in the sense that their titles were now inheritable, their social position remained somewhat ambiguous, as shown by a comparison of the place of the Bavarian nobility with the French, on the one hand, and with its counterparts in Swabia and Franconia, on the other. Among the many appellations and honors Duke Louis the Bearded from Ingolstadt listed after his name in the early fifteenth century, the title of

French count frequently appeared in second place, immediately following that of duke of Bavaria.[108] In France the duke was simply one among many nobles; at home he was a royal personage. The nobility under him, even though no longer unfree *ministeriales*, could attain a position comparable to their French counterparts only by acquiring the imperial status that would finally distinguish many of the aristocracy in Swabia and Franconia. The further circumstance that the Bavarian nobility reached new heights of emancipation under Louis of Bavaria, when the duke was also emperor, certainly reinforced their imperial aspirations. Until late in the fifteenth century the Bavarian nobility made constant appeals, sometimes accompanied by armed rebellion, for privileges comparable to those enjoyed by their Franconian and Swabian brethren.[109] For this reason, imperial political ideology was as strong among the Bavarian nobility as it was among the multitude of descendants of the imperial *ministeriales*, who lived more independently in the host of petty holdings and bailiwicks created out of the political ruins and fragments of the post-Hohenstaufen Empire.

The emancipation of post-Hohenstaufen south German *ministeriales* occurred at the same time that the lay religious movement for democratization of Europe's penitential system had culminated in the great year of Jubilee. At this point, we turn finally to statistical evidence to support the view that an eagerness among Bavarian liberated *ministeriales* to recruit popular support for Louis of Bavaria's campaign against John XXII led them to popularize *Umritte*, to participate in the massacre of Jews, and to promote the founding of new shrines—all in an attempt to establish more securely their own new dignity and authority. Since ordinary people often regarded the local seigneur as vicar of the neighborhood saint,[110] I propose to measure the degree of aristocratic influence on popular religious sentiment by comparing from one region to another the number of pre-Reformation shrines dedicated to saints with the number of pilgrimage places dedicated to Mary or to Christ. The results are so persuasive as to minimize the possibility of statistical distortion whether from uncertainties in the material gathered or from a presumed disappearance without trace of large numbers of medieval shrines in principalities that later became Protestant. Consider first the following figures from the north. From a total of 66 sites in the bishopric of Münster and the Province of Westphalia, I count 14 shrines dedicated to saints. In Pomerania only 1 of 15 pilgrimage places was founded for a saint. Not a single one of the 21 shrines in Brandenburg, none of the 7 in Mecklenburg, nor any of the 8 in Prussia, and only 1 of the 6 in Electoral Saxony had patron saints. Finally, of the 19 sites in Lower Saxony, from the same number in Schleswig and from the 17 in Silesia, I count respectively 4 saints in the first, 4 in the second, and 2 in the third region. In sum, a saint appears at only 26 of 178 pilgrimage places in north and east Germany—a ratio of almost 1 to 7. If Catholic Münster-Westphalia is left out, the ratio is close to 1 to 15.

Turning to the south, Bavaria (meaning here Upper and Lower Bavaria, the Innviertel[111] and the Upper Palatinate) boasted 151 saints from a total of 313 pilgrimage places. In Franconia, 60 out of 148 and in Swabia and Baden taken together, 101 out of 236 shrines were dedicated to saints. Altogether, saints worked their wonders at 312, or almost 45 percent of a total of 697 shrines. The ratio in Hesse, the Middle Rhine, and Thuringia was about the same, and nearly one shrine in three was dedicated to a saint in the Palatinate. Perhaps large numbers of pilgrimage sites disappeared without trace from northern and eastern territories, but coincidence alone cannot explain why some vast percentage of the allegedly vanished shrines were dedicated to saints. All the same, to exclude problems of probability from serious discussion, suppose momentarily that pure chance, or an unsuspected principle of human selection, may account for the aberrant typological distribution found among the surviving records of medieval shrines in northern Protestant lands. An explanation would then be needed as to why the Catholic territories of Westphalia and Münster—where the history of pilgrimage, with abundant sources, is the subject of flourishing local research—show no significant numbers of abandoned sites and they also eschew patron saints at shrines as do the neighboring Protestant states. Moreover, the pattern is not peculiar to Münster and Westphalia. A similar example is Ermland, a tiny ecclesiastical enclave in east Prussia, where loyalty to Rome persisted after the Reformation. After explaining how every holy site in the region had been preserved, a local historian thought it curious that "not a single pilgrimage to a saint" could be found among Ermland's eleven shrines, four of them medieval.[112]

To be sure, even after giving due weight to the cartography of *genossenschaftliche* pilgrimage clusters in Bavaria and allowing further for the southern image of local seigneurs as vicars of saints, a mere numerical tabulation, showing a southern plenitude and a northern paucity of shrines dedicated to saints, permits only a probable, not a necessary, inference of aristocratic influence on popular piety. Moreover, the great regional disparity in the proportions of shrines dedicated to saints demonstrates by itself no relation to subsequent confessional differences—especially considering that in the north few saintly sites appear in either Catholic or Protestant regions. But a closer look at the appended map does help to establish precisely these points. The 697 shrines located in Bavaria, Franconia, and the Swabia-Baden regions present two clearly visible features. First, the "agglutination" phenomenon is almost exclusively Bavarian, extending only in an attenuated form into Franconia (the Main area) and in the narrow stretch of land lying between the Duchy of Württemberg and the Bavarian frontier. Second, there is a clear correlation between the spatial distribution of medieval shrines and the geography of the subsequent south German Reformation. Areas rich in pilgrimage places remained Catholic, and those showing a paucity of sites embraced the Protestant faith.[113]

Here, amid a massive concentration of holy sites and an intensive tradition of pilgrimage research, it would be difficult to speak seriously of vanished shrines. The reasons for these curious patterns do not lie in the realm of chance; rather, they are to be found in the history of the aristocracy, especially in its vast regional differences. A few examples from territories in the northwest make the point clear. In Oldenburg, of 110 to 130 aristocratic family names appearing in fourteenth-century records, mostly lower nobility, only 16 survived down to 1500.[114] In the words of one historian, "the nobility was reduced to a species of great peasantry."[115] And the region turned Protestant in the Reformation. Lying immediately to the south, although intersected in the middle by part of the bishopric of Osnabrück, was the bishopric of Münster. Over half of Westphalia fell within its jurisdiction; the other part extended to the southeast. In contrast to Oldenburg, the territory saw a thorough consolidation of the lower nobility from the fourteenth through the middle of the sixteenth centuries.[116] And the area remained Catholic during the Reformation. One further important characteristic distinguished the Münster-Westphalian nobility: just like their counterparts in the northern part of Lower Saxony, the social distance between the aristocracy and the rich peasants or patricians was negligible in the fourteenth and fifteenth centuries. Intermarriage between the groups was very common.[117] Only in the sixteenth century did the Münster-Westphalian nobility set themselves clearly apart from wealthy commoners.

The progressive derogation of the Oldenburg nobility and the relative intimacy of later medieval Westphalian knights with people from the upper levels of plebeian life—a social custom diametrically opposed to Bavarian practices—had an important influence on aristocrat-peasant relations. Relatively free social intercourse saved the peasant from exaggerated fear or awe of the nobility. A mere mention of the famous battle of Hemmingstedt in Holstein on 17 February 1500, where Dithmarscher peasants successfully crushed an attacking army of knights and professional soldiers, testifies to the determination of rural folk to preserve their "free" *Bauernrepublik*.[118] Three centuries earlier, large-scale military efforts, solemn papal proclamations, and repeated crusades were required to overcome the powerful resistance to episcopal and lay authorities offered by Stedinger peasants on the lower Weser, in the Oldenburg-Bremen region.[119] And the well-known independence of ordinary

folk in the neighboring county of East Friesland, accustomed from the early Middle Ages to owning their churches and to appointing their own priests—a practice common to the upper third of north Germany west of the Elbe[120]—makes it clear that these rural people were not accustomed to regard nobles as earthly representatives of saints. Moreover, the rejection of aristocratic influence in northwest German religious devotion, far from being a phenomenon restricted to pilgrimage practices, was apparent in all forms of popular saint worship in these regions during the thirteenth century.[121] Nor is it possible to impute to men so jealous of their autonomy an enfeebled sense of past community experience. Surely their extraordinary passion for collective self-determination is connected with the weakness of the lower nobility in these areas through most of the high and late Middle Ages. And nothing could be more foreign to such a population than the closed circle of expiatory mutualities symbolized by the Bavarian shrines. This explains the demonstrable absence of pre-Reformation pilgrimage places dedicated to saints and makes more understandable why people in north and central Germany founded far fewer shrines of any description than did their countrymen in the south.

Indeed, the shrines of Münster-Westphalia powerfully confirm this view. For my research shows that seven of the fourteen sites dedicated to saints were founded before 1200, four between 1200 and 1360, and only three after 1360. In contrast, twenty-seven shrines were dedicated to Mary and to Christ *after* 1360. Thus there is an exact chronological and geographical correlation between the increase in pilgrimage places and the rise of lower nobility, and the virtual absence of holy places dedicated to saints after 1360 testifies to the relative integration of the nobility with the more prosperous commoners through most of the fifteenth century. Only one relationship remains to be explained. What is the connection between an upwardly mobile nobility and popular pilgrimage to shrines that were *not* dedicated to saints? The answer is clear: in the course of their ascent, the Münster-Westphalian nobility engrossed positions in church canonries, attaining a virtual monopoly in the late fifteenth century.[122] And because these clerical offices provided the major part of their wealth and influence, the nobility had a vital interest in enhancing the authority and splendor of these offices by establishing wonder-working shrines. But their social distance from ordinary people was too small to permit them to enter, as did their Bavarian counterparts, into intimate relations with the divine personages to whom common folk made pilgrimages. The evidence is now plain for both the northwest and the south. The curve of local shrines founded after 1300 rises in direct proportion to the number and importance of a lower nobility, reaching its steepest ascent and showing the highest numbers of shrines built for saints in regions where the knights placed a greater distance between

themselves and leading groups in plebeian society. Catholic and Protestant territories fall respectively in the upper and lower parts of the curve, but only in Bavaria does the largest body of small nobility combine with the longest tradition of vast social distance. Here I count twenty-three shrines established to saints before the year 1000; another twenty-one between 1000 and 1200; an additional sixteen between 1200 and 1360; and ninety-one holy sites, about 50 percent more than the combined number for all the previous centuries, dedicated to saints after 1360. The parallel ascent of pilgrimage saints and emancipated *ministeriales* dramatically confirms the nobility's crucial role in shaping popular piety in late medieval Bavaria.[123] Also, perhaps even more conclusive, the neighboring Duchy of Württemberg provides a striking example of a precisely opposite evolution. The virtual absence of a landowning lower nobility in fifteenth-century Württemberg explains at once the pronounced dearth of pilgrimage sites in the duchy and makes understandable Württemberg's subsequent role as the most powerful Protestant state in south Germany.[124]

The existence of a few diminutive Protestant enclaves in Bavaria—so small that they do not appear on standard maps of the Reformation—throws additional light on the role of nobility in the formation of popular piety. The *ministeriales* rose rapidly in the thirteenth century, partly because the old nobility simply was dying out. The surviving ancient houses, almost without exception, founded territorial dynasties and entered the *Reichsfürstenstand*. A very few former *ministerialis* families, such as the Hohenwaldecker in extreme south Bavaria, managed also to reach this exalted status, and they understandably acquired a consciousness of princely position similar to that of fellow rulers who possessed an immemorial lineage. Since sovereigns rarely or never founded holy sites to saints, these petty princelings imitated the duke of Bavaria or even the emperor himself when they dedicated shrines exclusively to Mary or to Christ in the independent enclaves: Hohenwaldeck, Ortenburg, and Haag. And *all three territories* turned Protestant after the Reformation! To speak here of the principle *cuius regio, eius religio* (a theme discussed below)—however important may have been the ruling houses' confessional choice in these instances—is to obscure the crucial fact that the sovereigns' decision that did actually conform to the local pattern of popular devotion was in fact made much earlier in the history of common worship. Indeed, folk attachment to the Reformation was notorious in all three territories and, in the case of Hohenwaldeck, grass-roots Protestantism proved sufficiently intolerable for the duke of Bavaria that he included it as one of the reasons for sending a military expedition against the little county.[125]

A much different, but extraordinarily revealing picture appears in

the lands lying to the east of the Elbe and Saale rivers. In Pomerania, for example, "relic worship . . . was never so popular [*volkstümlich*] as . . . in southern territories."[126] This is not surprising, since settlement of these lands, beginning around 1100, was undertaken by pioneering Cistercian monasteries with their small armies of *conversi*. The white monks had always prohibited relic worship and, correspondingly, they dedicated every Cistercian monastery to Mary. This piety pervaded the thinly populated rural areas.[127] Moreover, the low incidence of relic worship is related directly to a paucity of holy sites. East of the Elbe, late colonization and Christianization prevented the growth of traditions attributing the thaumaturgic powers of popular shrines to favors bestowed by God upon the distant forebears of local nobility.

Indeed, to encourage pilgrimage east of the Elbe, the papacy, beginning as early as 1250, probably sooner than elsewhere, directed a steady stream of indulgences to shrines located at monasteries, churches, and chapels. By the late fifteenth century the single shrine at the chapel built to Mary on the Gollen Heights overlooking the Pomeranian coast near Köslin received authority to grant indulgences to pilgrims in the years 1395, 1396, 1399, 1401, 1419, 1420, 1458, and 1490.[128] That this unusual flow of penitential remissions was connected with the long process of Christianization east of the Elbe is suggested by the issuance in the fifteenth century of indulgences to increase attendance at mass.[129] But whatever the effect of these efforts to transplant pilgrimage piety to colonial areas, they did not prevent the development of sharp regional differences in the devotional content displayed at local shrines. Holy sites situated in coastal regions, such as the one on the Gollen Heights, were frequently named *Stella maris*, for sailors said that the rays from their light towers appeared often miraculously, like a star in the heavens, to guide seamen through the darkness of night. An enormously popular shrine, the Gollen Heights chapel formed only one in a series of pilgrimage places erected at way stations along the continental Baltic coast.[130] Here worship of Mary was totally different from the devotion of Teutonic Knights, for whom the heavenly Queen was the celestial patron of a permanent crusade against populations that were more or less stubbornly resistant to Christian conversion. Since the Teutonic Knights prohibited the establishment of landowning monasteries, permitting only mendicant orders,[131] shrines founded in their territories differed from those located at monasteries in inland regions beyond their jurisdiction. The absence of saints from all of these holy sites suggests that local pilgrimages promoted from above, without regard for indigenous popular tradition, found little response from common folk. Apart from visits to the coastal areas, sacred treks were undertaken most frequently by people who could afford to travel long distances to worship at far-off shrines.[132]

In general, the distribution of sundry types of medieval shrines in time and in space shows that the vast regional differences in the content of German popular piety were becoming more pronounced on the eve of the Reformation. Two phenomena common to all Europe seem to have contributed in different ways to this development. First, aristocracies tended to grow more exclusive in western and central Europe after about 1470. Also, after approximately 1450–70 Europe experienced a powerful demographic growth that in turn caused an expansion in all areas of economic life, at least through the first quarter of the sixteenth century. Perhaps the increased numbers of wealthy roturiers aspiring to aristocratic status allowed the nobility everywhere to make entry into its ranks more difficult for newcomers. At any rate, economic prosperity helped to fund more masses for the dead and it encouraged greater financial support for ecclesiastical establishments and for every form of ritual practice —a phenomenon well known in the history of the Reformation.

Thus both aristocratic consolidation and a waxing prosperity, encouraging ecclesiastical endowments in wider sectors of society, contributed generally to a geographical expansion of institutions and practices associated with saint worship as well as to the intensification of the purgatorial cult in regions where it was already long established. The so-called "Catholic Reformation" or papal-oriented religious renewal that preceded the Protestant Reformation and established the spiritual foundations of the Council of Trent developed as part of this rich, ornate flowering of religious life after about 1470. These considerations have a special relevance for Bavaria, particularly the rich farm lands of Lower Bavaria, where the nobility was numerous, active, and far more powerful than elsewhere in the duchy. Agricultural prosperity, stimulated by the increase in population, had important consequences. On the one hand, the rising income from farm lands encouraged the Lower Bavarian nobility to press harder for the imperial status they had always sought; on the other, the increase in public revenue gave the central government far greater resources with which to combat aristocratic militancy. In this conflict, Duke Albrecht IV crushed the Lower Bavarian nobility in the famous *Löwlerkrieg* of 1488. Most important here, however, is the fact that Bavarian–south German pilgrimage worship grew most rapidly when ideological excitement among the Bavarian aristocracy was at its peak.

In this connection population growth had other important consequences. While high urban mortality rates had always caused some movement of people from the country to the city, these migrations rose substantially in periods of demographic expansion like the one beginning around 1450–70. Thus in the generation before Luther, the period of greatest pilgrimage activity, increasingly large numbers of rural folk poured into the south German cities—bringing with them the entire diapason of expiatory rites associated with village peregrinating practices. No wonder iconoclastic fury in the early years of the Reformation was a predominantly south German, urban phenomenon!

Finally, the close links between *Umritte*, pilgrimage piety, and the social and political aspirations of the Bavarian nobility throw light on unsuspected social aspects of rival modes of piety. Consider, for example, the special favor shown to the mendicant orders, particularly the Franciscans, in the lands of the Teutonic Knights. For Saint Francis's Rule of 1221 (Chapter 15) forbade members of his order to ride or to own horses.[133] Given the absence of other types of cloisters in these regions and the large numbers of feminine houses established elsewhere in the north—to say nothing of thousands of Beguine communities—observance of Saint Francis's precept would not have appeared strange; whereas in Bavaria, there was a craze for *Umritte* and a fascination with miracles associated with the hunt. No wonder that, in contrast to their northern brethren, south German Franciscans are notorious for militant support of Zwinglianism, a strikingly anti-aristocratic and anti-imperial form of Protestantism. The Reformation thus represents a mass popular rejection of a social and cultural as well as a religious system—a complex of devotional practices linked with purgatorial visions and an aggressively aristocratic ethos. This penitential system was incompatible with the social structure and with the moral, political, and spiritual attitudes of people who seldom worshiped saints at neighborhood shrines. That is the burden of argument in Part One of the essay. Part Two discusses the cultural dimension of the conflicting traditions of popular piety and focuses particularly on the links between intellectual life, patriotism and common lay devotion in late medieval and Reformation Germany.

PART TWO: POPULAR PIETY AND THE FORMATION OF GERMAN CULTURE

Pilgrimage and Patriotism: The Rise of South German Humanism and the Backgrounds to the Baroque

Although aristocratic consolidation and demographic growth were probably the chief external factors contributing to the expansion of pilgrimage processions, other reasons help both to explain proliferation of holy shrines after 1450–70 and to make clear how foreign this form of piety appeared to peoples outside the pilgrimage districts. The Turkish threat and the idea of crusade, especially after the fall of Constantinople in 1453, created enormous excitement in south Germany. Thousands of children from parts of the Rhineland and from Bavaria and adjacent areas left on successive pilgrimages from 1456 to 1459, sometimes in the dead of winter, to St. Michel at Mont St. Michel off the Normandy coast.[134] Sometimes actively encouraged by church officials, as in the Franconian episcopal See of Eichstätt, and sometimes by cheering on-lookers, the fledgling pilgrims wended their way to the distant shrine on behalf of the adult population. There they implored the militant arch-angel. Perhaps they reminded him that having so recently helped the "innocent maid," Joan of Arc, to rid France of her hereditary enemy, it was now all the more important for him to respond to entire processions of "innocents" and to help organize crusades to repel the heathen in-vader. This example of "substitution"—in origins a monastic principle—transformed into pathetic junior public initiative for penitential defense of the *respublica christiana* was incomprehensible to many north Ger-mans. For example, the writer of Lübeck's official chronicle did not know whether to ascribe the events to satanic or to celestial influences.[135]

Thus newly founded shrines show a precipitous rate of increase in a period of intense aristocratic militancy and unprecedented public agita-tion for crusades. The new surge of patriotic religiosity received its most enduring expression toward the end of the fifteenth century in the famous appellation: *Heiliges Römisches Reich deutscher Nation.* Meanwhile, on the crest of this ground swell of feeling for the Empire stood the bizarre, somehow faintly burlesque figure of the imperial knight. His enormous importance for south German literary life arose from his special position within the imperial church. Located principally in Swabia, Franconia, and the Rhine Valley, and escaping from the control of territorial lords, the imperial knights and imperial counts enjoyed a long de facto exis-tence before receiving belated official recognition—in Swabia from about 1450, then in Franconia (1540–70), and finally in the Rhine Valley (1729). They formed special confederations that recognized the emperor as their only political superior.[136] They owed this unique status to their monopoly of the canonry, permitting the knights to elect bishops from their number, who in turn represented them as ecclesiastical princes in the Reichstag. Thus, occupying a position crucial to the survival of im-perial benefices (*Reichsstifte*) generally, the knights, that is the richer among them, became so intimately related in the sixteenth century to the Imperial Church as to form separate parts of a single institution.[137] In some areas the local nobility moved after 1470 into the highest councils of rapidly growing territorial governments, rising as a group to mark the end of clerical predominance among state officials in the more centralized principalities. In others, however, the imperial knights institutionalized once again the old-fashioned arrangement whereby secular government became part of overarching ecclesiastical structures having no necessary territorial reference. True to the traditions of a corps that for centuries had staffed higher offices—lay and religious—the descendants of *Reichsministerialen* regarded the church as an institution important for their survival as a class of powerful officials active in political bodies everywhere in the empire. The knights did in fact give new strength to the medieval structure of the Holy Roman Empire, extending their control of imperial benefices from the later fifteenth through the eighteenth centuries. At the same time, they deplored the growing tendency of territorial governments to exclude clerics from secular offices—said to be subversive of traditional values—and they resisted centralization on the imperial level and rationalization of political authority in particular territories. In south Germany, the *Reichskirche*, which they dominated, steadily promoted the cult of the heavenly Queen throughout the Catholic Reform and Counter-Reformation. A document issued in 1519, entitled "A Friendly, Brotherly, and Neighborly Union and Contract . . . in Observation of a Christian and reasonable Police," shows the knights to have founded brotherhoods in her name. The paper contained articles pledging large numbers of imperial nobles in Franconia to a strict Christian life, "in the Name and Honor of the indivisible Trinity and in *highest praise of the most glorious heavenly Queen Mary*, in special pleasing obedience to . . . the Holy Roman Imperial Majesty . . . , to the preservation of our Noble Names, which are founded and dedicated alone to Virtue."[138] It is in the light of such pronunciamentos, written by proud descendants of crusading warriors, that we should read, for example, the rumbustious writings of the imperial Franconian knight Ulrich von Hutten, whose "basic criticisms of the church stemmed from his belief that the Curia and its minions had encroached on the Emperor's prerogatives and those of his imperial knights, and had violated the ancient liberties of the Empire."[139] His redoubtable friend and loyal supporter in the Reuchlin affair, Franz von Sickingen, played a special role in German letters. In the words of Hajo Holborn, "Hutten was the incarnation of chivalry on the spiritual side, Sickingen on the political."[140] The two figures expressed on a higher plane the qualities and values evident in the memoirs of Götz von Berlichingen: the union of soldierly brutality and literary accomplishment in the cause of empire, chivalry, and personal fame. To be sure, Hutten wrote to Erasmus saying that Sickingen "deserves to be immortalized in your letters," and Luther sent greetings to "our friends in the faith, Franz and Ulrich von Hutten."[141] But Erasmus and Luther remained as indifferent to the cause of Hutten and his *condottiere* companion as they were to Sebastian Brant's patriotic plans for reform of the empire and to his zealous defense of the Immaculate Conception. Another humanist, one much admired by Hutten, was Conrad Celtis, his famous fellow Franconian of peasant origins. Celtis, too, "entered the lists with the Upper Rhenish humanists against the Dominicans *in support of the dogma of the immaculate conception of Mary"*[142]—an appellation that was the doctrinal formulation for the heavenly Queen. Similar in spirit to Celtis was Jacob Wimpfeling, both in his adoration of the Immaculate Conception and in the patriotism informing his *Germania* (1501), which he wrote as the leader of a protonational literary circle in pre-Buceran Strassburg. The enthusiasm created by the restored imperial ideology flowed in many directions—the tumultuous lives of Sickingen, Hutten, and Berlichingen, and the general south German humanist obsession with the heavenly Queen. Perhaps its most vivid expression is the *Minneallegorie* of the forgotten Swabian poet Augustin von Hammerstetten: in recounting the story of a stag with golden antlers, between which an image of the Virgin appears, it recalls the hunting legends associated with many southern shrines. The emperors themselves took a hand. Maximilian celebrated the hunt in his literary works, both in the renowned *Weisskunig*[143] and in the highly publicized accounts of his personal exploits in German forests; his father, Frederick III, had named the twenty-eight-year-old Conrad Celtis in 1487 as the first poet laureate of the empire. Finally, the humanist sodalities founded by Celtis have a remarkable parallel in the almost simultaneous organization of the *Reichsritterkantone*, the basic administrative units in the confederation of imperial knights.

Thus the writings of the south German humanists before the Reformation reflect the distinctive religious, political, and social life of the region: notably a popular and militantly imperial piety, encouraged by imperial knights and promoted by a rebellious Lower Bavarian nobility.

Popular pilgrimage fervor appears to have been at least as great an influence on the style of public architecture as it was on the development of a distinctly south German literature. It reached its full flower only in the Counter-Reformation, which had a close relationship with the baroque style in art and architecture. It seems clear that the German baroque—an overwhelmingly southern Catholic phenomenon, attaining its most distinctive forms in Upper Bavaria—developed partly out of the triumphalism of late fifteenth-century pilgrimage piety, with its devotion to the heavenly Queen, the militant protectress of the Imperial Church. Besides this obvious association is a more fundamental consideration applying to the later Middle Ages. German late Gothic architecture was largely financed by indulgences[144] purchased by those who worshiped at churches being built or repaired from the income received from these remissions. The parallel with pilgrimage is striking. For pilgrims believed that the celestial patron was physically present at the holy place at which they left their offerings. Since the patron imparted sacred attributes to the image at the shrine, it could be repaired or replaced without affecting its supernatural properties. Location was the crucial factor.[145] For one to travel to a building site in order to obtain an indulgence implied a kind of piety indistinguishable from that displayed when traveling to a pilgrimage shrine. In both instances prayers and expectations were linked with architecture.

The sacred edifices and holy images of Baroque and Counter-Reformation south Germany symbolized a rural culture that was profoundly hostile to cities, disdainful of the literature they produced, and indeed rejected as heretical the introduction of the written word into popular religious life. The *Umritte*, in their bewildering variety, were another reflection of this rural piety. And this Bavarian–south German aversion to literate expression explains why the overwhelming majority of authors contributing to German vernacular literature between 1560 and 1789 were Protestant.[146] Only the massively nonverbal culture of Catholic Germany—which provoked Montesquieu's remarks about Bavarian mental regression[147]—could have the architectural and artisanal splendor that flourished along with every form of purgatorial rite and processional ceremony.

To assert that folk piety directly influenced higher levels of cultural accomplishment, however, is to raise a problem analogous to the one presented by the principle of *cuius regio, eius religio,* alleged to have been effective during the Reformation. Did authorities prescribe the outward ornaments of the commonweal in the same manner that they prescribed the faith of their subjects? Or, conversely, did royal decrees about religion, like those concerning aesthetic matters, reflect rather than shape the cultural contours of the society? Having argued that popular devotion influenced the character of south German literary and artistic life, I propose further to demonstrate that the schoolbook slogan *cuius regio . . .* is a sheer myth, repeated by generations of scholars who failed to inquire into the social background of the Reformation.

Suppose for a moment that William IV, duke of Bavaria (1503–50), was as zealous a Protestant as, for example, his contemporary, Philip, landgrave of Hesse. Would the Bavarian population also have adopted the new faith? A roughly similar situation existed in the Upper Palatinate, a small territory lying on Old Bavaria's northern border, and its history provides reasons to think that most Bavarians would have remained Catholic. Shrines and ossuaries were abundant in this tiny land. When the Rhenish Palatinate introduced Lutheranism, it achieved success in the cities, and even more radical teachings won prompt acceptance among the mine workers, yet Protestantism had little effect on rural pilgrimage practices. Indeed, even the later hard-fought and bloody triumph of Calvinism in the middle of the century failed to dampen pilgrimage ardor. Ernst Walter Zeeden explains:

The Visitation reports show that despite all prohibitions pilgrimage was not uprooted, indeed it was to a certain degree ineradicable. Even seventy to eighty years after the introduction of the Reformation and despite decades of severe countermeasures from the Calvinist government, the population sought out a large number of old pilgrimage sites within as well as without the Upper Palatinate territory—also conversely [people] from the neighboring lands of Bohemia *and Bavaria* continued to make pilgrimages into the evangelized Upper Palatinate.[148]

Surely the later Catholic reconversion of the Upper Palatinate during the Thirty Years' War proceeded as easily as it did precisely because rural pilgrimage had persisted for almost a century in the face of determined official efforts to abolish it. The contrast between a bloody introduction of Protestantism, especially Calvinism, and the subsequent peaceful character of reconversion—which applies also to other rural regions—is a phenomenon that, in the reverse situation, is directly comparable to the stubborn Lutheranism of people living in the three tiny Bavarian Protestant enclaves discussed above. Moreover, the further striking example of a single village in Protestant Haag, Albaching, in which every single inhabitant remained firmly Catholic, shows almost conclusively to what extent *cuius regio, eius religio* remained often a dead letter in rural regions of even the most diminutive territory.[149] Indeed, in the case of the microscopic county of Ortenburg, local historians emphatically deny that the count's official adoption of Lutheranism proceeded from the principle *cuius regio*.[150]

Finally, when we compare the Calvinist military conversion of the Upper Palatinate rural areas with, for example, the peaceful "Reformation from below" that occurred in the bucolic lands of the south Weser Valley,[151] we find that the religion of the ruling authorities merely reflected the dominant form of regional piety. The only exceptions are instances of official pressures on minority groups or, more rarely, decrees in lands so small as to be indistinguishable in size from large family estates. In the cases of the Calvinist Hohenzollerns and the Catholic convert Saxon king, August the Strong, ruling houses frankly abandoned the illusory principle that sovereigns alone determined the religious faith of their subjects. To be sure, examples of successful re-Catholicization in Habsburg territories during the Thirty Years' War—particularly in Bohemia and Styria—suggest a qualification; but the enormous military effort they required, along with the wholesale expulsion of the native nobility, show that *cuius regio* triumphed here only as a result of victory in a major civil war—scarcely evidence pointing either to the weakness of local popular piety or to proof of the effectiveness of *cuius regio* within the bounds of the more usual exercise of dynastic authority. Meanwhile, the persistence of Protestantism in Silesia after Habsburg re-Catholicization indicates that even these extreme measures did not always prove to be entirely successful.

Beyond the persistence of pilgrimage in areas where Protestantism was merely imposed from above, however, other evidence points to the depth of peregrinational devotion in Bavarian south Germany. Although Ulrich von Hutten wrote contemptuously of excited throngs milling about or "storming" holy shrines, he uttered no disparaging word about Emperor Frederick III's pilgrimage to Altötting in Bavaria in 1491, only two years after the first report of a miracle. For this was no ordinary shrine. Frederick's visit, almost at the time of its establishment, may be compared to the pilgrimage about a century later of Maximilian I of Bavaria, who inscribed his name with his own blood in the register of Altötting's congregation.[152] The behavior of emperor and duke reflects Altötting's unusual reputation as does the vast number of pilgrims who came to worship there from all of southern Germany and even from other parts of central Europe.[153] Indeed, persuasive evidence points to Altötting as a central shrine dedicated to the *Heiligen Römischen Reich deutscher Nation*. According to the Bavarian humanist Johannes Turmaier, known as Aventine (1477–1534), a student of Conrad Celtis and court historian to William IV, the Bavarians were converted to Christianity by Saint Rupert, who baptized Duke Dieter III of Regensburg and his brother Otto of Ötting. Each brother built a chapel dedicated to Rupert. But, Aventine continues, Charlemagne chose Ötting as the chapel he wished to visit in the company of other dignitaries of the empire.[154] Writing about a generation later, the historian Martinus Eisengrein says the chapel, built even prior to Saint Rupert's arrival, served the "common people [who] worshiped the seven planets."[155] Aventine's and Eisengrein's assertions are not entirely mythical. For modern research shows the edifice, dating from the early eighth century, to be a replica of the chapel erected to Mary in Würzburg (the first in Germany) by the great English missionary Boniface, Apostle of Germany. Indeed, this is the reason given by late fifteenth-century pilgrims for traveling to *unser lieben Frau ihr Capellen* (to the Chapel of our beloved Lady)![156]

In the first "miracle book" about Altötting, its author, the Canon Jakob Issickemer, writing in 1497, says that the "Holy" Charlemagne had "estranged" the chapel from the pagans in order "to consecrate it to the heavenly Queen." He goes on to say that

people from divers lands, of foreign birth and from all estates, cardinals spiritual, archbishops . . . exalted learned masters and doctors, also emperors, kings, dukes, landgraves, counts . . . simple people of both sexes come with their offerings. . . . Also out of no other reason than that God and His blessed Mother, the All Hailed *Queen of Heaven*, the Virgin Mary . . . announced in order that God's gifts be invested with profit, not buried fruitlessly in the earth, but distributed to our spiritual gain . . . that God chose the city of *alten öding* out of a special Grace and divine Providence. The same as He, for example, [commanded] that He be hailed and praised by emperors, kings, princes, and all the high born under the heavens in the Holy Temple of Jerusalem, so doth He [wish] to be honored, praised, and hailed through the Virgin Mary, the most blessed of women, *immaculate* and chosen [by Him] from all Eternity. Toward this end and for the protection of the Holy Christian Church . . . there arose in the heart of the Holy Roman Empire [meaning Altötting] through the intercession of the blessed Mother such a help and grace transmitted most conveniently to all parts of the same Holy Empire by the devout [pilgrims?].[157]

It is no surprise, therefore, to observe on the appended map that the highest density of shrines appears around Altötting, despite the fact that, unlike the shrine-rich regions immediately north and northwest of Lake Constance, the Altötting countryside possessed neither an unusual concentration of cloisters nor any other institutional arrangements known to encourage the founding of pilgrimage sites. Finally, it is important to refer again to the map showing the distribution of Austrian *Umritte* (unfortunately, no such reliable work seems to exist for other parts of Old Germany). For the Austrian map includes the Innviertel, a region that was part of Bavaria until 1779, when it was ceded to Austria by the Peace of Teschen. Inside a small area—a rectangle running roughly from the Innviertel border a few kilometers east of Altötting and continuing about sixty kilometers to the north, extending some thirty kilometers further eastward into the Innviertel—more *Umritte* appear than in all the rest of Austria! This fact along with further evidence gives us reason to suppose that the concentration on the present-day Bavarian side of the border was equally high.[158] All signs point to Altötting as the home of the heavenly Queen, Protectress of the Imperial Church and patron saint of the imperial knights. Furthermore, it would appear that Altötting, from the very beginning, was the pilgrimage capital of the entire Holy Roman Empire. Kösslarn had been the pilgrimage capital of Lower Bavaria,[159] but in 1488 Duke Albrecht IV crushed the local nobility's last bid for emancipation, and in the following year the first miracle was recorded at Altötting—the sudden appearance of the empire's highest dignitaries at a shrine in a chapel reputed to have been visited by Charlemagne. It is surely more than a coincidence that the relative eclipse of Kösslarn and the rise of Altötting took place in the few years immediately after Duke Albrecht's victory.

It is noteworthy that Altötting's appearance as the chief pilgrimage center of the Holy Roman Empire, occurring as it did during a decisive stage in Bavarian political centralization, corresponds with analogous events a generation later in France. Just as the fading of Kösslarn before the splendor of Altötting symbolized the triumph of Bavarian ducal sovereignty, so Francis I's prohibition of the use of relics in swearing oaths was part of a program to limit the power of the French aristocracy by making thaumaturgic powers an exclusive attribute of the crown—at least as far as they pertained to the exercise of secular authority.[160] Moreover, when we recall that even the most petty German sovereign rarely or never dedicated shrines to saints, preferring the more exalted figures of Mary and Christ, a pattern emerges that confirms a major theoretical principle formulated by one of England's most imaginative early anthropologists. Discussing the relation between political centralization and the religion of primitive tribes, A. M. Hocart, writing three years before his death in 1939, argued, "The whole struggle of monotheism v. polytheism is meaningless as long as we look upon it as a conflict of philosophies. What does it matter whether there be one God or many? Because by abolishing minor gods you abolish minor sovereignties."[161] Furthermore, the contemporary sociologist Guy E. Swanson finds that polytheism appears to be prevalent among those primitive societies where ancestral cults are most active[162]—a form of devotion strikingly similar to relic worship. Altogether, this evidence suggests that the founding of Altötting and Francis I's decree can be regarded as ritual concomitants to a process whereby "minor gods" are abolished in the course of establishing centralized political authority.

The point is fundamental for understanding some less obvious relationships between the history of political authority and the development of European national cultures. Swanson observes that polytheism appears in primitive societies where supernatural powers are regularly invoked to control moral relations between particular individuals.[163] In this respect, tribal peoples worshiping many deities resemble members of late medieval confraternities and *corpora mystica*. Moral acts are those which, being beyond the purview of judge or arbiter, are not susceptible to external adjudication. No such moral sphere is conceivable in corporations, where oaths bound members so closely to one another as to form a single personality. Oaths created infrangible relationships—their organic and involuntary character expressed by the term "brotherhood" as opposed to a word indicating "friendship." Men were inhibited from establishing an emotional distance from one another sufficient for them to claim an area of conduct that, being formally recognized as immune from official judgment, would permit them to develop that sense of personal autonomy upon which Western moral thought is founded.

To organize society around networks of oaths, each tiny plexus of *corpora mystica* bound to some higher supervisory structure by force of promises made in the sight of God, is to inspire the population with a fear of divine retribution for acts over which they had no direct control. No historian of late medieval or early modern Europe can fail to no-

tice the oppressive regularity with which entire communities sought to
propitiate God's anger for wrongs they could not identify. Every hail-
storm, drought, epidemic, or other natural disaster was perceived as
divine punishment for unspecified offenses. The enormous ideological
energy unleashed in late medieval and early modern Europe proceeds
from a common, profoundly emotional reaction of people who, having
come to doubt that every breach of oath was a direct affront to God,
refused to accept any longer the role of victims or sacrifices to be offered
up in appeasement for unidentifiable transgressions.

In this context, Francis I's monopolization of thaumaturgic powers
associated with relic worship throws light in two directions. On the
political plane, his ban of reliquary adjurations, making supernatural
justification for government an exclusive attribute of the crown, laid the
ritual and constitutional foundations for the doctrine of the divine right
of kings and helped to destroy a system of parcelized sovereignty. In the
cultural area, the corresponding inability of local authorities to regulate
interpersonal behavior through a system of divine sanctions helped to
emancipate common people from the constraints of collective responsibility and encouraged European populations to identify the development
of personal moral autonomy with some form of psychological participation in public affairs. At this basic level, the Renaissance, the Reformation, and the subsequent widespread popular support for the doctrine
of the divine right of kings express, in different ways, a common effort
to discredit the deeply rooted belief that every social organism has the
power to invoke supernatural sanctions. Here lie the popular roots of
political centralization and patriotic sentiment.

*Feminine Devotion and the Rise of Lay Piety
Above the Benrather Line*

The multitude of Bavarian shrines dedicated to saints testify to a
piety that was rooted in a popular identification of princely-seigneurial
paternalism with divine protection. Shrines were also numerous in politically fragmented regions where, unlike Bavaria, the population could not
attribute religious qualities to a single supreme sovereign. During the
Great Peasants' War (1524–25) religious insurrection raged in these min-
iature polities. There were two such areas of major importance. In the
south, insurrectional fury swept through the *Reichsstifte*, small enclaves
dominated by imperial knights and monastic establishments that promoted the founding of a plethora of widely scattered shrines. Although
many were dedicated to saints, they symbolized no wide pattern of community association, only a profusion of tiny communities isolated in the

local character of their devotion. In the north, peasant insurgence raged above all in the jumble of rural toparchies in Thuringia. But rural religious revolt, which was merely one part of the German Reformation, accounts neither for urban Protestantism and rural Lutheranism in the south nor for the particular form of piety, devoid of any regional or social reference, that was peculiar to Lutheran devotion in the north and in much of central Germany.

This northern spirituality developed out of social relationships very different from those associated with pilgrimage ardor or with biblically inspired rural rebellion. But merely to cite the relative absence of aristocratic influence in the north does not identify the kind of people who did help to form the character of popular religion in these regions. Curious as it may appear, a substantial body of evidence suggests that *il faut chercher la femme*! Women stood toward north German medieval popular piety as the local seigneur did to purgatorial saint worship in the lands of Louis of Bavaria. Subsequently, on the eve of the Reformation, when imperial knights infused southern humanist writings with the crusading vehemence of their thirteenth-century ancestors, north German literature reflected the feminine devotion of a previous age.

Although female religious organizations seem to have multiplied more freely in the empire than anywhere else in Europe, their distribution was very uneven. For example, consider the location of convents and Beguines or lay feminine religious communities around 1300, when they were probably most numerous. The Beguines were members of sisterhoods founded in the twelfth century in the Netherlands, who, taking no vows and having no common rule, mother house, or general superior, lived nevertheless in communities wherein they dedicated themselves both to a semimonastic life and to philanthropic works, especially to care of the sick and the poor.[164] In Germany they were a multitude. Max Heimbucher counts more than 141 Beguine communities in Cologne alone by 1246, 60 in Strasbourg, 57 in Frankfurt, and innumerable foundations in Aachen, Worms, Mainz, Wesel, Düsseldorf, Eisenach, Erfurt, Borken, Schüttdorf, Hamburg, Lübeck, Leipzig, Stuttgart, Braunschweig, Hannover, Magdeburg, Kaufbeuren, Augsburg, to name only some towns.[165] The Beguines were by no means alone, however, in the powerful female spiritual movement spreading through Germany during the thirteenth century. The 50 houses of the Mary Magdalene Order (after 1277) and the 44 houses of the Clarisses, Franciscan nuns (after 1237), as well as the 100 Dominican nunneries established between 1250 and 1303[166] and the rise in feminine recruitment among the Cistercians must also be included in an attempt to visualize the magnitude of the mounting tide of women entering religious organizations around 1300.

Moreover, when we consider that in 1277 there were but twelve

Dominican nunneries in Spain, France, and Italy;[167] that Beguines in Latin lands numbered only a tiny fraction of their German and Netherland counterparts; and that German Cistercian nunneries—over three times more numerous than the German Cistercian monasteries—far outnumbered the combined total of Cistercian female cloisters in most of western Europe;[168] the extraordinary dimensions of the German feminine movement become still more apparent. A further observation may be drawn from the work of Albert Hauck. He finds seventy convents in the empire as early as the year 900; by 1100 there were about one hundred fifty; in 1250 more than five hundred feminine foundations, exclusive of Beguines, were built in Germany.[169] But in Bavaria, with its shrines to the heavenly Queen and its miracles of the hunt, there were only thirteen nunneries in the duchy by 1300 and virtually no Beguine communities! The inference seems unavoidable: feminine religious activity appears weakest in regions where the spiritual significance of war and the hunt was most strongly established.

If women contributed so little to religious life in Bavaria, why did they gain so much spiritual influence elsewhere? Language and locality provide a clue. For the geography of language development shows that many women had long participated in religious and cultural life in regions outside the sphere of imperial, especially *ministerialis*, influence. Historians of language trace a series of phonological or sound displacements (*Lautverschiebungen*) in the spoken word, advancing on a broad front from south to north, from late Roman times until about the eighteenth century. Although the shift of different sounds over time and place varied widely, there is one phonological border, called the Benrather line, separating two major dialect groups: Low German to the north and center, and High German to the south. The eighteenth-century language frontier, running irregularly from Aachen and Düsseldorf in the west to Frankfurt-on-the Oder in the east, lies very close to the line of demarcation existing around 1250. This mid-thirteenth-century boundary, beyond which subsequent spoken sound shifted only imperceptibly further north, is virtually identical with a line above which we find no imperial *ministeriales*[170] and, to the south, no city belonging to the Hanseatic League (such minor geographical exceptions as Cologne remain unnoticed).[171]

Whatever the reasons for the boundary, the fact is that north of the Benrather line feminine influence in cultural and religious life has an extraordinary history, going all the way back to the Anglo-Saxon missions. In the eighth century, Boniface, the Apostle of Germany, founded nunneries in south and central Germany that were directed by Anglo-Saxon nuns, who, under his appointment, had left England for this purpose. Here as everywhere else in Europe at this time, nunneries were "places of residence and training schools for women of the ruling classes."[172] But the traditions of the Anglo-Saxon nuns took especially strong root in Saxony, that is, in territories then lying exclusively north of the later language frontier. Peculiar to the Saxon convents in the tenth and eleventh centuries was a confluence of Anglo-Saxon-inspired learning with an unusual political tradition enjoyed by the native nuns. As members of the imperial family, abbesses sometimes acted as guardians of the emperor or represented him during his absence from Germany. Indeed, nunneries even minted money, the coins bearing portraits, for example, of the abbesses of Gandersheim and Quedlinburg.[173] Moreover, the nuns of Herford, Gandersheim, and Quedlinburg contributed to the cultural life of their time in a measure without parallel among their contemporaries elsewhere in Europe. But to mention merely the more famous representatives of the great learned tradition of the Saxon sisters, such as the abbesses Hrotsvith (927) and Geberg II (959–1001), daughter of a duke of the Bavarians, would be to overlook more dramatic evidence. In the north Rhineland, in the tenth century, there were 18 monasteries founded as against 5 convents; in the south Rhineland 8 masculine houses and 1 feminine; in southeast Germany 25 male and 9 female houses; but in Ottonian Saxony 30 monasteries and no fewer than 28 nunneries were established. Thus, 33 of the 43 tenth-century convents lay north of the later language frontier. Even the figures from the ninth century are suggestive. At this time, southeast Germany possessed 109 monasteries as against 29 nunneries, the bishopric of Salzburg alone having 43 masculine and 7 feminine cloisters. In contrast, only 35 houses, 10 of them convents, one-third founded after 850, appear for all of Saxony.[174] From the earliest period of Saxon Christianization women played a principal role in the religious and cultural rise of Ottonian Germany, finding no parallel in any other region.

The long and singular history of women in Ottonian Saxony perhaps explains why much more powerful feminine movements, emanating from urban centers in the Netherlands during the twelfth and thirteenth centuries, followed widely different patterns north and south of the language frontier. The northern branch, predominantly lay and overwhelmingly *roturière*,[175] showed no connection with pilgrimage. But practices in the south were very different. Here aristocratic nuns founded a new, unprecedented form of shrine, dedicated to the *suffering* Mary. Between 1250 and 1303 about one hundred oversized Dominican nunneries were built in the Rhine Valley in Swabia, in adjoining Baden, in Switzerland, and in Alsace. The figure of the suffering Mary, a form of the Pietà or *Vesperbild*, originated among these convents around 1300.[176] Of a total of seventy-one shrines dedicated to her, sixty-four were located in the south—particularly in Swabia and Baden—and of the nine established in Bavaria, four stand only a few kilometers from the Swabian border. Meanwhile, although substantial numbers of Beguines lived in such southern urban centers as Augsburg, Stuttgart, or Kaufbeuren, they formed only a minority. The vast majority of Beguine houses were located in the north, and no shrine is connected with their name.

The south German Dominican sisters require further attention because their history suggests the strength of imperial piety among them and, by contrast, also a very different role and outlook among their northern counterparts. The German mystical tradition, made famous by Dominican friars like Meister Eckhard, Seuse, and Tauler, developed almost exclusively in the company of these nuns, many of whom were well-known authors of mystical writings. Expressing a profoundly personal, at times erotic relation to Christ, they combined their private adoration of the Eucharist with a more public effort to establish a form of peaceful pilgrimage, a type of worship dissociated from the imperial tradition of war and crusade. For example, a Dominican sister in the south, Margaret Ebner (1291–1351), who worshiped the suffering Mary, required a personal communication from God in order to overcome her compelling desire to admire the relics of the empire—the crown, the scepter, and the cloak—housed temporarily in front of her convent.[177] The need to call upon God himself suggests the attraction of imperial piety on this lady. If this interpretation is correct, a more conscious opposition to the prevailing form of public devotion would be difficult to conceive. Only recently established and intensely visible on the southern religious landscape, the *mulieres sanctae* were unable to deny the deeply rooted religious appeal of pilgrimage; they sought merely to dissociate it and perhaps to free themselves from its martial and imperial ethos.

All these women, however, appear to have been nuns; that is, most of them were from aristocratic families. Around 1300, when they first promoted shrines dedicated to the suffering Mary, significant numbers of middle-class and to a lesser extent perhaps even lower-class women entered Beguine communities, which, as we have seen, were lay rather than ecclesiastical organizations. This distinction, growing up after 1300, between southern aristocratic nuns, who dedicated shrines to the suffering Mary, and predominantly northern lay, mostly *roturière* Beguines, who had no institutional connection with pilgrimage, involved cultural and social differences as well as a fundamental spiritual division. And just as Low German, at least in its written form, developed as part of an urban culture, so did most Beguines live in cities. Conversely, the Dominican, Benedictine, and Cistercian convents—housing the aristocratic, predominantly southern ladies who founded pilgrimage sites dedicated to the suffering Mary—were built most frequently outside the town walls.[178] And their literary activity suggests a feminine continuation of chivalric culture transposed onto the religious plane.

Beyond urban-rural divisions and the absence or presence of pilgrimage affiliation, more important cultural and religious factors separated northern Beguines from southern aristocratic nuns. Consider two details in the history of Virgin worship. On the one hand, the cult of the Immaculate Conception was "almost totally unknown" in the Netherlands and, there is some reason to assume, in northern Germany generally, before 1477.[179] On the other hand, from about the middle of the thirteenth century—at least until the dramatic burning of four Dominicans in 1509 in Berne, during the notorious Jetzer scandal satirized by Thomas Murner[180]—the Dominicans had stalwartly opposed the doctrine of the Immaculate Conception, whereas the Franciscans zealously fostered it. The chief issues of contention centered on Mary's humanity. Since human nature originates in sin, and sin is the cause of man's suffering and mortality, it follows that if Mary suffered as a human being when her Son, Christ, was crucified, she must have been born in sin, and her body consequently putrefied after her death. But to deny that she was born in sin, and to assert, therefore, that her body did not putrefy after death, but instead rose physically intact to heaven, is to say that Mary did not suffer human distress at the sight of her Son nailed to the Cross.

Shrines dedicated to the suffering Mary—a figure symbolizing a doctrine contrary to the Immaculate Conception—originated among the approximately one hundred Dominican convents built in the later thirteenth century, largely in the Rhine Valley and in Swabia: the rival teaching of the Immaculate Conception, providing a doctrinal formulation for the heavenly Queen, also had a specific territorial reference.[181] In this light, the centuries of Marian dispute appear as a principally southern preoccupation—a struggle between antagonists and supporters of imperial piety. In northern lands, however, Mary was the subject of no major religious discord, for here common folk lived largely unaware of competing cults; there was no parallel to the southern contrast between regions that prayed more often to the suffering Mary (like Swabia and Baden) and those (like Bavaria) that favored the Immaculate Conception.[182] To be sure, northern people built a multitude of churches to the Virgin. Frequently she appears, as in the *Imitation of Christ*, in the role of maid or humble servant of God. But they portrayed her less commonly as ruler of a celestial court and nowhere picture her between the antlers of a stag. The relative absence of religious strife about the Mother of God, along with the comparative uniformity of celestial patrons among northern shrines, suggests doctrinal peace and some degree of cultural consonance. And the promptness of Low-German-speaking regions to embrace Beguine spirituality in the twelfth and thirteenth centuries also testifies to a distinct cultural unity. In the fourteenth and fifteenth centuries it was only in lands lying above the Benrather line that aristocrats and urban patricians alike celebrated the cult of King Arthur:[183] in the south, there was aristocratic hostility to fellow nobles who lived in cities or who married daughters of rich commoners. The situation is similar in the history of architecture. In the south Weser region, where the "Reformation came from below," cultural homogeneity uniting both city and country is reflected in a common late medieval building pattern shared by farmers and townsmen[184]—a phenomenon unknown in the south!

Further evidence points to the spirit of concord uniting north German urban and rural life, above all, the special character of confraternities in these regions. The *Elender-* and *Kalandsbruderschaften* associations, virtually unknown in the south, had literally hundreds of chapters in the north.[185] Apart from a duty to bury pilgrims who died far from home, the Elend—like the Kaland—brotherhoods also cared for poor strangers who were not pilgrims. Indeed, an obligation to minister to needy aliens is suggested by the very word, *der Elender*, which meant *stranger* in late medieval German. Of course, a responsibility to care for the souls of poor visitant strangers was virtually unknown in the closed circles of southern piety. The point needs no elucidation. More significant is a regional difference in urban confraternal attitudes toward charitable institutions. The distinction was made earlier between brotherhoods that did and those that did not enjoy formal church recognition. Ecclesiastical certification required a written agreement between the brotherhood and a monastery, church, or other religious body, specifying the nature of the good works undertaken and the types of indulgences and other spiritual benefits the church accorded to the association members. In the south, urban councilmen feared "spiritual," that is, clerically certified brotherhoods—in Nuremberg, for example, they constituted a veritable nightmare for city officials—because they raised the specter of urban revolution.[186] Erich Maschke has shown that the numerous highly differentiated artisanal *Zünfte* of southern towns, standing in sharp contrast to the merchant-dominated guilds of northern trading cities, had a much longer and incomparably more violent insurrectionary tradition than the relatively undeveloped artisanal associations in the *Hanse* towns.[187] Fearing all *kirchlichen Bruderschaften* to be fronts for conspiratorial activities, southern urban governments restricted the creation of new ones and regulated their practices.[188] As a consequence, organized charitable endeavor fell under their direct supervision.[189] In northern trading cities in contrast, certified spiritual brotherhoods—all self-administered institutions having important charitable responsibilities—multiplied almost as prodigiously as did the philanthropic houses of their lay sisters, the Beguines. Hamburg alone had over one hundred *geistliche Bruder-schaften*, Lübeck more than seventy, and in Electoral Saxony, one official died as a member of thirty-five brotherhoods.[190] Thus the Beguines and the spiritual brotherhoods, complementary communities reflecting the confederate, merchant-dominated structure of the *Hanse* "republic," expressed a lay piety that extended beyond the cities of their origin to bind urban and rural folk in common forms of devotion. This unity of town and country is the fundamental reason why the traditional cultural influence of the Netherlands continued to remain powerful in north Germany even as late as the seventeenth century.[191]

Lay religious endeavor was as specific to the social and constitutional structures of Germany above the Benrather line as clerical monopoly of spiritual leadership was to southern lands dominated by a long-established lower nobility. That is why northern women were able to establish institutions in which persons possessing no clerical status nevertheless performed important religious functions—preparing in this way the foundations for an indigenous lay piety. The long story of how they accomplished this task can be briefly summarized. In the late eleventh century the two terms "religion" (*religio*) and "religious life" (*vita religiosa*) were "synonymous with monastic orders and monastic life."[192] The term "lay" man meant a person who, standing outside clerical orders, was therefore incapable of higher spiritual attainment. For that reason, most heretical movements in the twelfth century, rejecting the Hildebrandine exclusive identification of religious life with clerical membership, proclaimed instead that poverty, preaching, and loyalty to ascetic ideals constituted the true principles of a spiritual vocation.[193] By about 1200, pressure, especially from urban centers, finally drove Innocent III to make the first important break with what was by this time the traditional and stark dichotomy between a life pursued within and without the monastery. Above all, by approving the mendicant orders, by announcing that urban-centered clerics living outside monasteries pursued a mission no less religious than that of monks, the papacy permitted the view that piety in thought and action was at least as important as mere clerical membership. Beyond the fact that this official recognition of the layman's new status in the scheme of salvation constituted a historic moment in the more general effort to democratize the Christian penitential system, the founding of the mendicant orders also had profound and immediate consequences for the development of feminine religious movements. For precisely because religious status for women had previously depended upon entry into the relatively paltry number of convents open to them, lay feminine piety developed chiefly under noncloistered mendicant sponsorship in the cities of the later thirteenth century. Thus, by about 1250, with only the rarest exceptions, women alone appeared capable of consistently establishing lay religious communities without incurring ecclesiastical censure. In contrast, lay pursuit of a spiritual mission by men, such as the Beghards, was comparatively infrequent and often provoked hostility from the Holy See.[194] In the urban centers of the Netherlands, in the *Hanse* cities as well as in rural regions influenced by Saxon feminine traditions, women alone appeared authorized to follow a religious life. In sum, not only did lay piety establish its strongest roots in regions where feminine religious traditions were most powerful, but it also had important anti-aristocratic implications. For the nobility controlled most higher church positions, and lay piety—a movement calling for spiritual equality among laymen and clerics—developed most in those regions where the lower nobility either was weak or was socially integrated with non-noble sections of the population.

The spectacle of large numbers of north German women calling themselves "religious," assembling in devout communities, and following the example of no saint, caused Matthew of Paris, writing from an English monastery in 1243, to exclaim:

At this time and especially in Germany, certain people—men and women, but especially women—have adopted a religious profession, though it is a light one. They call themselves "religious" and they take a private vow of continence and simplicity of life, though they do not follow the Rule of any Saint, nor are they as yet confined to a cloister. They have so multiplied within a short time that two thousand have been reported in Cologne and the neighbouring cities.[195]

Matthew of Paris's comments, indeed all the evidence adduced so far, suggest that fundamentally conflicting attitudes toward saint worship explain the division appearing a half-century later, about the time of the great year of Jubilee, between southern aristocratic nuns, founders of a new form of holy shrine dedicated to the suffering Mary, and their predominantly northern lay, mostly *roturière* Beguine sisters. For in the period after Matthew of Paris wrote, a golden age of saint worship and pilgrimage began—the widespread appearance of the feast and the procession of Corpus Christi, the granting of plenary indulgences to millions of pilgrims—along with the mass slaughter of Jews. This was a form of piety that must have appeared alien indeed to thousands of urban-based women, who—painfully conscious of their equivocal position in the church and in society—followed the rule of no saint and promoted ardently a popular devotion dissociated both from established ecclesiastical traditions and from a particular social class.

By the end of the fourteenth century, Beguine sisters were largely reduced to the position of inmates of poorhouses and could no longer dedicate their lives primarily to religious endeavor. Instead, male representatives of lay religious communities moved at this time into the foreground. To be sure, the Sisters of the Common Life, "springing from the ground like mushrooms,"[196] proved Beguine traditions to be far from dead. But the prominence of their Brothers and the high esteem which the Brethren earned from Rome reveal that, by the fifteenth century, the principle of lay religious communities finally received full recognition for both sexes. Indeed, brotherhoods multiplied prodigiously in this period. It should be noted, however, that a map showing the expansion of the Brethren of the Common Life, a most distinguished male lay order, reveals that except for half a dozen houses in Swabia, the *Devotio moderna* was welcome only north of the Main, principally in regions above the Benrather line.[197] This does not mean, of course, that people in the south universally rejected the principle of lay religious life. But the lay tradition was far weaker in the southern lands, for church-approved extraclerical spiritual movements were predominantly feminine at their inception, and the Beguines had always been overshadowed in the south by their cloistered sisters—virtually all of whom were aristocratic members of the regular orders. In contrast to the north, residents of the great southern imperial cities, tending increasingly after 1300 to identify spiritual ardor with civic patriotism, had long pursued religious renewal within a constitutional framework. Here women had no position comparable to that of their northern sisters.

Two German Reformations: North and South

Since the appearance of Bernd Moeller's *Reichstadt und Reformation* in 1962, a growing body of literature has established the existence of a distinctly south German form of civic piety.[198] The subject needs no further elucidation here. My purpose is rather to explain the theological and cultural consequences flowing from two Reformations: on the one hand, northern and central German Lutheranism, inspired by a feminine and strongly personal devotion; on the other hand, a southern artisanal tradition characterized by a militantly antipatrician, anti-aristocratic, and anti-imperial form of public worship. The gulf separating the two religious movements is most apparent in their conflicting conceptions of the Eucharist. All Reformation specialists agree that this single issue—the chief subject of the passions unleashed by the so-called "Sacramentarian Controversy" conducted between Luther and Zwingli in October 1529 at Marburg—lies at the heart of deep doctrinal differences that divided the Reformers and powerfully encouraged sectarian tendencies in the entire Protestant movement.

Since this basic conflict is my only concern here, little attention is paid to the much less divisive eucharistic disputes among the south German and Swiss Reformers themselves, particularly exemplified in the difference between Zwinglian and Buceran-Calvinist views. For this reason, it is convenient to refer simply to Lutheran and Calvinist traditions. It is also helpful to point out that Protestant theologians formulated doctrinal definitions of the Eucharist as direct expressions of particular forms of piety. For example, the affectionate moods and peaceful tones of feminine-inspired devotion appear clearly in Luther's conviction that neither human worthiness nor unworthiness is sufficient even to influence, much less to induce or to limit God's mercy. Luther's belief in God's forgiving nature permitted him to say that Christ continues to offer His body in the Eucharist irrespective of the character or even of the thoughts of the person receiving Him, the Lord, made incarnate by consecration of the material elements in the Host. For south Germans and Swiss Protestants, however, the corporate traditions dominating their urban centers were too strong to allow "unbelievers" or "nonmembers" to receive Christ. It was on this point that the sharpest difference occurred between the two Protestant traditions: "The Lutheran affirmation and the Calvinist denial that the unworthy receive the body of Christ."[199]

Luther says that the Lord offers Himself to believers and unbelievers alike; nevertheless, only the faithful benefit from the gift. For the Eucharist is not "the point of departure" in Luther's conception of the Communion rite, but the fulfillment, the ultimate actualization of the individual's faith in Christ's words as they are set forth in the Bible.[200] And because Christ's presence in the Host is at once a physical and a transcendental event, it follows for Luther that Christ cannot be contained entirely in the material elements of bread and wine, any more than He can be bound by the good or evil character of human action. Therefore, Luther explains, it is impossible to refer to the Eucharist as the locus of the Lord's body. The properties of Christ's human and divine natures are commingled so that Christ is present everywhere, both as man and as God. Christ is "in, under, and with" the bread, for the "whole living Christ," not just His corporeal human person, offers Himself to the faithful in order that they "can become one cake (*Kuchen*) with him."[201] Luther insists that the sacrament of the Eucharist causes the believer's faith to become manifest and to enter into common fellowship with the faith of other believers: the Communion thus defines the community— the true church—as an invisible assembly; it is, above all, an association whose spiritual qualities render it independent of local civic or political membership in precisely the same manner that Christ Himself, although actually present, occupies no *place* among the material elements of the Eucharist.

No eucharistic teaching could be more contrary to the civic and corporate tradition of south German and Swiss Protestant devotion. For

Calvin, very much like Zwingli, exalts not only the civilizing function of the political order, almost in the spirit of Thomas More, but argues further that proper maintenance of external worship and the right regulation of civil society are conditions indispensable to finding the heavenly Kingdom in ourselves:

The former [civil government], in some measure, begins the heavenly Kingdom in us, even now upon earth, and in this mortal and evanescent life commences immortal and incorruptible blessedness, while to the latter it is assigned, so long as we live among men, to foster and maintain the external worship of God, to defend sound doctrine and the condition of the Church, to adapt our conduct to human society, to form our manners to civil justice, to conciliate us to each other, to cherish common peace and tranquility. All these I confess to be superfluous, if the Kingdom of God, as it now exists within us, extinguishes the present life. But if it is the will of God that while we aspire to true piety we are pilgrims upon the earth, and if such pilgrimage stands in need of such aids, those who take them away from man rob him of his humanity.[202]

Calvin thought that good citizenship stood to the Christian life as the Old to the New Testament: the latter was the consummation of the former. Contrary to Luther, both Calvin and Zwingli conceived the spiritual and temporal realms to be complementary spheres "not adverse to each other."[203] The only important south Protestant Reformer who accepted Lutheran eucharistic views, Johannes Brenz from Württemberg, tried to join them to southern civic spirituality—an enterprise having no counterpart in the north.[204] Allowing for the exception of Brenz's attempt to bridge the gulf separating the two major branches of the German Reformation, it is possible to say that in south Germany and in Switzerland the Eucharist remained the quintessential symbol of the community in both its lay and religious dimensions. And just as differences in eucharistic doctrine were "entangled with political preferences and policies... wherever Germans of the Empire met Germans of the Confederacy,"[205] so Calvin—also inspired by urban and Swiss hostility to southern patrician and aristocratic imperial loyalties—formulated eucharistic teachings consistent with this form of public-minded religiosity. His view may be summarized by saying that, although consecration makes no change in its material elements, although Christ cannot be physically present, the Host is nevertheless a sacrament; it expresses the congregation's unity of worship in the sense that the Lord's nourishing, virtual presence in the elements, joined to the working of His spirit, make it possible for common devotion to be offered as a *corporate* act. The local church, that is, the assembled congregation, acknowledges the Savior's transcendence and His spatial separateness from the corruption of the world—truths revealed in the doctrine of the Ascension; these divine attributes, in demonstrating heaven to be the exclusive location of Christ's body, cause the community of the faithful to unite and to become one member of His person.

Calvin's denial of the physical presence implies that the Lord does not descend to the community, but, instead, that the congregation must "ascend" or "seek" Christ in heaven. This "upward-looking" *community* piety differs radically from the "inward" *personal* devotion characteristic of Lutheran spirituality. Luther says that Christ descends physically to offer His body to each individual, believer or unbeliever, who is present at the sacramental rite. Calvin denies that the unworthy can receive Christ's body, because to have them do so would destroy the corporate character of the sacrament.

> For the Lord so communicates his body to us there [the Lord's Supper] that he is made completely one with us and wè with him. Now, since he has only one body, of which he makes us all partakers, it is necessary that all of us also be made one body by such participation. The bread shown in the Sacrament represents this unity. As it is made of many grains so mixed together that one cannot be distinguished from another, so it is fitting that in the same way we should be joined and bound together by such great agreement of minds that no sort of disagreement or division may intrude.[206]

In sum, Calvin maintains that the community of believers, *not* the individual, receives Christ's body. The opposing view, distinctive of the feminine and north and middle German devotion, was expressed in Luther's conviction that the individual could possess God within himself. Still earlier were Meister Eckhard's teachings about the sacred *vünkelin der sele*, the notion of *synteresis*, and the spirit of *Gelassenheit* and *Abgeschiedenheit* (spiritual imperturbability and isolation from the world), prominent in, for example, the *Theologia Deutsch*—a treatise edited by the young Luther and condemned by Calvin as "the poison of the devil."[207] No group pursued eucharistic worship more passionately and in a more personal manner than the thousands of *mulieres sanctae*, who for many generations dominated the north German religious landscape. Excluded by their sex from participation in political life, they transformed a pronounced indifference to civic loyalties into an essential component of an intensely subjective form of eucharistic devotion. Their influence above all helps to explain both the popular and the mystical dimension behind Luther's tenacious defense of such seemingly abstruse principles as "the communication of idioms and the extension of the divine Person's ubiquity to the human nature of Christ."[208] Needless to say, most south German and Swiss Protestant Reformers found these traditions totally alien to their own spirituality.

Conflicting concepts of the Eucharist, corresponding to contrary notions of the spiritual and temporal communities, explain also the divergent tendencies in Lutheran and Calvinist doctrines of predestination.

Just as Luther believed that the individual received Christ's physical body, so he also understood original sin to take the parallel form of personal or individual guilt. Conversely, because Calvin denied the physical presence and insisted that Christ offered His single body to a community of believers, he regarded original sin as a collective fault or radical deformity inherent in human nature. A structural flaw requires not a personal but a collective or constitutional response: to organize civil society in the manner that, according to the Bible, God prescribed for man, that is, the community, and to receive His grace by means of the eucharistic sacrament. To say that original sin is connected with personal guilt is to deny the corporate origins of ethical norms. Calvin insisted that the community itself is "the source and fountain of ethical concern" because it is only as a community that men can receive the Lord's forgiveness by partaking of His body.[209] And since taking the Eucharist "is not a private act, much less a multitude of private acts formed together," good and bad qualities cannot be the subject of introspection.[210] The individual can look neither into his own nor into another person's soul. Luther, in contrast, thought acceptance of the Eucharist to be a supremely intimate act. Therefore he did not judge the ethical value of human behavior from its overt character, as did Calvin, but instead said that private intention was the principal criterion of moral judgment. To caricature his position, one could say that raping a woman might be a good deed if the actor's intentions were guided by God. The example is grotesque, but it is nonetheless reminiscent of similar assertions by William of Ockham, who, in his anticorporate zeal, also struggled to reconcile God's omnipotence with personal moral autonomy. The point is important because the bond uniting Luther with Ockham consists chiefly in the vehemence with which both men rejected corporate influences in religious life. It is worth recalling that Marsilius of Padua, like Calvin, denied the ethical value of private intention in order to enhance the moral quality of corporate endeavor. In short, the contrast between an "intentional" or introspective response to the problem of sin and a "constitutional" or structural response—the one proceeding from the personal nature of the Eucharist, the other from its collective character—corresponds to Luther's affirmation and to Calvin's denial of the individual's capacity to "know" he has been saved.[211] Thus Luther's optimistic and Calvin's pessimistic views of sin, grace, and predestination, far from reflecting either idiosyncratic traits or expressing mere professional disagreement among theologians, reflect concepts of community that developed respectively outside and within long traditions of corporate worship.

The full measure of the gulf separating Lutheran and Calvinist teachings, however, emerges more clearly when we compare their objections to Catholic notions of the mass—the central preoccupation of all Protestant Reformers. Directing the entire force of his criticism against "the clericalization of the Eucharist,"[212] above all, against private masses, Calvin explains: "I call it a private mass (that no man may be mistaken) wherever there is no participation in the Lord's supper among believers, even though a large multitude of men may otherwise be present . . . I say that private masses are diametrically opposed to Christ's institution, and are for that reason an impious profaning of the sacred Supper."[213] Protesting that the private mass "resembles a kind of excommunication" rather than a "communion ordained by the Lord," Calvin says that the deplorable practice began when priests, instead of following God's command "to take and divide amongst ourselves," appropriated the Lord's Supper and claimed to conduct "the sacrifice for the people."[214] And the evil that ensued from the hateful practice of permitting "priestlings to devour their victim . . . apart from the whole body of the faithful" may be seen today, says Calvin, in the bevy of priests offering "innumerable masses in all the separate corners of the churches, drawing the people hither and thither, when they ought to have formed one meeting, and thus recognized the mystery of their unity."[215] Behind Calvin's portrayal of "innumerable masses" held "in all the separate corners of the churches" we see the motley arrangements of side altars in the churches of France and south Germany, attended by priests reciting masses and dedicated to the patron saints of turbulent urban guilds. To speak of the mystery of the Eucharist in a rite that manifestly celebrated the community's factions and divisions was in Calvin's eyes to make a mockery of the sacred Supper that properly was "to be dispensed at the public meeting of the Church, to remind us of the communion by which we are all united in Christ Jesus."[216]

In contrast, Luther's protest against confraternities contains no hint of their being a divisive influence in the performance of church ritual. Instead, he complained that they had appropriated the priestly power to grant dispensations and indulgences. Luther also criticized "fraternities" for not undertaking "good works" in public charity, which was the principal reason for their existence.

The "fraternities," indulgences, letters of indulgence, butterbriefs, mass briefs, dispensations and the like, ought all to be drowned and destroyed as containing nothing good. If the pope can grant you a dispensation to eat butter, or from hearing mass, he should allow a pastor the power to grant it; indeed he had no right to deprive him of the power. I am also including [with the pope] the "fraternities" which grant indulgences, say masses, and prescribe good works. . . . If a "fraternity" were such that it subscribed funds to feed the poor, or otherwise gave help to someone, that "fraternity" would be sound, and would find its indulgences and merits in heaven. At present, however, their privileges lead only to gluttony and drunkenness.[217]

We have seen that in southern cities, where ecclesiastically certified brotherhoods were severely restricted among artisan guilds, the town councils—not confraternities—supervised charitable works. For that reason Calvin's lengthy, systematic attacks on Roman abuses contain no reference to the spiritual duties and the powers of penitential dispensation enjoyed by confraternities. Still less does he condemn the pope for authorizing brotherhoods that have usurped the clergy's powers of dispensation. In sum, the fundamental regional contrasts between northern and southern branches of German Protestantism appear clearly in their criticism of papal abuses—the one concern that drew them most strongly together.

Luther's and Calvin's conflicting perceptions of confraternities raise the issue of northern and southern understandings of God's covenant with man. Both men insist that the Eucharist is a sacrament to which a promise is connected. But each understands the Lord's promise in a different sense. Calling the mass "the greatest promise of all," Luther argues that

God presents two things to us, a word and a sign, in order that we may understand the word to be a testament, and the sign a sacrament. In the mass, the word of Christ is the testament, the bread and wine are the sacrament. Since greater power resides in a word than in a sign, so more power resides in a testament than in a sacrament; for a man may have, and use, a word or testament without a sign or sacrament. . . . Thus I am able daily, indeed hourly, to have the mass; for, as often as I wish, I can set the words of Christ before me.[218]

Luther insists that God's promise is a personal, not a community affair: "Therefore, this truth is irrefragable: each one stands for himself where the divine promise is concerned."[219] In contrast to Luther's lonely encounter with Christ, Calvin's emphasis on an "upward-looking" piety causes the community, not the individual, to find Christ. In the Old Testament, Christ is promised; in the New, "attestation is given that Christ has already been revealed."[220] God's promise finds its fulfillment in the supreme assurance which the eucharistic sacrament imparts to a congregation organized and prepared, as one body, to seek His person, physically located in heaven, in the manner He prescribed in the Bible.[221]

It was as a direct consequence of Calvinism, therefore, where God's promise and its fulfillment were indistinguishable from community worship, that the idea of covenant played an important role in seventeenth- and eighteenth-century political theory. For just as the New Testament testifies to the consummation of a pledge made in the Old, so in the political sphere the concept of an original covenant draws civil society closer to a pattern or a "constitution," whose very existence would fulfill a primal obligation. The covenant presented a secularized testament to man's faith and will to transform human institutions so that they would stand toward previous ages in a relation analogous to that of the New Testament to the Old. Lutheran Germany possesses few traces of covenant traditions in this communal and political sense. When this essay appears book-length I will discuss how the Lutheran Reformation institutionalized a form of piety that led men in the seventeenth and eighteenth centuries to think preoccupation with civil society to be an activity alien to the more noble pursuits of the human spirit—leading to the fateful and persistent tendency among Lutherans to divorce *Kultur* from *Zivilisation* and to sunder the "state" from "society" in a manner no less sharply than Descartes's dissociation of man's mind from his body. For almost a thousand years north and central German populations have excluded religious emotion from their thoughts about public life. Perhaps this explains why the civilizing themes most prominent in late nineteenth- and twentieth-century German nationalist writings emphasize the impersonal goals of organization and discipline to a degree compatible neither with the noetic content of *Kultur* nor with the meaning French patriots during the Revolution attributed to the term *civilisation*: an endeavor to integrate the achievements of the human mind with the aspirations of free citizens.

Cheese and Worms

The Cosmos of a Sixteenth-Century Miller

Carlo Ginzburg

Tout ce qui est intéressant se passe dans l'ombre. On ne sait rien de la véritable histoire des hommes. —Céline

In the past, historians could be accused of being interested only in the "deeds of kings." Things have changed now, of course. Historians are increasingly fixing their attention on matters their predecessors had avoided mentioning, rejected, or simply ignored. But it is not easy to extend an investigation far enough downward to reach the behavior and attitudes of the lower classes. "Who built Thebes of the seven doors?" —this question was already being asked by Brecht's "working-class reader."[1] Records say nothing about those anonymous masons, but that question has lost none of its force.

While the scarcity of sources is undoubtedly the most evident obstacle standing in the way of this sort of research, it is not the only one. Those who want to reconstruct the mentality of the lower classes in past centuries have to face a subtler difficulty: distortion of evidence. The thoughts, beliefs, and hopes of peasants and artisans of the past reach us through filters and media that inevitably warp them, more or less openly reflecting the ruling classes' ideology. In addition, there is the paradox of having to reconstruct an essentially oral culture on the basis of written sources. This impasse is so severe that some writers, lapsing into a sort of

This essay is an abridged version of *Il formaggio e i vermi: Il cosmo di un mugnaio del Cinquecento* (Turin, 1975). A first draft of it was discussed in the Davis Center seminar (fall 1973) and in the modern history seminar of the University of Bologna (spring 1974). I am deeply indebted to Lawrence Stone and to those who helped with their valuable criticism to eliminate weaknesses and mistakes from my text: Piero Camporesi, Jay Dolan, John Elliott, Felix Gilbert, Robert Muchembled, Ottavia Niccoli, Jim Obelkevich, Adriano Prosperi, Lionel Rothkrug, Jerry Seigel, Eileen Yeo, Stephen Yeo, my students in Bologna—and my translator, Marta Sofri. Obviously, the responsibility for what I have written is my own.

superficial neoskepticism, have wondered rhetorically whether "popular culture does exist beyond the act that suppresses it."[2]

These difficulties ought to be kept in mind when analyzing the case I am about to investigate: that of a miller from Friuli, who was tried and executed by the Holy Office at the end of the sixteenth century after having spent his life in complete obscurity. This case is unusual in many ways: it would be impossible mechanically to transpose to a general plane the conclusions I shall reach. However, the gulf existing between the judges' questions and the defendant's answers in the two trials (begun in 1583 and 1598) enables us to reach a deep and practically unknown vein of beliefs, ideas, and dreams. An analytic study on an individual scale therefore seems justified. Recent studies have shown the value of extending biographical investigation down to the lower strata of society.[3] Obviously, this sort of microscopic research does not impair the usefulness of large-scale, quantitative researches; in a certain sense, indeed, it is a necessary premise to them.

His name was Domenico Scandella, but he was known by the nickname of Menocchio. He had been born around 1532 (during his first trial he said he was fifty-two) at Montereale, a small village on the hills of Friuli, twenty-five kilometers north of Pordenone, right at the foot of the Alps. He had always lived there, excepting only for a period of two years of banishment for a brawl (1564–65), which he spent at Arbia, a nearby village, and in the mountains of Carnia. He was married and had seven children; four more had died. He declared to the judge, the *canonico* Giambattista Maro, general vicar of the inquisitor of Aquileia and Concordia, that his activities were "miller, carpenter, sawing wood, building walls, and other things." But his main activity was as a miller; he wore the traditional garb of millers, a robe, a cloak, and a cap of white wool. This is how he appeared at his first trial, all dressed in white.[4]

A couple of years later he told his inquisitors that he was "very poor": "I have nothing but two mills on rent and two fields on *livello* [a form of free tenancy, involving a short-term lease, often of nine years], and with these I provided and still provide for my poor family."[5] But undoubtedly he was exaggerating. Even if a large part of his harvest was needed to pay the rent for the two mills and the rent for the two fields, there certainly remained enough for his family to live upon and possibly also to find a remedy in times of trouble. When he was banished to Arbia, for instance, he immediately rented another mill. Undoubtedly, his social position in the microcosm of Montereale was important. In 1581 he had been mayor (*podestà*) of the village and of the surrounding "villas" (Gaio, Grizzo, San Lonardo, San Martino), and he had also been, at an unknown date, *camararo*, that is, administrator of the parish of Montereale.[6] Probably the main reason for his being given these offices was that he could "read, write, and do accounts." He was, in short, a peasant—but not an ordinary one.

On 28 September 1583, Menocchio was denounced to the Inquisition by the parish priest. He was accused of having pronounced "heretical and blasphemous" words about Christ. It had not been an occasional blasphemy. Menocchio had actually tried to explain and propagate his opinions: "predicare et dogmatizare non erubescit" (he is not ashamed of preaching and advertising his own ideas). This made his position all the more serious.

His attempts at proselytism were largely confirmed by the inquest opened a month later at Portogruaro and continued at Concordia and Montereale. "He always takes sides against people of faith in discussions; even against the parish priest," Francesco Fassetta told the general vicar. Another witness, Domenico Melchiori, said, "He was always bent on arguing with someone or other, and once, when he tried to start a discussion with me, I told him, 'I am a shoemaker and you a miller, and you aren't a scholar; why should we quarrel about these matters?'" Matters of faith are high and difficult, and beyond the reach of shoemakers and millers; one has to be very learned to be able to discuss them, and such learning belongs to clerks. But Menocchio said he did not believe that the Holy Ghost ruled the church, and he added: "Prelates keep us under them, and do all they can to keep us quiet, but *they* have a good time of it"; as for him, he "knew God better than they did." And when the parish priest brought him to the general vicar at Concordia to correct his ideas, telling him, "these whims of yours are heresies," he promised to stop meddling in these matters, but immediately started all over again.[7] In the streets, at the tavern, when he was going to Grizzo or Daviano or coming down from the mountains—everywhere and with everybody Menocchio had the habit of getting into conversation about matters of faith and of trying to win over others to his ideas.

It is not easy to discern how the villagers responded to Menocchio's propositions; nobody, of course, would have dreamed of letting the general vicar know that he had listened with approval to the speeches of one who was suspected of heresy. Some witnesses even took care to report their own indignant retorts. "Menocchio, please, for the love of God, don't let such words escape your lips!"—this is the answer Domenico Melchiori said he had given to Menocchio. And Giuliano Stefanut reported: "I told him several times, and particularly on one occasion when we were going together to Grizzo, that I'm very fond of him, but I can't stand the way he talks about religion; I'd always be ready to fight him, and even if he killed me a hundred times over and I came back to life every time, I'd still be ready to fight for my faith." The priest Andrea Bionima gave him a threatening hint: "Be quiet, Domenego," he told him, "don't say such things, because sometime you may come to regret them." Another witness, Giovanni Povoledo, tried to sum up Menocchio's position, although rather vaguely: "His reputation is bad; they say his opinions are of the stamp of Luther's."

But we must not be misled by the unanimity of this evidence. Almost all the persons who had been questioned declared that they had known Menocchio for a long time: some for thirty or forty years, some for twenty-five, some for twenty. One of them, Daniele Fassetta, said he knew him "since I was a child, because we belong to the same parish." It seems that some of Menocchio's statements had been uttered not merely a few days before, but "many years" before. During this long period, nobody in the village had denounced him, yet everybody knew his opinions. People reported and discussed them—with curiosity? shrugging their shoulders? In the evidence collected by the general vicar, no real hostility toward Menocchio emerges: at most, some disapproval. Some of these witnesses, it must be said, were relatives of his: for instance, Francesco Fassetta or Bartolomeo di Andrea, a cousin of his wife's. But even Giuliano Stefanut, who had vigorously contradicted him, declaring he was willing to die for his faith, had told him, "I'm very fond of you." This miller, who had been mayor of the village and administrator of his parish, certainly did not live on the margin of the community of Montereale. Many years later, during the second trial, a witness declared: "I see he associates with many people, and I believe he is a friend of everybody." Yet at a certain point somebody had denounced him, and the apparatus of the Inquisition had begun to move. Why?

Menocchio's sons immediately surmised that the anonymous denouncer was the parish priest of Montereale, don Oderico Vorai. They were right. There was a long-standing disagreement between Menocchio and the priest; during the last four years, Menocchio even went out of the village for confession. It is true that the priest's testimony, which closed the giving of evidence in the trial, was particularly elusive: "I can't remember in detail what he said, both because my memory is not very good and because I was hindered by other business." Apparently, nobody was in a better position than he for giving the Inquisition exact information on this matter; but the general vicar did not ask any more questions. This was because Vorai was the author of the detailed accusation that obviously formed the basis for the very precise questions that were put to the witnesses.

Whatever the cause for the hostility between Menocchio and the priest may have been, it is easily explained. Menocchio did not admit that the clergy had any particular authority in matters of faith. "Who

cares about popes, priests, or prelates! he used to say with scorn, because he didn't believe in them," reported Domenico Melchiori. With all
his discussing and arguing in the streets and taverns, Menocchio must
have become almost a rival to the priest. But what *did* Menocchio say?

To begin with, not only did he swear "immoderately," but he maintained that swearing was not a sin (another witness said that he declared
that swearing against the saints was not a sin, but swearing against God
was), and added wryly: "Every man has his own trade: some plough,
some harrow, and I ply my trade of swearing." And he expressed strange
opinions, which the villagers reported in a more or less fragmentary form
to the general vicar. For instance: "the air is God . . . the earth is our
mother"; "what do you imagine God is? God is nothing but a little
breath, and only what man imagines"; "all we can see is God, and we are
gods"; "when we are dead we are nothing, we are like worms and animals"; "can you really believe that Jesus Christ was born of the Virgin
Mary? It's not possible for her to have borne him and remained a virgin;
it's much more likely to have been the work of some good man, or of
some good man's son." They said he owned some forbidden books, in
particular a Bible in Italian: "He's always arguing with somebody or
other, he has a Bible in Italian and fancies he bases himself on it, and he
keeps obstinately to his arguments."

While this evidence was accumulating, Menocchio got wind of the
fact that something was brewing against him. He went to the vicar of
Polcenigo, Giovanni Daniele Melchiori, who had been his friend since he
was a child. Melchiori advised him to present himself of his own accord
to the Inquisition, or at least to go immediately if summoned, and gave
him this advice: "You must tell them what they ask, but not try to speak
too much or attempt to explain these things; you must only answer their
questions." Alessandro Policreto, a former lawyer Menocchio had met at
the house of a friend, a timber merchant, also advised him to present
himself to the judges, to admit his guilt, but at the same time to declare
that he had never really believed in his own heterodox statements. So
Menocchio went to Maniago, obeying the summons of the ecclesiastical
tribunal. But on the following day, in consequence of the way the inquest
was proceeding, the inquisitor himself, the Franciscan friar Felice da
Montefalco, had him arrested and "put in handcuffs" in the prison of the
Inquisition at Concordia. On 7 February 1584, Menocchio underwent
his first examination.[8]

In spite of all the advice he had been given to be prudent, he began
by being very talkative. He tried, however, to present his own position in
a more favorable light than that of the testimonies. He admitted that two

or three years earlier he had had some doubts about the virginity of Mary and had talked about it to several persons, including a priest of Barcis; but he added:

It's true that I said these words to some people, but I wasn't trying to persuade them into believing them, on the contrary I admonished many of them, saying: "Do you want me to show you the right path? You must try to do all the good you can, and follow the steps of my predecessors and the precepts of our holy mother the church." But the words I had said before had been uttered by me because I had fallen in temptation, and not because I believed them or meant to teach them to others; it was the devil who made me think of those things and spurred me to impart them to others.

With these words, Menocchio unknowingly corroborated the suspicion that in the village he had assumed a role of instructor of matters of doctrine and behavior ("Do you want me to show you the right path?"). As to the heterodox contents of this type of preaching, it was impossible to entertain any doubt—especially when Menocchio expounded an extraordinary cosmogony of his of which the Inquisition had already heard some vague echoes:

I said that, in my thought and belief, everything was chaos, I mean earth, air, water, and fire all together; and that volume, revolving, formed a mass, just like cheese does in milk, and in that mass there appeared some worms, and those were angels; and the most holy Majesty decreed that those were God and the angels; and in that number of angels there was also God, he, too, created by that mass in the same time; and he was made sovereign together with four captains, Lucifer, Michael, Gabriel, and Raphael. This Lucifer wanted to be master and equal to his king, the Majesty of God; and because of his pride God ordered him to be expelled from heaven with all his followers; and then God created Adam and Eve and the people in great multitudes to fill up the seats left empty by the banished angels. This multitude did not obey God's commandments, so God sent his son, and the Jews took him and crucified him.

He added: "I never said he let himself be hung up like an animal" (it was one of the accusations made against him; later on he admitted that perhaps he might have said something of that sort). "I did say," he went on, "that he let himself be crucified; and this man who was crucified was one of God's sons, because we all are God's sons and of the same nature as he who was crucified; and he was a man like all of us, but having a greater dignity, such as nowadays the pope has, who is a man like us, but with more dignity than us because he can do things; this man who was crucified was born of Saint Joseph and of the Virgin Mary."[9]

During the inquest, on hearing the strange rumors reported by the witnesses, the general vicar at first had asked whether Menocchio was "talking in earnest or joking"; later on he asked whether Menocchio was in his right mind. In both cases the answers had been very decided: Menocchio had talked "seriously" and was "right in the head, not crazy."[10] After the examinations started, one of Menocchio's sons, Ziannuto, acting upon the advice of some friends, began to spread the rumor that Menocchio was "crazy" or "possessed by an evil spirit." But the judges did not believe him, and the trial went on. They had probably been tempted, at a certain moment, to sum up Menocchio's opinions, and especially his cosmogony, as a pack of blasphemous but harmless eccentricities (the cheese, the milk, the angel-worms, the God-angel created from chaos); but they set aside this temptation. A hundred or a hundred fifty years later events might well have turned out differently, and Menocchio would have been termed "affected by religious obsession" and locked up in a hospital among lunatics;[11] but in the middle of the Counter-Reformation, mechanisms of exclusion were based on the identification and repression of heresy.

This was the solution the general vicar, Giambattista Maro, chose. During a pressing cross-examination on 16 February he tried to make the contradictions in Menocchio's statements emerge. But, faced with the dialectic ability of the general vicar, who was a doctor of the law *in utroque jure*, and with his command of theological terms, Menocchio only accumulated new contradictions, kept quiet, or shrugged his shoulders, saying: "I don't know . . . I don't know." Although apparently using the same words, the two men did not talk the same language. What did a phrase like "the most holy Majesty of God" mean to Menocchio? And how could it fit in with the opinions reported by the witnesses that "the air is God," "God is nothing but a little breath, and only what man imagines," "all we can see is God, and we are gods"? At first sight all Menocchio's remarks seem capricious and contradictory. For instance, after having insisted that Christ was a man, only a man, he declared on 1 May: "I believe that the person of the Son is the Holy Ghost, because in everything he acted according to God's will." Is it possible to find a consistency underlying all these contradictions—an *internal* consistency different from the one the general vicar was trying forcibly to impose on Menocchio's ideas? On a more general level, is it possible to expound these ideas without betraying them?

To answer these questions, we shall temporarily set aside Menocchio's cosmogony and follow the proceedings of the trial.

When Menocchio was put in prison, his son Ziannuto set to work at once to try to help him. He found a lawyer, a certain Trappola of Portogruaro; he went to Serravalle and talked to the inquisitor; he obtained from the local authorities of Montereale a written statement in favor of the prisoner and sent it to the lawyer, informing him that in case of necessity he could obtain other certificates of good conduct. Together with his brothers, he also coerced the parish priest of Montereale, to whom he imputed the principal responsibility for the whole business, into writing a letter (Ziannuto was illiterate) to Menocchio in prison. In this letter, Menocchio was advised to promise complete obedience to the church. It seems that Menocchio did not imagine that these words came from his enemy, the parish priest; he supposed they came from Domenego Femenussa, a wool and timber merchant, who used to come to his mill and had occasionally lent him money. But it obviously went against the grain for him to follow the advice contained in the letter. At the end of his first examination (7 February) he exclaimed, with evident reluctance, to the general vicar: "Sir, all I have said by inspiration of God or of the devil I cannot confirm to be either truth or falsehood, but I beg for mercy and will act as I am told to."[12] He was asking for pardon, but he was not taking back anything. "Don't try to talk too much," was the advice he had been given by the vicar of Polcenigo, who had been his friend since he was a child and knew him well. But Menocchio evidently could not restrain himself.

Toward the end of April, the affair suddenly took a new turn. The Venetian rectors requested the inquisitor of Aquileia and Concordia, the Franciscan friar Felice da Montefalco, to conform to the customary procedure of the republic, which required the presence of a secular magistrate by the side of the ecclesiastical judges in the Inquisition's trials. The conflict between the two powers was traditional.[13] We do not know whether on this occasion the lawyer Trappola intervened in favor of his client. Menocchio was brought to Portogruaro, in the palace of the mayor, to confirm in the mayor's presence the examinations that had already taken place. After this, the trial went on.

More than once, in the past, Menocchio had told the people of his village that he was willing, and even eager, to declare his "opinion" about matters of faith to the secular and religious authorities. Francesco Fassetta was one of the witnesses who reported this: "He told me that if ever he should fall in the hands of the authorities for this reason, he would cooperate, but if they used him ill, he would have many things to say against them for their evil deeds." In the presence of the mayor of Portogruaro and of the inquisitor of Aquileia and Concordia, Menocchio confirmed this evidence: "It's true that I said that if I weren't afraid of justice I could talk so much that everybody would be astonished; and I said, too, that if I had the possibility of being heard by the pope or a king or prince I might say many things; and then even if they killed me I wouldn't care."[14] At this point the inquisitors urged him to talk, and Menocchio dropped every trace of reserve. It was 28 April.

He began by denouncing the oppression the rich inflict on the poor through the use of an incomprehensible language like Latin in the courts: "My opinion is that to speak Latin is to betray the poor people, because in quarrels poor men can't understand what the others are saying and are ill treated, and if they want to say two words they are obliged to take a lawyer." But this was only one instance of a general exploitation in which the church conspired and took part: "And it seems to me that in this law of ours the pope, cardinals, and bishops are so great and rich that everything belongs to the church and the priests, and they maltreat the poor people: if they rent a couple of fields, they are sure to belong to the church, to such-and-such a bishop or such-and-such a cardinal." I have already mentioned that Menocchio had two fields on *livello* and that their owner is unknown. As for his Latin, it seems to have been limited to the *Credo* and the *Pater Noster*, which he had learned while serving at mass. And Ziannuto, his son, had had to obtain a lawyer for him as soon as the Inquisition had put him in prison. But these coincidences—or should we say these possible coincidences—must not mislead us: Menocchio's words, though starting from his own personal case, ended up by extending to a much larger sphere.

The need he felt for the church to abandon its privileges and become poor among the poor was connected with the formulation, in the wake of the Gospel, of a different religion, devoid of dogmatic emphasis and reduced to a core of practical precepts: "I would like men to believe in the majesty of God, and to be honest and to act according to what Jesus Christ said when those Jews asked him what law there should be: 'Love God and love your neighbor.'" In Menocchio's view, this simplified religion did not admit of confessional restrictions. He ardently extolled the equality of all religions based on an enlightenment given in equal measure to all men—"the majesty of God has given the Holy Ghost to everybody: to Christians, heretics, Jews, Turks; and all are dear to him, all will be saved in the same way"—but he ended up with a violent outburst against the judges and their doctrinal pride: "And you, priests and friars, you, too, think yourselves wiser than God, and are like the devil, and want to be gods on earth and possess God's knowledge, like the devil; and he who thinks he knows most, knows nothing." Throwing all restraint and all caution to the winds, Menocchio declared that he refused all sacraments, including baptism, as inventions of man, "merchandise," instruments of exploitation and oppression in the hands of the clergy: "I believe that the laws and commandments of the church are all merchandise the men of the church live upon." About baptism he said: "I believe that as soon as we are born we are baptized, because God, who has blessed everything, baptizes us; and that the other baptizing is an invention, and priests begin to eat the souls even before birth, and go on eating them continually till after death." About confirmation he said: "I think it is a merchandise, an invention of men, who all have the Holy Ghost, and make show of their knowledge but do not know anything."

About matrimony: "It was not made by God, but by men: once men and women used to plight their troth to each other, and that was enough; these inventions of men came later." About holy orders: "I believe that God's spirit is in everybody . . . and I think that anybody who has studied can be a priest without being consecrated, because those other things are all merchandise." About extreme unction: "I think it is nothing, and is worth nothing, because they anoint the body, but they cannot anoint the soul." About confession he used to say: "Going to confess to priests and friars is no better than going to talk to a tree." When the inquisitor reproached him for these words, he explained, rather patronizingly: "If that tree could give people the consciousness of repentance it would be enough; some men go to the priests because they don't know what atonement they are to make for their sins, and they want to find out; if they knew it, it wouldn't be necessary for them to go; and those who know never do go. These persons should confess to the majesty of God in their own hearts, and beseech him to forgive their sins."

Only the sacrament of the Eucharist escaped Menocchio's criticism —but he reinterpreted it in a heterodox manner. It is true, however, that the remarks reported by the witnesses sounded like blasphemies or scornful denials. One day, Menocchio had happened to come to the vicar of Polcenigo's house when they were making the wafers (ostie) and on seeing them he exclaimed: "By the Virgin Mary, how big these brutes (bestie) are!" On another occasion, while arguing with the priest Andrea Bionima, he remarked: "All I see there is a bit of dough, how can that be God? And what *is* God, anyway? Nothing but earth, water, and air." But to the general vicar he explained: "I said that the wafer is a bit of dough, but that the Holy Ghost comes down from heaven into it, and this I really do believe." Such ignorance seemed unbelievable to the vicar: "When your parish priest preached sermons about the holy sacrament of Eucharist, what did he say there was in that holy wafer?" But it was not ignorance on Menocchio's part: "He said it was Christ's body, nonetheless I believed it was the Holy Ghost, because I believe that the Holy Ghost is superior to Christ, who was a man, and that the Holy Ghost comes from God's hand."

"He said . . . nonetheless I believed": Menocchio seemed to take advantage of every chance of reconfirming, almost with insolence, his independence of judgment and his right to take a position of his own. He also told the inquisitor: "I like that sacrament when you have confessed and go to Communion and take the Holy Ghost, and your soul is contented . . . ; as for the sacrament of the Eucharist, it is something made for ruling men, found by men through the Holy Ghost; and saying mass was contrived by the Holy Ghost, like adoring the Host, to keep men from being like animals." So mass and Eucharist were justified from an almost political point of view, as means for civilizing men: in this remark he unconsciously echoed, reversing its meaning, his own exclamation to the vicar of Polcenigo when he had called the wafers "brutes."

What was this radical criticism of the sacraments based on? Certainly not on the Scriptures. Menocchio subjected the Scripture itself to a very unconventional examination and reduced it to "a very few words" forming its essential core: "I believe that the Scriptures were given to us by God, but that later men added to them; a very few words would be enough for these holy Scriptures, but they are like books about battles (*libri de bataia*), they've grown." The Gospels, too, with their discrepancies, were far from the brevity and simplicity of God's word: "As for the Gospel, I think that part of it is truth and part was added by the evangelists of their own accord, as you can see in the *passii*: no two of them say the same things." This explains why Menocchio told the people of his village that "the holy Scripture was made to deceive men" (he confirmed this statement during his trial). In short, he rejected the doctrinal aspect of religion, rejected even the Scriptures, and insisted exclusively on the practical side of religion. "He also told me he only believed in good deeds"; Francesco Fassetta reported that Menocchio had once said this to him while they were returning from a trip to Venice. And another time, while talking to Francesco, Menocchio had exclaimed: "All I want is to act rightly." In this sense holiness for him was a pattern of life, of practical behavior, nothing else: "I believe that the saints were honest men who did good deeds, and for this reason God made them saints, and I think they pray for us." It was wrong to venerate their relics or images: "As for their relics, such as an arm, trunk, head, leg, or hand, I think they are like ours when we are dead, and that we must neither reverence nor adore them . . . we must not adore their image, but only God who created heaven and earth; don't you know," Menocchio asked his judges, "that Abraham knocked down all the idols and images, and adored only God?" But the highest example of what a human life can be, in Menocchio's view, was represented by Christ. With his passion and death Christ had given men an example of a complete acceptance of the human condition: "He benefited all Christians, because he is a mirror for us: as he was patient in dying for our sake, so we must die and suffer for his sake, and not think it strange that we die, since God willed that his own son should die." But Christ was only a man: all men were sons of God "and of the same nature as he who was crucified." Consequently, Menocchio refused to believe that Christ had died to redeem men: "If a man has sinned, he must do his own penance."

Most of these opinions were expressed by Menocchio during a single, protracted examination. "I could talk so much that everybody would be astonished," he had said to people of his village; and undoubtedly the inquisitor, the general vicar and the mayor of Portogruaro were dumbfounded on hearing this miller expound with so much assurance and aggressiveness such an extraordinary series of ideas. Of their originality Menocchio was perfectly conscious: "I never associated with any heretics, but my mind is sharp, and I have searched for high things and things I did not know; I don't think what I have said is true, but I want to be obedient to the church. And I have had wicked opinions, but the Holy Ghost enlightened me, and I implore the mercy of God, of Our Lord Jesus Christ, and of the Holy Ghost, and may they let me die if I'm not saying the truth." He had at last decided to follow his son's advice; but first he had chosen to "say many things to the authorities about their evil deeds," as he had been wanting to do for a long time. Of course, he was aware of the risk he was taking. Before being brought back to prison, he implored his inquisitors: "I beg you, by the passion of Our Lord Jesus Christ, to set me free; and if I deserve death, put me to death, but if I deserve mercy, have mercy on me, because I want to live as a good Christian."

But the trial was far from ended. A few days later, on 1 May, the examinations were resumed; the mayor had had to leave Portogruaro, but the judges were anxious to hear Menocchio again. "During your previous examination," the inquisitor told Menocchio, "we told you that in the trial your mind appeared to be full of these humors and of evil doctrines; therefore the holy tribunal wishes you to finish speaking your mind." Menocchio replied: "My mind was full of pride, and wished for a new world and a new way of living, and hoped that the church might be less gorgeous, so there might not be so much pomp."[15]

I will discuss the significance of this allusion to a "new world" and a "new way of living" further on. But first we must try to understand how the ideas of this miller of Friuli had had a chance to come into being and be put into words.

During the second half of the sixteenth century, Friuli was a society with marked archaic characteristics.[16] The great families of the feudal nobility still had a preponderant weight in the district. Institutions like serfdom (*servitù di masnada*) had been preserved up to a century before, much longer than in the neighboring districts.[17] The ancient medieval parliament had kept its legislative functions, though the real power had long since passed into the hands of the Venetian *luogotenenti*. Venice's rule, begun in 1420, in fact left things as unchanged as possible. The Venetians' only concern had been to establish a balance of forces, so as to neutralize the rebellious tendencies of a part at least of the nobility.

At the beginning of the sixteenth century, contrasts within the nobility had become more acute. There were two parties, the *zamberlani*, favorable to Venice and headed by the powerful Antonio Savorgnan (who died after having gone over to the imperial camp), and the *strumieri*, hostile to Venice and headed by the Torreggiani family. An extremely violent class conflict wedged itself into this political rivalry between noblemen's factions. As early as 1508, the nobleman Francesco di Strassoldo had informed the parliament that in various places in Friuli the peasants were gathering in "assemblages," including up to two thousand persons; "foul and diabolical words" were spoken, "especially about wanting to slaughter prelates, gentlemen, townsmen, lords in their castles, and about starting a Vespro Siciliano [a general insurrection] and other execrable words of this sort."[18] And they weren't only words. On Carnival Thursday 1511, shortly after Venice's defeat at Agnadello, and coinciding with a plague epidemic, the peasants who were loyal to Savorgnan revolted, first in Udine, then in other places, killing noblemen of both factions and setting fire to castles. Class solidarity enabled the noblemen immediately to reunite their ranks and ruthlessly to quell the revolt. But the peasants' violence had frightened the Venetian oligarchy and at the same time had suggested the possibility of a bold policy for keeping the nobility of Friuli in check. During the decades following the brief insurrection of 1511, Venice's tendency to support the peasants of Friuli (and more generally of the mainland) against the local nobility increased. In this system of counterweights, there emerged an institution that was uncommon even in the Venetian dominions: the *contadinanza*. This organ had both fiscal and military functions: it collected a series of tributes and organized a peasant militia on a local basis (*cernide*). This last activity, in particular, was a real affront to the nobility of Friuli: the statute of the *Patria del Friuli* was so imbued with the feudal spirit that it went to the length of threatening the peasants who dared to hinder the noble sport of hunting by setting traps for hares or hunting partridges by night, and it included a heading "De prohibitione armorum rusticis." But the Venetian authorities, though allowing the *contadinanza* to maintain a series of unique features, were determined to make it become an official representative of the interests of the population of the countryside. The legal fiction that the parliament was the representative organ of the whole population had been even formally dropped.

The series of steps Venice took in favor of the peasants of Friuli was very long.[19] As far back as 1533, the *decani* of Udine and of other localities of Friuli and Carnia presented a petition, complaining that they were "much oppressed by various types of *livelli* that are paid in that *Patria* to nobles, non-nobles, and to certain other lay persons, because of the exaggerated price of grain that has been established during the last few years." They were granted the possibility of paying a part of their rents in money instead of in kind, on the basis of average prices determined once and for all; this, in a situation of rapidly increasing prices, was obviously very advantageous to the peasants. In 1554, after "a petition of the *contadinanza* of the *Patria*," all the rents fixed from 1520 on were reduced by more than 7 percent by a decree that was confirmed and extended eight years later. In 1574, the Venetian authorities also tried to limit usury in the countryside, decreeing that "one cannot take as pledge from the peasants of that *Patria* any animals, large or small, that can help in tilling the soil, nor any type of farming implement at the request of any creditor other than the owners themselves." Moreover, "in order to give relief to the poor peasants, whom the rapacity of creditors giving them things on credit deprives of their grain even before it is threshed, and during the period of the year in which its price is at its lowest," it was decreed that creditors could not demand their due before 15 August.

These concessions, whose main object was to keep under control the latent tensions in the countryside of Friuli, also established a bond of objective solidarity between the peasants and the Venetian authorities, as against the local nobility. To counteract the gradual reduction of the rents, the latter tried to transform the *livelli* into plain rents—that is, into a type of contract that decidedly worsened conditions for the peasants. These unfavorable terms of tenure now became common, but in Friuli they met with serious obstacles especially of a demographic nature. When hands are scarce, the terms of agricultural tenancies are not likely to become more favorable to the landowners. During the hundred years between the middle of the sixteenth and the middle of the seventeenth centuries, the total population of Friuli decreased, in consequence both of a series of epidemics and of an increase in emigration, especially toward Venice.[20] The reports of the Venetian *luogotenenti* during this period emphasize the poverty of the peasants. "I suspended all the collection of private debts until the harvesting period," Daniele Priuli wrote in 1573, reporting also that "creditors tore away the women's clothes they found wrapped around the babies, and even pried away the locks from doors, which I thought was inhumanly cruel." Carlo Comer, who wrote in 1587, stressed the natural poverty of the country: "It is very barren, because it is a mountainous region, and its flat part is pebbly, subject to flooding by its many rivers and to the damage of storms, very frequent in this country." He concluded: "Therefore, the noblemen of this country do not possess great riches, and the people, above all the peasants, are extremely poor." At the end of the century (1599), Stefano Viaro described a situation of decadence and desolation: "This country has been in such a scene of decadence during the last years, that there is no village that does not have two-thirds or even three-quarters of its houses ruined and abandoned, and little less than half of its lands uncultivated; this is a thing that arouses pity, because if the country's decline continues in this manner, as it will inevitably do if the inhabitants continue leaving it as they are doing now, only the most needy and wretched inhabitants will be left."[21] At a time when the first signs of decline were appearing in Venice, the economy of Friuli was already in a state of advanced dissolution.

But what could a miller like Menocchio know about this tangle of political, social, and economic contradictions? What view did he have of the enormous interplay of forces silently conditioning his existence?

Obviously, it was a rudimentary and simplified view; but it was a very clear one, too. There were many degrees of "dignity" in the world: there was the pope; there were the cardinals, the bishops, the parish priest of Montereale; there were the empress, the kings, the princes. But beyond all gradations of rank there was a basic division between "superiors" and "poor men"; and Menocchio knew he belonged to the second group. He had a decidedly dichotomous view of the class structure, typical of peasant societies.[22] In Menocchio's remarks, however, there were some indications of a more discriminating attitude toward the superiors. His attack against the supreme religious authorities was violent: "And it seems to me that in this law of ours the pope, cardinals, and bishops are so great and rich that everything belongs to the church and the priests, and they maltreat the poor"; but immediately afterward he criticized the political authorities in a much milder way: "It seems to me also that these Venetian princes allow thieves in that city: when a man wants to buy something, and asks: 'How much does it cost?' they answer 'a ducat,' although its worth is only three *marcelli*; and I wish they were fairer."[23] Of course, these words expressed above all the reaction of a peasant coming suddenly in contact with the forbidding reality of the city: the difference between Montereale or Aviano and a great city was enormous. But the fact remains that whereas the pope, cardinals, and bishops were accused directly of "maltreating" the poor, the Venetian "princes" were accused merely of "allowing thieves in that city." This difference in tone was certainly not due to caution: when he said those words, Menocchio was in the presence of the mayor of Portogruaro, the inquisitor of Aquileia, and his vicar. In his opinion, the chief embodiment of oppression were the ecclesiastical authorities. Why?

The first clue can perhaps be found in Menocchio's words: "Everything belongs to the church and the priests, and they maltreat the poor: if they rent a couple of fields, they are sure to belong to the church, to such-and-such a bishop or such-and-such a cardinal." As already noted, we do not know whether the church owned the fields he rented. From a land register of 1596[24] (that is, made twelve years after Menocchio's declarations), it appears that at least one of the fields presumably rented by him adjoined a holding that the local landowner, Orazio di Montereale, had rented, we do not know on what type of contract, to a ser Giacomo Margnano. The same land register, however, mentions various holdings possessed and rented by churches of the place or of neighboring localities: eight belonged to Santa Maria, one to San Rocco (both at Montereale), one to Santa Maria of Pordenone. Montereale was certainly not an isolated case: at the end of the sixteenth century the extent of the ecclesiastical property in Friuli (indeed in all the Venetian lands) was enormous. Wherever it had diminished in quantity, it had consolidated and improved in quality.[25] All this sufficiently explains Menocchio's words—even if he had never personally clashed with the ecclesiastical proprietors (who had always been explicitly excluded from the reductions of the rent rates introduced by the Venetian authorities).

The extensive presence of ecclesiastical property at Montereale and in its environs was enough to explain the asperity of Menocchio's accusations, but not their implications nor their extending to a more general level. The pope, cardinals, and bishops "maltreat" the poor: but in the name of what? with what right? The pope is "a man like us," except that he has power ("he can do things") and therefore has more "dignity." There is no difference between men of the church and laymen: the sacrament of orders is "merchandise"—like all sacraments and laws of the church—all are "merchandise" and "inventions" for fattening up the priests. Against this colossal structure based on the exploitation of the poor, Menocchio set up a very different religion in which all men are equal, because God's spirit is in everybody.

For Menocchio, then, the consciousness of one's own rights started from a specifically religious level. A miller could dare to explain the truths of faith to the pope, to a king, to a prince, because he had inside him that spirit God has given to all men. For the same reason, he could venture to "say many things against the authorities for their evil deeds." Menocchio was led vehemently to reject the existing hierarchy not only by his awareness of oppression, but also by his religious ideology. He believed in the presence of a "spirit"—sometimes called "the Holy Ghost," and other times "the spirit of God"—in every man.

At first sight it might seem that behind Menocchio's ideas there was the tremendous blow given to the principle of authority by the Protestant Reformation. But what connection did Menocchio have with the groups following the ideas of the Reformation?

"I believe that the Lutherans are those who teach people bad things, and eat meat on Fridays and Saturdays,"[26] Menocchio told the inquisitor. But this was disingenuous. At the time of his second trial in 1599, a chaplain from Portogruaro reported a conversation that had taken place the year before between Menocchio and a certain Simon, a converted

Jew. The two men had passed the whole night talking. Menocchio had said "really extraordinary things about faith": that the Gospels had been written by monks and priests "because they live in idleness"; that Mary, before marrying Saint Joseph, had had "two other children, and that's why Joseph wouldn't have her"; that he, Menocchio, had a "beautiful book," though unfortunately he did not have it at hand: from what he told him about it, Simon reckoned it was the Koran. Menocchio knew that his opinions would lead him to death, but he would not leave Montereale because a friend had vouched for him: "Otherwise I would have fled to Geneva." And he concluded: "When I die, some Lutherans will hear of it, and come and fetch my ashes."[27] So Menocchio was in touch with "some Lutherans," who were ready to consider him a martyr; he had planned to escape to Geneva; he read and praised the Koran. There is no doubt that his conversation with the converted Jew did take place: he alluded to it of his own accord. But we must remember that these facts —not all of them equally certain—emerge from a secondhand testimony. Besides, it is impossible to circumscribe them to an exact definition or doctrinal tendency. It will be better therefore to proceed cautiously, by gradual approximations.

Menocchio's ecclesiology, if it may be called so, as far as it can be reconstructed on the basis of his statements during the examinations at Portogruaro, has fairly well-defined characteristics. In the intricate religious setting of sixteenth-century Europe, some aspects of Menocchio's position are similar to that of the Anabaptists.[28] His emphasis on the simplicity of God's words, his refusal of sacred images, sacraments, and ceremonies, his denial of the divinity of Christ, his advocacy of a practical religion based on good deeds, the pauperistic tone of his criticism of ecclesiastic "pomp," his eulogy of tolerance, are all factors that connect him to the religious radicalism of the Anabaptists. True, Menocchio does not appear to have advocated adult baptism. But the Italian Anabaptist groups would soon reject baptism wholly, like all the other sacraments, and they admitted at most a spiritual baptism, based upon the interior regeneration of adults. Menocchio himself considered baptism entirely useless: "I believe that as soon as we are born we are baptized because God, who has blessed everything, baptizes us."[29]

The Anabaptist movement had spread largely in northern and central Italy, and especially in Veneto, but had been crushed toward the middle of the sixteenth century by a religious and political persecution after one of its leaders had turned informer.[30] But a few scattered clandestine groups survived for some time in Friuli. In 1557 the Inquisition imprisoned a group of artisans of Porcia who were in the habit of meeting at the houses of a tanner and of a wool weaver to read the Scripture and discuss "the renovation of life . . . the purity of the Gospel and the removal of sins."[31] Menocchio, whose heterodox positions dated to a period as far back as thirty years before, according to one of the witnesses, may very possibly have been in touch with these groups.

Yet he cannot be regarded as an Anabaptist, despite all the analogies indicated. The favorable opinon he expressed of the mass and Eucharist and also, within certain limits, of confession, was inconceivable for an Anabaptist.[32] Above all, an Anabaptist, considering the pope the embodiment of the Antichrist, would never have dreamed of saying what Menocchio said about indulgences: "I think they are good, because if God has put a man in his own place, that is the pope, and this man orders a pardon to be granted, it is valid, because it's like receiving it from God, the pardon having been granted by one who acted as his agent."[33] All this had emerged during the first interrogation at Portogruaro (28 April): Menocchio's proud and sometimes even insolent attitude at that time leads us once more to reject the conjecture that these words might have been suggested to him by considerations of prudence. Moreover, the texts that Menocchio indicated as the "sources" of his religious ideas are so diverse that nothing could be so far from the strict and sectarian exclusiveness of the Anabaptists. For the Anabaptists, the only source of truth was the Scripture—or even only the Gospel; for instance, this is what the wool weaver who headed the Porcia group said: "One should not believe in any other scripture save this one, and there is no salvation in any other scripture except the Holy Scripture."[34] In Menocchio's opinion, on the contrary, inspiration could come from various very different books: from the *Fioretto della Bibbia*, for instance, or from the *Decameron*. In conclusion, there were indubitable similarities between Menocchio's position and the Anabaptists', and these similarities can probably be explained by conjecturing that Menocchio may have met some Anabaptists or had contacts with them in Venice or somewhere in Friuli. These similarities, however, appear to be set in decidedly dissimilar contexts.

But if specifying Menocchio's position as being Anabaptist does not explain his case, would it not be better to employ a more generic term? Menocchio, it seems, admitted he was in touch with some "Lutheran" groups (in that period this term covered a very wide area of heterodoxy): why not be satisfied with the vague connection indicated from the start between Menocchio's attitude and the Reformation? This is not possible either. At a certain point, a significant dialogue took place between the inquisitor and Menocchio.[35] The former asked: "What do you think about justification?" Menocchio, usually ready to explain his own "opinions," this time did not understand. The friar had to explain to him "quid sit iustificatio," and Menocchio answered, as previously related, denying that Christ had died to save mankind, because "if a man has sinned, he must see to his own penance." His attitude toward predestination was the same: he did not know the meaning of the word, and only after listening to the inquisitor's explanation he replied: "I don't think anybody has been preordained to eternal life by God." Therefore, justification and predestination, the two issues on which religious debate hinged in Italy during the age of the Reformation, were completely meaningless words for this miller of Friuli.

This is all the more significant if we consider that even in Italy interest in these topics was not limited to the upper classes: "Il fachin, la fantesca e lo schiavon / fan del libero arbitrio anathomia / e torte della predestinazione" (Porters, maids, and servants anatomize free will, and make cake out of predestination), as the satirical poet Pietro Nelli, alias messer Andrea da Bergamo, wrote around the middle of the sixteenth century. A few years earlier, a group of Neapolitan tanners, after having listened to Bernardino Ochino's sermons, had debated heatedly about Saint Paul's letters and the doctrine of justification. An echo of the debates about the importance of faith and of works for salvation rings in the most unexpected contexts, for instance, in a petition presented by a prostitute to the Milanese authorities.[36] These cases were chosen at random, and many more could be quoted. But they all had a common element: all, or almost all, had taken place in the cities.[37] This is one of many indications of the deep gap that had long since opened in Italy between the cities and the countryside. The religious conquest of the Italian countryside might perhaps have been attempted by the Anabaptists had they not been crushed almost at the start by political and religious repression; it was achieved instead, years later, and under a very different banner, by the religious orders of the Counter-Reformation—the Jesuits, preeminently.[38]

This does not mean that during the sixteenth century the rural population in Italy did not show any sign of religious disquiet. But behind the thin curtain on which appeared the terms and topics of contemporary discussion, lies the massive presence of different, far older traditions.[39] This substratum of peasant beliefs and hopes had probably never been completely wiped out; now, however, it became much more evident than in the past, for two basic reasons. On the one hand, the Reformation, by breaking the crust of religious unity, had indirectly helped the emergence, especially in the countryside, of long-buried strata, of age-old sedimentations, among them a vein of autonomous peasant radicalism that in some ways was similar to Anabaptism, but was also something more, something quite different. On the other hand, the records accumulated by Counter-Reformation repression, and especially by an instrument such as the tribunal of the Holy Office, yield a mass of evidence on the attitudes of peasants in the sixteenth century that is infinitely superior, both in quantity and in quality, to the scattered and fragmentary facts usually available about peasants of earlier periods. This evidence creates an inevitable distortion of perspective.

The case of Menocchio is exemplary from both points of view: for its abundance of evidence and for its contents. In fact it becomes possible to understand Menocchio's confessions only if they are placed in that vein of peasant radicalism which the Reformation had helped to bring to the surface, but which was much older than the Reformation.[40]

To the inquisitors it seemed unlikely that a miller like Menocchio could have been able to formulate such a series of complex, though seemingly eccentric, ideas, without any outside influence. They asked the witnesses whether Menocchio had spoken seriously, or whether he had been joking or repeating words he had heard from other persons; they asked Menocchio to tell the names of his "companions." But in both cases his answers did not produce anything. Menocchio declared resolutely: "Sir, I have never met anybody who had these opinions, but what opinions I had, I took out of my own brain."[41] He was lying, at least in part. Fourteen years later, when denunciations against Menocchio began to arrive again at the Holy Office of Concordia, a priest from Montereale said that he had heard that "this Menocchio had learned his heresies from a certain Nicola da Porcia."[42] The name of this man—a "painter," otherwise unknown—had been mentioned during the first trial, too, and Menocchio's response had been a visible embarrassment. First he said he had met him during Lent and had heard him say that he fasted, but only "out of fear" (whereas Menocchio used to eat "a little milk, cheese, and a few eggs"). Immediately afterward, though, he began to digress, talking of a book Nicola owned, then changed the subject. Nicola, too, was summoned by the Holy Office, but he was immediately released because of the certificates of good behavior given him by two priests of Porcia.[43] During the second trial, an indication emerged of the influence exerted by an unknown person on Menocchio's heterodox opinions. During the examination of 19 July 1599, the inquisitor asked him how long he had believed—on the basis of a story from the *Decameron*—that every man could be saved within his own religion and that therefore a Turk was right in remaining a Turk and not converting to Christianity. Menocchio replied: "I may have had this opinion for fifteen or sixteen years, because we began to argue, and the devil put it in my head." "With whom did you begin to argue?" the inquisitor asked at once. Only after a long pause ("post longam moram"), Menocchio answered, "I don't know."[44]

So Menocchio had talked with somebody about religious matters fifteen or sixteen years before—in 1583 most likely, because at the beginning of the following year he had been put in prison and tried. This person most probably was the same one who had lent him the incriminated book, the *Decameron*. Menocchio mentioned his name a couple of weeks later: Nicola de Melchiori. Not only the name, but also the dates (a coincidence the inquisitors did not notice) lead me to identify this person as Nicola da Porcia; in 1584 Menocchio had not seen him for a year. It is not possible to ascertain when contacts between the two men had started. In any case, Menocchio's system of ideas had been formed long before the first trial.

"Do you want me to show you the right path? You must try to do all the good you can, and follow the steps of my predecessors and the precepts of our holy mother the church": these were the words, it will be remembered, that Menocchio, almost certainly lying, reported having said to the villagers of Montereale. In fact, Menocchio had taught them exactly the reverse, had led them to move away from the religion of their fathers, to reject the doctrines preached by the parish priest from his pulpit. To adhere to this nonconformist option for such a long period (perhaps even thirty years), first in a small community like Montereale, then in front of the tribunal of the Holy Office, required a moral and intellectual energy that it would not be exaggerated to call extraordinary. Not the distrust of friends and relatives, nor the reproaches of the parish priest, nor the threats of the inquisitors had been able to shake Menocchio's confidence. But what made him so confident? In the name of what did he speak?

In his first answers at the trial he ascribed his opinions to a diabolic inspiration: "I was saying those words because I was tempted . . . it was the evil one who made me believe those things." But at the end of the first examination, his attitude had already become less submissive: "What I said, by inspiration of God or of the devil." Fifteen days later he considered another alternative: "The devil or something else was tempting me." A little later he stated more clearly what this "something" that tormented him was: "What opinions I had, I took out of my own brain." From this position he never shifted during the whole course of his trial. Even when he resolved to ask the judges' pardon, he ascribed his mistakes to his own "subtle brain."[45]

So Menocchio did not boast of any particular revelation or enlightenment. In his speeches he emphasized instead his own powers of reason. This alone was enough to distinguish him from the prophets, visionaries, and wandering preachers who expounded obscure predictions in the streets of Italian cities during the late fifteenth and early sixteenth centuries. As late as 1550, a semi-literate former Benedictine friar, Giorgio Siculo, tried to relate to the fathers gathered for the Council of Trent the truths that Christ had revealed to him, appearing before him "in his own person."[46] But Menocchio's trial occurred twenty years after the end of the Council of Trent; the authorities had had their say; the long period of uncertainty about what the believers could and should believe was over. Yet this lonely miller, living in the seclusion of the hills of Friuli, went on revolving "high things" in his mind and opposing his own opinions in matters of faith to the decrees of the church: "I think . . . to my thought and belief . . ."

Besides reasoning, he consulted books. "Having confessed several times to a priest of Barcis," Menocchio declared during his first examination, "I asked him: 'Can it be true that Jesus Christ was conceived of the Holy Ghost, and borne by the Virgin Mary?' and I said I believed in it, but sometimes was tempted by the devil about this." This way of ascribing his doubts to a demoniac temptation reflected Menocchio's fairly cautious attitude at the beginning of the trial; he immediately explained the double foundation of his position: "This thought of mine was based on the fact that so many men are born in the world, and none of them are born of a virgin; and having read that the glorious Virgin was married to Saint Joseph, I thought that Our Lord Jesus Christ was Saint Joseph's son, because in some stories I read, Saint Joseph used to call Our Lord Jesus Christ 'son'; this I read in a book called *Il fioretto della Bibbia*."[47] This is an example chosen at random: Menocchio often indicated this or that book as the source (not the only one, in this case) of his "opinions." But what books had Menocchio read?

Unfortunately, we do not have a complete list of his books. When he was arrested the general vicar had his house searched: some books were found, but since they were not forbidden or suspect books, no inventory was made.[48] We can reconstruct with fair approximation an incomplete picture of what Menocchio had read, exclusively on the basis of some brief hints dropped by him during his examinations. The books he mentioned during the first trial were:

1. The Bible in Italian, "mostly in red letters."[49]
2. *Il fioretto della Bibbia*:[50] this was the translation of a medieval Catalan chronicle in which several sources were mixed, including the Vulgate, *Chronicon* by Isidoro, *Elucidarium* by Honorius of Autun, and a considerable number of apocryphal gospels. This work circulated in a manuscript form during the fourteenth and fifteenth centuries; later it was printed in some fifteen editions, under various titles (*Fioretto della Bibbia, Fiore di tutta la Bibbia, Fiore novello*) up to the 1550s.
3. *Il lucidario* (or *Rosario?*) *della Madonna*: this book can probably be identified as *Il rosario della gloriosa vergine Maria*, by the Dominican friar Alberto da Castello, which was printed several times during the sixteenth century.[51]

4. *Il Lucendario* (meaning *Leggendario*) *de Santi*: the translation of the much-read *Legenda aurea* by Jacopo da Voragine, edited by Niccolò Malermi, which appeared with the title *Legendario delle vite de tutti li santi*.[52]

5. *Historia del Giudicio*: a short poem in octaves by an anonymous author of the fifteenth century, which circulated in several versions of varying length.[53]

6. *Il cavalier Zuanne de Mandavilla*: the Italian translation, reprinted several times during the sixteenth century, of the famous travel book written around the middle of the fourteenth century and attributed to a fictional Sir John Mandeville.[54]

7. "A book called *Zampollo*": in reality *Il sogno dil Caravia*, printed in Venice in 1541.[55]

To these titles can be added a few others that were mentioned during the second trial:

8. *Il supplemento delle croniche*: the translation in the vernacular of a chronicle written at the end of the fifteenth century by an Augustinian hermit of Bergamo, Jacopo Filippo Foresti, and reprinted several times with additions up to the late sixteenth century, under the title *Supplementum supplementi delle croniche*.[56]

9. *Lunario al modo de Italia calculato composto nella città di Pesaro dal ecc.mo dottore maestro Camilo de Leonardis* (many reprints were made of this book, too).[57]

10. Boccaccio's *Decameron*, in an unexpurgated edition.[58]

11. An unidentified book that a witness conjectured to be the Koran (an Italian translation of it had appeared in Venice in 1547).[59]

How did Menocchio obtain these books? The only one we are sure he had bought was *Il fioretto della Bibbia*, "which," Menocchio said, "I bought in Venice for two *soldi*."[60] About three more—*Historia del Giudicio*, the *Lunario* and the Koran—there is no indication. Foresti's *Supplementum* was given to Menocchio by Tomaso Mero from Malmins.[61] All the others—six out of eleven, or more than half—were lent to him. These data are significant because they give a glimpse of this tiny community and its network of readers, who overcame the obstacle of their scarce financial resources by passing books on to each other. The *Lucidario* (or *Rosario*) *della Madonna*, for instance, was lent to Menocchio during his stay at Arba in 1564 by a woman, Anna de Cecho. Her son, Giorgio Capel, was summoned as a witness (his mother had died), and said he had a book called *La vita dei santi*; other books in his possession had been confiscated by the parish priest of Arba, who had given him back only two or three of them, saying that "they will want to burn" the others (meaning the inquisitors, of course). The Bible had been lent to Menocchio by his uncle, Domenico Gerbas, along with the *Legendario de santi*. The latter, "being wet, got torn." The Bible was given back to Menocchio's cousin, Bastian Scandella, who lent it to Menocchio again several times. However, six or seven months before the trial, Bastian's wife, Firo, had taken the Bible and burned it up in the oven. "But it was a shame to burn that book," Menocchio exclaimed. Mandeville's *Travels* had been lent to him five or six years before by the priest Andrea Bionima, chaplain of Montereale, who had found it by chance at Maniago, while rummaging among "certain notary's documents" (Bionima, however, maintained prudently that Menocchio had not borrowed the book from him, but from Vincenzo Lombardo, who, being able to "read a little," had probably taken the book to his own house).[62] *Il sogno dil Caravia* had been lent to Menocchio by Nicola da Porcia, who can probably be identified with that Nicola da Melchiori who had given Menocchio the *Decameron* through Lunardo della Minussa of Montereale.[63] As for the *Fioretto*, Menocchio had lent it to a young man from Barcis, Tita Coradina, who had read only a page of it (so he said); then the parish priest had told him it was a forbidden book, and he had burned it.[64]

So the circulation of books was intense and involved not only priests, which was easy to imagine, but also women. As far back as the beginning of the sixteenth century a school had been opened at Udine under the direction of Gerolamo Amaseo, with the object of "teaching reading to all sorts of persons, with no exception, both to children of townsmen and to children of artisans and of lower-class families, to persons of all ages, without any particular payment." Schools of grammar, where a little Latin was also taught, existed in such centers as Aviano and Pordenone.[65] Perhaps even in Montereale there was a school on an elementary level where Menocchio learned to "read, write, and do accounts," and where other of the villagers learned, too. It is surprising, however, to discover how much people read in a small hillside village like Montereale.[66] Unfortunately, in only a few cases are there indications of the social position of these readers. The painter Nicola da Porcia has been explained; Bastian Scandella, Menocchio's cousin, appears in the land register of 1596 as the holder (we do not know upon what basis) of a considerable number of plots; during the same year he was mayor of Montereale. But almost all of the others are only names. It is evident, in any case, that for these persons books were a part of a common experience; they were an object of normal use, to be treated without any particular care, and subject to the risk of being wet or torn. Menocchio's scandalized comment about the Bible burned up in the oven (no doubt to escape a possible search by the Holy Office) is significant; in spite of his ironical comparison with "books about battles, that have grown," he considered the

Scripture different from all other books because it contained a core given to man by God.

The fact that more than half of the books mentioned by Menocchio had been borrowed should be kept in mind when analyzing the characteristics of this list. Only in the case of the *Fioretto* is there certainty that Menocchio had made a choice, that he had decided to buy *that* book among the many others stacked up in the shop or stall of the unknown Venetian bookseller. The fact that the *Fioretto* had been a sort of *livre de chevet* for him is significant, as we shall see. Acquisition of *Mandavilla*, on the other hand, had been a mere chance: the priest Andrea Bionima had happened to find this book among the "notary's documents" at Maniago, and it had ended up in Menocchio's hands, probably as a consequence of an indiscriminate voracity for books rather than of a specific interest. This applies, probably, to all the other books he borrowed from people in his village. The list I have reconstructed shows a series of books Menocchio had a chance to read—it does not give a picture of his taste and conscious choices.

Moreover, the list is incomplete, which explains the predominance of religious books: six out of eleven, or more than half. Obviously, during his two trials Menocchio was most likely to mention this type of reading to justify his own ideas. Most probably a complete list of books owned or read by him would have presented a more varied picture, including, for instance, some of those "books about battles" that Menocchio had provocatively compared to the Scripture, such as *Il libro che trata di bataglia, chiamato Fioravante* (Venice: M. Sessa, 1506). But even this limited group of books, incomplete and one-sided as it is, enables us to make a few observations. Besides the Scriptures, religious texts, verse, and prose adaptations of the Scriptures, Menocchio read biographies of saints, an almanac, a semicomic short poem, a travel book, a chronicle. All the texts were in Italian (it seems that Menocchio knew little more Latin than what he had learned while serving mass), had been written two or three centuries earlier, were very widespread, and were read on different social levels.[67] Two books seem to stand out conspicuously in this list: the *Decameron* and (if Menocchio really did read it) the Koran; but these are exceptions to be discussed separately. All the rest are fairly obvious titles, but they apparently do not shed light on the problem of how Menocchio had managed to form what a man from his village had called "his fantastic opinions."

At this point, we have the feeling of having ended up again in a blind alley. At the beginning, on hearing Menocchio's extravagant cosmogony, we had wondered for an instant (as the general vicar did) whether Menocchio was crazy. This surmise having proved wrong, his ecclesiology was examined with the object of testing the possibility of his being an Anabaptist. This possibility having been discarded, too, the possibility arose, on hearing that Menocchio considered himself a "Lutheran" martyr, that he might have been connected with the Reformation. But the proposed link between Menocchio's ideas and beliefs and that deep vein of peasant radicalism brought to the surface by the Reformation but independent of it, now seems to be firmly contradicted by the list of books read by Menocchio and reconstructed on the basis of the evidence of the trial. How representative can as uncommon a figure as that of a miller of the sixteenth century who could read and write be considered? And representative of what? Certainly not of a vein of peasant culture, since Menocchio himself indicated a series of printed books as the source of his ideas. By knocking so many times against the walls of this labyrinth, we have worked our way back to the starting point.

Almost to the starting point. We have seen what books Menocchio had read. But how did he read them?

If the passages quoted by Menocchio are compared with the conclusions he drew from them (or even with his way of reporting them to the judges), a discrepancy, sometimes a deep gap, arises between the two versions. The temptation to consider these books as "sources" in the mechanical sense of the term is precluded by the aggressive originality of Menocchio's reading. It appears, then, that the most important factor is not so much the texts themselves as a sort of grid Menocchio unconsciously put between himself and the printed page: this grid let the light fall on certain passages, while hiding others, gave certain words an extreme meaning, while isolating them from their context, and acted on Menocchio's memory by distorting the very words of the texts.[68] And this grid, this approach to reading, sends us continually back to a different culture from the one expressed by the printed book—an oral culture.

This does not mean that books were for Menocchio a mere occasion, a pretext. Menocchio himself declared once that at least one book had disturbed him deeply, its unexpected statements leading him to think new thoughts. This clash between the printed page and the oral culture of which he was an unconscious carrier was what induced Menocchio to formulate—first to himself, then to the people of his village, last to the judges—the "opinions . . . taken out of *his* own brain."

I will now give a series of increasingly complex examples of Menocchio's approach to books.

During his first examination, Menocchio had said he did not believe Mary had conceived as a virgin by the Holy Ghost, both "because so many men are born in the world, and none were born of a virgin" and because, having read in a book called *Il Fioretto della Bibbia* "that Saint Joseph called Our Lord Jesus Christ 'son,'" he had inferred that Christ was Saint Joseph's son. Chapter 116 of the *Fioretto*, "How Jesus Was Sent to School," relates that Jesus cursed the teacher who had slapped him and made him instantly fall dead. Seeing the neighbors run up in anger, "Joseph said, 'You have punished him, my son, can't you see that these people hate us?'" "My son"—but on the same page, in the preceding chapter, "How Jesus while Playing with Other Children Brought Back to Life a Dead Child," Menocchio had certainly read Mary's reply to a woman who asked her if Jesus was her son: "Yes, he is my son, his only father is God."[69]

Menocchio's reading was obviously one-sided and arbitrary—almost as if he had been looking for a confirmation of ideas and beliefs he already firmly possessed. In this case, it was the certainty that "Christ was a man, born like us." It was unreasonable to believe that Christ had been borne by a virgin and that he died on the cross: "If he had really been God, he wouldn't have let himself be crucified."[70]

The quotation of passages from books like the *Fioretto*, based upon apocryphal gospels, is not surprising. When the terse simplicity of God's word—"four words"—is set against the unbridled proliferation of Scripture, the notion of "apocryphal" disappears. Apocryphal and canonical gospels are placed on the same level and considered merely human texts. On the other hand, contrary to what one might have expected from the evidence of the inhabitants of Montereale ("he always argues with some person or other, he has a Bible in Italian, and fancies he bases himself on it"),[71] Menocchio made very few precise references to the Bible during his interrogation. It would seem, indeed, that he was more familiar with the parascriptural adaptations of the type of *Il Fioretto della Bibbia* than with the translation of the Bible itself. On 8 March, answering a question of the general vicar, Menocchio exclaimed: "I say it is more right to love one's neighbor than to love God." This statement, too, was based on a text. Right afterward Menocchio added: "Because I have read in a *Historia del Giudicio* that when the day of judgment comes [God] will say to that angel: 'You are wicked, you have never done me any kindness,' and the angel will answer: 'My lord, I have never seen you, how could I do you any kindness?' 'I was hungry, and you didn't feed me; I was thirsty, and you didn't give me to drink; I was naked, and you didn't cover me; when I was in prison you never came to visit me.' For this reason I thought God was our neighbor, because he said, 'I was that poor man.'"[72]

Here is the corresponding passage of *Historia del Giudicio*:

> Dalla sinistra all'hor vorran parlare
> ma Dio gli caccierà con gran furore,
> dicendo: "Peccatori di mal affare
> gite a l'inferno al sempiterno ardore;

da voi non hebbi da ber né da mangiare,
né alcun ben facesti per mio amore;
andate maladetti al foco eterno
dove starete con duol sempiterno."

Risponderà quel popol doloroso:
"Quando, Signor, ti vedemmo giamai
morto di fame, afflitto e ancor penoso;
quando in prigion pattisti tanti guai?"
All'hor risponderà Cristo glorioso:
"Quando il pover cacciavi con guai.
Verso de miser non havesti pietade,
né mai a lor facesti caritade."[73]

(From the left they will then try to speak / but God will drive them away
with great fury, / saying: "You sinners with wicked hearts / go down to
hell in eternal heat; / from you I never had to drink or eat, / no good did
you ever do for my sake; / go, accursed ones, in perpetual fire, / where
you will live in pain for eternity." / That suffering people will answer: /
"When, O Lord, did we ever see you / dying of hunger, afflicted, in pain;
/ when did you suffer in prison such woe?" / Then glorious Christ will
answer: "When you rejected the moaning poor man, / To the wretched
you showed no pity, / and you refused to give them your alms.")

It is apparent that these crude octaves imitate, in a very unimagina-
tive way, a passage from Saint Matthew's Gospel. But Menocchio refers
to them, and not to the Gospel. In this case, too, the quotation from the
printed page—basically exact, the only exception being the curious mistake of the "angel"'s protesting instead of the damned—actually turns
out to be a remaking. But in the case mentioned before, the meaning of
the passage was forced by means of an omission: here the process is more
intricate. In comparison with the text, Menocchio takes a step forward—
apparently a very small step, in fact an enormous one: if God is our
neighbor, "because he said 'I am that poor man,'" it is more important
to love our neighbor than to love God. It was a deduction that strained in
a radical direction the emphasis on a practical, active way of being religious that was common to almost all the Italian heretical groups of this
period. The Anabaptist bishop Benedetto d'Asolo, too, preached a faith
in "an only God, an only Jesus Christ our Lord and intercessor," and
charity toward one's neighbors, because "on Judgment day the only
thing we will be asked is whether we have fed the hungry, given drink to
the thirsty, clothed the naked, assisted the sick, given hospitality to way-
farers ... these being the foundations of charity."[74] But Menocchio's
attitude toward this type of preaching—if it reached him, which is very

probable—was not merely receptive. A very decided tendency to reduce religion to morality is often perceptible in his speeches. When he explained to the inquisitors that swearing is not a sin, he used a marvelous argument, based as usual on concrete images: "Because when somebody swears, he only damages himself, and not his neighbor; for instance, if I have a cloak, and choose to tear it, I damage only myself and nobody else, and I believe that if someone does no harm to others, he doesn't commit any sin; and since we are all sons of God, if we don't harm each other, for instance, if a father has several sons, and one of them says, 'May my father be cursed,' his father will forgive him, but if he breaks the head of another man's son, he cannot forgive him unless he pays for it; that's why I said that swearing is not a sin, since it does not harm anybody."[75] Thus, if someone does no damage to his neighbor, he commits no sin: man's relationship with God becomes irrelevant compared with his relationship with his neighbor. And if God is his neighbor what need is there of a God?

Of course, Menocchio did not take this last step that would have led him to uphold an ideal, devoid of any religious connotation, of a society based upon justice. In Menocchio's opinion, love toward one's fellow creatures remained a religious precept—actually the very essence of religion. But his insistence exclusively on the evangelic message in its simplest and barest form opened the way to a tendency to reduce religion to morality. Even in the case of *Historia del Giudicio* it is obvious that the pattern of interpretation is far more important than the source.

Yet some texts had had a great importance for Menocchio. First of all (as he admitted) was *Il cavalier Zuanne de Mandavilla*, that is, *Mandeville's Travels*. When the trial started again at Portogruaro, the inquisitors urged Menocchio again, this time with threats, to tell the names of "all his confederates, otherwise more drastic steps will be taken against him; since it seems impossible to this Holy Office that he can have learned so many things without having any companions."

"Sir, I am not aware of ever having taught anything to anybody," was Menocchio's reply, "neither have I ever had any companions in these opinions of mine; and what I said, I said because of that book by Mandavilla I read."[76] More exactly, in a letter he wrote to the judges from prison, Menocchio listed the causes of his mistakes and put in the second place the fact that he had "read that book by Mandavilla about so many sorts of peoples and of different laws, that troubled me so much." What was the reason for his feeling so "troubled" and uneasy?

Mandeville's Travels were written in French, probably in Liège, around the middle of the fourteenth century, and attributed to an imaginary Sir John Mandeville. They are essentially a treatise based on geographic texts and on medieval encyclopaedias like the *Speculum* by

Vincent of Beauvais. After circulating widely in manuscript form, it was published in a series of printed editions in Latin and in the principal European languages; the Italian translation alone appeared in more than twenty editions between 1480 and 1567.

The *Travels* are divided in two parts, very different in contents. The first is an itinerary to the Holy Land, a sort of sightseeing guide for pilgrims. The second is a description of a trip to the East, stopping in increasingly distant islands and reaching India and Cathay (China). The book closes with the description of an earthly paradise and of the islands surrounding the coast of the kingdom of the mythical Prester John. Both parts are presented as direct testimonies; but the first part is full of accurate and well-informed observations, whereas the second is largely a work of the imagination.

"The folk of that contree han a dyuers lawe, for summe of hem worschipe the sonne, summe the mone, summe the fuyr, summe trees, summe serpents or the firste thing that thei meeten at morwen, and summe worschipen symulacres and summe ydoles."[77] This was reported by Mandeville almost at the beginning of the second part of his journey, in his description of Channe (Thana) a small island near India. Here we find an allusion, later repeated several times, to the "dyuers lawe," to the variety of beliefs and religious customs that had so "troubled" Menocchio. Mandeville's largely fabulous descriptions of remote countries broadened Menocchio's mental universe prodigiously. It was no longer bounded by Montereale, or Pordenone, or at the most Venice, the places of his miller's existence—it reached to India, Cathay, the islands of the man-eating people, of the pygmies, of the men with dog's heads. On the subject of the pygmies, Mandeville had written a passage bound to have an extraordinary success:

The folk ben of litylle stature, that ben but iii span long. And thei ben right faire and gentylle after here quantytees, bothe the men and the wommen. And thei maryen hem whan they ben half yere of age and geten children. And thei lyuen not but vi yeer or vii at the moste, and he that lyueth viii yeer men holden him there right passynge old. Theise men ben the beste worcheres of gold, syluer, cotoun, sylk, and of alle suche thinges of ony other that ben in the world. And thei han often tymes werre with the bryddes of the contree that thei taken and eten. This litylle folk nouther labouren in londes ne in vynes, but thei han grete men amonges hem of oure stature that tylen the lond and labouren amonges the vynes for hem. And of tho men of oure stature han thei grete skorn and wonder as we wolde haue among vs of geauntes yif thei weren amonges vs.[78]

The pygmies' scorn toward "tho men of oure stature" sums up all the feeling of bewilderment Menocchio must have experienced in reading this book. The variety of beliefs and customs reported by Mandeville led him to question himself about the basis of his own beliefs and actions.

Those largely imaginary islands provided him with an Archimidean point from which he could look at the world where he had been born and had grown. "So many sorts of peoples and . . . different laws," "many islands whose inhabitants live some in one way, others in other ways," "so many different sorts of nations, some believing in some things, others believing in other things": Menocchio insisted on this point several times during his trial. During those same years, a nobleman of Périgord, Michel de Montaigne, was experiencing a similar relativistic shock on reading the accounts of the natives of the New World.[79]

But Menocchio was not Montaigne, he was only a self-taught miller. His life had run its course almost exclusively within the walls of the village of Montereale. He did not know either Greek or Latin; he had read only a few chance books, though he had thoroughly digested every single word of those books. He had ruminated on them for years, words and sentences fermenting in his mind. An example can illustrate the workings of this slow, laborious process of transformation. In Chapter 148 of *Mandeville's Travels*, whose title, in the translation Menocchio read, was "About the island of Dondina, where people eat each other when they cannot survive, and about the power of its king, who is master of LIIII more islands and of many kinds of men who inhabit these islands," Menocchio had found this passage:

In that yle ben folk of dyuerse kyndes, so that the fader eteth the sone, the sone the fader, the husbonde the wif, and the wif the husbonde. And yif it so befalle that the fader or moder or ony of here frendes ben seke, anon the sone goth to the prest of here lawe and preyeth him to aske the ydole yif his fader or moder or frend schalle dye on that euylle or non. And than the prest and the sone gon togydere before the ydole and knelen fulle deuoutly and asken of the ydole here demande. And yif the deuylle that is withinne answere that he schalle lyue, thei kepen him wel. And yif he seye that he schalle dye, than the prest goth with the sone or with the wif of him that is seek and thei putten here hondes vpon his mouth and stoppen his breth, and so thei sleen him. And after that thei choppen alle the body in smale peces and preyen alle his frendes to comen and eten of him that is ded. And thei senden for alle the mynstralles of the contree and maken a solempne feste. And whan thei han eten the flesch, thei taken the bones and buryen hem and syngen and maken gret molodye. And alle tho that ben of his kyn or pretenden hem to ben his frendes, and thei come not to that feste, thei ben repreued for euermore and schamed and maken gret doel, for neuer after schulle thei ben holden as frends. And thei seyn also that men eten here flesch for to delyueren hem out of peyne. . . . Whan the flesch is tendre and megre, thanne seyn here frendes that they don gret synne to leten hem haue so long langure to suffre so moche peyne withoute resoun. And whan thei fynde the flesche fatte, than thei seyn that it is wel don to senden hem sone to Paradys, and that thei haue not suffred him to longe to endure in peyne.[80]

This description of a ritual anthropophagy struck Menocchio very hard, as emerges clearly from the examination of 22 February. The general vicar asked him, as he had already done many other times: "Tell me who were your companions and had the same opinions as yours." Menocchio replied: "Sir, I have never met anybody having these opinions, but what opinions I have, I took out of my own brain. It is true that once I read a book lent to me by a chaplain, the reverend Andrea Bionima, who is now living at Montereale; this book was called *Il cavalier Zuanne de Mandavilla*, I think it was French, it was printed in vernacular Italian tongue. . . . This same book by the knight Mandeville also told that when men were sick, and about to die, people went to their priest, and the priest prayed to an idol, and the idol told him whether the sick man was bound to die or not, and if he was bound to die, the priest would stifle him, and all together they would eat him; and if he was bad, he had committed many sins, and it had been ill-judged to let him live so long. And from that I took this opinion of mine, that when the body dies the soul dies too, because among so many different sorts of peoples, some believe one thing, others believe another."[81]

Once again Menocchio's ardent memory had melted, transposed, and remolded words and sentences. The slaughtered man whose flesh was too lean had become outright "bad" (bad tasting), the one with the fat flesh had become "good" (good tasting). The moral-gastronomic ambiguity of these terms (good, bad) had attracted to itself the allusion to sin, shifting it from the killers to the killed man. Thus, he who was good (that is, good tasting) was without sin, he who was bad (that is, bad tasting) was full of sins. At this point, Menocchio had jumped to the conclusion that there is no life after death, there are no future prizes or punishments, heaven and hell are on this earth, the soul is mortal. As usual, Menocchio aggressively distorted the text (obviously quite unintentionally). The torrent of questions he asked books went far beyond the printed page. But in this case the role of the text was important: "*and from that I took* this opinion of mine that when the body dies the soul dies too, *because among so many different sorts of peoples, some believe one thing, others believe another.*"

However, the emphasis on the variety of laws and customs was only one of the poles of Mandeville's report. At the opposite pole was the perception of an almost constant element in the midst of many dissimilarities: rationality, invariably accompanied by a faith in God as author of the world, as "God of kynde," "God of nature." After talking about the adorers of idols and images of the island of Channe, Mandeville added:

And thei that worschipen symulacres thei worschipen hem for sum worthi man that was sumtyme, as Hercules and many othere that diden many meruayles in here tyme. For thei seyn wel that thei be not goddes, for thei knowen wel that

there is a god of kynde that made alle thinges, the whiche is in Heuene. But thei
knowen wel that this may not do the meruayles that he made but yif it had ben be
the specyalle gifte of God. And therfore thei seyn that he was wel with God . . .
therfore thei worschipe him. And so seyn thei of the sonne because that he
chaungeth the tyme and yeueth hete and norissheth alle thinges vpon erthe. And
for it is of so gret profite thei knowe wel that myghte not be but that . . . God
hath youen it more gret vertue in the world. Therfore it is gode resoun, as thei
seyn, to don it worschipe and reuerence.[82]

"Gode resoun." With a soberly detached, almost ethnographic tone,
Mandeville recorded exotic realities or beliefs, showing how a rational
core was hidden under their monstrous or absurd appearance. It is true
that the inhabitants of the Island of Channe adored a divinity that was
half ox and half man. But they believed that the ox is "the moste holy
beste that is in erthe and most pacyent and most profitable than ony
other" and that man is "the most noble creature in erthe and also for he
hath lordschipe abouten alle bestes"; besides, wasn't it true that some
Christians superstitiously ascribed harmful or beneficent powers to certain animals? "It is no meruaylle thanne that the paynemes that han no
gode doctryne but only of here nature beleeven more largely for here
symplesse." The inhabitants of the Island of Nacumera, Mandeville reported, both men and women, had dog's heads and were called Cyno-
cephali; but he immediately added: "and thei ben fulle resonable and of
gode vnderstondynge." Thus, in the final chapter, having reached the end
of his account of his extraordinary travels, Mandeville could solemnly
declare to his readers:

And yee schulle vndirstonde that of alle theise contrees . . . and of alle the dyuerse
folk that I haue spoken of before and of dyuerse lawes and of dyuerse beleeves
that thei han, yit is there non of hem alle but that thei han sum resoun within hem
and vnderstondynge . . . and that han certeyn articles of oure faith and summe
gode poyntes of oure beleeve; and that thei beleeven in God that formede alle
thing and made the world and clepen Him God of Nature, after that the prophete
seyth, *Et metuent eum omnes fines terre*, and also in another place, *Omnes gentes
seruient ei*, that is to seyne, Alle folk schul serven Him. But yit thei cone not
speken perfytly, for there is no man to techen hem, but only that thei cone deuyse
be hire naturelle wytt.[83]

Thus, through *Mandeville's Travels*, an innocent narration inter-
woven with fantastic elements, translated and reprinted countless times,
an echo of the religious tolerance of the Middle Ages reached the age of
the wars of religion, of excommunications, of the burning of heretics. It
was probably only one of many different channels that fed a popular current—as yet very little known—that was favorable to tolerance: traces of
it can be seen here and there during the whole of the sixteenth century.
Another channel can be found in the persistent popularity of the medieval

legend of the three rings.[84] Menocchio heard it and was so shaken as to relate it in much detail during his second trial (12 July 1599) to the inquisitor who judged him, who was the successor of fra Felice da Montefalco, fra Gerolamo Asteo. After having admitted that he had once said ("but I don't remember to whom") that he had been "born a Christian, so he wanted to live as a Christian, but if he had been born a Turk he would have wanted to remain a Turk," Menocchio added:

> Listen to me, if you please, sir. There once was a great lord who declared that his heir would be the person who was in possession of a certain precious ring of his; and when he was about to die, he had two other rings made, identical to the first, because he had three sons; and he gave a ring to each son; each of them thought he was the heir and thought he had the real ring, but as they were so similar it was impossible to say with certainty which one was the real one. In the same way God, our father, has several sons he loves, that is, Christians, Turks, and Jews, and to each he has given the will to live according to their own law, and nobody knows which is the right one. That's why I said that, having been born a Christian, I want to remain a Christian, and if I had been born a Turk I would have wanted to live as a Turk.

"So you mean," the inquisitor asked, "that we do not know which is the right law?" Menocchio replied: "Yes, sir, I think everybody believes his own faith is the right one, but one cannot know which is the right one; but since my grandfather, my father, and all my relatives have been Christians, I want to remain a Christian and believe that this is the right faith."[85]

This was an extraordinary moment even in a trial like this one, extraordinary from beginning to end. The roles were temporarily inverted, Menocchio had taken the initiative, tried to convince the judge, while explaining to him his convictions: "Listen to me, if you please, sir." Who represented, here, the part of high culture, and who the part of popular culture? It is not easy to answer. The medium through which Menocchio had heard the simile of the three rings rendered the situation even more paradoxical. He declared that he had read it in "I don't know what book." The inquisitor immediately understood which book it was: "It is a forbidden book." Almost a month later, Menocchio confessed its title: "I read it in the book of *Cento novelle* by Boccaccio," which had been lent to him by "the late Nicolò de Melchiori"—probably the painter Nicolò da Porcia, from whom, according to a witness, Menocchio had "learned his heresies."

But all the evidence examined so far shows clearly that Menocchio was not slavishly repeating other persons' opinions or theories. His approach to books, his intricate and laborious declarations, are an undoubtable sign of an original elaboration. Of course, it had not been accomplished in a void. It has become increasingly evident that both popular and learned currents converged in it, in ways and forms that are yet to be defined. Probably the person who put a copy of the *Decameron* in Menocchio's hands was someone belonging to the upper classes. But that book, or at least a part of it—the third story of the first "giornata," which tells the legend of the three rings—produced a deep echo in Menocchio's mind. Unfortunately, we do not know how he responded to the other stories by Boccaccio. No doubt in the story of Melchisedec the Jew his religious attitude, so impatient of confessional limitations, must have found a corroboration. But the passage of Boccaccio's book containing the story of the three rings had been eliminated by Counter-Reformation censorship,[86] notoriously much more alert to religiously dangerous passages than to alleged obscenities. Menocchio must have seen an older edition, or in any case one that had escaped the intervention of the censors. At this point the clash between the inquisitor and canonist Gerolamo Asteo and the miller Domenico Scandella, nicknamed Menocchio, about the story of the three rings and the praise of tolerance contained in it, seems somehow symbolic. During this period, the Catholic church was fighting a war on two fronts: against the old and new high culture that could not be confined within the limits of the Counter-Reformation, and against popular culture. Between these two enemies, different as they were, there could sometimes be underground connections.

Menocchio's reply to the inquisitor's question, "So you think that we do not know which is the right law?" was subtle: "Yes, sir, *I think everybody believes his own faith is the right one, but one cannot know which is the right one.*" This was the theory supported by the advocates of tolerance; but Menocchio, like Castellione,[87] extended this tolerance beyond the three great historical religions to include heretics. And as in those contemporary theorists, Menocchio's defense of tolerance had a positive content: "The majesty of God has given the Holy Ghost to all: to Christians, to heretics, to Turks, to Jews, and he loves all of them, and all are saved in the same way." Rather than tolerance in the strict sense of the word, it was an explicit recognition of the equivalence of all faiths in the name of a simplified religion, a religion devoid of confessional or dogmatic qualifications, something similar to the faith in the "God of nature" that Mandeville had found in all peoples, even the most remote, even the most strange and monstrous—although, as we shall see, Menocchio actually rejected the idea of God as creator of the world. But for Mandeville that recognition was accompanied by the reassertion of the superiority of the Christian religion over the partial truth of the other religions. Once again Menocchio went far beyond his own texts. His religious radicalism, though occasionally nourished by the themes of medieval tolerance, was much closer to the sophisticated religious theories of contemporary heretics who had had a humanistic education.

We have seen how Menocchio read his books, how he isolated words and sentences, sometimes distorting them, joining different passages, making flashing, lightning-like analogies. Every time the texts have been compared with Menocchio's response to them, I have been induced to postulate a key to their interpretation that he must have obscurely possessed that cannot be explained by his contacts with this or that heretical group. Menocchio had a way of taking apart and transforming the things he read that was outside all known patterns. His most shattering assertions came out of his contact with harmless texts like *Mandeville's Travels* or *Historia del Giudicio*. It was not the book itself, but the contact between the written page and oral culture that formed an explosive mixture in Menocchio's mind.

We can now return to Menocchio's cosmogony that had seemed enigmatic at first. Its intricate, layered construction can now be determined. It began with the description of primordial chaos, thus differing from the start from the account in Genesis and its orthodox interpretation: "I have said that, as I think and believe, everything was chaos, that is earth, air, water, and fire all together" (7 February). During a later examination, the general vicar interrupted Menocchio while he was talking about *Mandeville's Travels* to ask him "whether this book said anything about chaos." Menocchio replied that it didn't, and once again revealed (in a conscious form, this time) the interweaving of written and oral culture already discussed: "No, sir, but I saw this in *Il fioretto della Bibbia*; but the other things I said about this chaos were formed by me out of my own brain."[88]

As a matter of fact, Menocchio's memory had played him false. *Il fioretto della Bibbia* did not precisely speak about chaos. The biblical account of creation was preceded, however, inconsistently, by a series of chapters mostly derived from *Elucidarium* by Honorius of Autun; in this book metaphysics is mixed with astrology, and theology is mixed with the doctrine of the four temperaments. The fourth chapter of the *Fioretto* ("*How God created man out of four elements*") begins with these words: "As we have said, in the beginning God made a great quantity of matter: which had no shape nor manner; and he made so much of it that he could take some out and do what he pleased with it, and he divided and distributed it in such a way as to make man out of it, forming him out of four elements."[89] Here a primeval indistinction of elements is postulated, but chaos is not mentioned. It is likely that Menocchio may have found this learned term in a book he mentioned incidentally during his second trial (but he had already seen it in 1584): *Supplementum Supplementi delle croniche* by the Augustinian hermit Jacopo Filippo Foresti. This chronicle was written at the end of the fifteenth century, but its structure is decidedly medieval. It begins with the creation of the world. After quoting Saint Augustine, patron of his order, Foresti wrote:

And it is said that in the beginning God created heaven and earth; we say he made heaven not because it existed already, but because it could exist in the future; as if in considering a tree we should say that the roots, the strength, the branches, the fruit, and the leaves are all there: not because they are there already, but because they are bound to be there. Thus we say that in the beginning God created heaven and earth, almost the seed of heaven and earth, the matter of heaven and earth still being in confusion; but since it was certainly bound to be heaven and earth, that matter was already called heaven and earth. This spacious matter, that lacked a definite form, was called chaos by Ovid in the beginning of his greatest work, and also by other philosophers; in the same book Ovid mentions this fact, saying: "Before the earth and the sea and the sky, that covers everything, existed, nature had only one image, which philosophers called chaos, of coarse and undigested matter: and it was nothing but an uncertain, sluggish weight all gathered in that same circle, and discordant and disjointed seeds of things to be."[90]

Having started with the idea of reconciling the Bible with Ovid, Foresti had ended up by expounding a cosmogony that was much more Ovidian than biblical. The idea of a primeval chaos, of a "coarse and undigested matter," struck Menocchio very much. From this he drew, by turning them over and over in his mind, "the other things . . . about this chaos . . . formed by *his* brain."

Menocchio tried to impart these things to the people of his village. "I heard him say," Giovanni Povoledo reported, "that in the beginning this world was nothing, and that the seawater was beaten to a froth and coagulated like cheese, and from this cheese a great multitude of worms were born, and these worms became men, and the wisest and most powerful of them was God, to whom the others paid obedience."

It was very indirect evidence, having passed through three persons: Povoledo was reporting what a friend had told him eight days before while "walking down the road going to market at Pordenone"; this friend had told him something he had heard from another friend who had talked with Menocchio. Actually, during his first examination, Menocchio had given a somewhat different version: "I said that, as I think and believe, everything was chaos . . . and this volume, revolving, formed a mass just like cheese does in milk, and in that mass there appeared some worms, and these were the angels, and the holy Majesty decreed that those were God and his angels, and in that number of angels there was God, *he too created from that mass in that same time*." Apparently, Menocchio's narration, having passed from one person to another so many times, had ended up by being simplified and distorted. A difficult word like "chaos" had disappeared and had been replaced by a more orthodox variant ("in the beginning this world was nothing"). The sequence of cheese-worms-angels-holy Majesty-God the most powerful of angels-men had been shortened to that of cheese-worms-men-God the most powerful of men.

On the other hand, in the version given by Menocchio, the beating of the seawater to a froth did not appear at all. And it is impossible to suppose that Povoledo might have invented it. The latter part of the trial showed clearly that Menocchio was willing to change this or that element of his cosmogony, though maintaining its essential features unchanged. So when the general vicar asked him: "What was this holy Majesty?" he explained: "I mean that that holy Majesty was *the spirit of God, who always existed.*" In a later examination he defined the matter with even more precision: on Judgment day men shall be judged by "that holy Majesty I mentioned before, *who existed before chaos came into being.*" And in yet another version he substituted God for the "holy Majesty" and the Holy Ghost for God: "I believe that the eternal God of that chaos I mentioned before has lifted up the most perfect light, just as we do with cheese when we pull out the best one, and with that light he made those spirits we call angels, and he elected the noblest of them and gave him all his knowledge, all his will, and all his power, and this is what we call the Holy Ghost, whom God placed above the structure of all the world." As to God's existing before chaos, he changed his mind once again: "This God was inside chaos like a man who is in the water and wants to free himself, and like a man who is in a wood and wants to free himself: so this intellect, having acquired knowledge, wants to free itself to create this world." At this point, the inquisitor asked: "So God was eternal and always with chaos?" "I believe," Menocchio replied, "that they have always been together, and that they never have been apart, that is, chaos without God or God without chaos."[91]

In all these variations of words (God in the place of the "holy Majesty," the Holy Ghost in the place of God), two points remained constant: his refusal to ascribe to the divinity the creation of the world, and his obstinate reassertion of the apparently most whimsical element: the cheese, the angel-worms born from the cheese.

It might be possible, perhaps, to consider this theme an echo of the *Commedia* (Purgatory X.124–25): "... vermi / nati a formar l'angelica farfalla" ("worms, born to form the angelic butterfly"), especially because Vellutello's comment on these lines is a word-to-word echo of another passage of Menocchio's cosmogony. Vellutello's comment was: "Angelic, that is divine, having been created by God *to fill those seats that the black angels lost when they were banished from heaven.*" Menocchio's words were: "and God then created Adam and Eve and the people in great multitudes *to fill up the seats left empty by the banished angels*."[92] It would really be strange if two such coincidences had met in one page by pure chance. But if Menocchio had read Dante—perhaps seeing him in the light of a sage, of a master of metaphysical and moral truths—why did *those* lines ("born to form the angelic butterfly") impress themselves in his mind?

In an ancient Indian myth, mentioned in the *Veda* and spread later among the shepherds of the Altai, the origin of life is explained with the coagulation, like milk, of the waters of the primeval sea, when they were beaten up by the creating gods. According to the Kalmucks, at the beginning of time the surface of the sea became covered with a thick layer, similar to the one that forms on the surface of milk; out of this layer there issued plants, animals, men, and gods.[93] "In the beginning this world was nothing, and . . . the seawater was beaten to a froth and coagulated like cheese, and from this cheese a great multitude of worms were born, and these worms became men, and the wisest and most powerful of them was God."[94] These, more or less, had been the words spoken by Menocchio (apart from the possible simplifications already mentioned). It really is an extraordinary coincidence—but it must not make us neglect a basic difference between the two accounts: Menocchio was talking of a very real cheese, not a mythical one; it was the cheese he had seen countless times while it was being made (or perhaps while he was making it himself). "From the most perfect substance of the world [the angels] were produced by nature *in similitude to the way worms are produced from a cheese*, but when they come out, they are given will, intellect, and memory by God, who blesses them." It is clear from this answer of Menocchio's that his insistent reference to cheese and worms had a purely analogic and explanatory purpose. Menocchio used the everyday experience of the appearance of worms in rotten cheese to explain the birth of living creatures—the first, the most perfect, the angels —from chaos, from "coarse and undigested matter," *without resorting to the intervention of God*. Chaos existed before the "holy Majesty," whose figure remained rather vague; from chaos, the first living creatures —the angels, and the foremost of them, God himself—were born by spontaneous generation, "produced by nature." Menocchio's cosmogony was essentially materialistic and scientific in tendency. The doctrine of the spontaneous generation of living beings from inanimate ones was shared by all the scholars of that period (up to the time of Francesco Redi's experiments, almost a century later), and was evidently more scientific than the creationist doctrine of the church, which followed the narration of Genesis. Even a man like Walter Raleigh could compare, under the sign of "experience without art," a woman making cheese (cheese!) to a natural philosopher: both know that rennet makes the milk coagulate in the churn, although they cannot explain why.[95]

In Menocchio's statements, then, a deep cultural stratum comes to the surface, as if through a deep crack in the ground: it is so unusual as to seem, at first sight, strange and unintelligible. What had unearthed this *different* culture was the Reformation and the spread of printing.[96] Thanks to the former, a simple miller had had the daring to speak and to express his opinions on the church and the world. Thanks to the latter, he had been able to find the words to express the obscure, inarticulate vision of the world that was simmering in his mind. The sentences or fragments of sentences he had wrung out of books had been for him the instruments for formulating his ideas and for defending them for years, first against an indifferent or hostile village population, then against a group of judges armed with doctrine and power.

Thus Menocchio in his own experience had bridged the gulf between the language of oral culture, based on gestures, mutterings, and cries, and the language of written culture, toneless, unchanging, crystallized on the written page. The former is almost an extension of the human body, the latter is "cosa mentale." The triumph of written culture over oral culture was above all a triumph of abstraction over empiricism. In the possibility of freeing oneself from particular situations lies the root of the bond that has always inextricably connected writing to power. The cases of Egypt and China, where the ruling elites long monopolized writing, are self-evident. The invention of the alphabet some fifteen centuries before Christ broke this monopoly for the first time, but was not sufficient to put the written language within everybody's reach. Only printing made this possibility become more real.[97]

Menocchio was proudly conscious of the originality of his own ideas; for this reason, he was eager to explain them to the highest religious and secular authorities. At the same time, though, he felt the need to become master of his enemies' culture. He understood that writing, and the ability to grasp and impart written culture, are sources of power. For this reason he did not confine himself to denouncing a "betrayal of the poor" in the use of a bureaucratic and priestly language such as Latin. The horizon of his criticism was much wider. "You can be sure of it, the inquisitors don't want us to know the things they know," he exclaimed, many years after the events I am relating, to a neighbor, Daniel Iacomel.[98] The opposition between "us" and "them" was clearcut. "They" were the superiors, the men who had power—not only those who were at the top of the ecclesiastic hierarchy. "We" were the peasants. Daniel was almost certainly illiterate (when he reported Menocchio's words during the second trial he did not sign his own testimony). Menocchio, instead, could read and write; but he did not believe, on the strength of this, that the long struggle he had begun against authority concerned only himself. He still thought that the desire to "search for high things" that he had ambiguously recanted twelve years before in front of the inquisitors at Portogruaro was not only legitimate, but potentially within every man's reach. The clergy's pretention to preserve the monopoly of a knowledge that could be bought for two *soldi* on a bookseller's stall in Venice must have appeared illegitimate, or indeed absurd, to him. The idea of culture as a privilege had been seriously weakened (but not killed, of course) by the invention of print.

In that very same *Fioretto della Bibbia* he had bought in Venice for two *soldi*, Menocchio had found the learned words that are mixed with everyday words in his confessions. So in his answers of 12 May, we find "a baby in its mother's belly," "cattle," "bricklayer," "bench," "work-people," "cheese," "worms," but also "imperfect," "perfect," "substance," "matter," "will, intellect, and memory." An apparently similar mixture of humble and sublime vocabulary can be found in the *Fioretto*, especially in the first part. But the linguistic and conceptual instruments Menocchio was able to appropriate were neither neutral nor innocent.[99] Here is the source of most of the contradictions, the uncertainties, the inconsistencies of his statements. Using a terminology imbued with Christianity, neoplatonism, and scholastic philosophy, Menocchio was trying to express the elementary, instinctive materialism of countless generations of peasants.

To make the living spring of Menocchio's deepest thoughts gush out, we must break the crust of that terminology. What did Menocchio really mean when he talked of God, of the holy Majesty of God, of the spirit of God, of the soul?

We must begin with the most striking feature of Menocchio's language: its abundance of metaphors. Those words belonging to everyday life—"a baby in its mother's belly," "cattle," "carpenter," "cheese," and so on—all introduce a metaphor. The images the *Fioretto* is dotted with have an evident and exclusively didactic aim: that is, they illustrate an argument with readily intelligible examples, so the reader can understand it without difficulty. The role of metaphors in Menocchio's speech is different, and in a certain sense opposite. In an intellectual and linguistic universe such as his, characterized by the most absolute literalism, even metaphors are meant to be understood in a strictly literal manner. Their content never is casual; it gives us a glimpse of Menocchio's real and unexpressed meaning.

To begin with, for Menocchio, God is above all a father. His use of metaphors gives a new meaning to such a worn-out and traditional epithet. God is a father to men: "We are all children of God, and of the same nature as he who was crucified." All—Christians, heretics, Turks, Jews— "are dear to him, and all are saved in the same way." Whether they like it or not, they always remain their father's sons: "He calls all of them to him, Turks, Jews, Christians, heretics, and all equally, like a father who has several sons and calls them all equally; even if there are some who don't want to obey, still they are always his sons." His love is so great that he does not care if his sons curse him: when somebody swears, "he only damages himself, and not his neighbor; for instance, if I have a cloak, and choose to tear it, I damage only myself and nobody else; and I believe that if someone does no harm to others, he doesn't commit any sin; and since we are all sons of God, if we don't harm each other, for instance, if a father has several sons, and one of them says, 'May my father be cursed,' his father will forgive him, but if he breaks the head of another man's son, he cannot forgive him unless he pays for it: that's why I said that swearing is not a sin, since it does not harm anybody."[100]

All this is connected, as we have seen, with the proposition that it is less important to love God than to love one's neighbor—and this neighbor must be understood in the most concrete and literal manner. God is a loving father, but he is far away from his children's lives.

But besides being a father, in Menocchio's eyes God is the very image of authority.[101] Menocchio talks several times of a "holy Majesty," sometimes apart from God, sometimes identified with the "spirit of God" or with God himself. Furthermore, he compares God to a "great captain" who "sent his son in this world as ambassador to men." Elsewhere he compares him to a gentleman: in paradise "he wants the people who sit on those chairs to see everything, and is like a gentleman who shows all his things." The Lord is, above all, and in a literal sense, a lord: "I said that if Jesus Christ had been the eternal God, he should not have let himself be caught and crucified; and on this subject I was not certain, but had doubts, as I have said, because it seemed to me a great wonder for a lord to let himself be caught in that manner; so I doubted that, since he had been crucified, he might not be God."

But the principal characteristic of lords is that they do not work, because others work for them. And so it is with God, too: "As for indulgences, I think they are good, because if God has put a man in his own place, that is the pope, and this man orders a pardon to be granted, it is valid, because it's like receiving it from God, the pardon having been granted by one who acted as his agent." But the pope is not God's only agent: even the Holy Ghost "is like an agent of God; this Holy Ghost afterward elected four captains, or shall I say agents, among those angels who had been created." Men were created "by the Holy Ghost according to God's will, and by his ministers; like an agent who executes the ministers' work, the Holy Ghost set to work."

So God is not only a father but also a master—a landowner, who will not soil his hands by working, but entrusts all tiring tasks to his agents. Even these, however, "set to work" only in exceptional cases: the Holy Ghost, for instance, created the earth, the animals, men, fish, and all other creatures "by means of the angels, his assistants." It is true that Menocchio, answering a question of the inquisitors', did not exclude the possibility that God might have created the world even without the angels' help: "When a man builds a house, he uses masters and workmen, but people say *he* built it; in the same manner, in building the world, God used the angels, and people say that God built the world; and just as a master can build a house by himself, though it will take him more time, so God in building the world could have done it all by himself, but it would have taken more time." God has "power": "Along with the will, it is necessary to have the power to do a thing; for instance, if a carpenter wants to make a chair, he must have tools to be able to make it, and if he doesn't have any wood his will is vain; in the same way, we say that besides will God must have power." But this "power" consists of "acting by means of his workmen."

These recurring metaphors are certainly connected with the necessity to make the central personages of religion closer to man and more understandable by translating them into terms of everyday experience. To Menocchio, who had declared to the inquisitors that his craft was, besides being a miller, being "a carpenter, sawing, building walls," God was like a carpenter, a bricklayer. But from this swarming of metaphors a deeper content emerges. The "building of the world" is, once again, a wholly material action—"I believe that it isn't possible to create anything without the materials, and not even God could have created anything without the materials"—a manual task. But God is a lord, and lords do not use their hands to work. "Has God made, created, produced any creature by himself?" the inquisitors asked. "He intended to give the will through which all things were made," Menocchio replied. Even if he is compared to a carpenter or a bricklayer, God always has "masters" or "workmen" in his service. Only once, when he was carried away by his ardor in speaking against the adoration of images, Menocchio mentioned "the only God who created heaven and earth." Actually, in his eyes God had not done anything; neither had his "agent," the Holy Ghost. Only the angels—the "workmen," the "assistants"—had worked at building the world. And who had created the angels? Nature: "From the most perfect substance of the world they were produced in similitude to the way worms are produced from a cheese."[102]

"The first creature that ever was created in the world," Menocchio had read in *Il fioretto della Bibbia*, "were the angels; and since the angels were created from the noblest material there was, they committed the sin of pride, and were deprived of their place." But he had also read: "And therefore you can see that nature is under God's dominion like the hammer and the anvil are under the smith, who makes whatever he likes, a sword, a knife, or other things: and although he makes them with his hammer and anvil, it was not the hammer, but the smith who made them."[103] This Menocchio could not accept. His obstinately materialistic outlook did not admit the presence of a creating God. It did admit a God—but a faraway one, like a landowner who has left his estate in the hands of his stewards.

A faraway God—or else (which, after all, was the same thing) a very near one, melted in the elements, identical with the world: "I believe that all the world, that is the air, the earth, and all the beauties of this world, are God . . . : because it is said that man was shaped after the image of God, and in man there is air, fire, earth, and water, and from this it follows that air, earth, fire, and water are God."[104]

And from this it follows: once again, with his intrepid reasoning, Menocchio picked his way among his texts (the Scripture, the *Fioretto*) with an extraordinary freedom of movement.

However, owing to a contradiction we cannot dwell upon here, Menocchio ended up by admitting a survival of the individual, although he identified man with the world and the world with God. The resurrection of the flesh seemed to him an absurd and untenable concept: "No, sir, I do not believe that on the day of judgment we will resuscitate with our bodies; it seems impossible to me, because if they were to resuscitate, the bodies would fill up the sky and the earth; and the majesty of God will see our bodies with his intellect, just as we do when we close our eyes and, wishing to create something, we put it in our mind and intellect, and so we see it with the said intellect." As for hell, he considered it an invention of the priests: "I like it when they preach that men should live in peace, but when the preaching is about hell, Paul says this, Peter says that, I think it is a merchandise, an intention of men who know more than the others. I read in the Bible," he added, hinting that the real hell is here, on this earth, "that David made the psalms while he was being persecuted by Saul." But then he inconsistently admitted the validity of indulgences ("I think they are good") and of prayers for the dead ("so God will put him a little further forward and give him a little more light"). Above all, he dreamed about Paradise: "I think it is a place that surrounds all the world, and from there you can see all the things of the world, even the fish in the sea; and for those who are in that place it is like being at a feast." Paradise is a feast—the end of work, the denial of everyday toil. In paradise there is no use for "intellect, memory, will, thought, belief, faith, and hope," that is, "the seven things . . . given by God to man, like a carpenter who wants to start a job, and just as a carpenter does his work with a hatchet, a saw, wood, and other instruments, so God has given those things to man so he can do his work." In paradise they are useless because "up there, there is no need to work." In paradise matter becomes pliable and transparent: "These bodily eyes of ours cannot see all things, but with the eyes of the mind we will be able to pierce everything, and to see through mountains, walls, and everything."[105]

"It is like being at a feast." Menocchio's peasant paradise was perhaps less akin to the Christian life after death than to the Moslem one, of which he had read a glittering description in *Mandeville's Travels*: "Paradys . . . is a place of delytes, where men schulle fynde alle maner of frutes in alle cesouns and ryueres rennynge of mylk and hony and of wyn and of swete water; and . . . thei schulle haue faire houses and noble, euery man after his dissert, made of precyous stones and of gold and of syluer; and . . . euery man schalle haue iiii wyfes alle maydenes, and he schalle haue ado euery day with hem, and yit he schalle fynden hem alleways maydenes."[106] When the inquisitors asked him, "Do you believe there is an earthly paradise?" he answered with bitter sarcasm: "I believe that earthly paradise is where there are gentlemen who have goods aplenty and live without ever getting tired."[107]

Besides dreaming about paradise, Menocchio longed for a "new world": "My mind was full of pride, and wished for a new world and a new way of living, and hoped that the church might be less prosperous, so there might not be so much pomp."[108] It is not easy fully to catch the sound those words had when they were spoken.

In societies based upon oral tradition, the community's memory tends unconsciously to mask and reabsorb changes. The comparative flexibility of material life is matched with a decided immobility in the image of the past. Things have always been as they are; the world is what it is. Only in periods of acute social transformation does there emerge the image, usually a mythical one, of a different and better past—a pattern of perfection that makes the present seem a period of degeneration, of decadence, in comparison. "When Adam delved and Eve span, who was then the gentleman?" The struggle for the transformation of the social order would then become a conscious attempt to return to that legendary past.[109]

Menocchio, too, felt the contrast between the rich and corrupt church he saw in his times and the poverty and purity of a mythical primitive church: "I wish the church were lovingly run as it was established by Our Lord Jesus Christ . . . these masses are pompous, Our Lord Jesus Christ doesn't want any pomp."[110] But, unlike most of the villagers of Montereale, his ability to read had given him the chance to take possession of an image of the past that went far beyond this crude comparison. *Il fioretto della Bibbia*, in part, but above all Foresti's *Supplementum supplementi delle croniche*, gave an analytic account beginning from the creation of the world and reaching the contemporary period. Both books mixed sacred and profane history, mythology and theology, descriptions of battles and of countries, lists of princes and of philosophers, of heretics and of artists. We have no explicit evidence of Menocchio's response to this reading. It certainly did not "trouble" him deeply as *Mandeville's Travels* had done. The crisis of ethnocentrism in the sixteenth century stemmed from geography, no matter how legendary it was, and not from history—and this was not to change for a long time.[111] However, an almost imperceptible clue gives a glimpse of Menocchio's state of mind in reading this chronicle.

The *Supplementum* was repeatedly reprinted and translated into the vernacular both before and after its author's death in 1520. Menocchio must have read a posthumous vernacular version that had been updated by an unknown author up to a recent period. So he saw the pages about the schism of "Martin, called Luther, friar of the hermit order of St. Augustine" written by the anonymous editor—probably a friar of the same order as Foresti, who also was an Augustinian hermit. The tone of this passage was benevolent, even though at the end it turned into a decided censure. "The cause of Luther's breaking into such an iniquity," the anonymous editor wrote, "seems to have issued from the supreme pontiff (although in truth it is not so); on the contrary it issued from a group of malignant and wicked men, who, under the appearance of holiness, performed very grave and truly excessive acts." These men were the Franciscans, to whom Julius II and Leo X had entrusted the preaching of indulgences.

And since ignorance begets all errors, and the familiarity with money had perhaps excessively inflamed the minds of the said friars with covetousness for money, these friars with clogs broke out in such insanity that they caused great scandal to the people for the insane things they said while preaching about indulgences. And among all the other parts of Christendom they were particularly active in Germany, and when they said something insane and some men (proficient in conscience and doctrine) wanted to censure them, they immediately said that they were excommunicated. One of these men was this Martin Luther, who really was a learned and literate man.

So the origin of the schism, according to the anonymous writer, was the "insane things" of the rival order, which, faced with Luther's justified reaction, had excommunicated him.

Then the said Martin Luther, who was a man of very noble blood and in high reputation with all men, began to preach publicly against these indulgences, saying that they were false and unfair. In a short time he brought on a great perturbation. And since there was a certain resentment between the spiritual and temporal estates, because the greatest part of their riches was in the priests' hands, he easily found a following among them, and began to preach a schism in the Catholic church. And seeing that many rallied around him, he separated himself completely from the Roman church, and established a new sect, and a new way of living with his various and several opinions and whims. So it has come to pass that a very large part of those countries have risen against the Catholic church, and do not obey it in any matter.[112]

"He established a new sect and a new way of living," "he wished for a new world and a new way of living, and hoped that the church might be less prosperous, so there might not be so much pomp." When he disclosed his desire for a religious reform that had been suggested to him by his "proud mind" (his allusion to a "new world" will be discussed later), Menocchio was echoing, consciously or not, the portrait of Luther he had read in Foresti's chronicle. Of course, he was not echoing Luther's religious ideas. In any case, the chronicle did not dwell on them, but confined itself to censuring the "new style of doctrine" proposed by Luther. Above all, Menocchio could not be satisfied with the reticent, and perhaps ambiguous, conclusion of the anonymous writer: "And in this fashion he has blinded the ignorant crowd; and those who possess knowledge and doctrine, on hearing about the evil operations of the ecclesiastical estate, follow him, without considering that it is not right to draw such an inference. Clerks and ecclesiastics lead an evil life, nonetheless the Roman church is good and perfect; and although Christians lead an evil life, nonetheless the Christian faith is good and perfect." The "laws and commandments of the church" seemed to Menocchio "all merchandise" to fatten the priests: in his view, a moral renewal of the clergy and a deep change in doctrine must take place at the same time. Through the unexpected medium of Foresti's chronicle, Luther was presented to Menocchio as the very prototype of the religious rebel—as the man who had been able to unite "the ignorant crowd and those who possess science and doctrine" against the ecclesiastical hierarchy, taking advantage of the "resentment" of the "temporal estate" against the "spiritual estate" because of the fact that "the greatest part of their riches was in the priests' hands." "Everything belongs to the church and the priests," Menocchio had exclaimed to the inquisitor. Perhaps he also considered the similarities between the situation in Friuli and the situation in the areas beyond the Alps where the Reformation had triumphed.

Nothing is known about the contacts Menocchio probably had with "those who possess science and doctrine," though he does say something about his persistent attempts to spread his own ideas among the "ignorant crowd." But it seems that nobody listened to him. In the sentence that closed the first trial, this lack of success was considered a mark of divine intervention that had saved the innocent souls of the inhabitants of Montereale from being corrupted.

There had been an illiterate carpenter, Melchiorre Gerbas, "reputed a person of scant wit," who had given heed to Menocchio's remarks.[113] People said "in taverns that he doesn't believe in God, and swears violently"; and several witnesses had associated his name with Menocchio's because he had "gossiped and spoken ill of the things of the church."[114] The general vicar tried to find out what relationship he had with Menocchio, who had just been put in prison. At first, Melchiorre maintained that their connection was related only to their work ("he gives me wood to work with, and I pay"); but later he admitted that he had sworn in the taverns of Montereale, repeating a sentence he had heard from Menocchio: "Menocchio having told me that God is nothing but air, and I believe this too."[115]

This attitude of blind subordination is not difficult to understand. Menocchio's ability to read, write, and argue gave him almost a magic halo in Melchiorre's eyes. After having lent Menocchio a Bible, Melchiorre went and told everyone, with a mysterious air, that Menocchio had a book with which he was able to "do marvelous things." But people were well aware of the difference between the two men. "He . . . is suspected of heresy, but he is not like the said Domenego," a witness said, referring to Menocchio. Another said that Melchiorre "says the sort of things that proceed rather from madness, and because he gets drunk."[116] The general vicar, too, had understood that this was a man of a very different calibre from the miller. "While you were saying that there was no God, did you really believe in your heart that there was no God?" he asked suavely. And Melchiorre promptly answered: "No, father, because I believe that God is in heaven and earth, and that he can make me die whenever he pleases; and I said those words only because they had been taught to me by Menocchio."[117] The judges gave him some slight penance to do and let him go. This was the only follower—at least the only self-acknowledged one—that Menocchio had at Montereale.

Apparently Menocchio had not confided even in his wife and children: "God save them from having these opinions." In spite of all his ties in the village, he must have been very lonely. "That evening," he confessed, "when the father inquisitor said to me 'Come to Maniago tomorrow,' I was almost desperate, and wanted to go away, wandering around the world, and doing evil acts . . . I wanted to kill priests, and burn churches, and live as a desperate man; but, because of my two small children, I restrained myself."[118] This outburst of impotent despair shows his isolation. Faced with the injustice they were doing him, only one reaction had flashed into his mind—individual violence, to avenge himself, to become a bandit—and he had promptly repressed it. A generation before, the peasants had burned the castles of the noblemen of Friuli. But times had changed.

All that was left to him was his longing for a "new world." Time has flattened out these words, like a coin that has passed through too many hands. We must try to recapture their original significance.

Menocchio did not believe that the world had been created by God. He explicitly denied original sin and claimed that man "starts sinning when he begins to feed on his mother's milk, when he comes out of her belly."[119] And Christ, in his opinion, was merely a man. Accordingly, any idea of religious millenarianism was foreign to his point of view. In the course of his confessions he never mentioned the second advent. The "new world" he craved was human reality, to be gained by human means.

In this manner, though, we are taking for granted the trivially metaphoric use of an expression that still had all its depth of meaning to Menocchio. Indeed, it was a double metaphor. At the beginning of the century, a letter addressed to Lorenzo, son of Pietro de' Medici, and signed by Amerigo Vespucci, had been printed under the title of *Mundus novus*. Giuliano di Bartolomeo del Giocondo, who translated the letter from Italian into Latin, explained in the introduction the reason for the title: "Superioribus diebus satis ample tibi scripsi de reditu meo ab novis illis regionibus . . . *quasque novum mundum appellare licet*, quando apud maiores nostros nulla de ipsis fuerit habita cognitio et audientibus omnibus sit novissima res."[120] (During the previous days, I wrote to you in a fairly detailed manner about my return from those new regions . . . *that it is allowable to call new world*, since our ancestors knew nothing about them, and for everybody they are something quite unheard-of.) They were not the Indies, as Columbus had believed, nor even new lands, but really a new world, unknown up to then. "Licet appellare": the metaphor was new, so he almost apologized for it. With this meaning, it spread and entered into common use. But Menocchio used it in a different sense, to indicate not a new continent but a new society yet to be built.

We do not know who was the first to effect this shift of meaning, but underlying it there was the image of a rapid and radical transformation of society. In a letter to Butzer written in 1527, Erasmus spoke with bitterness of the tumultuous turn taken by the Lutheran Reformation and observed that, first of all, the consent of princes and bishops should have been sought, in order to avoid a revolt; then, that many things, including mass, could have been "changed without tumults"; last, he remarked that there were persons who no longer accepted anything from tradition ("quod receptum est"), as if a new world could be suddenly established ("quasi subito novus mundus condi posset").[121] On one side, a slow and gradual transformation, on the other, a rapid and violent (we would say revolutionary) overthrow: the contrast was clear-cut. In Erasmus's words, however, the term "novus mundus" had no geographic implication whatever: its connotation was indicated by the word "condere," used to indicate the founding of cities.

The shift of the "new world" metaphor from a geographic to a social context is explicit, instead, in utopian literature on various levels. An instance is *Capitolo, qual narra tutto l'essere d'un mondo nuovo, trovato nel mar Oceano, cosa bella, et dilettevole* (A Chapter, giving a complete description of a new world found in the Ocean Sea, a lovely and delightful thing), by an anonymous author, published at Modena toward the middle of the sixteenth century.[122] It was one of many variations on the ancient theme of the country of Cuccagna[123] (which was explicitly mentioned in the earlier *Begola contra la Bizaria*). In the *Capitolo* this country is placed among the lands discovered on the other side of the ocean:

> By voyagers in the Ocean Sea
> a beautiful, new country has been found
> that no one had every seen or heard of.

The description echoes the usual themes of this grand peasant utopia:

> A mountain of grated cheese
> alone is seen amid the plain,
> and on its top a cauldron they have brought . . .
> A river of milk flows from a cave
> and runs across the land,
> its banks are made of cottage cheese . . .
> This country's king is Bugalosso,
> they made him king because he is the laziest of all,
> and he is as big and fat as a straw-stack . . .
> and from his ass manna comes out,
> and when he spits, he spits marzipan,
> and his hair is full not of fleas, but fish.

But this "new world" is not only a country of abundance: it is also a country that does not know the restraint of social institutions. It does not know the institution of the family because sexual freedom is complete:

No need is there of gowns or jerkins
of shirts or breeches at any time,
boys and girls all naked go.
It is never hot or cold in any season,
they look at each other and touch each other as much as they like,
O what a happy life, O what a jolly time . . .
They don't mind having lots of children
to bring up, as they do here,
for when it rains, it rains pastry.
Nor do they trouble to marry off their daughters,
because they sell like hot cakes,
and everybody satisfies his own appetite.

They do not know what property is because there is no need to work,
and they share everything:

Everybody gets what he wants in any case,
and if a man dared to talk of working
they'd hang him, and heaven would not save him . . .
There are no peasants there, nor villeins,
each man is rich, each man has what he wants,
because the plain is laden with goods . . .
The fields are not divided, nor the lands,
because things are everywhere in excess,
so the country is all in liberty.

All these elements can be found (though with a less full treatment) in most sixteenth-century versions of the *Paese di Cuccagna*; they probably are a heightened version of the already legendary image that the first travelers had given of the lands discovered beyond the ocean and of their inhabitants: nakedness and sexual freedom, absence of private property and of all social distinction, against the background of an extraordinarily fruitful and friendly nature.[124] Thus the legend of the Paese di Bengodi (the "land of enjoyment"), which already existed in the Middle Ages, assumed a strong coloring of primitivistic utopianism. Contents that were not only serious, but even forbidden, could circulate freely provided they were fitted into a paradoxical, ludicrous, hyperbolic context, with owls who excreted cloaks and donkeys tied up with sausages—duly made fun of at the end with the customary formula:

Chi lì vuol andar, vuo' dirli la via,
vada imbarcarsi al porto Mamalucco,

> poi navicando per mar di bugia,
> e chi v'arriva è re sopra ogni cucco.

(Whoever wants to go there, I'll show him the way: / embark at Port Dupe, / and cross the Sea of Lies: / and if he ever gets there, he's king of all dunces.)

A very different language was used by Anton Francesco Doni in one of the first and best-known Italian utopias of the sixteenth century, a dialogue, inserted in *Mondi* (1552), whose title was "A new world."[125] The tone here is extremely serious, and the content is different. Doni's dialogue is not a peasant utopia like that of the *Paese di Cuccagna*, but a strictly urban one, placed in a star-shaped city. The inhabitants of the "new world" described by Doni live a sober life quite opposite to the roistering of Cuccagna: "What I like about this order is that it has wiped out the shame of drunkenness ... of lingering five or six hours at the table gorging on food." But, Doni, too, merged the ancient myth of the golden age[126] with the description of primitive innocence and purity given by the first accounts of the American continent. The allusion to those lands was only implied; the world described by Doni was simply "a new world different from the one we are living in." Thanks to this ambiguous phrase, for the first time in utopian literature the pattern of a perfect society could be projected into the future, instead of being projected into space, into an inaccessible land.[127] But the travelers' accounts (and also More's *Utopia*, which Doni himself had published, writing an introduction to it) were the source of the most important feature of this "new world": the sharing of women and of goods. As we have seen, these characteristics were present also in the image of the land of Cuccagna.

Menocchio must have read the few short passages about the American discoveries contained in Foresti's *Supplementum*;[128] perhaps he was thinking of them when he remarked, with his usual unconventionality: "Having read that there are so many different sorts of peoples, I think that more than one of them have been created in various parts of the world."[129] On the other hand, he probably never read about the urban and sober "new world" imagined by Doni, nor about the countrified, merrymaking one of the *Capitolo*. That is unfortunate, because both of them contained elements he would have liked. In the world described by Doni, the religion without rites (despite the massive presence of the temple in the center of the city) and with only one commandment, to "know God, thank him, and love one's fellow creatures"[130] was very similar to the creed Menocchio had formulated during his trial: "I wish people believed in the majesty of God, and were honest, and acted according to what Christ said to those Jews who asked him what law they should follow: 'Love God and love your neighbor.'" In the world described by the *Capitolo*, Menocchio would have liked the image of a happiness based on abundance, on the enjoyment of material goods, on the absence of work. It is true that when Menocchio was accused of having broken the Lent fast, he justified the fast, although in dietetic and not in religious terms: "The fast is made for the benefit of the intellect, so that those humors won't come down; on my part I would like it if people ate three or four times a day and did not drink any wine; this way those humors would not come down." But this defense of temperance turned immediately into a polemical outburst, perhaps against the friars who were before him (the notary's transcription is incomplete here): "and not do like these . . . who eat more in one meal than many do in three."[131] In a world full of social injustices, over which the threat of famine always loomed, the image of a uniformly temperate life sounded like a protest.

> In the earth we dig
> for strange and different roots,
> and that's what we live on,
> and we are lucky if we find some every day.
> An ugly thing is famine.

These verses were in the contemporary *Lamento de uno poveretto huomo sopra la carestia* (Lament of a wretched man upon famine). But *L'universale allegrezza dell'abondantia* (The universal joyfulness of abundance), published together with it, replied:

> Let's enjoy ourselves and feast,
> all together merrily,
> since the cruel famine
> no longer makes us suffer . . .
> Hurrah for bread, hurrah for wheat,
> for plenty and abundance
> come, poor men, let's all sing,
> for hope has come for us at last. . . .
> After darkness comes light,
> after evil comes good,
> abundance, our guide and beacon,
> comes to take us out of pain,
> bringing with it wheat in plenty,
> this alone keeps us alive,
> white and lovely, tasty bread.[132]

This disputation in verse gives a realistic parallel to the hyperbolic fancies of the land of Cuccagna. Compared to the "strange and different roots" of times of famine, the "white bread" one could eat with his friends in periods of plenty was a "feast." "It is like being at a feast," Menocchio had said about paradise: a never-ending feast, safe from the periodic alternation of "darkness and light," of famine and plenty, of Lent and Carnival. The land of Cuccagna beyond the ocean, too, was an enormous feast. Who knows how closely the "new world" dreamed of by Menocchio resembled it?

In any case, Menocchio's words bring to the surface for an instant the deep popular roots of utopias, both those in a learned style and those in a popular style, too often considered mere literary exercises. Perhaps the image of a "new world" contained many elements that were very old, connected with mythical memories of a remote age of well-being.[133] For it did not break the cyclical image of human history, typical of an age marked by the emergence of the myths of *Re*naissance, of *Re*formation, of New Jerusalem. The image of a more just society was consciously projected into a noneschatological future. It was not the Son of Man high up above the clouds who was to bring the "new world," but the struggle of men like Menocchio—men, for instance, like the peasants of Montereale, whom he had vainly tried to win over to his ideas.

The examinations ended on 12 May. Menocchio was brought back to prison. A few days elapsed. At the end, on 17 May, he refused the lawyer they offered him and gave the judges a long letter in which he asked to be forgiven for his past errors—that same letter his son had fruitlessly asked him to write three months before.

In the name of the Father, of the Son, and of the Holy Ghost.

I, Domenego Scandella, called Menocchio, from Montereale, I am a baptized Christian, and have always lived as a Christian and acted as a Christian, and have always been obedient to my superiors, and to my spiritual fathers as much as I could, and always, mornings and evenings, I crossed myself with the sign of the holy cross, saying, "In the name of the Father, of the Son, and of the Holy Ghost," and have said the pater noster and ave Maria and the credo with a prayer to the Lord and another one to the Virgin Mary. It is true, as it appears in my interrogations, that I have thought and believed and said things against the commandments of God and of the church. I said them by the will of the false spirit who had blinded my mind and memory and will, making me think and believe and say false things and not the truth, and so I confess I have thought and believed and said false things and not the truth, and so I said my opinion, but I did not say it was the truth. I would like to say a few words briefly taking as an example Joseph, son of Jacob, who talked with his father and his brothers about certain dreams he had had whose meaning was that they must adore him, and so they got angry with him and wanted to kill him, but it was God's will that instead of killing him they sold him to certain merchants from Egypt, who brought him to Egypt, and in consequence of certain mistakes he was put in prison, and then the king Pharaoh had a dream in which he saw fat cows and lean cows, and nobody was able to explain this dream. He was told there was a young man in prison who could explain it to him, so he was taken out of prison and brought into the king's presence, and he told him that the fat ones meant seven years of great abundance, and the lean ones seven years of great famine, when you cannot find wheat to buy. And so the king believed him and made him prince and governor of all the kingdom of Egypt, and so there was abundance and Joseph provided wheat enough for more than twenty years; then there was famine and you couldn't find any wheat to buy, and Jacob heard that in Egypt they sold wheat, so he sent ten of his sons with animals to Egypt, and they were recognized by their brother, and by the king's order he sent for his father and all his family and goods. And so they lived all together in Egypt, and the brothers were uneasy and afraid because they had sold him, and Joseph, seeing they were uneasy, said to them: "Do not be uneasy because you sold me, because it was not owing to you but to God's will, because he wanted to provide for our necessities, so be of good cheer, because I forgive you with all my heart." And so when I talked to my brothers and spiritual fathers they accused me before the reverend father inquisitor of having sold myself, and he had me brought to this Holy Office and put in this prison, but I do not say it was owing to them, but to God's will, I don't know whether they are brothers or spiritual fathers, but pardon all of them who were cause of it, so God may forgive me as I forgive them. But God has caused me to be brought to this Holy Office for four reasons: first, so I can confess my mistakes; second, so I can atone for my sins; third, to free me from the false spirit; fourth, to give an example to my sons and all my spiritual brothers, so they will not fall into these mistakes. So if I have thought and believed and talked and acted against the commandments of God and of the holy church, I am sorry and wretched, repentant and discontented, so I say "mea colpa mea colpa mea masima colpa," and for the remission of all my sins I ask forgiveness and mercy to the most holy Trinity, Father, Son, and Holy Ghost, and also to the glorious Virgin Mary, and to all the saints, male and female; of paradise, and also to your most holy and venerable and illustrious justice, that you may forgive me and have mercy on me, and so I beg you by the passion of Our Lord Jesus Christ not to sentence me with wrath nor with justice, but with love and charity and mercy. You know that Our Lord Jesus Christ was merciful and forgiving, and still is so and always will be so; he forgave Mary Magdalen who was a sinful woman, and Saint Peter who denied him, and the robber who had stolen, and the Jews who crucified him, and Saint Thomas who would not believe until he could see and touch; and so I firmly believe that he will forgive me and have mercy on me. I have done penance a hundred and four days in a dark prison, to the shame, infamy, ruin, and desperation of my home and sons, so I beg you for the love of Our Lord Jesus Christ and of his mother the glorious Virgin Mary to change it to charity and mercy, and not be the cause of my being separated from company and from the children God has given me for my joy and comfort; and so I promise never to fall again into these mistakes, but to be obedient to all my superiors and to my spiritual fathers in all their commands and nothing else. I await your most holy and reverend and illustrious sentence along with the teaching to live as a Christian, so I can teach my sons to be true Christians. These have been the causes of my errors: first, I believed in the two commandments, to love God and to love one's neighbors, and that this was enough; second, because I had read that book by Mandavila about so many sorts of different peoples and different laws that troubled me so much; third, my intellect and memory led me to know things I didn't need to know; fourth, the false spirit always molested me to make me think false things and not the truth; fifth, the disagreement between me and our parish priest; sixth, that I went to work and got tired out and exhausted, and for this reason could not follow in everything the commandments of God and of the holy church. And so I make my defense with a prayer for forgiveness and mercy and not for wrath or justice, and so I implore Our Lord Jesus Christ and you to show me mercy and forgiveness and not wrath or justice. And do not look at my falseness and ignorance.[134]

The very appearance of the pages written by Menocchio, with their letters traced one next to the other almost without any link between them (as is the habit, according to a contemporary calligraphy treatise, of "foreigners, women, and old men"), clearly shows that their author was not very familiar with the use of the pen. Very different on first sight is the appearance of the fluid and sensitive handwriting of the priest Curzio Cellina, notary of Montereale, who became one of Menocchio's accusers at the time of his second trial.[135]

Of course, Menocchio had never been to a school of a superior type, and it must have cost him an enormous effort to learn to write. His effort even was physical: it shows in certain letters that seem rather carved in wood than traced on paper. He was evidently much more used to reading. Although he had been shut up in a "dark prison a hundred and four days," certainly without any books at hand, he had managed to recover in his memory the sentences he had absorbed slowly, protractedly, from the story of Joseph he had read in the Bible and in the *Fioretto*. This familiarity with books is the source of the unusual features of the letter Menocchio sent to his inquisitors.

We can distinguish seven sections in this letter: (1) Menocchio asserts he has always lived as a good Christian, though he admits he has broken God's and the church's commandments; (2) he declares that the origin of this contradiction is the "false spirit" that induced him to believe in false things, though he presented them as his "opinions" and not as truths; (3) he compares himself to Joseph; (4) he states four reasons why God made him be imprisoned; (5) he compares the judges to Christ, the merciful; (6) he beseeches the judges to pardon him; (7) he states the six causes of his errors. This orderly external structure is matched, internally, by a language rich in correspondences, alliterations, and such rhetorical forms as the anaphora and the *derivatio*.[136] It is sufficient to examine the opening sentence of the letter: "I am a baptized *Christian*, and have always lived as a *Christian*"; "and I have *always* . . . and *always* . . . and *always*"; "et *sempre* matina et *sera* io *son se*gnato col *se*gno de la *sa*nta cro*ze* . . ." (Always, mornings and evenings, I crossed myself with the sign of the holy cross.) Of course, Menocchio was using the art of rhetoric unconsciously, just as he was unaware of the fact that the first four "causes" listed by him were final causes and that the other six were efficient causes. However, the frequency of alliteration and rhetorical forms in his letter was not accidental, but was dictated by the necessity to create a language that could be memorized easily. Before he arranged those words on the page in the form of letters, he no doubt had long ruminated on them. But they had been thought up from the start as written words. The language Menocchio used when speaking—as far as is indicated from the records of the examinations written by the notaries of the Holy Office—was different: to begin with, it was full of metaphors, which are completely absent in the letter he sent to the inquisitors.

The connections Menocchio established between himself and Joseph, and the one he wished for between the judges and Christ, were not of a metaphoric type. The Scripture provides a network of *exempla*, and present reality conforms, or must conform to it. But it is precisely the formula of the *exemplum* that reveals, beyond Menocchio's intention, the latent contents of the letter. Menocchio considers himself a sort of Joseph, not only because he is an innocent victim, but also because he is capable of revealing truths that are unknown to everybody else. Those who accused him and had him imprisoned, like the parish priest of Montereale, are comparable to Joseph's brothers, who were involved in God's inscrutable plans. But the chief character is Menocchio-Joseph. He forgives the wicked brothers, for he understands that they really are blind instruments of a superior will. This parallelism belies in advance the pleas for mercy that close the letter. Even Menocchio felt there was a jarring note, and added: "but I do not know whether they are brothers or spiritual fathers," trying to reestablish a relation of filial reverence denied in fact by his whole attitude. But he was not blindly following his son's advice sent him through the parish priest to promise "complete obedience to the holy church." Though admitting his own errors, on one hand he fitted them into a plan of Providence, on the other hand he explained them with motives that (with only the exception of the "false spirit") conceded very little to the inquisitors' point of view. These motives were probably listed in an order of decreasing importance. First, there are two references to texts, one implicit and the other explicit: to a passage of the Scriptures (Matt. 22:36–40), interpreted in a literal manner, and to *Mandeville's Travels*, read from the viewpoint already discussed. Then there were two motives of an internal sort: he was tormentingly goaded by his "intellect and memory," and tempted by the "false spirit" that, as he had said during his trial, lives in the "dark" part of men's hearts. Last, there were two external circumstances: the hostility between "us" (Menocchio and his sons) and the parish priest, and the physical weakness with which he had sometimes justified his violations of prescribed fasts. In short, to explain himself, he cited books; his response to books ("I believed in the two commandments . . . had troubled me so much"); the inferences he drew from books; last, actions. In this apparently heterogeneous list of motives, there was an indubitable connection. In spite of his final, pathetic plea, he did not give up discussing and arguing.

The same day they received Menocchio's letter, the judges met to give out the sentence. During the course of the trial, their attitude had changed imperceptibly. First they had pointed out to Menocchio the contradictions he was falling into; then they had tried to put him back on the right track; at the end, seeing his obstinacy, they had given up all attempts at persuasion and had limited themselves to asking him exploratory questions, as if merely wishing to obtain a complete picture of his aberrations. Now they unanimously declared Menocchio "non modo formalem hereticum . . . sed etian heresiarcam." So on 17 May the sentence was pronounced.[137]

Its length is striking: it is four or five times longer than ordinary sentences. This is a symptom of the importance the judges attached to Menocchio's case, and above all of the difficulty of making his unheard-of statements fit into the stereotyped formulas of this type of document. The judges' astonishment was so strong that it showed through the dryness of the judicial language: "invenimus te . . . in multiplici *et fere inexquisita* heretica pravitate deprehensum" (we have found you entangled in a manifold and *almost unprecedented* heretical wickedness). So this extraordinary trial was ending with an equally extraordinary sentence (it was accompanied by an abjuration that also was very long).

From the beginning, the judges emphasized that Menocchio had explained his heretical opinions and argued against the Catholic faith, "non tantum cum religiosis viris, sed etiam cum simplicibus et idiotis" (not only with religious persons, but also with simple and ignorant persons), greatly endangering their faith. This evidently aggravated his offense; the peasants and artisans of Montereale had to be kept away from such dangerous doctrines. Then there was a meticulous refutation of Menocchio's theories. With a rhetorical crescendo, quite unusual in a sentence of the Inquisition, the judges insisted on the culprit's daring and obstinacy: "ita pertinacem in istis heresibus," "indurato animo permansisti," "audaciter negabas," "profanis et nefandis verbis . . . lacerasti," "diabolico animo affirmasti," "intacta non reliquisti sancta ieiunia," "nonne reperimus te etiam contra sanctas conciones latrasse?", "profano tuo iudicio . . . damnasti," "eo te duxit malignus spiritus quod ausus es affirmare," "tandem polluto tuo ore . . . conatus es," "hoc nefandissimum excogistasti," "et ne remaneret aliquod impollutum et quod non esset a te contaminatum . . . dicebas," "tandem latrabas," "venenum apposuisti," "et quod non dictu sed omnibus auditu horribile est," "non contantus fuit malignus et perversus animus tuus de his omnibus . . . sed errexit cornua et veluti gigantes contra sanctissimam ineffabilem Trinitatem pugnare coepisti," "expavescit coelum, turbantur omnia et contremescunt audientes tam inhumana et horribilia quae de Jesu Christo filio Dei profano ore tuo locutus es." (So obdurate in these heresies, you maintained your obstinate state of mind; you boldly denied; with profane and nefarious words you tore; with a diabolical spirit you affirmed; you did not leave inviolate the sacred fasts; haven't we found you barking even against the holy sermons?; with your profane judgment . . . you condemned; the evil spirit has led you so far astray that you have dared to affirm; and you even attempted with your filthy mouth; you conceived this most nefarious thought; and, so that nothing might be left unpolluted and not contaminated by you . . . you denied; and addressing your evil-speaking tongue . . . you said; last you were barking; you poisoned; and, what is horrible not only to say but also for anybody to hear; your malignant and perverse spirit was not content with all this . . . but raised its head and, like the giants, began to attack the most holy and ineffable Trinity; the heavens are appalled, everybody is shaken, and those who listen to you tremble at the unhuman and horrible things you have said with your profane mouth about Jesus Christ, son of God.)

There is no doubt that with these emphatic literary proceedings the judges were trying to express a very real feeling: their astonishment and horror at a mixture of unheard-of heresies, which must have seemed to them a volley coming straight from hell.

But "unheard-of" is not quite accurate. It is true that these inquisitors had carried out dozens and dozens of trials in Friuli against Lutherans, witches, *benandanti*, swearers, even Anabaptists, without ever meeting with anything like Menocchio's ideas. Only regarding his belief that in order to confess it was enough to tell God one's sins, they recalled a similar theory advanced by the "heretics," that is, by the followers of the Reformation. As for the rest, they looked for sporadic similarities and precedents in a more remote past, making use of their philosophical and theological learning. They compared Menocchio's allusion to chaos to the doctrines of an unnamed ancient philosopher: "In lucem redduxisti et firmiter affirmasti vera fuisse alias reprobatam opinionem illam antiqui filosofi, asserentis aeternitatem caos a quo omnia prodiere quae huius sunt mundi" (You brought to the light and firmly maintained the truth of that opinion, elsewhere reprehended, of the ancient philosopher who posits the eternity of chaos from which all things of this world stemmed.) Menocchio's contention that "God is author of good, but does not do any evil, but the devil is author of evil and does not do any good" was connected with the Manichean heresy: "tandem opinionem Manicheorum iterum in luce revocasti, de duplici principio boni scilicet et mali" (last, you brought back to light the belief of the Manicheans, that is, the one about the double principle of good and of evil.) With a similar proceeding the inquisitors identified the theory of the equivalence of all faiths with the Origenian doctrine of apocatastasis: "heresim Origenis ad lucem revocasti, quod omnes forent salvandi, Iudei, Turci, Pagani, Christiani et infideles omnes, cum istis omnibus aequaliter detur Spiritus Sanctus." (You brought back to light Origen's heresy that everybody is going to be saved, Jews, Turks, Pagans, Christians, and all infidels, because the Holy Ghost is given equally to all of them.) Some of Menocchio's assertions seemed to the judges not only heretical, but even contrary to natural reason: for instance, "when we are in our mother's belly, we are like nothing, like dead flesh," or the assertion of the nonexistence of God: "circa infusionem animae contrariaris non solum Ecclesiae sanctae, sed etiam omnibus filosofantibus. . . . Id quod omnes consentiunt, nec quis negare audet, tu ausus es cum insipiente dicere 'Non est Deus.'" (As to the infusion of souls you have set yourself not only against the holy church, but even against all philosophers. . . . As to something on which everybody agrees and nobody dares to deny, you have had the daring, like the fool, to say "there is no God.")

In Foresti's *Supplementum supplementi delle croniche*, Menocchio had had a chance to read a few scant allusions to the doctrines of Origen and of the Manicheans.[138] But in identifying them as the precedents of Menocchio's theories, the judges were obviously going too far. The sentence corroborates a fact that had been apparent during the trial: the deep gulf between Menocchio's culture and his inquisitors' culture.

It was the inquisitors' task forcibly to bring back the culprit under the church's influence. Menocchio was sentenced to abjure publicly every heresy he had maintained, to wear always a "little robe" with a cross on it as a mark of repentance, and to pass all the rest of his life in prison: "te sententialiter condemnamus ut inter duos parietes immureris, ut ibi semper et toto tempore vitae tuae maneas."

Menocchio stayed almost two years in prison at Concordia. On 18 January 1586, his son Ziannuto presented, in his brothers' and mother's name, a petition to the bishop Matteo Sanudo and to the inquisitor of Aquileia and Concordia, who at that time was Evangelista Peleo. The petition was written by Menocchio himself:

Although I, poor Domenego Scandella, prisoner, have already implored the Holy Office of the Inquisition to consider me worthy of being pardoned, perhaps in order to let me atone better for my error, now induced by extreme necessity I again beseech them to consider that this is the third year that I am deprived of my work, condemned to such a cruel prison that I do not know why I have not died yet from the badness of the air, deprived of seeing my dear wife because of the distance of the place, burdened with a family and with sons who will be forced to abandon me because of their poverty, after which I cannot but die of poverty. Therefore, repentant and sorry for my great sin, I implore forgiveness first of Our Lord, then of this holy tribunal, and entreat them to show me mercy and set me free, and I give them an adequate assurance that I will live according to the Holy Roman church's precepts, and will do all the atonement this Holy Office will enjoin on me, and so I implore all blessings on them from Our Lord.

Behind the conventional humility of these formulas we can guess the intervention of a lawyer. Menocchio had expressed himself in a very different way indeed when, two years before, he had written his own defense. This time the bishop and the inquisitor decided to extend to Menocchio that mercy they had denied him in the past. First they sent for the jailer, Giovanni Battista de' Parvi. He told them that the prison Menocchio was shut up in was "strong and secure," barred by three "strong and secure" doors, so "there is no stronger or harsher prison in the city of Concordia." Menocchio had never left it, except to say his abjuration on the door of the city cathedral, with a candle in his hand, on the day of the sentence and on the day of Saint Stephen's fair, and to hear mass and receive Communion (but he usually received Communion in prison). He had fasted on many Fridays, "except during a period he was so seriously ill we feared he would die." After his illness, he had stopped fasting, "but many times when there were other days of abstinence, he would say to me, 'Tomorrow bring me only a piece of bread, because I want to fast, and do not bring me any meat or anything fat.'" "Several times," the jailer added, "I came silently near his door to hear what he was doing or saying, and I heard him say some prayers." Other times Menocchio had been seen reading a book the priest had brought him or "an *Officio della Madonna* where there are the seven psalms and other prayers"; he had asked for "an image to say his prayers, so his son bought it for him." A few days earlier, he had said that "he always entrusted himself to God and admitted that he was suffering because of his own sins and mistakes, and that God had helped him, because he did not believe he would survive fifteen days suffering as he did in prison, and yet he had endured up to then." He had often talked to his jailer "about the insane things he once used to believe, saying he knew quite well that they were really insane, but he had never adhered to them so far as to believe in them firmly, but through the devil's temptation such strange and extravagant thoughts came into his mind of their own accord." In short, he seemed really to have repented, although (the jailer prudently remarked) "the hearts of men cannot be so easily understood, except by God."

Then the bishop and the inquisitor summoned Menocchio himself.

He wept, pleaded, knelt on the ground, and humbly begged to be forgiven. "I am most seriously repentant for having offended God, my Lord, and wish I had not said the insane things I said, having fallen into them most senselessly, blinded as I was by the devil, and not knowing what I was saying. . . . I did not find it hard to do the penance I was given, and to stay in that prison, but I felt such a rejoicing for it, and God comforted me so much because I prayed to him continually, so I felt as if I were in paradise." If it hadn't been for his wife and sons, he exclaimed, clasping his hands and lifting his eyes to heaven, he would have stayed in prison all his life to atone for his offense to Christ. But he was "very poor": with two mills and two fields on rent he had to keep his wife, seven children, and several grandchildren. The prison—"most hard, cold, damp, and dark"—had completely ruined his health: "It took me four months to get up from bed, and this year my legs were swollen, and my face is still swollen, as you can see, and I am almost deaf, and have become almost weak-headed and out of my mind." "Et vere," the notary of the Holy Office remarked, "cum haec dicebat, aspectu et re ipsa videbatur insipiens, et corpore invalidus, et male affectus" (Indeed, while he was saying these things, in appearance and fact he appeared to be out of his wits, in bad health, and afflicted by disease.)

The bishop of Concordia and the inquisitor of Friuli saw in all this the marks of a real conversion. They immediately summoned the mayor of Portogruaro and several local noblemen and proceeded to commute the sentence. They assigned the village of Montereale to Menocchio as his prison for life and forbade him to leave it. They expressly forbade him to talk of his evil opinions or mention them to anybody. He was to confess regularly and always wear the "little robe" with the cross on it over his clothes, as a mark of infamy. A friend, Daniele de Biasio, vouched for him, binding himself to pay two hundred ducats in case of Menocchio's transgression.[139] Quite broken down in body and mind, Menocchio returned to Montereale.

He resumed his place in the community. In spite of the trouble he had had with the Holy Office, in spite of his disgraceful conviction and imprisonment, in 1590 he was again appointed administrator of the church of Santa Maria at Montereale. There may have been some connection between this designation and the new parish priest, Giovanni Daniele Melchiori, a childhood friend of Menocchio's (what happened to the previous parish priest Oderico Vorai who had denounced Menocchio to the Holy Office will be discussed later). Apparently, nobody was shocked by the fact that a heretic, or, even worse, a heresiarch, should administer the funds of the parish.

The office of administrator was often given to millers, probably because they were able to advance the money that was needed for running the parish. The administrators, however, were inclined to take advantage of their position by putting off the transmission of the tithes paid by the congregation. In 1593, when the bishop of Concordia, Matteo Sanudo, happened to pass through Montereale in the course of a diocesan visitation, and asked to see the accounts of the administrators of the last seven years, it turned out that included among the debtors was Domenico Scandella, that is, Menocchio: he owed two hundred lire, making his debt the highest after Bernardo Corneto's.

Such cases were common and were regularly complained about in the pastoral visits in Friuli during that period. In this instance, too, the bishop (who certainly did not connect the name of Scandella with the man he had condemned nine years before) tried to introduce a more strict and accurate administration. He ordered the administrators to pay their debts, "under penalty of being forbidden to enter the church and of being deprived of ecclesiastical rites when they die"; within six months the parish priest was to bring to Portogruaro the accounts for 1592, under penalty of a fine and of the suspension a divinis. We do not know whether Menocchio paid his debt in the end; it seems likely, because during the next pastoral visit, made in 1599–1600 by the same bishop, Sanudo, the administrators who owed money were entered beginning from 1592.[140]

Another piece of evidence confirms that Menocchio's standing among the people of his village had not been injured. "Some slight difficulty" had arisen between the count Giovan Francesco Montereale and one of his tenants, Bastian de Martin, about two plots of land and a farmhouse. At the count's request, two appraisers were appointed to evaluate the extent of the improvements effected by the preceding tenants on the house: one was Piero della Zuanna, for the count, and the other was Menocchio, for the tenant. It was a difficult case, since one of the parties involved was the feudal lord of the place, but evidently people trusted Menocchio and his ability to argue and rebut.

During the same year, Menocchio and his son Stefano rented a new mill in a place called sotto le siege de sora (under the hedges in the upper part). The rent agreement was for nine years; the tenants promised to pay every year four staia of wheat, ten of rye, two of oats, two of millet, and two of buckwheat, and a pig weighing 150 pounds; a clause stated the exact amount of money (six soldi per pound) that was to be paid in case the weight of the pig was more or less than the one that had been agreed upon. Besides this, there was a "fee of honor" to be paid: a couple of capons and half a linen cloth. This last tribute was symbolic, for the mill was used for milling fabrics. The two tenants took it over equipped with "bonis atque idoneis," a wheel (leviera), and six fulling mills, and bound themselves to return it "potius melioratum quam deterrioratum" to the landlords, who were the tutors of the heirs of the late Pietro de Macris. The previous tenant, Florito di Benedetto, who turned out to be insolvent, promised to pay his arrears within five years. At his request, Menocchio and Stefano stood surety for him.

All this indicates that the two Scandellas' economic situation probably was fairly solid. Menocchio fully took part in the life of the community. In the same year, 1595, he was entrusted with a message to the mayor from the lieutenant of the district and was appointed one of the fourteen representatives of the district of Montereale with the power to elect those who were to draw up the land register.[141]

After a while, however, Menocchio must have been in difficulty because of the death of one of his sons (probably Ziannuto) who supported him. He tried to support himself with other types of work: teaching in a school and playing the guitar at parties. At this point he was more anxious than ever to get rid of the "little robe" that marked his disgrace and of the prohibition to leave Montereale. So he went to Udine and asked the new inquisitor, fra Giovan Battista of Perugia, to exempt him from both those obligations. Regarding the "little robe," the answer was no because, the inquisitor explained in a letter to the bishop of Concordia under the date of 25 January 1597, "this exemption must not be given so easily"; but he gave him permission to "ply his trade freely in any place, excepting suspicious ones, so he can somehow help himself and his family in their poverty."[142]

The after-effects of the trial were gradually being eased. But in the meantime, without Menocchio's knowledge, the Inquisition had started investigating him again.

During the Carnival period of the previous year, Menocchio had left Montereale and had gone to Udine, with the inquisitor's permission. On the main square of the town, at the hour of Vespers, he had met a certain Lunardo Simon and had fallen into conversation with him. The two men were acquainted because Lunardo went around playing the fiddle at parties, as Menocchio did with the guitar. Sometime later, having heard of the recent bull against heretics, Lunardo had written to the vicar of the inquisitor, fra Gerolamo Asteo, to report his conversation with Menocchio; afterward he confirmed orally the contents of his letter. The conversation in the square had run more or less as follows.

"I have heard," Menocchio began, "that you mean to become a friar: is it true?"

Lunardo answered: "Isn't it a good idea?"

"No, because it's a beggarly thing to do!"

Lunardo threw back Menocchio's sally at him: "Mustn't I become a friar to be a beggar?"

"Of all the saints, hermits, and such like who have led a holy life, nobody knows where they have ended up."

"The Lord doesn't want us to know these secrets."

"If I were a Turk, I wouldn't want to become a Christian, but I am a Christian, so I don't want to become a Turk."

"*Beati qui non viderunt, et crediderunt.*"

"I don't believe, and I don't see. I do believe that God is father to all the world, and that he can do or undo all he pleases."

"So do the Turks and Jews, but they don't believe he was born from the Virgin Mary."

"When Jesus was on the cross, the Jews said to him, 'If you are Christ, come down from the cross,' but he did not come down: what does this mean?"

"It was because he wouldn't obey the Jews."

"It was because he couldn't come down."

"So you don't believe in the Gospel?"

"No, I don't. Who do you think writes these Gospels, if not priests and friars who have nothing else to do? They think up these things and write them down one after the other."

"The Gospels weren't written by priests or friars, they were written long ago," Lunardo rejoined; and he went away, thinking that his interlocutor was a "heretical man."

God as a father and a master, who can "do and undo"; Christ as a man; the Gospels as the work of priests and friars; all religions as equivalent—notwithstanding his trial, his disgraceful abjuration, his period in prison, and his striking display of repentance, Menocchio had started expressing his old opinions again. In his heart of hearts he had evidently never given them up. But Lunardo knew him only by his nickname ("a man called Menocchio, miller of Montereale"), so, in spite of the report that this man was a recidivist, already condemned by the Holy Office "as a Lutheran," Lunardo's accusation was dropped. Only two years later, on 28 October 1598, by chance or during a systematic review of the previous record, the inquisitors suspected that Menocchio and Domenico Scandella might actually be the same person. So the apparatus of the Holy Office began to move again. Fra Gerolamo Asteo, who in the meantime had become general inquisitor of Friuli, began to collect new information about Menocchio. It turned out that don Odorico Varai, author of the accusation that had brought Menocchio to prison years before, had paid dearly for it: "He was persecuted by Menocchio's relatives and driven away from Montereale." As for Menocchio, "people have believed and believe that he still entertains the false opinions he used to have." At this point, the inquisitor went to Montereale and questioned the new parish priest, don Giovanni Daniele Melchiori. The priest reported that

Menocchio had stopped wearing the "little robe" with the cross on it and went out of the village, infringing the orders of the Holy Office (this, as we have seen, was only partly true). However, he confessed and received Communion several times a year: "On my part I consider him a Christian and an honest man," he concluded. He did not know what opinion the villagers had of Menocchio. But after making and signing these statements, Melchiori changed his mind; he was obviously afraid that what he had said might expose him to risks. To the sentence, "I consider him a Christian and an honest man," he asked his interviewers to add, "as far as one can see from the outside."

Don Curzio Cellina, chaplain of San Rocco and notary of the village, was more frank. "I consider him a Christian because I've seen him confessing and receiving Communion," he confirmed. But behind this appearance of submission, he could feel Menocchio's old restlessness: "This Menocchio has certain humors; when he sees the moon or the stars or when he hears thunder, he immediately wants to give his opinion on the matter; and at the end he submits to the opinion of the majority of people saying that all the world must know more than he alone can. And I believe that this humor is evil, and that he submits to other people's opinions out of fear." So the sentence and the prison of the Holy Office had left a deep mark on him. Menocchio, it seems, no longer dared to talk with the insolent freedom he had shown of old. But not even fear had been able to stifle his intellectual independence: "He immediately wants to say his opinion." What was new was his bitter and ironic consciousness of his own isolation: "He submits to the opinion of the majority of people, saying that all the world must know more than he alone can."

His isolation was chiefly inward. Even don Cellina remarked: "I see he associates with many people, and I think he is a friend of everybody." As for himself, he declared he had neither "a close friendship nor an enmity toward this Menocchio, but I love him as a Christian, and make use of him as I do of all the others, when I need some work from him." Outwardly, Menocchio had been fully reinstated in the village community; he had been appointed administrator of the parish for the third time, and together with his son had rented a third mill. Nonetheless he felt excluded—perhaps also because of his economic difficulties he had had during the last years. The "little robe" was the tangible symbol of his exclusion. Menocchio was obsessed by it. "I know," Cellina reported, "that for a long time he had worn a robe with a cross on it, given him by the Holy Office, and that he wore it secretly under his clothes." And Menocchio had told him that "he meant to go and ask the Holy Office for permission not to wear it any more, because he said that people, seeing that robe with the cross, avoided talking or associating with him."

He was wrong, of course; he associated with everybody, was everybody's friend in the village. But he found it hard not to be able to express his opinions as he had done in the past. "When they heard him talking" of the moon and the stars, Cellina remarked, "people told him to hold his tongue." Cellina did not remember exactly what Menocchio had said on that subject, not even when the inquisitor suggested that perhaps Menocchio believed that the planets were able to override men's free will. However, he denied most decidedly that Menocchio might have been joking: "I think he was talking seriously, and that he has an evil humor."

Once again the Holy Office interrupted its investigation. It is not difficult to understand why: all things considered, the heresiarch miller had been reduced to silence, to outward conformity; he was no longer dangerous to the faith of the villagers. In January 1599, during a meeting of the Holy Office, it was decided that the "culprit," Menocchio, should be cross-examined again. But this plan, too, was dropped.

Yet the conversation reported by Lunardo shows that Menocchio, beneath his seeming compliance with the rites and sacraments of the church, held obstinately fast to his old ideas. More or less in the same period, a certain Simon, a converted Jew who wandered about begging, happened to pass through Montereale and was given hospitality by Menocchio. The two men talked of religious matters for a whole night. Menocchio said "really extraordinary things about faith": that the Gospels had been written by priests and friars "because they live in idleness" and that Mary, before marrying Saint Joseph, had had "two other children, and that's why Joseph wouldn't have her." They were practically the same themes he had argued about with Lunardo on the main square of Udine: the polemic against the parasitism of the clergy, the rejection of the Gospel, the denial of Christ's divinity. That night, though, he also talked about a "beautiful book" that unfortunately he had lost and that Simon "thought was the Koran."

Perhaps his rejection of the central dogmas of Christianity—beginning with the dogma of the Trinity—was what had led Menocchio, like other heretics of that period, to take up the Koran with curiosity. Unfortunately, Simon's assumption that the book mentioned by Menocchio was the Koran is not certain; and in any case we do not know what Menocchio assimilated out of that mysterious "beautiful book." Of course, he was sure that sooner or later his heterodoxy was bound to be discovered: "he knew he would die because of this," he confided to Simon. But he did not want to run away because fifteen years earlier a friend of his, Daniele de Biasio, had vouched for him in front of the Holy Office: "Otherwise I would have fled to Geneva." So he had decided to remain at Montereale. He already envisaged his own end: "When I die, some Lutherans will hear of it, and come and fetch my ashes."

Who knows what "Lutherans" Menocchio had in mind. Perhaps he had kept secretly in touch with some group or with some individual he had met, possibly many years before, and later lost sight of. The fact that Menocchio saw his own death haloed in a light of martyrdom makes us suspect that his talk was nothing but the pathetic daydreaming of an old man. He had nothing else left. He was alone now: his wife and his dearest son were dead. He probably was on bad terms with his other sons: "And if my sons want to do as they like, so much the better for them," he declared contemptuously to Simon. But the mythical Geneva, the land (he believed) of religious freedom, was too far away. This, and his stubborn loyalty to the friend who had stood by him in a difficult moment, had kept him from fleeing. It was evidently impossible for him to stifle his passionate curiosity about matters of faith—so he remained in Montereale, waiting for his persecutors.

A few months later, as Menocchio had expected, the inquisitor received a fresh denunciation against him. He had uttered, it seems, a blasphemous sentence that was on everybody's lips from Aviano to Pordenone; people were shocked and horrified. A tavernkeeper of Aviano, Michele del Turco, nicknamed Pignol, was questioned, and reported that he had heard that seven or eight years before Menocchio had exclaimed: "If Christ had been God, he would have been a . . . to let himself be crucified." "He didn't say what Christ would have been," the tavernkeeper added, "but I guessed he meant Christ would have been a bloody fool, if you'll excuse my using such an ugly expression. . . . When I heard these words, my hair stood on end, and I changed the subject at once so as not to hear such things, because I consider him worse than a Turk." Menocchio, he concluded, was "obstinate in those old opinions of his."

By then the inhabitants of Montereale were not the only people who reported Menocchio's sayings to each other. The notoriety of this miller, whom not even the Holy Office's prison had been able to set right, had crossed the narrow boundaries of the village. His provocative questions and his blasphemous jokes were repeated, sometimes even years later: "How can you believe that Christ or God was the Virgin Mary's son, if that Virgin Mary was a whore?" "How can it be possible for Christ to have been conceived by the Holy Ghost if he was born of a whore?" "Saint Christopher was greater than God, since he carried all the world on his shoulder." "I think he had an evil mind, and did not dare to talk because he was afraid," was the opinion of Zannuto Fassetta of Montereale, who had heard Menocchio "make music." But his usual impulse led Menocchio to discuss religious matters with the people of his village. One day, while returning to Montereale from Menins, he asked Daniele Iacomel: "What do you think God is like?" "I don't know," the other man replied, surprised or embarrassed. "He is nothing but air," Menocchio said. He was still brooding over his old thoughts, he was not giving up. "Believe me, the inquisitors don't want us to know the things they know." But he felt equal to facing them: "I would like to say four words of the *Pater noster* to the father inquisitor, and see what he says or answers."

This time the inquisitor must have thought he had gone too far. Toward the end of June 1599, Menocchio was arrested and put in prison at Aviano. After a while he was moved to Portogruaro. On 12 July he was taken before the inquisitor, fra Gerolamo Asteo, the vicar of the bishop of Concordia, Valerio Trapola, and the mayor of Portogruaro, Pietro Zane.

Fifteen years had elapsed since Menocchio had first been questioned by the Holy Office. He had spent three years in prison during this period. He was an old man, now, thin, white-haired, with a grizzled, almost white beard, dressed as always in his miller's garb, a white robe and cap. He was sixty-seven. After his condemnation he had worked at many trades: "I worked as a carpenter, as a miller, as a tavernkeeper, I taught children to read, write, and keep accounts, and I also play the guitar at feasts." He had tried to support himself somehow or other by making use of his abilities—including the ability to read and write that had been one of the sources of his troubles. When the inquisitor asked him whether he had ever been tried by the Holy Office, he replied: "I was summoned . . . and questioned about the *Credo* and about other fancies that had come into my head because of having read the Bible and of having a sharp wit; but I always was, and still am, a Christian."

His tone was meek ("fancies"), but his proud consciousness of his own intellectual abilities remained. He explained in detail that he had carried out all the penance assigned to him, that he had confessed and taken Communion, that he had left Montereale only a few times and with the inquisitors' permission. He excused himself only on the matter of the "little robe": "I swear upon my faith that sometimes during holidays I used to put it on and sometimes I didn't; and during workdays, in the winter, I always used to wear it, but under my clothes," because when he had it on "I lost the earnings I made by being called for assessments and other jobs . . . because men thought I was excommunicated when they saw me with that robe on, so I didn't wear it." His entreaty to the inquisitor had been in vain: "He would not give me permission to stop wearing the robe."

But when the inquisitors asked him whether he still had doubts about the matters for which he had been condemned, Menocchio was unable to lie. Instead of answering decidedly no, he said: "Many fancies came into my head, but I never would believe them, and I never taught anything evil to anybody." And when the inquisitor pressed him, asking him if he had ever "argued with anybody about the articles of faith? And who are these persons, and when and where?" he answered that he had "talked about the articles of faith with some persons in jest, but upon my faith I don't know with whom, or where, or when"—an incautious reply. The inquisitor reproached him with severity: "What, you were joking about matters of faith? What do you mean by this word, 'jest'?" "Saying a few lies," Menocchio answered feebly. "What lies were you saying? Tell us exactly!" "I don't know, really."

But the inquisitor was insistent with his questions. "I don't know," Menocchio replied, "somebody may have misunderstood me, but I have never had any feeling contrary to faith." He tried to parry each blow as it came. He had not said that Christ had not been able to come down from the cross: "I believe Christ had the power to come down." He had not said that he did not believe in the Gospel: "I believe that the Gospel is truth." And here he made a false step: "I did say that priests and friars, who have studied, have made the Gospel through the instruction of the Holy Ghost." The inquisitor was prompt in following up his advantage: Had he really said this? When, where, and to whom? And who were those friars? Menocchio was exasperated: "How can I tell? Upon my faith I don't know." "Why did you say it if you didn't know?" "The devil sometimes tempts us to say certain words."[143]

Once again Menocchio was trying to attribute his tormenting doubts, his restless brooding, to a diabolical temptation—only to reveal, immediately afterward, their rational basis. In Foresti's *Supplementum delle croniche* he had read that "various people have written Gospels, Saint Peter, Saint James, and others [apocryphal], and justice annihilated them."[144] Once again the corrosive power of analogy had been at work in his mind. If some of the Gospels are apocryphal, why not all of them? Thus all the implications of what he had said fifteen years before—that the Scriptures could be reduced to "four words"—came to light. During all that period, he had obviously continued following the thread of his old ideas. And now he had a chance to express them to someone who (he thought) was able to understand them. Blindly, he abandoned all caution, all prudence: "I believe that God is made of all things, that is earth, water, and air." "And what about fire? Who made fire?" the inquisitor asked with supercilious irony. "Fire is everywhere, like God," Menocchio replied, "but those other three elements are the three persons: the Father is air, the Son is earth, and the Holy Ghost is water." And he added: "It seems like that to me; but I don't know if it's the truth; and I think that those spirits that are in the air fight each other, and that lightning is the sign of their anger."

Thus, in his laborious backward journey, Menocchio had unconsciously gone beyond the Christian image of the cosmos and reached that of one of the ancient Greek philosophers. This peasant Heraclitus had picked out fire, the most mobile and indestructible of elements, as the prime element. The whole of reality was bathed in it ("it is everywhere"); reality, in spite of the variety of its manifestations, was unitary, swarming with spirits, pervaded by divinity. For this reason, he claimed that fire was God. It is true that Menocchio had also worked out a minute, pedantic correspondence between the other three elements and the persons of the Trinity: "I believe that the Father is air, because air is higher up than water and earth, and I say that the Son is earth, because he issues from the Father; just as water comes from air and earth, so the Holy Ghost comes from the Father and the Son." But behind this parallelism (denied at once, with belated and useless caution, by Menocchio: "But I don't want to maintain these things"), his deepest belief comes to the surface: that God is one and that he is the world. On this point the inquisitor launched his attack: did he believe God had a body? "I know Christ had a body," Menocchio replied evasively. It was not easy to get the better of such an interlocutor. The inquisitor drew out, from among the paraphernalia of his school learning, a syllogism. "You say that the Holy Ghost is water; water is a body; so the consequence would be that the Holy Ghost is a body?" "I say these things only as a simile," Menocchio answered, maybe with a touch of conceit: he, too, was able to argue, he, too, knew how to use the tools of rhetoric.

At this point the inquisitor renewed his attack: "It appears in your trial that you have said that God is nothing but air." "I don't remember having said this, but I did say that God is all things." "Do you believe that God is all things?" "Yes, my lords, upon my faith I do." But what did this mean, more exactly? The inquisitor was puzzled. "I believe that God is everything he chooses to be," Menocchio explained. "Can God be a stone, a serpent, a devil, or something of that sort?" "God can be everything that is good." "So God might be creatures, since creatures are good?"

"I don't know what to say," Menocchio answered.

In fact, the distinction between the creator and the creatures, and the very idea of a creator God, were alien to him. He was well aware that his ideas were different from the inquisitor's; but at a certain point the words to express this difference failed him. Of course, fra Gerolamo Asteo's logical traps could not convince him that he was wrong, just as the judge who had tried him fifteen years before had not been able to convince him. He tried at once to get the upper hand, actually reversing the procedure of the examination. "Listen to me, if you please, sir. . . ." Through the narration of the legend of the three rings, Menocchio, as we have seen, corroborated the doctrine of tolerance he had already formulated during his first trial. That time, though, his argument had been religious: that all faiths are equivalent, including heresies, because "God has given the Holy Ghost to everybody." Now, instead, his arguments focused rather on the equivalence of the various churches as realities connected with social life: "Yes, sir, I do believe that everybody believes his own faith to be the right one; but since my grandfather, my father, and all my family were Christians, I want to remain a Christian, and believe that this is the right faith." The fact that only traditional religions were considered was justified by his reference to the legend of the three rings, but we can hardly help considering these words as the bitter product of the experience Menocchio had undergone after his conviction by the Holy Office. It was better to sham, to comply outwardly with those rites that he inwardly felt were "merchandise." This retreat led Menocchio to give less emphasis to the subject of heresy, of an open and conscious separation from traditional religion. At the same time, though, he was stressing much more than in the past his view of religion as a purely worldly reality. It took a considerable critical detachment for someone to say he was a Christian merely by chance, by tradition—the same detachment that led Montaigne to write, during those same years: "Nous sommes Chrestiens à mesme titre que nous sommes ou Périgordins ou Alemans."[145] But, as we have seen, both Montaigne and Menocchio, each in his own way, had passed through the shattering experience of the relativity of creeds and institutions.

This acceptance—conscious, not passive—of the religion of his fathers was merely external. Menocchio heard mass, confessed, and took Communion, but in his mind he went on ruminating old and new thoughts. He told the inquisitor he thought he was "a philosopher, an astrologer, and a prophet," but he added, apologetically and in a subdued voice, "prophets used to make mistakes, too." And he explained: "I thought I was a prophet because the evil spirit made me see vanities and dreams and persuaded me I knew the nature of the heavens and other things of that sort; and I believe that the prophets used to say what the angels dictated to them."

During the first trial, Menocchio had never referred to supernatural revelations. Now, instead, he alluded to experiences of a mystical type, though ambiguously denying them as "vanities," "dreams." Perhaps he had been influenced by the Koran (the "beautiful book" identified by the converted Jew Simon), that the archangel Gabriel had dictated to the prophet Mohammed. But these are mere conjectures. There is no proof that the "beautiful book" Menocchio had talked about with enthusiasm really was the Koran; and even if there was proof, we could not reconstruct how he read it. A text so totally remote from his experience and culture must have struck him as enigmatic—and for this reason must have led him to project his own thoughts and daydreams upon it. But we do not know anything about this projection, if ever there was one. And, more generally, we can guess very little about this last stage of Menocchio's intellectual life. Unlike fifteen years before, he was gradually led by fear to deny almost everything the inquisitor rebuked him for. But he found it hard, this time, too, to lie; only after having remained "aliquantulum cogitabundus," he asserted that he had never "doubted that Christ was God." Almost at once he contradicted himself by saying that "Christ did not have his father's power, being a human body." "You are mixing things up," someone objected, and Menocchio replied: "I don't know what I am saying; I am an ignorant man." He humbly explained that when he had said that the Gospels had been written by "priests and friars who had studied," he meant the evangelists, "who, I think, had studied, all of them." He tried to say all the things they wanted him to say: "It's true that the inquisitors and our other superiors don't want us to know the things they know, so we must keep quiet." But sometimes he was not able to restrain himself: "I did not believe that paradise existed, because I didn't know where it was."

At the end of his first examination, Menocchio gave the inquisitors a paper he had written about the words of the *Pater Noster*, "et ne nos inducas in tentationem, sed libera nos a malo," adding: "And so I wanted to beg for the mercy of being freed from these sufferings." Then, before they brought him back to prison, he signed it with his old man's trembling hand.

Here is what he had written:

In the name of our Lord Jesus Christ and of his mother the Virgin Mary and of all the saints in paradise that I implore for help and counsel.

O great, almighty, and blessed God, creator of heaven and earth, I beseech you in your saintly kindness and infinite mercy to enlighten my spirit and soul and body so I may think and say and do everything your divine majesty wishes; and so be it, in the name of the holy Trinity, Father, Son, and Holy Ghost, amen. I Menego Scandela unhappy man fallen in disgrace of the world and of my superiors to the ruin of my home and of my life and of all my poor family, so I don't know what to say or do but say these few words. First: "set libera nos a malo et nos in ducas in tentazionem et demite nobis debita nostra sicut ne nos dimitimus debitoribus nostris, panem nostrum cotidianum da nobis hodie": and so I implore our Lord Jesus Christ and my superiors for pity's sake to give me some help, with little damage to them. And I Menego Scandela wherever I go I will beg faithful Christians to obey all commands of our holy mother the Roman Catholic Church and of its superiors, that is, the inquisitors, bishops, vicars, parish priests, chaplains, curates of its dioceses, and that they may learn from my experience, I Menego did think death would take me out of all this dread, so I might not give trouble to anybody, but she did everything the wrong way round, she carried away a son of mine who was able to relieve me of every trouble and pain; then she chose to take away from me my wife who was my only stay; and these sons and daughters who are left make a fool of me and say I have been their ruin, and that is the truth, I wish I had died when I was fifteen, so they might not have had any trouble from me unhappy man.

And if I have had some evil thoughts or said some vain word, I have never believed in them nor acted against the holy church, because Our Lord has made me believe that all I thought and said was vanity and not wisdom.

And this I think is the truth, so I do not want to think or believe anything but what the holy church believes, and do what my curates and my superiors will order me to do.[146]

At the bottom of this paper there were a few lines written by the parish priest of Montereale, Giovan Daniele Melchiori, at Menocchio's request, and dated 22 January 1597. The priest declared that "si interioribus credendum est per exteriora," Menocchio led a "Christian and orthodox" life. This caution, as we know (and perhaps the priest knew it, too) was most opportune. But the wish to submit that was expressed in the writing was undoubtedly sincere. Rejected by his sons, who considered him a burden, a disgrace in front of the village, the ruin of his family, Menocchio was anxiously trying to get reinstated in the church that had once turned him out, marking him visibly as a reprobate. For this reason he was paying a pathetic tribute to his "superiors," to "inquisitors" first of all, as was natural, then progressively to "bishops and vicars and parish priests and chaplains and curates." It was a useless tribute, in a certain sense, because when Menocchio's paper was being written, the Holy Office's investigation of Menocchio had not yet started. But his uncontrollable impulse to "search for high things" tormented Menocchio, filled him with "trouble and pain," made him feel guilty in front of the world, "fallen in disgrace of the world." So he desperately invoked death. But death had forgotten him: instead, his wife and son had been taken. So he cursed himself: "I wish I had died when I was fifteen," before he grew up to be the man he was, his own and his sons' disgrace.

After a new examination (19 July), Menocchio was asked if he wanted a lawyer. He answered: "I don't want to make any other defense, but I only ask for mercy; but if I could have a lawyer I would take him, only I am a poor man." At the time of his first trial, Ziannuto had fought for his father and had procured him a lawyer; but Ziannuto was dead now, and his other sons did not lift a finger to help him. Accordingly, the court appointed a counsel for the defense, Agostino Pisensi; on 22 July he presented to the judges a long defense "pauperculi Dominici Scandella." This paper said that the evidence was secondhand, contradictory, or vitiated by an evident ill will of the witnesses toward the defendant; the evidence showed the "mera simplicitas et ignorantia" of the defendant; therefore his absolution was requested.

On 2 August the Congregation of the Holy Office met, and Menocchio was unanimously declared "relapso," that is, a recidivist. The trial was over. The judges decided, however, to subject the culprit to torture in order to wrench the names of his accomplices from him. This was done on 5 August; the day before, a search had been made in Menocchio's house, and, in the presence of witnesses, all his chests had been opened and all "books and writings" confiscated. We unfortunately have no information about what these "writings" were.

They asked him to confess who his accomplices were, if he wanted to avoid the torture. He answered: "Sir, I don't remember having ever argued with anybody." They had him undressed and visited, as the rules of the Holy Office prescribed, to see if he was fit for torture. Meanwhile, they went on questioning him. He answered: "I argued with so many persons that now I can't remember them." So they had him tied up and asked him again to tell the truth about his accomplices. Again he replied: "I don't remember." They brought him to the torture chamber, always repeating the same question. "I have been thinking and imagining," he said, "trying to remember the people I argued with, but I haven't been able to remember." They prepared him for the strappado; "O my Lord Jesus Christ, have mercy, Jesus, have mercy, I don't know if I argued with anybody, may I die if I have had any school or companion, but I read all by myself, O Jesus, have mercy." They gave him a first tug of the cord: "O Jesus, O Jesus, oh poor me, oh poor me." "Whom did you argue with?" they asked, and he answered, "Jesus, Jesus, I don't know anything." They urged him to tell the truth: "I will tell it gladly, let me down so I can think it over."

They lowered him. He remained absorbed in thought for a while, then said: "I can't say I argued with anybody, or that anybody had the same opinion as mine, and I'm sure I don't know anything." They ordered him to be given another tug of the cord. While they were hoisting him up, he said: "Woe is me, woe is me martyr, O my Lord Jesus Christ." Then: "Sir, let me down, and I'll say something." When they put him down on the ground, he said: "I talked to the Lord Zuan Francesco Montereale, and told him no one knew which was the true faith." (The following day he added: "The said Lord Giovon Francesco reproached me for my folly.") They were not able to get anything else out of him, so they untied him and brought him back to prison. The notary remarked that the torture had been applied "cum moderamine." It had lasted half an hour.

What the judges' state of mind was, behind their monotonous repetition of the same question, we can only try to imagine. Perhaps it was the same mixture of boredom and disgust described during the same years by the nuncio Bolognetti, when, writing about the Holy Office, he complained about "the nuisance of having to listen to the foolish things said by a great number of persons, while writing them down word by word, a sort of torture for anyone who is not made solely of phlegm."[147] The old miller's obstinate silence must have seemed incomprehensible to them.

Not even physical pain had been able to get the better of Menocchio. He had uttered no names, or rather, he had mentioned only the feudal lord of Montereale, a name that seemed calculated to discourage the judges from too deep an investigation. He undoubtedly did have something to hide; but when he said that he had "read all by *himself*," he probably was not very far from the truth.

With his silence, Menocchio chose to emphasize to the last that his thoughts had originated in isolation, in contact only with books. But, as we have seen, he projected upon the printed page elements that came from a very old oral tradition.

This tradition, deeply rooted in the European countryside, explains the tenacious persistence of a peasant religion intolerant of dogmas and ceremonies, closely connected with the rhythms of nature, basically pre-Christian. It often was alien to Christianity, as in the case of the cowherds from the countryside of Eboli who, toward the middle of the seventeenth century, appeared to the shocked Jesuit fathers as "men who were human only in their outward appearance, and in ability and knowledge were not very different from the animals they took care of; quite ignorant of prayers and of all other particular mysteries of our holy faith, and even of the very notion of God."[148] But even in situations of less severe geographic and cultural isolation it is possible to find the traces of a peasant religion that had assimilated and remolded all alien contributions—starting from the Christian ones. The old English peasant who thought of God as a "good old man," of the soul as a "great bone in his body," of the hereafter as "a pleasant green meadow" where he would go if he acted right, obviously did not ignore the dogmas of Christianity: all he did was to translate them into images that fitted his experience, his aspirations, his dreams.[149]

In Menocchio's confessions, too, we can see such a translation. His case is more complex because it involves both the medium of print and the crumbling of traditional religion under the blows of the radicals of the Reformation. But the process is the same, and Menocchio's is by no means an exceptional case.

Let us take as an example the case of another miller, Pellegrino Baroni, nicknamed Pighino, "the fat one," who lived in a village in the Appennines near Modena, Savignano sul Panaro.[150] In 1570 he was tried by the Holy Office of Ferrara; but five years earlier he had been forced to abjure certain of his errors in matters of faith. The people of his village considered him "an evil Christian," a "heretic," a "Lutheran"; someone called him "a whimsical, scatter-brained man," or even "rather a fool than not." Actually, Pighino was far from being a fool: during his trial he was able to keep the inquisitors at bay, showing he possessed not only a considerable amount of steadfastness and courage, but also a subtle, almost sophistical intelligence.

But the villagers' bewilderment and the parish priest's indignation at Pighino's propositions are not difficult to understand. Pighino denied the saints' intercession, confession, the fasts prescribed by the church—and up to this point he still remained within the limits of a vague "Lutheranism." But then he went on to assert that all sacraments, including Communion (with only the exception of baptism, it seems) had been established by the church and not by Christ and that one's soul could be saved without them. Moreover, he maintained that in paradise "we will all be equal, great men having the same grace as small ones"; that the Virgin Mary "was born from a servant"; that "there is no hell nor purgatory, for they were all inventions of priests and friars to make money with"; that "if Christ had been a good man, he wouldn't have been crucified"; that "when the body dies, the soul dies too"; and that "all faiths were good for those who observed them strictly." Though tortured several times, Pighino obstinately denied ever having had accomplices and asserted that his opinions were the result of an illumination that had come to him while reading the Gospels in the vernacular—one of the four books he had read. The other three were the Book of Psalms, the *Grammar* by Donato, and *Il fioretto della Bibbia*.

Pighino's ultimate fate turned out to be different from Menocchio's. He was condemned perpetually to reside in the village of Savignano; finally he ran away to escape the hostility of the villagers, but almost at once gave himself up to the Holy Office of Ferrara, to his torturers, asking for forgiveness. His spirit was quite broken down, and he was in poor physical condition. The inquisitor was charitable with him and eventually found him a place as servant in the bishop of Modena's household.

These two millers came to different ends; but the similarities between their lives are surprising and probably more than an extraordinary coincidence.

In preindustrial Europe, even very small centers had at least one water- or windmill. The miller's trade therefore was one of the most common. Consequently, the presence of a great number of millers in heretical sects during the Middle Ages is not at all surprising.[151] Yet when, toward the middle of the sixteenth century, the satiric poet Andrea da Bergamo asserted that "a real miller is half Lutheran," he seemed to allude to a more specific connection.[152]

The age-old hostility between peasants and millers had corroborated the image of millers as cunning, thieving, swindling men, automatically predestined to hell. This negative stereotype is widely exemplified in popular traditions, legends, proverbs, fairy tales, and short stories.[153] A Tuscan folk song goes:

> I went to hell and saw the Antichrist,
> and hanging from his beard there was a miller,
> and under his feet there was a German,
> on each side a butcher and a host;
> I asked him which of them was the most wicked,
> and he said: Listen, and I will tell you.
> Look at the man with the grasping hands,
> it's the miller who makes the snow-white flour.
> Look at the man with the snatching hands,
> it's the miller who makes the snow-white flour. . . .
> the miller is the most thievish of them all.[154]

The accusation of heresy fitted this stereotype very well. A fact that nourished it was that the mill was a place where people met, where social relationships flourished in that predominantly narrow and static world. It was also a place, like the tavern and the shop, where ideas circulated. No doubt all sorts of matters were discussed among the crowd of peasants gathered outside the mill, on "the soft and muddy ground / fouled by the urine of the village mules" (this is Andrea da Bergamo's description),[155] waiting for their wheat to be milled. And the miller certainly took part in the discussion. It is not difficult to imagine scenes such as the one that took place one day in front of Pighino's mill. The miller, talking to a group of peasants, began to murmur against "priests and friars" —until one of the villagers, Domenico de Masafiis, came back and persuaded everybody to go away, saying: "Fellows, you had better let the priests and friars say office and not speak ill of them, and not heed Pelegrino di Grassi" (that is, Pighino).[156] The very conditions they worked in made millers (as well as innkeepers, tavernkeepers, and wandering artisans) a professional group that tended to be open to new ideas and inclined to spread them. Moreover, mills, usually located outside built-up areas, were very suitable for clandestine gatherings. The case of Modena, where in 1195 a persecution of the Cathari led to the dismantlement of the *molendina paterinorum* ("mills of Paterini"), was probably not exceptional.[157]

The millers' social position tended to isolate them from the community they lived in. The hostility the peasants bore them has been mentioned. To this must be added the tie of direct dependence that traditionally bound millers to local feudal lords, who had remained for centuries the holders of the privilege of milling. We do not know whether this was the case at Montereale, too: the fulling mill rented by Menocchio and his son, for instance, belonged to a private individual. But an attempt such as Menocchio's to convince the local feudal lord, Giovanni Francesco of the family of the counts of Montereale, that "one doesn't know which is the real faith" on the basis of the story of the three rings, was made possible, probably, by the atypical character of Menocchio's social position. Being a miller marked him out from the anonymous crowd of the peasants: with *them* Giovan Francesco Montereale never would have dreamed of arguing about religious matters. But Menocchio also was a peasant who tilled the soil, described as "a peasant dressed in white" by the former lawyer Alessandro Policreto, who met him for a short moment before the first trial. All this perhaps helps to explain the intricate relationship between Menocchio and the community of Montereale. Although nobody, except Melchiorre Gerbas, had approved of his ideas (though it is difficult to evaluate the possible reticence of witnesses facing the Inquisition), a long period had elapsed, perhaps even thirty years, without Menocchio's being denounced to the religious authorities. And in the end, the person who denounced him was the parish priest, instigated by another priest. In spite of their singularity, Menocchio's propositions must have appeared to the peasants of Montereale as something not foreign to their own life, beliefs, and aspirations.

Unexpected analogies occasionally emerge from under the deep difference in language between the basic trends of the peasant culture I have tried to reconstruct and those of the most advanced sectors of sixteenth-century high culture. To explain these analogies as a mere diffusion from the top downward would be to accept the theory—quite undemonstrated as yet—that ideas originate exclusively from the ruling classes. A refusal of this simplistic explanation, on the other hand, implies a much more complex conjecture as to the relationship between the culture of the dominant classes and that of the subordinate classes in this period.

A more complex conjecture, and, partly, an undemonstrable one. The nature of the documentation reflects, as is obvious, the nature of the power relations between the classes. An almost exclusively oral culture, such as that of the subordinate classes of preindustrial Europe, has a tendency to leave no traces, or only distorted ones, hence the symptomatic importance of an extreme case such as Menocchio's. It forcefully raises once more a problem whose significance is just beginning to be appreciated: the problem of the popular roots of a considerable part of European high culture, during the Middle Ages and later. Figures such as Rabelais and Bruegel probably were not splendid exceptions, but they closed an age characterized by fruitful underground exchanges, in both directions, between high culture and popular culture.[158] The period that followed was characterized both by an increasingly strict distinction between the culture of the dominant class and that of the artisan and peasant, and by a one-way indoctrination of the popular masses. The chronological division between these two periods is the second half of the sixteenth century,[159] in significant coincidence with the sharpening of social differentiation following the price revolution. But the decisive crisis had taken place a few years before, with the Peasants' War and Münster's Anabaptist reign. From that moment, the dominant classes were dramatically faced with the necessity of restoring their rule, ideologically as well as politically, over the popular masses that threatened to escape every form of control from the top; but at the same time they had to preserve, or indeed to emphasize, social distance between classes.

This renewed hegemonic effort took on different forms in various parts of Europe; but the evangelization of the countryside by the Jesuits and the widely ramified family-based religious organization established by the Protestant churches can both be ascribed to the same trend.[160] Corresponding with this, taking the form of repression, was the intensification of witchcraft trials and the strict control over such marginal groups as tramps and gypsies. This background of both the overt and implicit repression of popular culture is the setting in which Menocchio's trial took place.

Even though the trial was over, Menocchio's adventure had not yet ended. In a certain sense, the most extraordinary part of it had just begun. When evidence against Menocchio had begun to accumulate for the second time, the inquisitor of Aquileia and Concordia had written to the Congregation of the Holy Office to inform them of what was happening. On 5 June 1599, one of the members of the Congregation, the cardinal of Santa Severina, answered, insisting that they must make haste and imprison as soon as possible "that person from the diocese of Concordia who *had* denied the divinity of Our Lord Jesus Christ . . . because his case is most serious, especially since he has already been condemned as a heretic." The cardinal, moreover, gave orders for Menocchio's books and "writings" to be confiscated. The confiscation took place; some "writings" were found, though their nature is unknown. Seeing that Rome was interested in the case, the inquisitor of Friuli sent the Congregation a copy of three accusations against Menocchio. On 14 August, the cardinal of Santa Severina wrote another letter, saying, "That recidivist . . . in his examinations turns out to be an atheist," therefore it was necessary to proceed "according to due terms of justice also to discover his confederates"; the case was "most serious," therefore "your reverence is requested to send a copy of the trial, or at least a summary." The following month the news came to Rome that Menocchio had been sentenced to death, but the sentence had not yet been carried out. Probably owing to a belated feeling of clemency, the inquisitor of Friuli was hesitating. On 5 September he wrote a letter to the Congregation of the Holy Office (this letter has disappeared) to inform them of his doubts. The reply written on 3 October by the cardinal of Santa Severina in the name of the whole Congregation was most harsh: "I tell you by order of the Holiness of Our Lord that you must not fail to proceed with the thoroughness required by the gravity of this case, in order that this man's horrible and execrable excesses may not remain unpunished, but on the contrary that they may be an example to others in that region with their due and strict punishment: therefore do not fail to execute him with all possible solicitude and severity of mind, because this is required by the importance of the case, and is the explicit wish of His Holiness."

The supreme head of the Catholic church, the pope himself, Clement VIII, had bent down toward this humble subject of his who had become a diseased limb of Christ's body and demanded his death. During those same months, in Rome, the trial against the former friar Giordano Bruno was drawing toward its conclusion. This coincidence may be considered emblematic of the double struggle, toward the top and toward the bottom, that the Catholic authorities were carrying on during those years to enforce the doctrines approved by the Council of Trent. Hence their pitiless persecution—otherwise incomprehensible—against the aged miller. Shortly afterward (13 November), the cardinal of Santa Severina insisted again: "Your reverence must not fail to proceed in the case of that peasant of the diocese of Concordia accused of having denied the virginity of the most holy Virgin Mary, the divinity of Our Lord Jesus Christ, and the Providence of God, according to what I previously wrote to you by an explicit order of His Holiness: because there can be no doubt that the examination of cases of such an importance belongs to the Holy Office. Therefore you must sternly carry out all that is necessary according to the terms of justice."[161]

It was impossible to resist so strong a pressure; shortly afterward Menocchio was killed. That he was executed is certain from the testimony of a certain Donato Serotino, who, on 6 July 1601, told the commissary of the inquisitor of Friuli that he had been at Pordenone shortly after "Scandella . . . had been put to death by the Holy Office" and that he had met there a tavernkeeper who had told him that "in that town . . . there was a man called Marcato or Marco, who claimed that when the body is dead the soul is dead too."[162]

We know many things about Menocchio. About this Marcato, or Marco—and about many others like him, who lived and died without leaving any trace—we know nothing at all.

The Catholic Response to Protestantism
Church Activity and Popular Piety
in Rouen, 1560–1600

Philip Benedict

Our understanding of the Counter-Reformation has been transformed in recent years by the work of a number of French historians
following the trail blazed by the great sociologist of religion, Gabriel
Le Bras. These scholars have directed attention away from the kinds of
studies that dominated church history until recently: studies of church administration, of the papacy, of church-state relations, and of the thought
and actions of an elite of saints and theologians. Instead, they have
attempted to write the history of the Catholic church as a religious institution encompassing millions of believers, not just a coterie of saints,
bishops and doctors. Two questions in particular have engaged their
attention: (1) What was the state of the clergy and how did it conceive
and carry out its pastoral functions? and (2) How fully did the average
member of the church understand the elements of the faith and participate in the ritual life of the church? In focusing their attention on these
questions, these French historians have shown the Counter-Reformation
to have been a remarkably successful campaign by the church to elevate
the quality and status of the clergy, improve religious instruction, quicken
popular piety, and eradicate, or at least drive underground, competing
beliefs labeled as heretical or superstitious.[1]

In at least one respect, however, all of the recent historians of the
French Counter-Reformation owe a strong debt to the preceding generations of scholars who have written on the subject. For centuries church
historiography generally began accounts of the Counter-Reformation

An earlier version of this essay was presented to the seminar of Denis Richet at the
Sixth Section of the Ecole Pratique des Hautes Etudes. I would like to thank the members of
that seminar, as well as those of the Davis seminar, for their critical comments.

with the generation of saints of the early 1600s. Perhaps these scholars wished to acquit the religious revival of seventeenth-century France from any possible connection with the violent and occasionally radical excesses of the Wars of Religion. The more recent students of religious life have followed this tradition, beginning their studies in the 1620s or later. In consequence, the second half of the sixteenth century has been largely neglected in the recent historiography.[2] Yet this is an exceptionally interesting period. In these years French Catholicism faced its most direct challenge from Protestantism. The Reformed Church blossomed into a major nationwide presence in the late 1550s and early 1560s, reaching its peak strength around 1565. In precisely these same years the Council of Trent was laying down its blueprint for Catholic reform. One Catholic response to the threat posed by the rapid growth of Protestantism was violence and repression: the second half of the sixteenth century is the age of the Wars of Religion. But is there any evidence from the period of the kinds of innovative devotional, missionary, or educational activities that were characteristic of the Counter-Reformation? Was there any increase in popular Catholic piety in reaction to the violent attacks of the reformers on such popular devotional practices as the adoration of the Virgin and the Eucharist? These questions raise the issue of how an ecclesiastical establishment responds to radical challenge and speak directly to the classic debate over whether the renovation of Catholicism in the sixteenth and seventeenth centuries was primarily a reaction against the growth of Protestantism or an autonomous movement of spiritual renewal growing out of sources within the church. So far, however, they have rarely been examined.

I have chosen to investigate these questions through a local study of the important Norman city of Rouen. At once a provincial administrative capital, an important manufacturing center, and a leading port, Rouen housed over seventy thousand inhabitants around the mid-sixteenth century, making it in all probability France's second largest city at that time.[3] It was the seat of an archbishopric and the site of numerous convents and monasteries, including houses of all four mendicant orders. In the course of the sixteenth century it also became one of the chief centers of Protestantism in northern France.[4] Thus, the city provides an excellent locale in which to study the Catholic response to the rise of Protestantism.

The first section of this essay will examine the most important measures taken by the Catholic church in its effort to reawaken the faith of the masses, improve their level of religious instruction, and integrate them more fully into the life of the church. Particular attention will be paid to discovering which elements of the church responded actively and imaginatively to the Protestant challenge and which remained passive or even hindered innovation. A second section will then attempt to discover how successful the measures taken by the church were in stimulating popular piety and whether or not the second half of the sixteenth century saw any revival of Catholic sentiment among the urban masses. Several quantitative tests of popular attachment to certain devotional practices will be used for this purpose. This study will, I believe, provide a bridge between the Council of Trent and the rather late take off of the Counter-Reformation in France, as well as sketching the outlines of the religious history of this neglected period.

In the seventeenth century, it became almost a commonplace among Catholic prelates to interpret the growth of Protestantism as a providential warning to the church to put its own house in order. The notorious failure of many members of the hierarchy to live up to the standards set for them had to be ended, and the church's champions had to try both to convince those who had left the church of the error of their ways and, perhaps more important, to inoculate against heresy the great silent majority of Catholics, a group often poorly instructed in the basic tenets of the creed and more conforming than fervent in its faith. Did Rouen's clergy interpret the increasing headway made by Protestant ideas from 1520 onward in this same fashion? It would appear not. Their initial response was limited and strictly defensive. Internal reform was barely discussed. Ambitious or innovative efforts to stimulate Catholic fervor—the establishment of new religious orders or confraternities, for example, or the introduction of catechetical instruction—were slow to appear.

In 1528 the first heretic to be condemned to death in Rouen during the Reformation era, one Pierre Bar, was burned at the stake in the town marketplace. Following his execution, the Cathedral Chapter staged a solemn procession that wound its way through the city to the Carmelite monastery, where the prior of the order delivered a sermon "pour l'instruction du peuple, afin qu'il s'abstienne des erreurs de la lecture des livres de l'ecriture sainte transcrits en langue vernaculaire."[5] This was the church's first response to the rise of Protestantism. It dusted off its two great weapons of communication and propaganda, the sermon and the procession, and used them in conjunction with legal means of repression to warn the population of the dangers to society and the state purportedly posed by heresy.

As the true mass medium of the era, the pulpit had long been the essential tool for popular religious instruction, and it was now the natural place from which to attack Protestantism. The frequent sermons that formed a regular part of the religious calendar were directed against the heretic. Contemporaries were not shy in their estimates of the numbers of souls that an effective orator could regain for the church; the governor of Dieppe credited the sermons of the famous Jesuit Antonio Possevino, or

Possevin, with reconverting no less than twenty-five hundred Huguenots by his sermons.[6] But the Jesuits were exceptional in this period in that they tried logically to confute Protestant doctrine. Most preachers seem to have aimed their sermons less at any Protestants who might have been in the audience than at those who were still faithful, warning them in no uncertain terms of evils associated with the Calvinist *preche*. While no sermons actually preached in Rouen have survived, the published sermons of a leading Parisian champion of Catholicism, the Franciscan Thomas Beauxamis, can serve as an example of the thrust of most Roman attacks on Protestantism. His *Resolution sur certains pourtraictz et libelles intitulez du nom de Marmitte* (Paris, 1562), originally a series of sermons countering a widely distributed piece of Protestant propaganda, is a prolonged denunciation of the "Satanic troop" of Huguenots, whose assemblies are little other than orgies and whose doctrine is nothing but an excuse for giving lubricity free rein.[7] That similar attacks were pronounced from Rouen's pulpits is certain: the city's magistrates repeatedly had to reprimand Catholic preachers for stirring up popular violence with their denunciations of the Huguenot.[8]

Processions through the city's streets attempted in symbolic fashion to give the faithful the same warning of the dangers of heresy. Although processions to combat heresy are often associated with the period of the Catholic league, the ceremonies of that era were merely the most extravagant processions of the period. The sight of a long train of clerics and laymen carrying the *chasse* of the Virgin or the Corpus Domini through the streets and singing hymns in their honor would long have been familiar to Rouen's inhabitants. From 1528 onward, special processions were regularly staged in the wake of important Protestant attacks on objects the Catholics held sacred—incidents of iconoclasm, for example—and during the periods of civil war.[9] These usually served a double function. They presented a dramatic, ornate public spectacle of reverence for a person or doctrine attacked by Protestantism, usually the Virgin Mary or the doctrine of the Real Presence, and thus reaffirmed their sacred character. They were also rites of purification, attempting to mitigate God's wrath and cleanse a city polluted by heresy. They commonly included purificatory symbols such as the burning of candles or ringing of church bells. The message thereby conveyed to the onlooking crowds was that the Protestants formed a polluting force within society that threatened to provoke divine retribution against the city unless measures were taken to purify it. Occasionally the purpose of a procession was simply commemorative. A solemn procession was held annually from 1563 through 1577 to celebrate the anniversary of the city's recapture by Catholic forces in October 1562, ending the short-lived Huguenot domination.[10]

If the church's initial response to Protestantism was negative—simply to denounce the new faith, thereby fostering the climate of religious violence that was to characterize the period of the civil wars—signs of positive efforts to revitalize Catholic devotional life began to appear as the Wars of Religion approached. Significantly, these were not the work of the local clergy, but of laymen and of members of the new religious orders brought into the city by the archbishop.

The earliest efforts came on the eve of the religious wars and took the form of public reaffirmations of elements of the faith that had been called into question by Calvinism. Thus, as Huguenot attacks on idolatry mounted in frequency, Catholics responded by showering especial respect on the statues of religious figures that adorned many of the city's houses. Militant public gatherings were held before these street-corner images. These are known to have begun around 1559 in Paris, where, according to Jacques-Auguste de Thou, crowds of water carriers, servants, and other elements of the "lie du peuple" gathered regularly before statues of the Virgin and saints to light candles and sing canticles. Boxes were placed nearby and donations solicited from passers-by, who faced the prospect of being labeled Huguenots and beaten if they proved too niggardly.[11] By 1560, such wildcat devotions had clearly spread to Rouen as well. In that year, three chaplains were pursued by the authorities after they snatched a tennis racket from a youth and used it to break his collarbone when he refused to genuflect before a statue, in front of which bands of children regularly assembled in the evening to sing "Ave Maris Stella."[12]

In the following year, 1561, a number of Catholics sprang to the defense of another heavily criticized element of the faith, the doctrine of the Real Presence, by establishing the General Confraternity of the Holy Sacrament. This *Confrérie* du Saint-Sacrement, not to be confused with the secret, seventeenth-century *Compagnie* du Saint-Sacrement, was founded by twelve laymen: one *conseiller aux Eaux et Forêts*, two *huissiers au Parlement*, four *praticiens au Parlement*, and five *marchands bourgeois*. The association welcomed members from all of the city's parishes, who were to assemble each week in a different church to hear a special mass paid for by the members on a rotating basis. This mass was followed by a sermon and then, in the afternoon, an *ave verum*, a *salve*, and a small procession around the church and its cemetery in which the Holy Sacrament was carried in honor. In addition to these small weekly processions, the confraternity held larger semiannual ones through the entire city "pour s'esmouvoir le peuple a devotion." Members of the four mendicant orders, the city militia, the students of the four paupers' schools, and a large number of six-year-olds dressed in white and carrying burning candles marched in these larger parades, which also honored the Holy Sacrament.[13] These processions bear a striking resemblance to those staged by the great seventeenth-century missionaries at the start of a mission, and indeed, the activity of this confraternity could be viewed as a sort of urban mission symbolically defending Catholic doctrine.[14]

Did this confraternity represent a conscious effort to counter the Calvinist denial of the doctrine of the Real Presence? Confraternities in honor of the Eucharist had been a common feature of Catholic religious life from the late fourteenth century onward, and an earlier Confraternity of the Holy Sacrament had been founded in Rouen in 1435.[15] It may be purely coincidental that this second confraternity was founded at a time of growing Protestant strength, but this does not appear to be the case. Louis Marc, one of the founders and the first *maître* of the confraternity, was also one of the most zealously anti-Protestant figures in Rouen.[16] Furthermore, a myth of anti-Protestant origins seems to have been passed down orally within the organization, for in the brief account of its foundation written in 1590, on the first page of its list of new members is the declaration that the confraternity was founded at a time when the Protestants were masters of Rouen and trampling the Holy Sacrament underfoot.[17] In fact, the Huguenots did not take over the city until a year after the association was formed, but the error is a significant revelation of the confraternity's self-image as an organization devoted to rescuing the Host from the Protestants who were trying to vilify it. This task seemed so urgent in 1561 that within the first year of its existence the group had attracted over thirteen hundred members.[18]

The Catholic reaction in 1561 was unable to check the buoyant rise of Protestantism, but only exacerbated tensions and pushed France closer to the civil war that erupted the following year. During this First Civil War, Rouen's Huguenots seized control of the city, pillaged its churches, and banned Catholic services for six months until the town was besieged, retaken, and sacked by a royal army. This period of Protestant domination further embittered relations between the members of the two confessions, and the following decade was marked by almost annual violence between them. Yet despite the tense religious atmosphere and the continued presence of a sizable Calvinist minority within the city, the inertia of the parish clergy and the Cathedral Chapter during the first decades of the religious wars is striking. Since the archbishop of Rouen, the cardinal of Bourbon, was one of the leading political figures of the realm and hence away at court most of the time, the canons of the Cathedral Chapter were the true administrators of the archdiocese. The registers of their deliberations, however, are devoid of any major attempts to combat Protestantism beyond staging processions and dispatching an occasional delegation to court to protest some measure or other of toleration granted the Calvinists.[19] Several important innovations foundered against their indifference or outright hostility, as shall be seen later in this essay regarding the foundation of the Jesuit college. If the parish priests took any measures to combat Protestantism, no traces remain in the surviving records.

Any evidence of innovation and concern within the church is provided by the archbishop and the members of the new religious orders he introduced into the city. The cardinal of Bourbon was not a reforming bishop in the manner of Carlo Borromeo; he fit the stereotype of the pre-Tridentine courtier-bishop far more closely. Yet while his visits to Rouen were rare, his concern for church reform cannot be entirely discounted. In 1581 he convened the first archdiocesan council in France to deliberate how to put the reforming decrees of Trent into practice. He also championed the establishment of two of the most important new religious orders of the period, the Capuchins and the Jesuits.[20]

The provincial council of 1581 provides evidence that a concern for internal reform was beginning to stir within the local hierarchy and reveals its limited success. The assembly adopted a series of articles that both echo the Tridentine decrees and suggest some of the problems of the archdiocese.[21] Discipline was ordered to be tightened up at all levels of the hierarchy—from the bishops, who were to be deprived of their income when not in residence in their diocese, down to the parish clergy, which was instructed to take care to wear garb appropriate to its station at all times. Dignity was to be maintained in all church rites, and rites that had fallen into disuse, notably confirmation, were to be revived. A spirit of reverence was to be enforced within church buildings at all times: no secular matters were to be announced from the pulpit, and the choirboys were to cease their "badinerie" on the Feast of the Innocents. To ensure tighter control over the opinions and devotions of the laity, lists of forbidden books were to be read from the pulpit and all confraternities were ordered to obtain the permission of their curate for their assemblies. Special attention was to be paid to detecting any signs of witchcraft, libertinage, or atheism, all of which were said to be spreading alarmingly as a result of the license being accorded heresy by the edicts of pacification that allowed Protestantism liberty of conscience.[22] Finally, a seminary was to be created in each diocese within the province to provide better training for the clergy and, it was hoped, to fill the reputed lack of priests in Normandy. But it is hard to find any evidence that these decrees became anything other than statements of good intentions. The seminary did not open its doors until 1659, the frequent episcopal visitations the council called for were not carried out, and the abuses it attacked appear to have continued unabated.[23] Cases of canons reprimanded for maintaining a mistress dot the deliberations of the Cathedral Chapter as liberally after 1581 as they did prior to that date.[24]

The new religious orders founded by the cardinal undoubtedly had more impact on the city's religious life than did the articles of the provincial council, but its record, too, is one of failure as much as of success. Little is known about the early history of the Capuchins of Rouen except that their house was founded in 1580, that their numbers grew rapidly for a while but diminished after many died giving dedicated service to those stricken by the plague, and that their popularity was so great that their little chapel could not hold the crowds attracted by their sermons, so the fathers were often forced to preach from a boulder outside the chapel so that all could hear.[25] The Jesuits, on the other hand, have left much more copious documentation of their activities.[26] In 1565, the archbishop first announced to his Cathedral Chapter that he intended to found a Jesuit college in Rouen. Although the school did not open until 1593, the Jesuits were not inactive in the city in the intervening years. Individual members of the order are known to have made five visits to the town: in 1565, 1569–70, 1580, 1583, and 1588.[27]

The description left by Father Possevino of his two sojourns in Rouen in 1565 and 1569–70 give an idea of what a remarkable organizer could do in a short period. Possevino preached three times a week before audiences whose size he estimated at several thousand, among them curés taking notes on what he said. He organized an association of women drawn from the best families of the city, who visited the Hôtel-Dieu regularly and assisted the nurses. He attempted to promote the devotion of the Eucharist by having the Host exposed on the altar of all of the churches of the city. Above all, he devoted himself to introducing organized religious instruction to Rouen by promoting that important sixteenth-century innovation, the catechism.[28]

The catechism was first introduced by the great Protestant reformers as a means of conveying to the masses a firm grasp of the elements of the faith. It was quickly adopted by the Catholics and spread particularly by the Jesuits. While in Rouen, Possevino gave lessons from the catechisms of Canisius and Auger, encouraged their sale, and attempted to train priests in the rudiments of pedagogy so that they could continue the lessons after he departed. During his second visit, street vendors circulated throughout the city crying, "Voici le catéchisme enseigné par le Père Prédicateur." Sales of the books were so great, Possevino claims, that six new editions had to be ordered from Paris to keep up with the demand.[29] Unfortunately, it is not clear whether catechistic instruction continued after Possevino left Rouen. A letter of the period declares that his visits had a great effect on the people for a short while,[30] but it is hard to imagine they exercised a permanent influence unless others carried on his work between his visits.

One aspect of Possevino's visit of 1569–70 was surely a failure. He had come to Rouen to oversee the establishment of the Jesuit college, which the cardinal of Bourbon had endowed with a *rente* of two thousand livres, but this project foundered against the combined hostility of the four mendicant orders, the Cathedral Chapter, and the Parlement. Encouraged by the canons, the mendicants had instituted a suit against the Jesuits on the grounds that the proposed college infringed upon their right to control all educational establishments within the city. Even though Possevino had attempted to earn the Parlement's gratitude by aiding it in pacifying a mob that had been threatening Huguenots who refused to take Easter communion, the court ruled against the Jesuits, and the attempt to establish the college was dropped for a time.[31]

The cardinal of Bourbon tried to revive his project in 1583 by granting the society a new *rente* drawn against the revenues of his rich Abbey of St. Ouen. This time his plan ran afoul of the general of the society, who feared that this money might be difficult to collect in the event the cardinal's successor as abbot opposed the alienation of his revenue for such a project. The general consequently deemed the financial security of the college inadequate, and he would not allow it to open.

As the initial failure of the Jesuits to establish their college in Rouen demonstrates, the city's clergy and its monastic orders not only took very little positive action to reform or revitalize Catholic religious life; they actually formed an obstacle to innovation and innovators.

Several explanations of this inertia come quickly to mind, each undoubtedly containing a measure of truth. First, many members of the first estate lacked zeal. Studies of the Catholic clergy in the sixteenth century suggest that many clerics were poorly trained, that nonresidence was widespread, and that timeservers were numerous.[32] The failure of the city's archbishops to carry out any episcopal visitations, combined with the absence of registers of ordinations dating from the period, make a detailed investigation of Rouen's clergy an impossibility. The mere fact, however, that no visitations were carried out indicates something about the state of church administration. All of the surviving evidence indicates that Rouen's clergy, if perhaps better trained than the bulk of clerics of the age because rich urban benefices attracted well-educated priests, nonetheless lacked zeal in performing its duties. In 1535 fourteen of the city's thirty-six parishes were headed by nonresident curates.[33] Attendance at the meetings of the Cathedral Chapter was sparse.[34] The most telling condemnation is provided by the provincial council's denunciations of simony and of the preferment accorded the illegitimate offspring of church officials, as well as by the fate of its decrees.

A second consideration may have tempered the concern of certain clergymen about the rise of Protestantism: they felt a certain openness to the movement. This was especially true of a group of men within the Cathedral Chapter who were strongly influenced by humanist intellectual currents.[35] The works of Erasmus and, to a lesser extent, Lefevre d'Etaples were heavily represented in the libraries of several canons, and occasionally suspect or even heretical works found their way onto their bookshelves.[36] One canon, Claude Chappuys, resigned his position early in 1562 because of his pro-Calvinist sentiments, only to resume it later because the court backed him; he sat in the chapter for over a decade. Others, although not Protestants, had Huguenot relatives.[37] In short, a substantial part of the Cathedral Chapter, which drew its members from the better educated of the urban elite, held tolerant, latitudinarian religious views both because of Erasmian conviction and family feeling. There is no evidence that these men were ever numerous or outspoken enough to form an active group of Erasmian or evangelical reformists within the chapter, but they were unlikely to press for vigorous measures against heresy.

Vested interests rarely appreciate the creation of rival institutions, and this must be accounted a third obstacle in the way of a vigorous riposte to Protestantism. The established religious orders were jealous of their position in society and resisted newcomers like the Jesuits. They were also suspicious of each other after generations of interorder combats, and these ancient enmities undermined chances for concerted action. In 1570, the grand vicar of the cathedral told the Parlement, which was scandalized by a bitter dispute it was investigating between a Dominican and a Franciscan, that if the court looked into every conflict between mendicant fathers, such affairs would keep a whole Parlement busy full time.[38]

But the most important reason for the clergy's inertia in moving toward religious reform probably lies in a fourth consideration: the normal reactions to radical challenge of men vested with power, wealth, and a sense of their sacred dignity. That in this particular case the men may also have been stung by an often biting Protestant satirical literature probably only added to the already great likelihood that they would respond to attack, not with internal reform, but by vilifying and attempting to squelch their attackers. Those who saw the growth of Calvinism as a sign that the church needed to change its ways were generally already convinced for other reasons of the need for internal reform. The great majority of the clergy believed that the crisis required firm action. And while a liberal conscience may not wish to admit it, such a policy was by no means doomed to failure. The anti-Huguenot violence that became common in the first decade of the Wars of Religion, together with intermittent government measures of proscription, shattered Rouen's Reformed Church. After peaking around the mid-1560s, the congregation's numbers plummeted by 89 percent over the subsequent decade.[39] By the mid-1570s the threat that Protestantism might become dominant locally had been successfully beaten back. The pressure of popular intolerance, encouraged by the clergy, had indeed met the crisis. Why would other measures to bolster the faith seem necessary?

To jolt the church into measures beyond the simple vilification of Protestantism apparently required a truly alarming crisis that could not be resolved through violence against a local enemy. Such a crisis occurred late in the religious wars, with the death of the duke of Anjou and the emergence of the Protestant Henry of Navarre as the heir-apparent to the throne. This caused a veritable explosion of Catholic devotional innovations that stands in striking contrast to the inertia of the preceding decades.

Many Catholics were convinced that if Henry of Navarre became king, the outlawing of the mass and a severe repression would inevitably follow. Both the Huguenot takeover in 1562 and the example of England stood as warnings of what happened to Catholicism when Protestants ruled, and the lessons of these events were especially vivid in a city that had suffered a disastrous sack as a result of the Huguenot occupation and was a center for Catholic refugees from England.[40] Here was a threat to the faith that came from outside the city and could not be countered by overcoming the Protestants locally. It was also a threat that strongly suggested the warning hand of God. Just as kings were God-given, so presumably were heirs-apparent, and if God chose to make the heir-apparent a Protestant, He was undoubtedly sending France a message about its sinful ways.[41]

What was to be done about this threat? Politically, the Holy League was formed, or, more properly, reformed, becoming the sort of nation-wide organization that was needed to carry on a crusade against a more-than-local threat. But many of the pamphlets of the period provide a two-part prescription: arm for the struggle and pray to God.[42] The second part of this prescription was no less important than the first. The same situation that produced the political activities of the league also stimulated the feeling that religious devotions must be redoubled and morals reformed lest God send a heretical king to scourge the people of Rouen for their sins.[43] The crisis, to borrow a phrase from Denis Pallier, made penitents as well as militants out of the Catholic population.[44]

Perhaps the most important religious activity of this period is the establishment of the Jesuit college, at last, in 1593. The college's financial situation was no more secure at this time than it had been a decade previously, and the college had to be granted special subsidies soon after its doors opened.[45] The general of the society nonetheless relented in his opposition to erecting a college on unsteady financial foundations because the attitude of Rouen's judicial, ecclesiastical, and municipal authorities changed. The Cathedral Chapter and the municipal government had both written the Society of Jesus urging the establishment of the college, and the city had granted the Jesuits a two-year pension, while the members of the Parlement raised money among themselves to help finance the costs of setting up the institution.[46] With their support, it was established quickly.

Why this change of attitude on the part of corporations previously hostile to the Jesuits? All of these bodies were now controlled by the Holy League, and the Jesuits had been allied with the League elements within the city since before Rouen's Day of the Barricades. Their sermons had, in fact, played an important role in preparing for the Sainte-Union's triumph in the city. In August 1588—after the Day of the Barricades in Paris, but when Rouen was still royalist—two Jesuits arrived in the city. They had been sent from the League-controlled capital by the man who later headed the League council in Rouen, Michel de Monchy, the grand vicar of the cathedral and a *conseiller clerc* in the Parlement.[47] The chapter, still controlled by more moderate elements, forbade them to preach. Nonetheless, following the assassination of the duke of Guise it was one of the Jesuits, Commolet, who first broke the silence imposed on all of the city's preachers after that event by the governor. His sermon is movingly recounted by an English sister of the order of St. Bridget, which had taken refuge in Rouen in 1580:

When he came into the pulpytt, all eyeis and mowthes gapying upon hym, the good man was in such a passyon that he seemyd lyke to burst and could scars bryng out hys words for weepyng, the passyon of that tyme had so alteryd his voyce. Hys matter was of blessyd St Thomas, declaryng to the people the cause of hys martirdome in the behalfe of Chrystes churche, and of the quarrel betwyxt hym and the kyng, and how hys braynes were stroke out uppon the pavement before ye alter. Thys thyng was so apt for hys purpose that the people could by and by apply ytt that the preacher had no soner namyd the slaughter of theyr 2 Prynces but thatt all fell out into weepyng, and the preacher ther sobbyng alowde could saye no more. Butt after a preatty space, stryving with hymself to speake, he clappyng of hys hands cryed aloude, o pover eglese galicane, and so came downe, the people and all so movyd as we never have seene nor shall see ye lyke.[48]

In the long run, the Collège de Bourbon, as the Jesuit college was named, was undoubtedly the most important of the institutions founded in Rouen during the period of the League. Within a decade of its creation some eighteen hundred students were enrolled, receiving the characteristic Jesuit education, at once theologically orthodox and pedagogically innovative, that shaped unmistakably the ideas and interests of generations of Rouennais, among them Pierre Corneille and the Cavelier de la

Salle.[49] In the short run, however, a second innovation of these years may have made a more dramatic impact on the inhabitants of the city, addressing more directly the fears aroused by the perilous state of the church. This was the practice contemporaries referred to as the *oratoire*, known today as the perpetual adoration.

Introduced to Rouen early in 1588, the practice of the *oratoire* involved displaying the Holy Sacrament amid a collection of relics on a richly decorated altar for a week at a time in each of the city's churches. Services were held daily in the parish where the Host was on display and were accompanied by special sermons.[50] Each week the Host was carried to the next church in a great procession in which many participants marched barefoot. A journal of the period declares that the *oratoire* stimulated "plus de dévotion qu'il estoit possible de dire," and this opinion is confirmed both by Elizabeth Sanders, the English nun, who speaks of the "mervelous devotyon" of these years, and by the large sums of money collected in the basins placed alongside the altar.[51] But this practice was apparently discontinued after 1593, as all mention of the *oratoire* disappears from the accounts of the parish treasuries.

The other two important initiatives of this period were primarily the work of one man, Jehan de Quintanadoines, a fascinating individual whose biography deserves a brief excursus. His life shows the confessional struggle as it was played out within a single family.

The Quintanadueñas were originally important wool merchants in Burgos. Members of the family emigrated to several of the major north European ports with which the family traded, one line establishing itself in Rouen around 1519. Within a generation, the family had been assimilated into the city's leading circles.[52] One mark of the degree to which the Quintanadueñas, their name now frenchified to Quintanadoines, had drifted away from their Spanish origins was the conversion of two members of the second generation to Protestantism. One of these two was Fernande, seigneur de Brétigny, Jehan's father.[53]

Jehan was born in the parish of St. Etienne-des-Tonneliers in 1555. Sometime in 1562, he was—curiously—sent back to Spain, where he was to receive Catholic education from private tutors in his uncle's house in Seville.[54] It is highly improbable that a Protestant father would of his own volition choose to give his eldest son a strongly Catholic upbringing. The most plausible explanations of this peculiar action are either that pressure from the rest of the family was brought to bear on Fernande or that he left the city briefly following the Catholic reconquest and that his son was sent away in his absence. Another member of the Quintanadoines clan was in Rouen around 1562, a cousin Antoine, who was born in Burgos and returned there before marrying, but was clearly the head of the clan during his years in Rouen.[55] Antoine was a zealous Catholic, as is evident from the fact that he fled the city during the Huguenot occupation and some 10,889 livres worth of his goods was confiscated, while the Rouen-born brothers, even the Catholics, stayed in the city and lost no property.[56] Clearly, the family was divided on religious grounds, and in the extended families characteristic of the leading merchant and *officier* circles it does not seem impossible that the leader of the clan might command the authority to determine the form of his cousin's education.[57] The suspicion that young Jehan was sent away to remove him from his father's heretical influence is strengthened by the fact that Fernande reconverted to Catholicism in 1569 and Jehan returned home the following year.

The relations between father and son in the ensuing years were ambivalent, to say the least. The elder Quintanadoines wanted his son to marry and continue as a merchant. Jehan, already deeply pious but also very timid, wanted to enter holy orders but also to obey his father's wishes. Twice marriage arrangements were on the brink of being concluded when Jehan fell mysteriously ill. During his second illness, as he hovered on the brink of death, his father agreed to allow him to become a cleric. Jehan miraculously recovered.[58]

This long family drama seems to have affected Jehan profoundly. He grew up to be extremely afraid of speaking in public and once was struck dumb in the pulpit when forced by his superior to preach. In his later years, he often suffered from such attacks of extreme scruples that he would on occasion refuse to say mass without a confessor nearby lest he sin on the way to the altar.[59] A remarkable spiritual dialogue between himself and God, which he wrote in 1610, shows that he had a sense of being virtually paralyzed by guilt and the feeling that he had wasted the few moments given him on earth. In it he echoes the prodigal son: "Father, I have sinned against heaven and before you; I am no longer worthy to be called your son."[60]

Despite his timidity and sense of personal unworthiness, Quintanadoines' accomplishments during the period of the Holy League and shortly thereafter were far from negligible. The most important of these was the role he played in the establishment of the female order of the Carmelites in France. The Carmelites were first introduced to France in Paris in 1603 thanks to the influence of the circle around Mme Acarie and Bérulle. The first attempt to establish this great Spanish order in France, however, was made in Rouen during the period of the league.[61] After Quintanadoines' first betrothal-induced illness, he was sent to Spain. There he was introduced to, and greatly impressed by, the spiritual activities of the Carmelite disciples of Saint Theresa. His goal became to carry back with him to France the Carmelite rule.

The opportunity to realize this goal came during the years of the league. To fulfill a vow of thanksgiving made when the siege of Rouen of 1591–92 was raised, Quintanadoines undertook with the encouragement of the widow of the duke of Joyeuse (who was also the protectoress of the violently *ligueur* Capuchins of Caen[62]) to convince Rouen's Cathedral Chapter and the duke of Mayenne to back his project. In this he was successful, but his subsequent voyage to the Escorial to convince Philip II to permit the transfer of several Carmelite sisters to France failed for reasons that are not clear. The enterprise had to be abandoned for a time. On Quintanadoines's return from Spain, though, he translated from Spanish to French a biography of Saint Theresa, and this work caught the attention of Mme Acarie and led her to support the project. These religious activities of the years of the League clearly are linked to those of the *dévot* circles of the early seventeenth century—the same kind of link that can be found in the biographies of many of the leading Parisian *dévots* including Mme Acarie herself.[63]

A few years before his attempt to found a Carmelite convent in Rouen, Quintanadoines was instrumental in establishing a confraternity —the Penitents—about whose activities in the city very little can be discovered, but which is of great interest because of its role in recent historiography. The number, size, and importance of the companies of Penitents in the Midi throughout the ancien régime have been revealed by the recent studies of Marguerite Pecquet, Marc Venard, and Maurice Agulhon.[64] These authors do not note that the Penitents also expanded into northern France during the period of the League.[65] Confraternities were founded in the second-level cities of Abbeville and Laon as well as in Paris and Rouen, and traces of other groups could probably be found elsewhere in northern France during this period if one searched diligently.[66]

Because Rouen's Penitents disappeared with the fall of the League and left no documents, only fleeting references to their activities and membership remain. They were founded in 1588 by Quintanadoines after Spanish models, with the goal, according to Elizabeth Sanders, "to reforme the people."[67] Their first meeting was held in the chapel of the English nuns of Saint Bridget, which became during these years a center for *ligueur* spirituality, even as the nuns themselves became living symbols of the persecution that befell Catholics under Protestant rulers and were therefore honored in league propaganda.[68] The members of the Penitents, said to include "un grand nombre de personnes, même d'une naissance distinguée," gathered regularly to perform the extremely dramatic ceremonies characteristic of the group, such as torchlit nocturnal processions inside the cathedral.[69] The precise links, if any, between the Penitents and the *ligueur* elements within Rouen are not clear, but elsewhere, in Laon, Bourges, and most probably also in Paris, the ties were so strong that the Parlement of Paris abolished the confraternities following the fall of the Sainte-Union.[70] It is tempting to hypothesize that one reason the Penitents were found exclusively in the South in the seventeenth and eighteenth centuries is that these groups had become popular there several decades before the period of the League. Consequently, they were not closely associated with the movement and did not suffer from the opprobrium that fell after 1594 on all things *ligueur*, which explains the disappearance of the Penitents in the North after that date.

The Penitents, like the *oratoire*, may have disappeared from Rouen with the fall of the League, but while each lasted they provided perfect forms of expression for the anguished penitential piety of this period of political crisis. The novel devotional activity of these years has not often been remarked upon except in offhand comments about "fanaticism," but it seems to have accompanied the League in many cities in which the movement was dominant and probably ought to be regarded as an essential element of the Catholic reaction to the specter of Henry IV's succession. Just as evidence is easily found of companies of Penitents created in northern cities besides Rouen, so, too, local studies and published memoirs show that the *oratoire* was introduced in other cities.[71] In Laon, the Penitents, the *oratoire*, the Jesuits, and the league were all inextricably linked. Shortly after the Sainte-Union assumed power in that town, the new *ligueur* authorities petitioned the Jesuit order to establish a college. The Society lacked the personnel to staff an entire college, but a single Jesuit father, Antoine Tholozan, was dispatched to the town. A man of remarkable learning and rhetorical skill, he soon had the entire city in his thrall. Among the activities he championed were the introduction of the *oratoire* and the establishment of a company of Penitents. This group soon included "la plus saine partie des habitans," and, as such, became an essential element in Tholozan's efforts to keep the League in power in the late days of the movement when zeal began to flag. All members of the confraternity were required to confess at least once a month, and Tholozan threatened those whose commitment to the League he feared was slackening with revealing the secrets they had confided to him in the confessional.[72] In other cities, cases can be found where a religious confraternity served more directly as a tool of League political activity. The Parisian *confrères* of the Name of Jesus, for example, pledged in obedience to their statutes both to take frequent Communion and to arm themselves for the defense of the city against the heretic, swearing never to recognize Henry of Navarre as king.[73]

Such direct linkage between League political activity and novel forms of Catholic devotion (here, frequent Communion) was more the exception than the rule. There is no evidence that any of the new confraternities founded in Rouen in this period served directly as cells of anti-

Protestant militancy as the Confraternity of the Name of Jesus and others like it did.[74] Political activism had limited appeal for many thoroughly zealous Catholics. Such was the case for Jehan de Quintanadoines, who, despite his importance on the religious scene, never appears in the political or administrative records pertaining to the period of the League. Other men saw the devotional and political activities of the period as but two aspects of the same struggle. This was true of Michel de Monchy, whose name is found throughout the documents of the period. This nephew of the cardinal of Pellevé was the man who invited the Jesuits to Rouen in 1588. He also directed the League's provincial *conseil de l'Union* and sat in the Parlement as a *conseiller-clerc*, until his extremism ran him afoul of the governor, the duke of Villars, who expelled him from the city in 1593. As archdeacon of the cathedral, Monchy toured the parishes under his charge "assisté de personnages de rare doctrine et piété pour confuter les hérétiques, instruire le peuple, et corriger le clergé."[75] He was apparently linked to the Penitents in some manner, since it was he who announced to the other canons when the company desired to hold a procession in the cathedral.[76] The contrast between de Monchy and de Quintanadoines reflects the broader split within Catholic religious currents of the time between those encouraging activism in the world (here de Monchy's link with the Jesuits is surely more than fortuitous[77]) and those for whom retreat and contemplation were the highest possible forms of service to the community.

All of the activities so far discussed, from the creation of the Confraternity of the Holy Sacrament in 1561 to the establishment of the Jesuit college in 1593, were the work of a relatively small number of men drawn almost exclusively from the upper strata of Rouennais society. Occasionally, when the documents speak of "mervelous devotyon" or inform us that thirteen hundred members rapidly enrolled in the Confraternity of the Holy Sacrament, there are indications that the new institutions or devotional forms struck a receptive chord among the anonymous mass of the Catholic population. It is a persistent temptation of religious history to seize upon such indications and proclaim triumphantly that they show that the new forms voiced the aspirations of that elusive entity, the people. But even a confraternity of thirteen hundred members, while undoubtedly having considerable mass appeal, represents less than 5 percent of Rouen's adult population. For surer evidence about the attitudes of the bulk of the population, quantitative tests that chart the opinions of the otherwise voiceless must be employed. Only on such a basis can more confident statements be made about whether the sorts of activities so far discussed truly influenced and represented something that might fairly be called popular religion.[78]

In recent years, many French historians and sociologists of religion have recognized the importance of devising quantitative tests of mass religious belief and have devoted a great deal of energy to searching for sources that permit the construction of reliable indices of popular fervor.[79] Sources for many of the indices they now use, such as the degree of abstention from Easter Communion, number of individuals entering holy orders, or frequency with which testators left money for masses for their souls, do not exist for the period of Rouen's history studied here.[80] Nonetheless, it is possible to calculate two measures of popular attachment to Catholic religious practices. Neither of these provide what might be called "panoramic" measures of religious opinion—measures that survey each and every member of a community (or at least a representative sample) and therefore indicate the full spectrum of belief and unbelief within it. The "great unknown" in the religious history of this period— the percentage of the population thoroughly indifferent to organized religion and to the confessional struggle of the era—must remain an unknown insofar as Rouen is concerned.[81] The indices available are diachronic measures. They reveal changes in the degree of fervor among the city's nominal Catholics. They therefore can provide some indication of whether or not the pattern of piety discernible among the elite responsible for the highly visible expressions of religiosity also characterized the evolution of mass religious concern over the course of the wars of religion.

During the early Middle Ages, the church rigorously forbade all believers to engage in sexual relations during Lent. This requirement was softened into a pious recommendation over the course of the later Middle Ages, but confessors continued to encourage abstention from sex during Lent through the sixteenth century and beyond. The extent to which a dip in conceptions appears during Lent on a graph of monthly fluctuations in the number of baptisms provides a rough indication of the extent to which the mass of the faithful heeded these counsels.[82] It can thus serve as an approximate guide to popular fervor, and perhaps is particularly apt for indicating the extent to which Rouen's inhabitants shared in the privacy of their beds the impulse toward communal purification which the public religious ceremonies of the period of the League paraded so ostentatiously.

Rouen's Catholic parish registers are numerous from the 1560s onward, so the seasonal movement of baptisms and conceptions during the final forty years of the sixteenth century can be computed easily. Figure 1 sets forth the results obtained for the periods 1563–77 and 1580–94 for two contrasting groups of parishes: five small, well-to-do parishes in the central and western sections of the city; and two large, poorer parishes in the east of town, St. Maclou and St. Vivien.[83] (The index must be calculated for intervals of at least fifteen years to eliminate the influence of

Figure 1. Monthly Movement of Conceptions

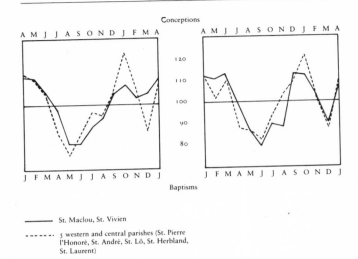

Conceptions

	St. Maclou, St. Vivien

- - - - - -	5 western and central parishes (St. Pierre l'Honoré, St. André, St. Lô, St. Herbland, St. Laurent)

Baptisms

random annual fluctuations in the pattern of births.) The graphs reveal a clear difference between the two groups of parishes. The curves of the five western and central parishes show an equally deep drop in conceptions in March in each of the fifteen-year periods. An equally large percentage of the population clearly practiced sexual abstinence during Lent throughout the Wars of Religion in these parishes. In St. Maclou and St. Vivien, on the other hand, the March trough does not appear at all in the first period but is quite marked in the second. The inhabitants of these popular parishes apparently began to follow this practice only in the later years of the civil wars, around the period of the League.

Because it must be calculated in fifteen-year segments, this first measure does not permit a very close analysis of changes in popular fervor, although it does suggest a certain growth in religious concern around the period of the League. The second index permits finer discrimination. This is based on the sums collected in the basins that were placed in several locations in each parish church to receive the offerings of the faithful. Each church had several basins, most commonly one dedicated to the Virgin and one, the "bassin de l'oeuvre," for the upkeep of the church. A few parishes also maintained a basin of the relics. The sums collected annually in these receptacles are noted in the accounts of the parish treasuries. Relatively complete sets of these accounts have survived from the early sixteenth century onward for thirteen parishes, permitting a study of the volume of pious offerings in a representative sample of the city's parishes.[84]

The adoration of the Virgin was, of course, one of the most violently contested and most passionately defended Catholic practices, so the donations to the basin of the Virgin would appear an excellent test of the popular response first to Erasmian and, especially, Protestant critiques of the cult, then to the Catholic counterattack. The significance of gifts to the *bassin de l'oeuvre* is more difficult to interpret, but such donations probably reflected an interest in the physical adornment of the parish church, again a point of contention between Catholics and Protestants. In any case, the curves of the *bassin de l'oeuvre* parallel almost exactly those of the basin of the Virgin in parishes where both were recorded separately in the account books.

Figure 2 is a cumulative index arrived at by combining figures for all of the basins in the thirteen parishes.[85] It shows, first, a marked drop in the amounts collected in the decades prior to the outbreak of the Wars of Religion. The decline is evident from the 1540s on and is particularly dramatic in the years just preceding the civil wars. As the city's overall population was stable or expanding throughout these years, this decline clearly must represent changes in religious sentiment rather than in the city's economic situation. The diffusion of Protestantism has to be accounted the chief reason. Significantly, two parishes proved exceptions to the general trend, the semiagricultural faubourg St. Gervais and the cloth-working parish of St. Nicaise, the poorest parish in the city proper. This suggests that the poorest and least educated people of the city remained relatively untouched by the new ideas. Both St. Gervais and St. Nicaise remained strongly Catholic throughout the century, and the drapers of St. Nicaise distinguished themselves in a number of the violent

Figure 2. Cumulative Index, Bassins de La Vierge, de l'oeuvre, et des reliques Combined, All Parishes

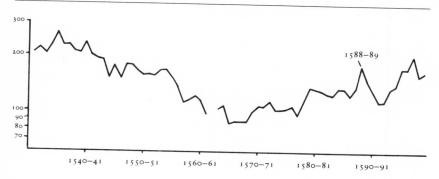

clashes that were common between members of the two confessions.[86]

Following the iconoclasm and the banning of Catholic services that accompanied the period of Protestant domination in 1562, the reestablishment of the mass and the work of reconstructing the defaced churches might have been expected to lead to a larger number of gifts offered by the Catholic faithful, who were thankful to be able to worship once more as they pleased. But in fact, following the gap in the curve caused by the outlawing of Catholicism, the cumulative index falls to its lowest point of the century in the later 1560s. It then rises slowly for the next two decades, the rise being most marked in the poorer parishes. This slow increase, totaling approximately 40 percent, is difficult to interpret. The city declined a bit in size during these years, and inflation was rampant. Grain prices almost doubled in Paris between the five-year periods 1563–67 and 1583–87, and only in the parishes of St. Godard, St. Gervais, and St. Nicolas did gifts rise as rapidly.[87] The effect of inflation on the level of donations is not at all clear. On the one hand, people had more spending money in their pockets; on the other hand, somebody who was used to giving four sous to the Virgin every Easter may not have felt that, with the rising cost of living, a larger gift was necessary to gain Her patronage. It is impossible, therefore, to state with assurance whether the rise in giving in these years ought to be considered the product of inflation or the reflection of a slow reawakening of Marian devotion. All that can be declared with certainty about the period 1562–67 is that there was no dramatic trend in either direction.

The jump in donations coincident with the early years of the Holy League is subject to no such ambiguities. In nine of the twelve parishes for which the registers exist, the amounts collected reached their highest level of the entire period of the religious wars between 1587 and 1591. In three, they more than doubled the amounts collected in the surrounding years. Clearly, the dramatic public manifestations of religious fervor were part of a deeper upsurge of concern during these troubled years.

A sharp drop in donations followed quickly on the heels of this upsurge that must be attributed to the severe economic crisis of the period of the League and growing popular disaffection with the movement. A new upsurge occurred after the return of peace and prosperity under Henry IV. This rise seems to continue strongly until at least the middle of the seventeenth century, at which point the parish accounts began to be maintained differently, making further comparison impossible.[88] The great flowering of the Counter-Reformation is reflected here, as well as in the extraordinary spate of new religious foundations that resulted in the creation of seventeen convents and monasteries in the city over the course of fifty years.[89]

In 1589, the parishioners of St. Michel brought a suit against their parish priest. They alleged that Sunday mass was never celebrated at any fixed hour; instead, the curé held it whenever it suited him, often so late in the day that the parishioners missed the afternoon sermons at the cathedral or the city's monasteries. They urged the ecclesiastical authorities to make sure that the curé carried out his duties more punctually in the future.[90]

The concern shown by these ordinary churchgoers lest they miss the afternoon sermons seems characteristic of the early years of the League. These were the years that, to recapitulate, most clearly witnessed an upsurge of Catholic fervor. The rapid advances made by Protestantism in the late 1550s and early 1560s had provoked some early defense of the elements of the faith under attack, most notably Mariolatry and the doctrine of the Real Presence. But these seem mostly to have involved the already deeply committed Catholics, for the parish account books reveal that devotion to the Virgin declined among the population as a whole in the years just prior to the outbreak of the Wars of Religion. In the ensuing years of the civil wars, the church hierarchy demonstrated little concern for the revitalization of Catholic religious life within the city. The exception was the new religious orders. The Jesuits in particular were prominent because of their sermons and catechetical work; they clearly deserve their reputation as the spearheads of the Counter-Reformation. But their efforts had encountered considerable opposition and were slow to bear fruit until the specter of a Protestant successor to the throne jolted the population from its complacency and the Day of the Barricades swept the Catholic League into power. The highly emotional atmosphere of the ensuing years bred unusual religious ferment, in which the introduction of new religious orders and devotional forms went hand in hand with the multiplication of traditional pious gestures among the mass of the people.

Until further research has been done on this period, it will be impossible to say just how representative Rouen's experience was compared to France as a whole. Richard Gascon's work suggests that Lyon witnessed some vigorous efforts to counter Protestantism by reinvigorating Catholic devotional life as early as the 1560s, with the Jesuits playing the critical role[91]; the first decades of the religious wars may not have been a period of inertia everywhere in France. Certainly the ferment of the years of the League was shared by a number of other major French cities.

Such activity indicates that the origins of the French Counter-Reformation cannot be cut off as completely as they have been from the political struggles of the wars of religion. There is, in particular, a fascinating duality about the religious initiatives of the period of the League. In many ways, they point backward to the late Middle Ages; the spate of processions and devotions can be interpreted as an attempt at communal self-purification—the sort of mass breast-beating in the face of natural and political calamities that occurred often from the Black Death onward. Yet many aspects of the initiatives of the period suggest the Counter-Reformation: the *oratoire*, very like the devotion of the Forty Hours; the often central position of the Jesuits; the attempt to establish the Carmelites. Furthermore, it is possible to see how, through a process of mobilization and disillusion, the combination of political and religious activism awakened by the crisis of the League could have become transmuted into the more inward-directed and less overtly political Catholic activism of the early seventeenth century. The alarm caused by the possible accession of a Huguenot king undoubtedly provoked an intensification of religious activity by many members of the urban elite, as well as a political movement challenging the power of the monarchy. The subsequent excesses of this political movement could then have served to discredit mass politics among this group, prompting a retreat toward, on the one hand, mysticism, and, on the other, secret underground pressure groups such as the Compagnie du Saint-Sacrement.

More detailed research will be needed before any confident statements can be made about specific links between the League and the development of the Counter-Reformation. In particular, we need investigations of whether or not those active in the new confraternities that accompanied the Sainte-Union also were involved in the early centers of Counter-Reformation spirituality.[92] It may well turn out, however, that the wellsprings of the Catholic religious revival included more radical sources than earlier generations of church historians have liked to admit. The case of Rouen shows clearly that violent intolerance and little else dominated Catholicism's initial reaction to the Protestant challenge, but it also suggests that the movement of internal revitalization that subsequently developed received a strong boost from the crisis awakened by the threat of a Protestant king. The movement may truly merit the title "*Counter*-Reformation" to a greater degree than most work of the past several generations would seem to indicate.

The Wonderyear

Reformed Preaching and Iconoclasm in the Netherlands

Phyllis Mack

I cannot write you in ten sheets of paper the strange sight I saw there —organs and all, destroyed. . . . Yet they that thus did, never looked towards any spoil, but break all in pieces, and let it lie underfoot . . . [and] as I do not understand they neither said nor did anything to the nuns: but when all was broken, left it there, and so departed.—Richard Clough, describing the iconoclasm at Antwerp in 1566[1]

A Protestant crowd corners a baker guarding the holy-wafer box in St. Médard's church in Paris in 1561. "Messieurs," he pleads, "do not touch it for the honor of Him who dwells here." "Does your god of paste protect you now from the pains of death?" was the Protestant answer before they killed him.—Natalie Davis, describing the iconoclasm at Paris in 1561[2]

In the spring of 1566, Dutch Calvinist ministers secretly made their way home to the Netherlands from churches of exile in England, Germany, France, and Switzerland.[3] A clandestine Reformed movement had existed there for over twenty years, and when the government issued a decree that limited the activities of the Inquisition against heresy, many ministers in exile returned home expecting to find religious toleration. In the early summer they began preaching publicly to huge audiences in the countryside. In August small bands of Reformers broke into the churches and demolished the images of Catholic worship; within a few days the iconoclasts had destroyed the interiors of over four hundred churches in Flanders alone. Triumphant, the ministers moved into the "purified" buildings and began holding formal religious services, but within a few months they found themselves under siege by government troops. When the duke of Alva arrived from Spain in 1567 to inflict the king's punishment on the heretics, the era of Reformed worship and Reformed violence was already over. Contemporaries called it the Wonderyear.

The troubles in the Netherlands shocked contemporaries because the image-breaking was so explosive and so thorough, not because it was unique. Indeed, violence directed against the inanimate symbols of the church and, on occasion, against the living defenders of the church, was a universal element in the Reformed movement. At times the violence was apparently chaotic and without focus, as in cases of murder and pillage. At other times, acts of violence were clearly motivated by political ambition; Reformers attempted to take control of local governments by maneuvering Protestants into positions of power in city councils or by subsidizing members of the Protestant nobility who recruited mercenary armies to fight for the Reformed cause. But the most characteristic form of religious violence among Protestants was iconoclasm, the destruction of the images of Catholic worship. Image-breaking occurred wherever the Reformed movement had penetrated. Some iconoclasts were government officials upholding the law, as in Zurich; some were lawbreakers with no formal connections to the Reformed leadership, as in France. But whatever the position of individual Reformers regarding the legality of religious violence, the destruction of religious art was a clear expression of the spiritual goals of the movement.

To the ordinary layman, whether participant or witness to the destruction, image-breaking was less the expression of a religious principle than an act to test the claims of the ministers against the magical efficacy of the church's ornaments and rituals. Certainly, many people had exaggerated ideas about the magic the priests were able to perform. Some thought that they used magic powders and strange objects to ward off the devil. Under one altar the iconoclasts discovered a number of vases filled with powders, raisins, and other objects which they took to be the equipment of sorcerers; they believed that these objects explained the numerous signs of the cross made by the priest in case the demon was nearby and could not be intimidated by a single sign. It was also rumored that the clergy practiced black magic.

Some said that the hangman was regularly summoned to the Dominican cloister, where he decapitated people who were brought there in secret; others said the monasteries housed torture instruments, secret jails, and other horrors.[4] Marcus van Vaernewijck, a Catholic burgher of Ghent, discounted these reports as superstition, but he agreed that the priests simulated miracles in order to increase their revenues.[5]

Iconoclasm must have given immense vicarious satisfaction to those who were convinced that the priests were evil magicians. They must have felt that the new ministers had finally proved their superiority by demolishing the appurtenances of the Catholic stronghold without being destroyed in a burst of heavenly lightning.[6] This was, after all, the method used by medieval jurists to verify evidence; since God always protected the innocent, it made eminent sense to subject the accused to torture or trial by ordeal in order to elicit the truth. The iconoclasts dealt the same way with the images; not only did they break them to pieces, but they selectively "tortured" them by breaking off noses, heads, and limbs.[7] The iconoclasts treated the images as filth, as polluting elements that were to be given a function fitting to their nature. In the villages of East Flanders, one iconoclast stole a mass book and used the pages to wrap herbs and powders; another took home a three-dimensional picture of Christ which he used as a pig trough.[8]

In short, while acts of iconoclasm may have been triggered by hostility toward the clergy as a privileged social group, by persecution by the authorities, or by hunger, the specific goal of breaking images was to disprove the church's spiritual authority; it was more satisfying to urinate in the Communion wine cup than to pawn it. Thus the iconoclasts at Ghent hurled a statue of Saint Maurice into the river and watched it sink, crying, "Look, look, this is a miracle! Although completely armed, this saint still knows how to swim!"[9] And the Protestants who murdered the baker in St. Médard's church in Paris ridiculed their victim: "Does your god of paste protect you now from the pains of death?" In breaking down images and attacking members of the Catholic church, the iconoclasts in both countries were demonstrating in the most irrefutable and dramatic way possible that churches or statues of saints were not beloved of God, since God had not chosen to save them from destruction. The violence of the image-breakers must have expressed the feelings of those who were not avowed Calvinists of disequilibrium or anxiety about the real source of religious truth, an anxiety that must have been intensified when the symbols of the Catholic gods were tested and found to be nothing more than pieces of painted wood. "These changes, so radical and so sudden, terrified many people, to the point where they cried out, And the air doesn't change! finding it unbearable that God had not seen fit to show signs of His anger . . . Others became sick; men and women passed the nights sighing and weeping, wringing their hands."[10] At the same time, iconoclasm verified the superiority of the Reformers' miraculous powers, since the ministers were able to commit scandalous actions against the church and remain unpunished; in the autumn of 1566 one worshiper pulled the grass from the spot a preacher had been standing on and took it home as a relic.[11]

Since religious violence had very great significance in the minds of contemporaries, it is surprising that there was so little of it. One of the strangest aspects of the iconoclasm in the Netherlands, despite its explosive character, was the passivity of the masses; only a small number of people actually took part—a few hundred at most, in the biggest cities—while the masses observed these events without taking action either to prevent or to assist the image-breakers. "For that when they entered into some churches [there were not] above ten to twelve that spoiled . . . but there were many in the church looking on. . . . This thing was done so quiet and so still, as if there had been nothing ado in the churches; all men standing before their doors in harness, looking upon these fellows passing from church to church, who as they passed through the streets, required all men to be quiet."[12] In Basel and Wittenberg, in contrast, iconoclasm was committed by the mass of the population, and in France contemporaries referred to the crowds of image-breakers who terrorized the Catholic populace.[13] Equally important are the striking differences in the quality of violence in France and in the Netherlands. The day after the iconoclasm began in West Flanders, Richard Clough wrote, "As far as I can learn, these matters will break out, and that out of hand. God be merciful unto them, and to us all. For and if they do once begin, it will be a bloodie time; for it is marvelous to see how the common people are bent against the papists."[14] But there was no "bloodie time." With rare exceptions, violence in the Netherlands was perpetrated solely against images; almost no violence was done to people, even to members of the hated Catholic clergy. Many people undoubtedly loathed the clergy, but their attacks on priests were verbal, not physical. As one Catholic witness remarked, "It has been said that the Calvinists killed a hundred priests in the city, cutting some of them to pieces, and burning others over a slow fire. I remember very well everything which happened on that abominable day, and I can affirm that not a single priest was injured."[15] In France, on the other hand, violence against images was accompanied by atrocities against both the Catholic clergy and innocent Catholic bystanders.[16] The quotations that introduce this essay describe similar activities, the desecration of the symbols of Catholic worship. But the incident in France culminated in a murder; that in the Netherlands ended in the crowd's quiet departure. In sum, the violence in the Netherlands was both more limited and more refined than elsewhere; in France the violence was more obscene.

This absence of widespread participation and personal or random violence is especially curious because of the degree of anticlerical and iconoclastic activity in the years before 1566 and because the iconoclasm came after almost three months of public preaching in which the ministers spoke against idolatry and evils of the Roman clergy to audiences of several thousand. It becomes more curious when we realize that in many cases the iconoclasts were drunk; numerous contemporary accounts speak of people breaking into wine and beer cellars in the cloisters and wading up to their ankles in drink: "The wine confused their senses and made them deaf."[17] The absence of violence seems even stranger when the troubles of 1566 are compared with the behavior of the Reformers only six years later. In 1572, when the Beggar chiefs entered a city, they guaranteed the lives and goods of ecclesiastics—and then proceeded to murder the priests and expel the magistrates.[18]

But, having observed this absence of violence, both in degree and in kind, does it not remain true that acts of ritualized violence were the most striking and therefore the most significant aspect of the Troubles? Given the modern historian's predilection for analyzing movements of social protest, it would seem natural to assume that the violence was an important indicator of mass sentiment and that the positive gestures of outrage, not their absence, need to be explained. Thus one historian, ignoring the fact that the iconoclasm was committed by only a few people, demonstrates that these few belonged to the lower classes.[19] He identifies the interests of these image-breakers as "lower-class interests"—the desire to express hostility against the wealthy clergy—and concludes that the images in the churches did not appear to these people as religious idols, but as symbols of the social and economic establishment in its most sacred form. These arguments seem to me to be somewhat beside the point. They do not explain why so little was stolen, especially in an area like Ghent, where there had been a grain riot the day before the iconoclasm, nor do they explain why so little violence was done to persons.[20] Finally, they do not explain the *absence* of activity by almost everyone. And this certainly is the point to be explained; for even if every iconoclast in Ghent belonged to the lower classes, that does not mean that the iconoclasm was a lower-class movement, since over 99 percent of the lower class declined to participate in it.

I think that this negative aspect of the Troubles requires attention at least as much as the positive and more easily discernible feature of violence, even though it is far more difficult to explain why people did not do things than why they did. For the fact is that in the Netherlands, violence was not a mass exercise. There was no aggressive attack against priests, magistrates, or images. Certainly the Reformers were capable of violence, as they demonstrated only two years later, when three priests were murdered in the Flemish town of Reninghelst.[21] And certainly there were differences in the patterns of violence between one area and another. But violence done to persons was not an element of the appeal of Calvinism as a mass movement. Priests were not mutilated or murdered, nor was a significant portion of the church's property stolen in 1566; the violence began only after the mass movement had been totally suppressed and punished.

Clearly, the main characteristic of the Troubles as a mass movement was not the iconoclasm but the public preaching that preceded it; for while the iconoclasts numbered only a few hundred, audiences at the hedgepreaching, or *prêche*, were usually estimated to be over ten thousand. The congregation would assemble in the fields outside town and group themselves in order around the minister, who would conduct the service: sermon, sacraments, marriages, the distribution of alms, and —what was most striking to contemporary observers—the singing of biblical psalms.[22] These religious services and the singing and display of armed strength that accompanied them attracted the mass of the population, and so it would be logical to direct our attention to the *prêche* as the real expression of mass sentiment during the Troubles.

But does it make sense to examine the hedgepreaching in this way? The *prêche*, after all, was not a spontaneous riot but an organized meeting with a preconceived agenda; how can it be described as an expression of popular feeling? If hedgepreaching is taken as evidence of religious sentiment, whose sentiments do we mean? Since the *prêche* was led by the ministers, it seems reasonable to assume that the meetings took the form they did because the ministers structured them; far from being a spontaneous collective demonstration, the hedgepreaching may have been the product of the ministers' charismatic authority and powers of manipulation. If this was the case, we should be able to explain the popularity of the hedgepreaching by reference to the personality and goals of the Reformed clergy.

Most observers would probably accept this definition of the relationship between charismatic leaders and their followers without argument. Max Weber described charismatic authority as something imposed from above: the leader stands above and outside the social order, and he changes the course of social development by his introduction of a unique and original message. "The natural leaders in distress have been holders of specific gifts of the body and spirit; and these gifts have been believed to be supernatural, not accessible to everybody. . . . The holder of charisma seizes the task that is adequate for him and demands obedience and a following by virtue of his mission. . . . It is the duty of those to whom he addresses his mission to recognize him as their charismatically qualified leader."[23] Thus the audiences at the hedgepreaching were somehow *forced* to recognize the authority of the ministers; they did not choose their own patterns of behavior.

Given what we know about the ministers' performance, Weber's definition of charismatic authority seems to make a good deal of sense as an explanation of the Troubles. Public preaching was a relatively conservative way of expressing religious sentiment, compared to the mass riots that occurred in France, and as a group, the Netherlands ministers tended to be far less radical than their French colleagues. Witnesses of the hedgepreaching agreed that the sermons were not seditious. The preachers attacked idol worship and the practices of the Roman clergy, but they also offered prayers for the king.[24] They did not promise an apocalyptic reversal of fortune or the coming of an earthly or heavenly utopia, nor did they titillate their audiences with miraculous demonstrations of their superior powers as the Anabaptists had done at Münster. When their detractors complained that the preachers did not perform miracles, the ministers answered that the true miracle was the simple Word of God and the moral improvement of society.[25] A few ministers did participate in the iconoclasm and many preached immediately before or after the violence; but all repudiated the image-breaking in public, and all claimed to act with the express approval of the Catholic high nobility.[26]

Weber's theory of charisma seems to provide an acceptable explanation of popular behavior in 1566: the relative restraint of the crowds was apparently an act of obedience to their leaders, an imitation of the ministers' own restraint. But if the Troubles are explained by an analysis of the leaders, it is not enough to show that both leaders and followers acted in similar ways; we must establish that the conditions for the exercise of charismatic authority, as Weber saw it, actually did exist, that these leaders were in total control of the people they were supposedly manipulating. But did the ministers really have a "unique and original message"? And were they really in a position to "demand obedience by virtue of [their] mission"? What was the actual extent of Reformed organization and propaganda in the Netherlands in the years before the Troubles?

The Reformed leaders did not attract and hold a following by virtue of their original message.[27] It was not the novelty of the Calvinists' theological doctrines that made the Reformed ministers so attractive to the followers of the hedgepreaching. Popular Reformed theology, as it was purveyed in catechisms, psalms, and the hedgepreaching itself, was probably indistinguishable from the anticlerical, Erasmian sentiments that had been presented for years in the plays of the Chambers of Rhetoric. The Reformed preachers exhorted their followers to a life of ethical behavior and trust in God. They emphasized the power and mercy of Christ and attacked the cult of the saints as idolatry and the Catholic clergy as idol worshipers, as did the plays of the Chambers of Rhetoric.[28] Almost every play written during the 1560s was anti-Roman, and several were openly sympathetic with the Reformers; in one play the Jewish nation was identified with the church and the heathens with Catholic idolaters, and the words of the prophet were spoken by a "preacher."[29] In another the curtain opened on a scene of a painter finishing his work. A man entered, obviously a Protestant, who became violently angry about "these paintings which God forbids."[30] Several of the more notorious plays were either printed whole or transformed into popular ballads; they provided an excellent introduction to the principles and the slogans that were later applauded with much enthusiasm at the hedgepreaching.[31]

Thus the theology presented by the Reformed ministers did not burst upon the average layman with the force of prophecy; nor was it noticeably different from the doctrines preached by the Lutherans and Anabaptists. In both cases, popular preaching centered positively on the omnipotence and mercy of Christ and negatively on the evils of the Roman clergy. In 1563 a priest at Kiel, later condemned as a Lutheran, spoke to his congregation about the sins of man. By trusting in the priests, he said, the sinful man has only half of God; he must give himself wholly to Christ, for only Christ and the sacraments can save him: "Christ is the honest shepherd. It is He we must follow. There are many wolves and tyrants who would lead us from Him to idolatry. . . . Jezebel persecuted the truth and the prophets of truth. . . . There are the Jesuits or Jezebelites, who hide behind the pillars with their books and paternosters, to keep our Lord from hearing anything else." The preacher compared the lambs of Christ, who need no other advocates, with priests and Pharisees; many heathens wear the clerical habit, he said, but they are all hypocrites.[32]

The theology of the Anabaptists was different from that of the Calvinists and Lutherans concerning the doctrines of baptism and the incarnation of Christ. But the Anabaptists in the southern provinces were similar to the "magisterial" Reformers in their rejection of chiliastic beliefs and in their emphasis on ethical behavior. "Through the Word of God you receive godly senses that are exercised to discern both good and evil, for the holy Scriptures testify to God's goodness, and make the ignorant . . . wise to fear God . . . and do good."[33] Their notion of the priesthood was radically different from that of the Catholics, but not from that of the Calvinists. According to one Anabaptist minister, Jacob de Rore, Christ was the only high priest; before Him all men are equal in authority.[34]

It would be foolish to belabor the similarities of theology among Protestant groups in the Netherlands; certainly the Anabaptists gladly went to the stake to affirm the integrity of their doctrines against the challenges of both Catholics and Calvinists. My point, however, is that the theological doctrines of the Mennonites would not have impressed outsiders as being radically different from those of other Protestant groups. These Anabaptists were not anarchistic, nor did they prophesy the coming of an apocalypse.[35] And the average Catholic layman probably found the idea of spiritual regeneration by adult baptism a good deal more palatable than the Calvinist doctrine of predestination. Or perhaps the average layman was merely indifferent to these theological differences; the Catholic van Vaernewijck certainly thought so: "If the Anabaptists . . . the Martinists or the Libertines had come here to spread their propaganda, they would surely have attracted as many partisans as the Calvinists. One can see this at Antwerp, where some follow Calvin [and] some Luther. . . . The Calvinist preachers haven't produced any new doctrines . . . only the lesson of the Apostles."[36]

When the Calvinist pastor Gaspar van der Heyden arrived in Antwerp as a religious refugee, he saw his host reading the Bible late at night and knew immediately that he was a member of the Reformed community. Adherence to Scripture was probably the most obvious and popular definition of Protestant worship, particularly since the ministers of every confession continually challenged each other to public debates in which the one with the greater knowledge of Scripture would be declared the "winner," the bearer of religious truth. The Reformed ministers added particular nuances to this basic definition of Protestantism, but it was not their theology that made them leaders of a mass movement.

A more common explanation for the ministers' apparent control of their mass audience is the success of Calvinist methods of organization. Indeed, simply to say that the ministers were Calvinist is sufficient to conjure an image of a fanatically dedicated party member, an obedient official in the Calvinist system, a participant in consistories, colloquies, synods, and international debates—a servant of Geneva. The mystique of the Calvinist genius for organization extends to every level of religious activity. One historian remarks that whereas Anabaptist conventicles were small meetings for sympathetic listeners, the Calvinist conventicles were formal religious services. The life of a believing Calvinist, he writes, was comparable to that of a cloistered monk: "His rule of life in the cloister had the same charismatic quality as discipline in the Calvinist community."[37]

The ministers who preached in the years before the troubles would probably not have recognized themselves in this description. The Calvinists had more sophisticated methods of ecclesiastical organization and a larger and more disciplined pastorate than the Lutherans, and they enjoyed greater prestige among Reformers than the Mennonites. But there were too few ordained pastors, who were trained in too many different Reformed centers, to make an overall network of consistories, with a shared system of ecclesiastical government, feasible at this time. The cities of Antwerp, Tournai, and Valenciennes had had consistories since the 1540s; in these centers of the Reformed movement, consecrated pastors were almost continuously active in the years before the hedgepreaching. But in the smaller cities and in communities where the Inquisition was powerful, the Reformers' activities were superficial and intermittent. Breda, for example, was served primarily by one Lodewijck de Voghele, who had failed the examination for ordination at Emden. The only other ministers who visited Breda before the hedgepreaching were Jan Lippens, a lay preacher, and François du Jon, a pastor from Antwerp; both appeared—and departed—in 1565.[38] The smaller towns of East Flanders were sometimes visited by ministers from Ghent and Antwerp; the villages of Axel and Hulst once welcomed Pieter Hazard, who conducted a Communion service and discussed the Netherlands Confession of Faith. But the main source of spiritual enlightenment for these communities was a merchant named Jan Claeyssone, who had established relations with the mother church at Antwerp and continued to practice his trade while serving as an itinerant preacher in the area. There is no evidence of a local consistory, and the majority of believers remained Catholic in name.

Calvinist discipline did not exist before 1566,[39] partly because of the increase in persecution in the three years before the troubles. In most cities Reformers were active in the early 1560s, even conducting public services; but the Reformers were forced underground after 1563, and several pastors who had been active in the early years of the movement were in exile during the period immediately before 1566; to my knowledge, only nine consecrated pastors were continuously active in the southern provinces in the three years before the Troubles.[40] Undoubtedly these pastors were successful in introducing Calvinist doctrines into communities where the people had rejected Catholic rituals and attended occasional meetings to discuss Scripture. But it is hard to believe that this network of Reformed communities and the secret conventicles that sustained them in the years before the Troubles can really be called a Calvinist underground. An underground may have existed in the minds of the ministers in exile who corresponded with consistories at home, but it did not exist on the popular level outside the major Reformed centers. In many cases, Calvinist consistories were introduced only after the Troubles had begun and the Calvinists had been accorded the right to preach in public. If this was true in an important city like Ypres, it was undoubtedly true in smaller communities where connections with the Reformed movement had been sporadic. In these instances, it seems, Calvinist organization did not cause the success of the hedgepreaching and the iconoclasm; on the contrary, the success of the hedgepreaching and the iconoclasts enabled the Reformers to introduce the structure and practices of organized Calvinism into numerous towns and villages where Calvinist discipline was known only by repute.

This lack of extensive organization before 1566 was not only caused by pressure from without; it was also a product of the ministers' confusion about their own status, both within the Reformed community and in relation to the local government. For these ministers were in no sense a unified corps of pastors; they were not shock troops dispatched by Calvin to foment religious revolution, like the Huguenot ministers in

France. On the contrary, the Netherlands ministers were divided on almost every conceivable issue. They spoke two different languages. They had been educated in different countries, and they turned for guidance to different mother churches that often disagreed among themselves; Calvin advocated compromise with the Lutherans, while the Emden church opposed it, and Beza's hostility to the notion of compromise paralyzed the ministers even after they had managed to formulate a unified policy toward the Lutherans in 1564.[41] At home the ministers were forced to rely on lay preachers to assist their efforts, preachers whose activities sometimes jeopardized the entire movement. The persecution of 1563–66 was a result of public demonstrations conducted chiefly by these lay preachers, without the approval of the leading pastors.[42] In exile, dispersed among refugee churches in England, Germany, France, and Switzerland, the ministers were treated with hostility by both Lutherans and Catholics, who identified them with the radical Netherlands Anabaptists at Münster. But while they were united in their adherence to the Reformed movement and in their eagerness to return home, the ministers were uncertain whether they were returning as loyalists or as rebels; for like everyone else, they were ignorant of the king's real intentions toward religious dissidents.

The ministers therefore became defensive.[43] They argued incessantly among themselves about questions of authority—their authority to punish members of the community, their authority to act independent of the mother churches, and their authority to commit violence. The ministers' public behavior was also defensive. Their pretensions to membership in an international elite made them strive to act dignified rather than theatrical, and they were supremely concerned to assert their moral superiority over both the priests, whom they regarded as corrupt magicians, and the Anabaptists, whom they feared as anarchists. This concern for moral legitimacy was reinforced by pressures from outside the Reformed community. In exile, they had little claim to the loyalties of the Netherlands nobility and no claim to the favor of the crown, and yet they wished that both the nobility and the crown should welcome them home.

All of this does not mean that the Reformed movement was unpopular; the eagerness of local Reformers to welcome ministers from Antwerp or Tournai is clear evidence of the movement's early success outside the main centers of Calvinist worship. It does mean that the organization of Calvinist churches in the Netherlands was less extensive than contemporaries supposed and that the degree of organization and discipline that existed was not sufficient to explain the sudden success of the public preaching in 1566. Calvinist organization does not explain why so many people were inspired by Reformed services, why the popular, clandestine Reformed movement became a mass movement. Indeed, by voting to begin public preaching after the Lutherans had already begun public preaching in Flanders and Antwerp, the Antwerp consistory could hardly claim to have led a Calvinist conspiracy to introduce Reformed worship in the Netherlands.[44]

How, then, and to what degree, did the Reformed ministers influence behavior during the Troubles? Granted that the Calvinists were better organized than the Lutherans and Anabaptists and possessed greater unity and fervor than either of these groups, it is still fair to say that the image of the actual unity and power of the Netherlands Calvinist elite that has been presented both by contemporaries and by most modern scholars is exaggerated. These exaggerated claims for the authority of the Reformed leadership have been sustained, I think, largely because of the basic assumptions that have been made about the relationship between charismatic leaders and their followers. Most observers have accepted Weber's notion that charisma is somehow embodied in an extraordinary leader, a man of apparently supernatural gifts, and they have tried to account for the success of the Calvinist movement by discovering what these gifts were; hence their interest in Calvinist theology and methods of organization and their willingness to attribute greater powers of communication and discipline to the ministers than they actually possessed. My own study of these leaders has shown that the interests of the ministers seemed to parallel the behavior of the crowd, but I have been unable to determine in what way the ministers actually caused this behavior.

A more recent and, I think, more acceptable theory of the nature of charisma has been advanced by the anthropologist Peter Worsley. Worsley rejects Weber's notion that the exercise of public authority is a one-way process—a charismatic leader acting upon a passive audience. In many cases, he observes, charismatic authority may be diffused among several leaders. More important, in order for the message of the leader to be accepted, it must reflect what people already hope to hear; in a fundamental sense the message is imposed from below, not from above: "Followers . . . cleave to an appropriate leader because he articulates and consolidates their aspirations."[45] Worsley uses the example of soapbox orators in Hyde Park: one becomes a popular leader while another is called a crackpot, but this is only partly because the first man is a better speaker or conveys a more potent message; it is also because he speaks to some need already present in the minds of his listeners.

How can Worsley's theory of charisma be applied to the phenomenon of the hedgepreaching? Instead of simply assuming the charismatic superiority of the Calvinist ministers over other potential leaders, we should assume that people listened to the Calvinists because they saw in the Reformed movement something they wanted very much to see. If the hedgepreaching was not hysterical, if the ministers were not flamboyant, if there was no revival of the apocalyptic millennarian craze of the 1530s, this was only partly because Calvinist theology forbade such practices. It was also because the people sought other means of self-expression; they accepted Calvinist leaders, and not other leaders who were more or less radical, because the Calvinist message was an articulation of their own anxieties and aspirations. In this context it becomes less important to examine the ministers' objective qualities—their theology, their connections, their methods of organization—and more important to examine the society in which both leaders and followers lived and tried to survive.

Every student of Netherlands society is well aware that during the mid-sixteenth century, political authority had utterly broken down. Margaret of Parma, the king's deputy in the Netherlands, was an ineffectual regent; Granvelle, her counselor, was forced out of power by the nobility in 1564, and Philip himself had not set foot in the Netherlands for over five years. His letters came sporadically, and when he did send instructions to the regent she had no means of enforcing them, for she in turn depended upon the great nobles whom, unfortunately, she did not trust.

The great nobles had traditionally acted as mediators between the cities and provincial estates on the one hand and the royal government on the other. But during the 1560s many no longer consented to function as executors of the royal will. Not only had they resented Granvelle's attempts to control the government without consulting them; they also resented Philip's efforts to control religious practice through his institution of the new bishoprics and the Inquisition. And because the nobles were unwilling to function as obedient servants of the king and as active governors on their own lands, the town magistrates, whether Catholic or Calvinist, had no confidence in their authority or physical power to effect the policy of the regent; certainly they were unable to suppress or to moderate the activities of the Reformers with any consistency.

This virtual absence of political authority in the period before the Troubles was even more painfully evident during the hedgepreaching, when local magistrates found themselves utterly unable to intimidate the Reformers. Listen to Richard Clough, an Englishman writing home from Antwerp on 22 July: "There was a proclamation that no man should go to the sermons upon pain of hanging, whereupon on Sunday went out of the town to the sermon above sixteen thousand persons; and so, after the sermon, [they] returned to the town and went to the high bailiff's house, and commanded him to deliver a prisoner; which he refused. Whereupon they went to the prison and broke it, and delivered the preacher; and so everyone departed."[46]

When the Prince of Orange arrived in Antwerp to restore order, he found the city full of mutual enemies:

For the magistrates did put no trust in the burgesses, and much less in them of the [Reformed] religion. On the other side, the inhabitants . . . distrusted the Court and much more their magistrates. Then they of the religion feared and distrusted, not only the Court and the magistrates, but also all the members of the town, and what is more, they were jealous of one another, they of the Confession of Augsburg on the one side, and those of the Reformed religion on the other.[47]

But when Orange wrote to Margaret asking for authorization of a lieutenant to take his place, she deferred the matter. And during the iconoclasm the Antwerp magistrate fled to the city hall while the cathedral was sacked; as one witness tersely put it, "The Margrave came into the church with half a dozen men, who being willed to leave, stayed not." The response of the nobility was even less strident; in October, the count of Hornes wrote to the king that he simply had no idea what to do.[48]

In short, the Calvinists were active in a society where the breakdown in the lines of authority was so extreme that van Vaernewijck, himself a magistrate, believed that it was a sign from God. "When God . . . wishes to inflict some calamity on a country, city, village or family, he blinds the wise and experienced leaders, and makes them grope about in broad daylight as if they were in shadow."[49] A Spanish adviser, writing to Philip about the breakdown in the chain of authority between the king and his subjects, called the Netherlands "a body without a head."[50] And a Catholic academic, speaking at Louvain in 1565, already envisioned the collapse of universal order: "How is it that all things are done in a confused tumulte, nothinge advisedly and in order? That the highest and lowest without distinction are mingled and ruffled together? That cold and heate, drowthe and moisture strive and contend with continual discord."[51]

What was the significance of this breakdown of authority, this "continual discord" which contemporaries perceived in society, in religion, in government, and in nature itself? Two points are obvious. First, there was a surprising similarity in the behavior exhibited by Catholics and Protestants. Both groups seem to have felt inhibited about the use of violence. Much as the Calvinists valued the opportunity to effect a spiritual revolution, they were unwilling to kill priests; much as the Catholics dreaded the destruction of the established order, they were unwilling to massacre Protestants. Thus it was not simply a matter of the Calvinists choosing to behave peaceably because of their theology or their leadership; probably the Calvinists would have been far more violent in their behavior if the Catholic soldiers who appeared at the *prêches* had fired into the crowd or arrested the ministers—but this seldom happened. In France the Huguenots at Sens held a public *prêche* after obtaining letters of safeguard and a captain to protect them; the crowd was massacred by Catholics.[52] At Tournai, the crowd attending a *prêche* on 3 July returned quietly to the city, "And the other workers gave them no hindrance, nor did they pour forth insults or sharp words, which was much the contrary of what happened to them . . . [in] France . . . where similar *prêches* were held in the fields and outside the cities." The witness remarks that in France the Huguenots were often massacred on the way home.[53]

Some observers have explained this Catholic passivity as evidence of their indifference to the fate of the Roman clergy and their sympathy with the Reformed movement; but if this were so, then it is hard to understand why the Calvinists were not doubly successful in taking over the churches and obtaining official and exclusive recognition of the Reformed cult. Certainly my original hypothesis—that the behavior of the crowd was determined by the policy of their charismatic leaders—is even less useful as an explanation of this general behavior, since the Catholic bystanders were presumably not affected by the ministers at all. It would make far greater sense to assume that if the behavior of Catholics and Protestants differed so little, the two groups must have been acting from similar motivations.

The second observation that should be made about the behavior of Catholics and Calvinists is that the ideal of legitimacy was tremendously important to both groups. I have already discussed the ministers' concern to establish their authority both within the Reformed community and in relation to the society at large. But the Calvinists were not the only ones who talked about the duties owed to the magistrate or the need for a legal mandate to take violent action; the Catholics also expressed anxiety about questions of public authority—but their problem was not so much to establish their relationship to the government as to discover why the sources of public authority seemed to have evaporated.

Many observers, both contemporary and modern, have offered excellent explanations for the violence that occurred in 1566: the spiritual goals of the Calvinists, the popular hatred of the Catholic priesthood and the Inquisition, and increasing economic hardship. But the expression of this violent activity seems to have been constantly inhibited on both sides; and this absence of extreme violence can be explained only if we grant that the desire to act legitimately was more important to many people than the desire to express anger against the Catholics or allegiance to the Protestants—or simply to attack the rich. The behavior of contemporaries during the troubles becomes understandable if we take them at their word rather than assuming that their protestations of loyalty to the government were rationalizations for more devious or radical motives. For the fact is that while all groups may have been willing to acquiese in the destruction of the churches, none were willing to assume the initiative and to exercise public authority in a crisis: the magistrates because they had no noble mandate to do so, the nobles because they were unsure of Philip's position, the ministers because they had based their entire authority to act as spiritual leaders on their alliance with the nobility and their loyalty to the crown.

But what about the average man or woman? Surely the ordinary person was far less affected by the breakdown of local government and the absence of the king than those groups in society who were actively involved in government and social control. Since my object is to understand the Troubles as a mass movement, how can it be determined that these political factors actually caused *popular* behavior more than, say, the rising cost of food? My argument is that the breakdown of political authority had a very great negative effect on every person in the Netherlands because society had not become polarized into hostile parties; it had become fragmented into an infinite number of groups with confused loyalties, and hence the adherents of any one group—whether political or economic or religious—could not amass a large, united following or view the other half of society as an enemy to be exterminated. In short, the political breakdown of Netherlands society effectively short-circuited the attempts of isolated groups—whether workers, nobles, or Calvinist radicals—to incite a violent mass movement, and the very real economic frustration which the average person suffered was not articulated in any strong collective action. Economic grievances might have created a general disposition to engage in some form of collective activity, but in fact there was little reflection of that kind of concern in the religious violence that did occur. The evidence of popular behavior during the Troubles might have indicated that the ordinary person was not willing to do violence against his enemies, even when these were made of wood, without the apparent sanction of the constituted authorities.

Hence the character of the iconoclasm was strangely limited. The ministers always defended the violence as legitimate, dictated by the nobles or by the court. At Hulst, Gaspar van der Heyden sent two delegates to the city hall with a list of thirty people assigned to break images; the magistrates were asked to cross off those who were considered rebels.[54] At Ghent, a Calvinist appeared before the high bailiff and announced that his people were ready to destroy idols on the express orders of the count of Egmont. The mob proceeded to a church, where one of the group knocked down a statue of Christ. "That's clear enough!" the people cried. "In breaking images like that, we are executing the orders of the high bailiff!"[55] At Poperinge, the minister Sebastien Matte stood before his congregation with a letter that sanctioned acts of iconoclasm; the letter, he assured them, bore the seal of Philip II.[56] At Tournai, the ministers declared that since they were under the protection of the no-

bility, "therefore [the iconoclasm] must be attributed to the said nobles."
Of course, the ministers had no royal mandate to break images. But
whether or not they believed they were telling the truth is irrelevant; the
point is that they were regarded by the general public as emissaries of the
government. "Things reached the point," wrote van Vaernewijck, "that,
of one hundred persons, there was barely one who didn't imagine that
the iconoclasm was ordained and determined by the magistrates."[57]

The Catholics did little to stop the violence. The magistrates and the
majority of the populace may have been horrified by the image-breaking,
and they were not willing to commit violence on their own account; certainly the magistrates and bourgeois citizens would have been reluctant
to destroy church property which they themselves had donated. On the
other hand, they were anxious to believe that a higher magistrate in
Brussels was actually issuing commands for them to follow, and many
Catholics were clearly not averse to watching the destruction of the symbols of clerical authority. Van Vaernewijck, describing the iconoclasm in
West Flanders, observed that a number of Catholics watched the burning
of an important relic, refusing to compromise themselves to help the
Catholic clergy. He adds that they believed that since the authorities did
nothing, the court must have secretly supported the Reformers.[58] And in
fact, certain nobles had assisted at the iconoclasm; the most notorious
was the count of Culembourg, who fed the Host to his parrot.

Perhaps more important, the actual violence committed in the
churches showed almost no evidence of hostility toward the upper
classes. The facts indicate that the opposite was the case; the iconoclasm,
among other things, reflected popular respect for the nobility. Almost no
one proposed to attack the sepulchers of the nobles or the houses of the
rich. Tombs were damaged, but there was, to my knowledge, only one
instance of a noble corpse being disinterred and mutilated.[59] At Ghent,
the iconoclasts, like executioners, broke off the heads of the statues, but
no one dared to touch the pedestal that supported the lions and insignia
of the Toison d'Or. Compare this with the behavior of the image-breakers
in France, who systematically desecrated the bodies they uncovered in
the churches.[60]

Popular anxiety about questions of authority not only determined
these negative aspects of the Troubles; it also determined why people
looked to the Reformed ministers as the ideal type of public leader.
Nearly everyone seemed to believe in the invincibility of the Reformed
clergy. After the iconoclasm, van Vaernewijck observed that the ministers, instigators of all the evil, were not arrested. He attributed this to
influences emanating from the court protecting the preachers. Clearly
people exaggerated the powers of the Reformed ministers because they
wanted to believe in the existence of a genuine center of authority. But

they also wanted to believe that this authority was legitimate; they did not idealize their leaders as revolutionaries. The fulfillment the ministers offered their followers was not a new theology or the promise of liberation from political oppression or from the taxes of the Catholic clergy; least of all was it the possibility of revolution. The ministers offered their audience a sense of restored authority, of the ideal reintegration of society at a time when society seemed to be falling apart. The Calvinist preachers were seen as the providers of this new spiritual, social, and political authority not because they were really able to take control, either through the inspiration of their theology, their advanced methods of organization, or their alliance with the Protestant nobility, but because they were extraordinarily concerned to assert their own authority, both within their own consistories and in relation to the outside world. The Calvinists, as we have seen, were preoccupied with questions of legality, and they were concerned above all to present themselves as members of a legitimate, orderly reform movement. This concern was reflected in their propaganda, which was legalistic in tone; the ministers demanded the removal of the Inquisition because it was an outrage against local privileges. More important, the ministers went to great lengths to publicize their connections with the nobility and with Reformed leaders abroad. Thus, while the Lutherans may have had more actual ties to the centers of political power in the Netherlands, the Calvinist ministers communicated an image of importance and legitimacy much more effectively.

In analyzing the popularity of the Reformed ministers, we should remember that the choice of these men as leaders of a mass movement was not inevitable. The ministers and their consistories were not powerful enough to organize and sustain a movement of this kind, and even if they were, it is certainly possible that other, more radical leaders could have appeared on the fringes of the movement as time went on. It is in this context that we should consider the behavior of the 149 lay preachers who were active in the southern provinces during the Troubles. The lay preachers were not members of the Calvinist elite, trained in a particular theology and discipline. Most had never preached before, and the great majority, according to contemporary records, never preached again.[61] These were obscure laymen, mainly from the Flemish working class, who responded spontaneously to Reformed propaganda and to the preaching of the Reformed ministers; many had formed part of the ministers' audience during the early summer. Hence their behavior as preachers may be viewed as a reflection of the attitudes of Netherlands society —more accurately, of the more discontented elements of that society. It may also be viewed as an indication of the fulfillment that many ordinary people hoped to gain by their participation in the Reformed movement.

Judging from their outward behavior, the lay preachers were not attracted to the Reformed movement from a desire for personal attention or to express their hostility to the government or to the Catholic clergy. In the first place, they were not outrageous exhibitionists. There are no reports of eccentric or hysterical behavior by the preachers; on the contrary, their impulse was apparently to imitate the behavior of the pastors in Antwerp or Tournai or Valenciennes. Thus Maurice Watelet, a weaver's son, attended a Communion service conducted by the pastor François du Jon. Later he was arrested for holding a *prêche* in the woods near his home; he had recited and then explained a psalm of David, led prayers, and read from a book of martyrs printed in England.[62] Jehan Louchard attended several meetings in Artois, where he sat as close as he could to the minister; later he went to live in La Gorgue to "instruct and entice the people."[63] A few months earlier, one Leonard Xhoka, a vicar of Limbourg, had announced to his congregation that he would no longer hold mass, saying "that he had abused the good people for a long time, praying their forgiveness, saying that he had received the holy spirit."[64] Martin de Smet also announced to his parishioners that he had been converted; weeping, he asked their pardon for not sincerely fulfilling his ministry and offered to return the money he had collected from them.[65]

Contemporaries described these lay preachers as vagabonds, implying that they were both poor and itinerant. But the records indicate that although they were poor, they moved very little; most preachers appear to have been active in only one community or in the area of one major city. More important, the most active lay preachers were also the ones who had established some contact with the organized Reformed movement. Guillaume de Hollandère left the Augustinian cloister at Ypres in August 1566 and began to preach in the area; two months later he had become *pasteur en titre* at Rousbrugge, where he stayed for several months, building his own temple with materials donated by the congregation.[66] Martin de Smet offered his services to the Antwerp church, which sent him to Mechelen in November 1566; de Smet held outdoor services and conducted negotiations with the local magistrates until February, when he was arrested and hung without trial.[67] Often the preacher was recruited by a lay Reformer who brought him to a community or he acted as a sort of backup to a more important Calvinist minister. After the iconoclasm at Limbourg, Leonard Xhoka moved into the parish church. When the pastor François du Jon arrived in October, Xhoka preached in the fields outside the city; when du Jon fled, he resumed his activities as the preeminent preacher in the town.[68]

But the most interesting fact about the behavior of the lay preachers is that only forty-five committed any violent acts during the Troubles, and of this number, thirty-nine had also established contacts with the orthodox Reformed movement. One of the most notorious preachers was a young man known only as Julien. On 10 August 1566, Julien conducted a public service in the church cemetery at Richebourg, accompanied by an armed guard of five hundred men playing tambourines and fifes. When the priest entered the pulpit to deliver his sermon, the Reformers entered the church and began to insult him. It was said that he died a month later of the shock. "And as [the priest] was consecrating the Host, the *sectaires* pronounced execrable words . . . and after the presentation they came to take the altar to divest it of its ornaments."[69] Julien was certainly no Calvinist; the Reformers who accompanied him admitted that since he was young and ignorant, one had to have patience with him.[70] But he was proud of his attachment to the Reformed community and boasted to his congregation that he had been summoned to court by the princes. In this, Julien was typical of the most radical lay preachers. Thus Jan de Vlameng broke images in Hasselt under the direction of the pastor Herman Moded. And Mailgaert de Hongère, who led an abortive invasion of the city of Ypres, was consecrated in 1566 by the minister Pieter Hazard.

This general absence of violent behavior on the part of the lay preachers is curious. The popular response to the Calvinist ministers might have been expected to trigger a second, less restrained movement led by the lay preachers, many of whom were described as very young men, and as a result of their activities the iconoclasm might have become more violent, more formless, certainly more prolonged, than it actually was. But to assume that the restraint of the lay preachers derived from their dedication to Calvinism would be wrong. The lay preachers may have attended synods, dealt with local magistrates, and helped to organize consistories, but few had any prolonged training in Reformed doctrines. Indeed, in many cases the consistories seemed to have controlled the lay preachers. Julien's relationship to the Reformers who accompanied him was probably of this nature; at any rate, his knowledge of Reformed doctrine was perhaps less than that of his "congregation." What did motivate these lay preachers, aside from religious conviction, was less the desire for personal attention than the opportunity to operate in a group and to assume a share of what many felt to be a genuinely legal, not personal authority. This hypothesis is supported by their overall patterns of behavior. There was much less movement from place to place than contemporaries supposed; even though the preachers did not all join churches, they tended to preach in one community, if only for a short time. And their general behavior was not hysterical or original but restrained and imitative; thus the vicar of Oostwinkel broke images in his own chapel because he had seen the Calvinists in Ghent do the same.[71]

The lay preachers thus enjoyed a borrowed charisma. They copied the behavior of the Reformed ministers instead of parading as demagogues or eccentrics; some, like Julien, were undoubtedly exhibitionists, but they did not, like John of Leyden, wear robes and crowns. They ridiculed the Catholic clergy, as did the pastors, but they did not molest them. This general restraint explains why the most active lay preachers were also accepted as members of the orthodox Reformed movement and why they were accepted as popular leaders in local communities. If people had been inclined to violence or revolution, they could have rejected the preaching of the Calvinist ministers and followed other leaders or they could have created their own leadership—lay preachers who ignored the pastors' exhortations to peaceable behavior and committed violence on their own authority. Thus the charisma of the ministers cannot be understood in the conventional sense of manipulating an audience or inciting a certain type of behavior. Charisma really meant popularity: the ability to articulate the sentiments of the congregation in a manner of which they themselves were incapable but with which they could completely identify. If people chose to identify with leaders who adhered to the example of more prominent ministers and who, by and large, avoided personal violence, then we may infer that they did not view the hedgepreaching as a prelude to the destruction of social institutions and political authority. For pastors and lay preachers as well as for their audience, the hedgepreaching was a ritual that symbolized the ideal, peaceful reintegration of society.

The *prêche* was essentially a socializing experience. In a sense, it was also a leveling experience, a ritual that invited the participation of all members of society on an equal footing.[72] The physical form of the *prêche* was usually a circle. At Ghent the "pulpit" was mounted on a wagon in the center of a field, and the congregation, carrying pikes and weapons, was entirely surrounded by wagons and by peddlers of forbidden books.[73] The general atmosphere was informal, even festive. At a *prêche* held at Bruges cries of "Ghent! Ghent!" or "Eekloo! Eekloo!" were heard as groups from different towns gathered under their own banners, while wagonloads of food were prepared and beer was served.[74] Two pulpits were set up in the open field, and the people camped overnight and listened for two days to sermons by four ministers, speaking in both French and Flemish. The ceremony was also cooperative and informal. At Axel, after the sermon, a child was baptized with water carried to the pulpit from a nearby stream.[75] At St. Amand, the Communion table was set with a plate of coarse bread, sliced "as if to eat eggs with," and two glasses of wine, similar to the glasses used at ordinary meals.[76] At Antwerp, the preacher distributed bread and wine to an assembly of several hundred, who stood around the Communion table, passing the sacrament from one to the other.[77] At Ghent, people formed groups of two or three hundred and walked through the streets arm in arm during the evenings to sing in unison psalms the preachers had taught them.[78]

Not only did the ministers create an atmosphere of community; they also directed their attention to the poor, the uneducated, and the degenerate members of society. At Valenciennes, the poor could receive alms denied them by the city charity laws.[79] At Ghent, benches were set aside for the children's catechism, and during the evenings there was instruction in psalmsinging. At Antwerp, the cabarets were deserted: "People of dissolute habits, notably a number of married women whose misconduct had caused a scandal, and men whose vices had caused them to be cast out by their families, threw themselves into the new party."[80]

But the ritual of the *prêche* also served to reinforce social differences. The congregation was usually seated according to sex or status in the community. An eyewitness at Ghent wrote, "The Calvinists have a certain order in their *prêches*: the women sit in the middle in a circle, fenced in by stakes . . . around them soldiers hold watch."[81] Sometimes the seats directly under the pulpit were reserved for rich tradesmen and their wives, and the entire group was surrounded and protected by armed men on horseback, who were often members of the nobility. In the town of Reckheim, near Maastricht, the minister was provided with the use of the church by the local nobleman, who attended the service, while the burghers from the city sat with their backs to the altar, like chairmen at a meeting, and remained seated even during the elevation of the Host.[82] At Culembourg, the count and his family sat next to the raised pulpit, apart from the congregation, and left by a separate door.[83] At Ghent, there seems to have been a hierarchy of preachers as well; the elite of the city followed Pieter Dathenus and Jean Micheus, who preached in the new temple, while the other ministers preached outside, to satisfy the crowd. Even the group singing was sometimes organized according to status; at Ghent, van Vaernewijck noticed a group of shoemakers returning from a *prêche*, singing and marching in unison.[84]

Thus the function of the *prêche* was not to give people a sense of equality, a feeling that social and economic barriers had been dissolved, as they might have felt at a mass rally, where the consciousness of the group is surrendered to the preaching of a demagogue. Nor did the *prêche* function as a ritual in which social roles were symbolically inverted, as in the French charivaris, where those in power or their effigies were ridiculed by those who were ordinarily deprived of power. On the contrary, at the preaching of 1566 the traditional position of social and economic groups was upheld and, with few exceptions, the personality of the minister was deemphasized; many were not even known by name.

The relationship of the phenomenon of the hedgepreaching to the larger society was ambiguous. Many people attended the *prêches*, at least in part, because they believed it was a legitimate activity. Once there, they enjoyed a sense of participation in activities that were peaceful, communal, and sanctioned by the nobility; the ritual of the *prêche*—the seating arrangement, the variety of activities, both mundane and spiritual —might be seen as a microcosm of society as a whole, but a society that was ideally integrated, as the real society of the Netherlands certainly was not. Thus Herman Moded boasted in his *Apologie*: "Then there was quarreling and disunity between man and wife . . . then there was quarreling and disunity between friends . . . with judging, haggling, deceiving. . . . Haven't we seen this wickedness stopping everywhere? . . . Where does one hear now of so many homicides, murders, robberies and thieveries, outside as well as inside the cities, as we have seen and heard of everywhere before the public teaching and exercise of the holy Evangile?"[85] At the annual religious procession at Antwerp in August 1566, the tableaux began with scenes of "Discord" and "Disorderly Nature." But there was a third display, entitled "God's Providence," which consisted of three horsemen, "Wise Counsel," "Prudent Inquiry," and "United Community." These were followed by an orator who recited a poem, telling of God's power to reconcile differences between men. Then another personage appeared, holding in one hand a flaming sword, "The Word of God," and in the other a book, "Evangelical Teaching." Then came several figures bearing biblical quotations and, finally, the figure of Grace.[86]

Conversely, the *prêche* was also a display of power. The message of the sermons, clearly reminiscent of Old Testament prophecy, was implicitly hostile to the social order, both in its anticlericalism and in its hostility to the repressive policies of the royal Inquisition. There was also an element of class hostility against the wealthy clergy; a popular song went, "You dress those wooden blocks in velvet suits, and let God's children go naked."[87] The impact of this message was intensified by the atmosphere of violence that coexisted with that of the general camaraderie, so that the group singing must have often reverberated like hymns of battle. Indeed, the scene of the hedgepreaching, wrote van Vaernewijck, looked like a battlefield: "Everywhere the eye was struck by trophies of arms as for a troop in the field."[88]

The violence remained implicit, but it was symbolic, not overt. It was expressed visually, in the aspect of weapons and armed horsemen, and verbally, in the threats uttered by both Catholics and Calvinists. Most people apparently were willing to express their hostility to the priesthood and their attraction to the new faith, but they were willing to express this hostility only in a form that demonstrated the fundamental unity of society as it had existed before the breakdown of public authority. Once aggression became overt, there was less enthusiasm for the Reformed movement. In this sense the *prêche* expressed a feeling of passivity as well as one of violence. The monk Cornelis expressed this double nature of the *prêche* when he preached to his Catholic congregation at Bruges: "Bah, see how they come here with wagons and carts, with baggage, with food . . . with pot and kettle; . . . bah, hear how they call Ghent, Ghent, Eekloo, Eekloo; bah, see how they stand there in order, as if going to the slaughter [*slacht-ordenen*], . . . bah, see [their] weapons, . . . hear how they call vive les Geus."[89] Of course, the enemies of the movement saw the hedgepreaching as seditious, and individual Reformers contemplated a transference of political power from the Catholic magistrates to the Calvinists. But the *prêche* itself did not represent a symbolic alternative to the existing political hierarchy; on the contrary, for the majority of the ministers' adherents political reality had not changed at all.

How could people have believed that the *prêche* was not seditious? In the first place, the ministers did not behave violently. Because of the magistrates' inactivity there was no need for any minister, whether moderate or radical, to consider taking violent action to defend the faith. The confederates' actions in Brussels and their occasional presence at the *prêches* gave a further stamp to the Reformers' claim to legitimacy. Most people did not know that the ministers had been unable to conclude a formal alliance with the members of the high nobility or that William of Orange had written privately that the Calvinists were not to be trusted. They saw only that the ministers were preaching peacefully, that they seemed to be having a positive effect on social behavior, and that they, more than the municipal authorities or the regent, seemed to know what they were doing. In one sense the ministers' dedication to the aggressive Reformed movement was an important reason for their success during the hedgepreaching, as long as they continued to defend law and order; they undoubtedly appeared to be more energetic than the Mennonites, who were dedicated to secrecy and the triumph of the spirit in the next world.

The government also seemed to be behaving more sympathetically toward the Reformers in 1566, and Philip was as yet an unknown quantity, so that even if there had been a popular impulse toward rebellion, there was no tangible enemy to rebel against. Moreover, while many people saw the preachers as prophets of a new spiritual order, there is no reason to believe that they viewed their attendance at the preaching as a heretical act, since the ministers' sermons invariably praised the king and since Reformed doctrines closely approximated those of the Catholic Chambers of Rhetoric. In short, many people found it possible to ignore the seditious elements in the hedgepreaching and to accept the presence of the nobles as proof that the *prêche* was, in fact, a restoration of genuine order and might even be tolerated by the court; even the Catholic burgher van Vaernewijck became more, not less, sympathetic toward the preachers as the summer wore on.

But the hedgepreaching was an illusion; the social and political conflicts were muted only temporarily. The confederates made the situation potentially explosive by pursuing an alliance with the German Lutherans and alienating themselves from the conservative high nobility; during the autumn they issued a beggar's seal, stamped with a picture of the iconoclasm. More important, the situation was explosive because of the absence of political authority and of recognized social norms. Whereas the English ministers returned home at the beginning of a period of stability, the Netherlands ministers returned home to a political vacuum. Any innovative action on their part, even a new seating arrangement at a worship service, inevitably increased the anxiety of the magistrates, who knew that they were incapable of controlling the people if violence should occur. Thus the ministers' preaching excited both fear and hope: fear that any open clash with the Roman church could not be controlled, and hope that the Reformers might be able to elevate religious life and protect the people from the Inquisition. Finally, the situation was aggravated by the Reformers' own beliefs. The ministers conveyed a sense of restored authority, but their ultimate goal was not to defend the sanctity of the renovated Catholic church but to restore a godly society that had no need of Roman Catholicism. It is by no means certain that the thousands who attended the preaching perceived this or that they would have accepted the formal institution of Calvinist worship even if it were approved by the nobility. The people might have felt both comfortable and exhilarated at the *prêches*—but not all of them were Calvinists.

The Reformers appeared to be at the height of their power in the period following the iconoclasm. At a synod held in Antwerp, delegates from all the provinces discussed the issue of resistance to the magistrate and organized a campaign to collect funds for a military treasury.[90] At Valenciennes, the Reformers took over the essential functions of local government and commenced regular preaching in the churches. At Axel and Hulst, the consistory sent to nearby communities for help in besieging the city hall and spoke about throwing the Catholics out of town.[91] But the iconoclasm not only gave the Reformers an opportunity to take over the churches; it also revealed the conflicts among the ministers, the nobility, and the conservative Catholic populace. Many members of the nobility backed away from the movement after the iconoclasm, either because they considered the violence premature or because they disapproved of the image-breaking on principle. The Lutherans, who had willingly discussed proposals for an alliance with the Calvinists, made every effort to disassociate themselves from the movement after August.[92]

When the mob at Axel and Hulst called for assistance against the magistrates, too few people came, and the siege was ended.

The iconoclasm proved effective in the short run, since it enabled the ministers to preach for a time in the Catholic churches and, in a few cities, to assume control of the local government. But in the long run the iconoclasm destroyed the power of Calvinism as a mass movement. The hedgepreaching had provided the illusion of a peaceful, ordered society, of the possibility of social transformation without social upheaval. The behavior of the ministers seemed to synthesize, for a moment, their energy and dedication to radical reform and their concern that the reform be accomplished by legitimate means. But when this sense of moral community was destroyed during the iconoclasm, other groups in the society withdrew their allegiance to the movement. The iconoclasm had made clear the incapacity of these groups to unify in real life, as they had done so effectively in the ritual of the *prêche*.

The observer who hopes to interpret the Troubles must try to bridge the gap between abstract ideas and practical behavior, specifically, between the doctrines of Calvinism and the rituals and violence that occurred in the Netherlands in 1566. Both contemporaries and historians have perceived this relationship of ideas and behavior as an either/or situation: either Calvinist ideology inspired the Troubles and the Dutch Revolt or it did not. Some historians have observed that Calvinist ministers had been a part of Netherlands history since 1544 and that the leaders of the Dutch Revolt were Calvinists. They have concluded that Calvinist ideology became an element in the formation of Dutch nationalism in the same way that the Enlightenment doctrine of individual happiness is supposed to have inspired the leaders of the American Revolution. According to these historians, Calvinist ideas were secretly introduced by the early ministers, spread underground despite persecution, burst upon the national consciousness during the hedgepreaching, and found ultimate expression in the iconoclasm. The image-breaking would thus appear as the symbolic inauguration of the Dutch Revolt, when religious ideology was fused with nationalist sentiment. The alternative to this interpretation has been to reject the influence of ideas altogether and to view the preaching and the violence as evidence of social and economic discontent. In this context, the preachers used Calvinist doctrines as slogans, but they might just as well have used the slogans of the Anabaptists or the Catholics.

It seems clear that Calvinist ideas did not cause the Troubles in the sense I have just described. People were not moved to applaud the hedgepreachers and to commit violence because they believed in a revolutionary ideology that had been imposed on them from above by an

organized, international elite. In fact, Calvinism apparently was not perceived as a revolutionary ideology even by many of its own leaders. But
this is not to deny that popular behavior was caused by ideas. Attendance
at the hedgepreaching and participation in the iconoclasm was at least
partially determined by what people thought about the Calvinists and
their powers of self-discipline and organization. But the ritual of the
prêche was not the product of a Calvinist conspiracy; it was the product
of the need of many people to believe in the stability of a higher social
and spiritual authority and of their belief that the ministers had the
practical and spiritual capacity to provide that authority. It was also a
political gesture. The nobles and magistrates of the Netherlands had a
vision of something called the national interest, but they conceived of
that ideal in terms of their own traditional privileges—their personal
right to legislate on religious matters and dispense patronage within their
own spheres of jurisdiction. An overall political authority was needed,
but every attempt to impose administrative and political order had failed
by 1566. Philip's efforts to centralize the government and reform the
bishoprics had failed because they depended on the acceptance of the
Inquisition and the sacrifice of provincial authority; the nobles' efforts to
deal collectively with religious matters in the States-General also failed
because Philip insisted on submitting the religious edicts to each provincial council separately—to control the people by fragmenting them. "The
meeting of the States-General was considered by all sensible people to be
the only remedy against the Troubles," wrote an Antwerp official.

What else could be concluded when neither the supplication of the nobles, nor
the desire of various provinces and towns . . . had succeeded in persuading the
court to do it? There seemed to be nothing left to give them hope that the
promises to the nobles might be kept, or that the inhabitants might be released
from the hated persecutions and odious inquisition. . . . Despair made those who
dissented in religion more obdurate. . . . This was the reason why they started to
hold their meetings and services each day more openly, thus getting so many
adherents.[93]

The failure to call a meeting of the States-General was commented on
and resolved in the *prêche*, which achieved orderliness, restrained enthusiasm, and the synthesis—not the disappearance—of disparate elements:
different social groups, localities, languages. In symbolic terms the *prêche*
accomplished what the States-General had been meant to achieve; it was
a statement of collective solidarity against the Inquisition and the foreign
government and a defense of the separate identity and authority of local
magistrates, guilds, and nobles. Both as worshipers and as citizens, the
people would have liked real life to reflect the *prêche*: organized, hierar-
chical, harmonious, with the ministers and nobles as the guardians of the
spiritual and political integrity of the country.

But if the ministers and their adherents were willing to act as public authorities during the *prêche*, why were they—even the nobles and local magistrates, who had a legal mandate to act as public officials—also willing to defer to authority during and after the iconoclasm?

Merely citing the breakdown of political and ecclesiastical offices in the period before the Troubles does not sufficiently explain this behavior, because in France, where there was a similar breakdown or division of public authority, individuals showed themselves more than eager to assume these public functions. During the iconoclastic riots in France it was common for Catholics to murder Protestants in the belief that they were acting in place of the magistrates, who were unable to protect the state; it was equally common for Protestants to attack Catholics because they believed that was what the magistrates should have done if they had seen the truth.[94] In the Netherlands, Catholics and Calvinists quarreled over the number of sacraments and the significance of Communion, and they often attacked one another as heretics, but they did not seem to view each other as ultimate enemies, as deviants who had to be exterminated in order to preserve society. In France, on the other hand, arguments about the nature of the sacraments could lead to the disembowelment of a pregnant Huguenot woman by a Catholic to ensure that the unborn child should not come into the world a heretic. Why this immense difference in perception and behavior? Why was society in the Netherlands so much less polarized than in France?

In the first place, the divisions in Netherlands society were less acute because of the absence of the king. The Calvinists viewed Philip neither as an ally nor as a confirmed enemy. The Reformers were cynical about Margaret's intentions toward them, but no one, not even Margaret herself, was really certain about the policies of the king toward the Protestants and the nobility.[95] This absence of a confirmed enemy prevented the Reformed ministers from formulating a political ideology either as adherents to the crown or as revolutionaries; it also prevented the high nobles who were vaguely sympathetic to the Calvinists from taking a stand in support of the Reformers and the Confederates. A second reason for the absence of clear divisions in Netherlands society was that there were many more alternatives; until Alva's Council of Blood had defined everyone as either a loyal Catholic citizen or a Protestant traitor, it was possible to be a Catholic who was also hostile to the Inquisition, a Lutheran, a Calvinist, or simply a liberal skeptic.

More important, perhaps, was the Netherlanders' experience with militant Anabaptism. Both Catholics and Protestants considered the Anabaptists to be deviants and anarchists. The Calvinist ministers were constantly attempting to convince the public authorities, both at home and in exile, that they were not to be identified with the Anabaptists who had

brought about the disasters at Münster. Their desire to establish themselves as dedicated to the protection of the constituted authorities was at
least as intense as their commitment to advance the cause of the new
religion, at least until Philip had finally shown himself to be intractable.
The ministers wanted to convince the Catholics that if a circle could be
drawn around the members of the social order that would exclude those
who were criminals, enemies of that order and that system of values, the
circle should be drawn around themselves and the established authorities,
and it should exclude the Anabaptists. Even the Anabaptists were eager
to disassociate themselves from the Münsterites; during the Troubles the
Mennonites were by far the most pacifist group—no one accused them of
participating in the image-breaking. Thus the differences between these
religious groups were, at this point in their history, no more striking than
the similarities; for Catholics, Calvinists, and Mennonites, the evil to
be eradicated was not heresy but anarchy. This anxiety to believe that
society was secure, integrated, and above all normal, did not prevent a
relatively small group from committing iconoclasm and taking over a
number of cities; but it did prevent these acts of violence from becoming
elements of a mass movement.

Thus there is no reason to view the Troubles as a rehearsal for the
Dutch Revolt simply because there was considerable popular discontent
in the Netherlands during this period. It seems much more likely that
most people would have been satisfied to participate in the hedgepreaching as an alternative to more radical forms of protest. The average member of the Reformed congregations probably found Calvinism appealing
not as a radical doctrine promising greater personal and political freedom, but as a promise of greater security within the established political
hierarchy. But if Calvinism was not widely perceived as a revolutionary
ideology in the period of the Troubles, what was the relationship of
Calvinism to the Dutch Revolt? Did the ministers help to cause the revolution? At what point did the myth of Calvinism become a nationalist
ideology? It seems that Calvinism was accepted as a revolutionary ideology by members of the high nobility and by moderates within the Reformed clergy only when they were forced to accept it to survive against
the duke of Alva; ironically, it was not the preaching of the Reformers
but their renewed persecution in 1569 that led to the popular acceptance
of Calvinism as a revolutionary doctrine. For in this latest wave of executions, not only the Calvinists were persecuted but the entire society of
the Netherlands. The wholesale massacre instigated by the duke of Alva
created a situation of theatrical extremes in which the forces of good and
evil could be clearly discerned by everyone and in which all elements of
Netherlands society could feel unified against the malevolent foreigner.
For the ministers it must have appeared that a sign from Providence had

finally come and that God intended them to strike down the tyrant.

In this situation of extreme pressure, the Netherlands pastors formally adopted the doctrines of Calvin and rejected the possibility of compromise with the Lutherans; the majority of them became political revolutionaries. Thus Pieter Carpentier, who had been a moderate during the Troubles, wrote to the London refugee church from Holland during the revolt: "I hope that you will pray for all the ministers, especially for those of this country, not forgetting the Prince of Orange. . . . May the Lord destroy the enemy, so that our people may be more encouraged."[96] For Jean Taffin, who had also taken a conciliatory position during the Troubles, the iconoclasm later became part of the nationalist myth: "Those of the Religion wonderfully advanced in Flanders, Brabant, and in several other provinces of the Low Countries; and affairs came to such a pass that . . . the images in the temples of Antwerp were broken . . . with a swiftness which was unbelievable to the simple people."[97]

The Witches of the Cambrésis

The Acculturation of the Rural World in the Sixteenth and Seventeenth Centuries

Robert Muchembled

"What, they say that all women are witches!"—Aldegonde de Rue, seventy years old, sentenced to be strangled and burned at Bazuel, in the Cambrésis, 31 August 1601 (ADN 8 H 312)

At first glance, witchcraft in the north of France appears very much as it does in the rest of Europe in the sixteenth and seventeenth centuries.[1] Here, as elsewhere, the trial judges—whose mentality has been the object of considerable study[2]—ordered countless pyres to be set alight for hapless victims, most of whom were ignorant of how they came to be accused. The trial records, however, paint a picture not only of the victims and their executioners, but also of the social groups to which the victims belonged. This essay will explore the sociological dimension of the witchcraft phenomenon. I exclude from my study urban and convent witchcraft, both of which deserve full-scale studies of their own, and confine my remarks to rural witches in the province of the Cambrésis. Through these trial records we can recapture the sense of social malaise

This essay was conceived and written at Princeton University during the fall semester 1973. I would like to thank the Shelby Cullom Davis Center for Historical Studies for giving me, as a Davis Fellow, the time as well as the financial support necessary for the completion of this study. I owe a debt of gratitude as well to the faculty and students of the History Department and to the other Davis Fellows, who participated in the research seminar on popular culture and religion. The exchange of ideas at these meetings, based on our experience of different periods and geographical areas, proved an invaluable source of inspiration for me. Finally, I wish to thank most warmly my colleagues and friends, Carlo Ginzburg (University of Bologna), Lionel Rothkrug (Sir George Williams University, Montreal), and Jay P. Dolan (Notre Dame University), from whose conversation I learned so much. The essay was translated by Susan Darnton.

All the references to unpublished source materials are drawn from the *Archives Départementales* of the North, at Lille (cited as ADN, followed by the source quotation).

that overtook this area in the second half of the sixteenth century, as widespread efforts to Christianize the popular masses were accompanied by important economic changes. In fact, this period marks the beginning of a genuine acculturation of rural life in the Catholic Low Countries, a profound movement whose dimensions I underestimated when I treated it, in an earlier article, as a simple clash between two conflicting cultures.[3]

I hope now to show that the rural witches of the Cambrésis were neither outcasts nor deviants but expiatory victims chosen by their fellow villagers to satisfy a confused, ritualistic need for sacrifice, as a result of the unconscious tensions born of the total and complete dismantling of structures (destructuration) in their world.[4]

I shall first attempt to construct a witchcraft "model" for the southern Catholic Low Countries and then will look at the witches of the Cambrésis and the French Hainaut in their village setting. Most of the texts I use in the first two sections are well known but have been exploited in only the most partial and partisan fashion. Moreover, a rereading of them from a different angle will, I hope, lead to a fundamental alteration of the way these problems have been interpreted in the past.

The Scope of Witchcraft in the Southern Catholic Low Countries from the Fifteenth to the Eighteenth Centuries

The Cambrésis and the French Hainaut make up what is today the western part of the French department of the Nord. In the sixteenth and seventeenth centuries, witches abounded there, as they did in the Douaisis, along the Flanders coast, and in the countryside around Lille.[5] A brief outline of the principal characteristics of the southern Catholic Low Countries will help to situate this witchcraft "model" in its regional context.[6]

Three important phenomena marked this area between the time of the collapse of the Burgundian state in the fifteenth century and the French takeover (1667–78): war, economic change, and the post-Tridentine religious revival. The first two were closely interrelated in their effects: the reign of Charles V, which has been depicted, perhaps wrongly, as the golden age of the Empire,[7] gave way, in Flanders and the Hainaut in particular, to an economic crisis, which Charles Verlinden has situated "between 1580 and 1590 principally."[8] During this same period, the military reconquest of the southern provinces was completed, except for Cambrai, which the French continued to hold. When Cambrai was taken in 1595, the whole area embarked upon an era of peace and demographic growth that lasted until 1632. In that year, at Bouchain, war broke out again, spreading in 1635 to Artois and the Flanders coast. The entire

Northern France

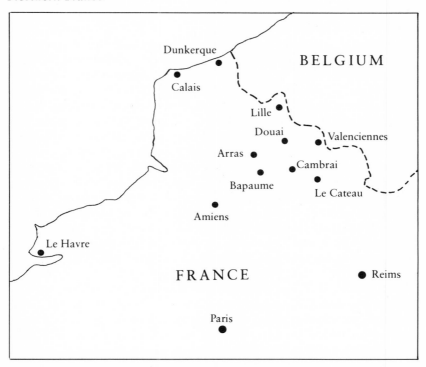

Dunkerque

BELGIUM

Calais

Lille

Douai

Valenciennes

Arras

Cambrai

Bapaume

Le Cateau

Amiens

Le Havre

FRANCE

Reims

Paris

- - - *Modern Boundary of France and Belgium*

region was repeatedly ravaged, first by the Thirty Years' War, then by the wars of conquest of Louis XIV, until, finally, Douai and Lille were captured in 1667 and Cambrai and Valenciennes ceded to France in 1678.[9] Throughout this period changes were occurring in the economic structure: the Flemish economy, which had stagnated "in mediocrity" during the fifteenth century,[10] weakened progressively in the course of the next century, as Liège and Brabant came to the fore.[11] The interior of Flanders and Hainaut, with its little villages, had shown a sharp economic decline by the seventeenth century, but Lille was thriving.[12] A survey of smaller economic units confirms this general impression, particularly in these areas that are the subject of this essay. In the region of Saint-Amand, for example, after a crisis in the weaving industry at Valenciennes during the sixteenth-century religious upheavals, local trade and crafts began to redevelop, only to have the wars of Louis XIV exert a "direct effect of depression upon the economy of the area."[13] In the Cambrésis, where, in the fifteenth and sixteenth centuries, the economy was mainly dependent upon wheat, the seventeenth century saw the production of fine linen cloth (the *mulquinerie* industry) spread gradually throughout the countryside.[14]

The principal characteristic, however, of the economic changes, independent or not of wars, in the "French Low Countries" in this period was their enormous regional variation. A Lille geographer, writing in 1963, has noted twelve separate urban and sixteen rural areas within the north of France.[15] Given such a wide range of regional particularities in the present day, I would like to emphasize in this essay local economic traits rather than those that are common to the region as a whole.

The third force at work in the sixteenth and seventeenth centuries in what is now the French Nord was a religious revival precocious for its time that conquered urban, and especially rural, areas from the reign of Philip II on. I shall discuss in greater detail this singular acculturation of the countryside that, church historians have shown, took hold here much earlier and much more rapidly than in other parts of France.[16] The Low Countries had experienced in the fifteenth century "a veritable brushfire of heresy" at Lille, Tournai, Douai, and at Arras, in particular, where fourteen Waldensian witches were burned in 1460 alone.[17] In fact, Charles V had already instituted a sort of state inquisition directed against Protestantism and Anabaptism.[18] Further religious upheavals in the second half of the sixteenth century had suggested that Catholicism could not survive without total reorganization and that repression alone was not the answer. In this setting, the Counter-Reformation burst upon the scene in the first third of the seventeenth century, to join battle with every weapon at its command in this part of Europe.[19] Hence the war against witchcraft can be seen as the result of a marked change in re-

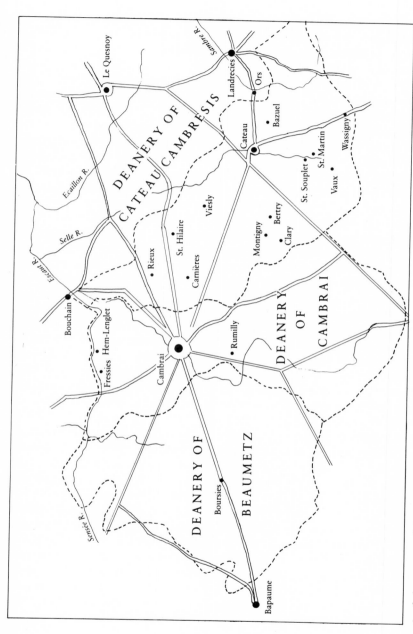

Archdeaconry of Cambrésis

ligious thinking occurring within the context of an evolving economy. But before looking more closely at rural Cambrésis, I will describe the victims, generally, throughout the whole region.

From the end of the sixteenth century on, prosecutions for witchcraft were on the rise in the Catholic Low Countries: Flanders, Brabant, Luxemburg, Hainaut, Namur, and Limburg were particularly affected.[20] I shall limit myself to a discussion of the situation in what is now the department of the Nord and those border lands immediately adjoining it to the north and south. The work of Villette[21] and the unpublished trial records give us an idea of the numbers involved here (see Table 1).[22]

A statistical survey by decades reveals two very distinct phases in the witch hunt (see Figure 1). The first and most important, from 1590 to 1630, with two peak periods in 1590–1600 and again in 1610–20, corresponds to an era of peace and demographic growth, thus giving the lie to H. R. Trevor-Roper's theory that the persecution of witches in Europe was directly linked, after 1560, to the wars of religion.[23] On the contrary, there is evidence that the edict of 20 July 1592, which was "a true code of magic," and the publication of antiwitchcraft literature, such as the "Disquisitio magicarum libri sex" by the Jesuit del Rio, were "directly responsible for the multiplication of legal suits" in the Catholic Low Countries.[24] The edict of 1592 was reinstituted in 1606 by the archdukes, and repressive measures grew more severe, particularly in Hainaut.[25] This judicial campaign correlates clearly with the peak periods of 1590–1600 and 1610–20 for this region. But, as a study of Cambrésis shows, it alone cannot account for the popular attitudes toward witchcraft.

The second important phase of persecution, from 1640 to 1680, though preceded by a decade in which there was little witch hunting, coincided with a period of unremitting warfare. Could the transition from peace to war about 1635 have been related to the subsequent increase in prosecutions? The characteristics of this second era of activity are quite different from those of a half-century earlier. Again, by taking the Cambrésis as an example, these points can be studied in more detail.

The incidence of witch trials in the area under study is similar to that of the Franche-Comté in the period 1599–1667, when 40 percent of 157 cases documented resulted in the death sentence.[26] Both of these regions belonged at that time to the Spanish crown. Neither reflected the severity of the Catholic and Protestant judges in Baden-Württemberg between the years 1560 to 1670.[27] Evidence from the north of France also suggests strongly that the severity of the courts differed according to the sex of the defendant. Four women were accused of witchcraft for every one man. But, once his case had come to trial, the man always had less chance of

Figure 1. *Variations by Decade, 1500–1700, Comparative Incidence*

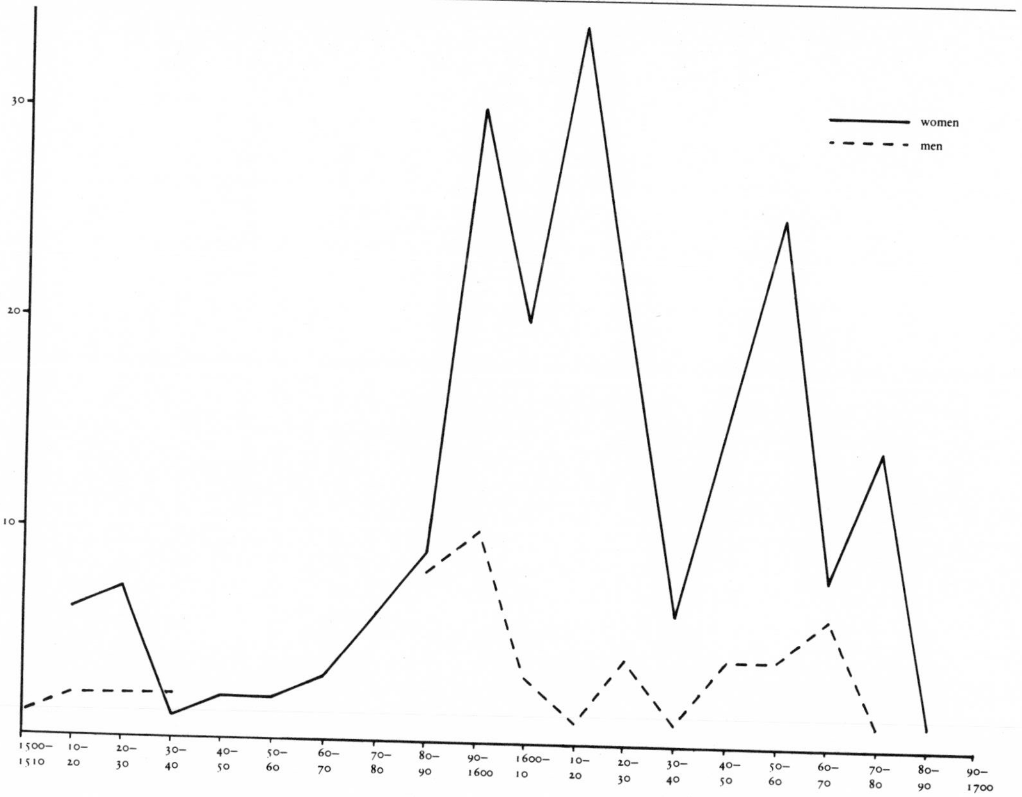

women —————
men – – – – –

Table 1. Defendants in the North of France, 1371–1783

Years	Women		Men		Totals
	Number	Percentage	Number	Percentage	
1351–1400	1	50	1	50	2
1401–1450	7	100			7
1451–1500*	10	91	1	9	11
1501–1550	16	70	7	30	23
1551–1600	50	74	18	26	68
1601–1650	97	88	13	12	110
1651–1700	48	81	11	19	59
1701–1790	3	50	3	50	6
Totals and average percentages	232	81	54	19	286

*The inclusion of the Arras Waldensians in the statistics for this period would result in completely atypical data—39 percent women, 42 percent men (and 19 percent undetermined)—whereas even in the fourteenth and eighteenth centuries, when the statistics reflect an unusually small number of cases documented, the percentage of male defendants never exceeded the females (Arras: chef-lieu of the Pas-de-Calais). See also Table 2.

escaping the death penalty than the woman (see Table 2). Though much more work remains to be done, these statistics suggest that historians have underestimated the number of men brought to trial in this area and perhaps elsewhere in Europe as well. More questions arise from the observation that between 1580 and 1600 the persecution of men preceded, then continued alongside, the first great wave of trials of women.[28] Finally, as study of the Cambrésis will show, and as E. W. Monter has shown for the Jura, "not all . . . witches were poor or lonely or obviously deviant. . . . Some Jura families . . . produced suspected witches over a long span of time."[29]

All indications are that the accused were not, for the most part, marginal characters in the society of their time and that, on this subject, the perspective of historians has perhaps been faulty. The witches should not be seen as a target of the seventeenth-century campaign against corruption and scandal that sought to "excise from civil society" the poor, beggars,[30] and deviants of all kinds. They should instead be considered in relation to the normal, rather than the pathological, aspects of their culture and time.[31] This bizarre sacrifice of women, and of men and children as well,[32] cannot help but pique our curiosity; the key to this strange phenomenon can no doubt be found in the rural world of the sixteenth and seventeenth centuries, particularly in its villages.

Table 2. *Outcome of Cases, 1371–1783*

	Death	Banishment	Misc. Punishments	Acquittals	Unknown	Total	Percent Death
Including the Arras Waldensians in 1460							
Women	115	59	5	20	42	241	47
Men	37	10	4	6	12	69	54
Unspecified	6				2	8	75
Total	158	69	9	26	56	318	49
Excluding the Waldensians							
Women	109	59	5	19	42	234	47
Men	31	10	1	0	10	52	60
Total	140	69	6	19	52	286	49

Table 3. Male Defendants and the Sentences They Received, 1580–1680

Dates	Executed	Percent Executed	Banished	Misc.	Unknown	Total
1581–1590	4	50		1	3	8
1591–1600	9	90			1	10
1601–1610	3	100				3
1611–1620			1			1
1621–1630	2	50		1	1	4
1631–1640			1			1
1641–1650	1	25	1		2	4
1651–1660	4	100				4
1661–1670	3	50	3			6
1671–1680				1		1
Total	26	62	6	3	7	42

Witches and Villagers in the Cambrésis

In contrast with the county of Essex during the Tudor–Stuart era, when 229 villages out of a total of 426 had some experience of witchcraft,[33] and in contrast also with the Jura, where "nearly every village produced some witch trials," between 1560 and 1680, and where witch hunts were "endemic rather than epidemic,"[34] the rural districts of the southern Spanish Low Countries seem not to have uncovered hordes of witches in the same period. Out of 286 documented defendants (see Table 1), many were of urban origin, though it is not always possible to differentiate longtime city-dwellers from recent rural emigrants or from those country folk who happened to be brought to the city for trial, like Denise and Barbe Le Jay, from Wandignies, imprisoned at Douai in 1575 at the request of their local bailiff and aldermen.[35] In hundreds of villages throughout Flanders, Artois, the Cambrésis, Hainaut, and Tournai, not the slightest trace of a witch can be found. The county of Artois, though predominantly rural, seems to have escaped completely the epidemic of witch hunting that was going on to the north and east. We can only conclude that witchcraft, in these areas, was limited to certain towns and villages. The former lie outside the scope of my study, for urban witchcraft sprang up in a very different economic and political atmosphere. Only Douai and Dunkerque, and, to a lesser extent, Cambrai, Valenciennes, Lille, Bouchain, and Saint-Amand, were the epicenters of the phenomenon.[36] Rural witchcraft seems to have been just as localized: four villages alone in the southern part of the Cambrai diocese accounted for 28 of the 286 rural and urban trials for which statistics are available covering the years 1599–1652 (see Tables 4, 7, and 8). Apart from these, no more than four or five trials for each of some other villages are cited in the Cambrai archdiocese,[37] which, even after the reorganization of 1559 that removed the archdeaconries of Brussels and Antwerp, amounted to no less than 500 parishes and 109 missions.[38] The proportion of villages exposed to witchcraft is here quite different from Essex, even including, in addition to the figures noted above, the instances of rural sorcery out of 366 defendants that have been identified in the county of Namur, which, in the period in question, 1509–1646, still fell within the archdiocese of Cambrai.[39] In point of fact, rural witchcraft, in the part of the Low Countries that today is French, seems to have been localized in the great archdeaconry of the Cambrai archdiocese, which encompassed the villages of Bazuel,[40] Rieux,[41] Fressies, and Hem-Lenglet,[42] and in the eastern tip of the diocese of Arras (located between that great archdeaconry, on the south, and the Tournai diocese to the north). Those areas (i.e., in the diocese of Arras) which the archival sources indicate were centers of witchcraft—the Douaisis, Valenciennois, Bouchain, and Saint-Armand—all lie within the boundaries of this meeting ground between the three dioceses.[43] The Bouchain region, northeast of Cambrai, deserves special attention: 183 persons were accused of witchcraft there between 1595 and 1614, according to an unsubstantiated source;[44] child witches were known in the area;[45] and there was an accompanying rash of trials in the villages of Rieux, Somain, Villers-au-Bois, and Campeau, all of which fell within its jurisdiction.[46]

Before we step into the world of these witches, that is, back into village life in the Hainaut and Cambrésis, we must reexamine the witchcraft trial procedures.

Some authors—notably P. Villette, writing on the north of France—would have us believe that these witches described before the tribunals a form of satanic religion, a reverse image of Christian faith. Abbé Villette distinguishes three stages of witchcraft: initiation, sabbath, and spellcasting. His first article is organized in three parts, corresponding to these three stages, and he makes it plain that the initiation is "a parody of the rites of baptism and marriage, while the sabbath is a parody of the mass."[47] The third stage of witchcraft corresponds to the fact that "sorcerers were capable of all kinds of evil," for they were servants of the devil, who is himself the "principle of Evil" incarnate.[48] Though Villette does not say so precisely, we may assume that their evil doings were meant to represent the Christian ethic, based on the conception of good, turned inside out.

This interpretation, which echoes the conclusions of demonologists such as Bodin, Boguet, de Lancre and the authors of *Malleus Malefica-*

rum,[49] errs in two important ways. First, it accepts without question the intellectual assumptions of the judges and inquisitors of the fifteenth, sixteenth, and seventeenth centuries, for whom the central article of faith was the existence of the devil and his ability to act in the world.[50] This seems to me a fundamental flaw, even though the author equivocates by suggesting that he himself belongs with "the majority who have ceased to believe" [in witchcraft] ever since the end of the seventeenth century.[51] In his second article, though, he soft-pedals his interpretation somewhat, assigning responsibility for the persecution rather to those demonologists who forged the system of persecution and to those credulous masses who flocked to view the execution spectacles and found in them a reinforcement of their faith.[52] My second point—and it is related to the first—is that these authors completely distort historical reality by neglecting a number of facts that do not fit their preconceptions. A closer look at the trials in the Cambrésis and Hainaut will help to remedy these errors.

First, I will consider the form of the trials. When carried to their conclusion, they consisted of three separate segments, which will be seen to have little relation to Villette's schema:

1. A preliminary investigation, consisting principally of a review of witnesses for the prosecution, who generally came forward spontaneously and who were, for the most part, neighbors of the accused.[53]

2. The interrogation of the accused; with or without torture as an accompaniment. I have been able to find no trace of lawyers or witnesses for the defense, as there were in some urban trials.[54]

3. The punishment, which, in the case of a death sentence, functions as a sort of exclusion rite.[55]

Turning to the content of the trials, a fundamental difference is found between the first two stages: the witnesses never introduce an antireligious element; this appears only with the arrival of the judge on the scene. The witnesses usually testify along the same lines: they are well acquainted with the accused, and they are aware that he or she is widely reputed to be a witch.[56] They then offer concrete accusations against the suspect, such as damages he or she may have done to their goods, notably their crops, to their animals, or to their fellow villagers, often citing the death of young children.

Taking the trial of Reyne Percheval, widow of Estienne Billot,[57] as an example, there are important differences in the notion of witchcraft as it is described by the witnesses and as it comes to be understood by the close of the trial. The fact that there is no record of her sentence forces us to leave aside the problem of punishment in this case.

It is September 1599; six witnesses pass before the alderman of Bazuel (see Tables 4 and 5).[58] The first, Pierre Wattelier, a thatcher, thirty

Table 4. *Witchcraft at Bazuel, 1599–1627*

Date (beginning and end of trials)	Name	Age	Remarks	Verdict	References (ADN)
2–13 September 1599	Reyne Percheval, widow of Estienne Billot		Born in B.; lived there all her life; tortured	Unknown	8 H 312
18 July–13 August 1601	Aldegonde de Rue, widow of Olivier Grotart	70	Born in B.; had several daughters; tortured	Condemned to be strangled and burned[a]	8 H 312
19 January–7 March 1621	Marie Lanechin, widow of Jean de Vaulx	62[b]	Born in B.; lived several years in Landrecies;[c] tortured	Condemned to be strangled and burned	8 H 312
10–21 March 1621	Maxellende Vasseur, widow, remarried to Marin Berseillon	60	Accused by the above; lived in various spots in the Cambrésis; had resided in B. for 17–18 years	Released	8 H 312
10–22 March 1621	Pasquette Barra, wife of Jacques Piettre	54	Accused by Marie Lanechin; illegitimate, born in Valenciennes;[d] had always lived in B.	Released	8 H 312
13–19 July 1627	Pasquette Barra, second accusation			Unknown	8 H 312

B. = Bazuel.
a. Error by Villette, "Sorcellerie dans le Nord," p. 148, who has wrongly stated that she was acquitted.
b. Ibid., p. 149; he lists her as 65.
c. Nord, *arrondissement* of Avesnes-sur-Helpe, *chef-lieu du canton.*
d. Nord, *chef-lieu arr.*

Table 5. *Witnesses at Witchcraft Trials in Bazuel, 1599–1627*

	Name	Age	Profession or status	Charges brought by the witnesses
1599, against Reyne Percheval	Pierre Wattelier	30	thatcher at Bazuel	Death of one of his cows; accused the defendant of witchcraft to her son-in-law
	Nicolas Bridoux	50	weaver (*mulquinier*) at Bazuel	Death of his daughter Marye, the granddaughter of the defendant
	Jean Lenain	60	alderman of Bazuel	Confirms the preceding testimony
	Georges Clocquette		sergeant of the town of Le Cateau[a]	Tries to make the witch confess
	Laurence Maughier, widow of Denys Wattelier	41		Illness of Jean Parmentier's family; a Waldensian kept company with the witch
	Jean Parmentier	50	alderman of Bazuel	Confirms the preceding; birth of a skinless calf
1601, against Aldegonde de Rue	Jean Morut	68	sergeant of Bazuel	Death of one of his cows
	Magdelaine Morut, widow of Jean Gillart	38	daughter of the above	Confirms her father's testimony
	Andrieu Doyen		*carlier* at Landrecies[b]	Death of two horses belonging to one of his tenants, Gérard de Briatte, a neighbor of the defendant, to whom he rented a house
	Gérard de Briatte	46	innkeeper at Landrecies[b]	Confirms the above
	Jacqueline Bourguignon, wife of Jean Debonnaire		husband: butcher at Landrecies[b]	Strange illness of her daughter, aged 8–9 years
	Margheritee, widow of Andrieu Florent	56	"hostess" at Landrecies[b]	A stranger to her, in her house, accused the defendant of being "a *caroigne* carrion witch"

Name	Age	Status	Testimony
Toussaint Lesaige	22	unmarried, from Bazuel (?)	The accused sent for him in prison to ask him to give the message to her daughter that she should commend herself to God and confess if she had "any temptation or vision"
Marye Bourguignon, wife of Claude Canoisne	40	husband: bourgeois of Le Cateau[a]	An Italian soldier, in her house, had accused the defendant of being a witch
Grégoire Florut and Anthoinette Warocquier, his wife		*censier* (rich tenant farmer) at Bazuel	One of his horses died as though in a fit
1621, against Marie Lanechin			
Nicolas Deramp		weaver's employee (*mulquinier*) in the lodgings of Mathieu Hennocq, at Bazuel	Death of a tenant farmer (*censier*) of Bazuel 17 or 18 years ago; death of the husband of the defendant; death of his master's daughter, aged 12, ten years earlier; illness of his neighbor, Andrieu Deramp; illness of Jean d'Avesnes, son of Nicolas, during the winter of 1620; he accuses the defendant of poisonings
Andrieu Deramp	30	inhabitant of Bazuel	Confirms his illness and notes that he had to be exorcised two times by the dean of Bazuel
Pierre Cauchy (Cauchie)	36	villein of Bazuel	Death of his wife and of a young infant still nursing
Catherine Leclercq, wife of Mathieu Hennocq		inhabitant of Bazuel	Death of her daughter
Andrieu de Braibant	70	shepherd at Bazuel	He saw the witch dance, hair disheveled, near a wood
Antoine Nicaise	60	day laborer at Bazuel	He saw her once, at daybreak, "all disheveled and wild-haired"

Name	Age	Profession or status	Charges brought by the witnesses
Nicollas Cauchie		inhabitant of Bazuel	He saw the defendant lying in a hedge near the house of a blind man who had been burned for witchcraft. She left upon catching sight of him.
Christoffe Avaine		inhabitant of Bazuel	At the wedding of Jean d'Avesnes the suspect told him that she didn't dare show herself in the street because of the rumors about her
Mathieu Hennocq			He confirms the story of the death of his daughter; some say she caused the death of her husband; he confirms the testimony of Pierre Cauchie
Francoise Regnier	22	unmarried, inhabitant of Bazuel	She saw the accused turning about, with her head down, near a fountain
Nicolas d'Avesnes		alderman of Bazuel	He confirms the death of his son Jean
Guillain Regnier	24–25	unmarried, resided at Bazuel	Eight to nine years ago, in summer, while passing with Gabry Bernard near a fountain about 11 o'clock in the morning, they spotted the suspect in the middle of a thick "mist" about 15–20 feet across, though the air was otherwise perfectly clear. Gabry Bernard cried: "Zounds, woman, you're a witch."
Marie Nicaise, widow of Gabry Bernard	40	inhabitant of Bazuel	Her husband forbade her to sell faggots to Marie Lanechin, because he said she was a witch; the pastor who gave him extreme unction said that the husband of the accused had been bewitched

1621, against Pasquette Barra	Saincte Avaine, wife of Andrieu Mortier	inhabitant of Bazuel	Death of her husband
	Jean Parmentier	(cf. trial of 1599)	Death of one of his chickens, followed by others; death of two horses belonging to him
the same, 13 July 1627	Pierre Wattelier	(cf. trial of 1599)	His son, Melchior, has been sick for six weeks; Pierre Wyart died shortly before

a. See n. 41.
b. See n. 41.

years old, relates how a sick cow of his, which he suspected Reyne of having bewitched, was cured after he threatened to retaliate by setting her house afire. He adds that he confided his suspicions to Reyne's son-in-law, but that Reyne herself, upon learning of them, showed no visible emotion.

Nicolas Bridoux, a weaver (*mulquinier*), fifty years old, had been previously married to Jacqueline Billot, daughter of the accused, and with her had had a daughter, Marye. Five or six years earlier, this child, on her sickbed, recounted to her father how her grandmother had promised to cure her illness if she could be trusted never to tell of it. Five or six days after making this confession she died.

Jean Lenain, a local alderman, aged sixty, speaks in confirmation of the preceding testimony, adding that he knew Bridoux's daughter well and that the incident had taken place seven or eight years before.

Georges Clocquette, sergeant for the town of Le Cateau and for the abbey court of Saint-André, who had been given the assignment of bringing in the defendant, tells of how he tried to convince her along the way to confess, citing the example of one Isabeau Dubaille, and of how she appeared upset at this, saying, "What, and she [Isabeau] didn't dare lately to come to Valenciennes?"

Laurence Maughier, widow of Denys Watterlier, forty-one years old, relates how the entire household of Jean Parmentier, finding that they had fallen ill as a result of a spell, set out for Bertry,[59] "to speak to a woman, who had given them some kind of brew to cure them, which woman from Bertry had told them that in order to take this potion they would do well to go somewhere else other than their home . . . and that when they took the brew in question, the sorceress who had concocted it would appear in that house despite all efforts to stop her."

Jean Parmentier, she continues, did go to take his potion in another house, but, at the crucial moment, he "fell in a faint." His wife took him for dead and began to raise a hue and cry, which drew "several persons, . . . among them Reyne . . . , who must have come running in a great hurry, for in her haste she had lost one of her shoes or house slippers in the mud." Parmentier, upon regaining consciousness, forbade Reyne to come in, and, when she persisted, threw a burning ember in her face. His wife recovered the ember and began to beat the witch, who made no effort to defend herself.

The same witness notes that "a Waldensian who lived at Saint Souplet[60] often came to Bazuel and went to see Reyne Percheval . . . even, according to some folks, sleeping there on occasion."

The sixth witness, Jean Parmentier, a Bazuel alderman, aged sixty, confirms his role in these events, which took place some sixteen to eighteen years earlier. He refers to Reyne as his "neighbor," and he explains that the healer of Bertry assured him that the witch who had cast a spell over his family would of necessity appear in the house where he took his cure, "when the street was full of fire and water." He also confirms the tale of the Waldensian, adding that Reyne had bewitched one of his cows, which "had disgorged [given birth to] a calf's head without flesh or skin" and from whose belly men had withdrawn all the calf's missing bones minus the skin.

All these witnesses, with the exception of Georges Clocquette, are residents of Bazuel. Every one of them admits to a long acquaintance with Reyne. And though they all claim to know that she is indeed a witch, they make no mention of the demonologists' initiations or sabbaths. The judges' interrogation is another matter. At her first questioning, on 2 September 1599, Reyne denies all the charges brought by the second and third witnesses, which were no doubt already known to the judges, even though they were not officially entered in the record until two days later. She is also accused of having laughed and mocked, with her daughter, at the grieving followers of two funeral processions that passed by her. She denies this in the case of the second, and for the first occasion, offers the explanation that her daughter had indeed laughed, but only at the sight of a drunkard trying unsuccessfully to chant with the priests, and that she had struck the girl in order to quiet her. She also denies having sent a Waldensian into the fields to find a certain Jean Avaine to ask for his daughter's hand, which the peasant refused. Finally, in response to the charge that she had been present at the execution for witchcraft of the wife of Merlin d'Ors[61] but that she had left just as the fire was set alight, she denies leaving at that moment and rejects the contention that one of those present remarked at the time: "Go on, go on, it will be your turn next."

On 6 September she categorically denies the charges brought against her by the first four witnesses. The aldermen of Bazuel refer her case to the court of Le Cateau, who rule, on the thirteenth, that she may be put to torture. This is done later that day; Reyne again denies all the charges against her, but, several hours later, she can no longer hold out under torture and at last she confesses all her "crimes": she did kill her son-in-law's daughter by putting a certain powder in her pâté, for, as she explains, Bridoux "often tormented" her. This same "powder" she used to bring about Jean Parmentier's illness and the birth of the deformed calf, but she did not mean to harm Pierre Wattelier, or even Jean Parmentier, who, she testifies, must have happened by chance to come in contact with the powder sprinkled on his manure heap.

From this point on in the interrogation, the judges seem to be imprinting the answers to their questions in the defendant's head. Here at last the devil comes upon the scene, in the person of one Nicollas Rigaut, who had had sexual relations with the accused. He knew her as Marghot, and, after persuading her to renounce her "chrism and baptism" and to give up her soul to him, he marked her with his sign. At the judges' bidding, Reyne describes her sabbath and her repertory of spells, for which she receives one *gros* per animal or human. She names her companions in the sabbath dance, among them Isabeau Dubaille, and admits to having practiced her art for seventeen or eighteen years. When the judges ask what she did with the Hosts she received in church, she replies that she was beaten by her devil because she refused to surrender them. And, finally, in response to their questions about the toads she kept, she explains that she has raised four of them, dressed them in red, green, and yellow cloth, and used their venom mixed with water to make "a dense drizzling rain" that could rot apples and pears.

We have no record of the verdict, but after testimony such as hers, there can be little likelihood that Reyne Percheval escaped the death sentence.

This long trial presents a very useful frame of reference for my study. Its first two stages are clearly distinguished, and there are material differences between the witnesses' accounts and the "confessions" of the defendant. The first are rooted in the common superstitions of country people of that time, while Reyne's testimony seems to be an amalgamation of these same superstitions with the satanical antireligion of the demonologists. Of course, the witnesses could not be expected to have been able to describe a sabbath or a pact with the devil because such knowledge would cast suspicion on them! One wonders how well versed the villagers were in the notion of diabolism which the judges were attempting to link to the defendant. For, though many of the local people must have been familiar with it, through their experience of trials and public executions, at which the sentence and the "crimes" of the witch were read aloud,[62] it is striking how few of them refer to it. Their rare allusions to diabolism are very indirect: for example, a seventy-year-old shepherd testifies to having seen, near Bois-l'Evêque, "a disheveled woman who whirled in a dance," whom he believes to be Aldegonde de Rue, accused of witchcraft at Bazuel in 1601. His description is bound to suggest to the judges the image of the nocturnal dance. And yet, among the dozens of witnesses who appeared at the five Bazuel trials, this shepherd and a sixty-year-old laborer who confirmed his testimony are the only ones to come forward with this kind of accusation. Even if we assume that they responded instinctively to a secret desire on the part of the judges to get this brand of testimony in the record, is it not surprising that they could think of no other detail to add to their accusation? In fact, the testimony of witnesses at these trials can be read as a declaration of orthodoxy, in which they were encouraged to emphasize the aberrations of the defendant in contrast to their own behavior. It is my feeling —and this conclusion merits a separate study—that the trials reveal two types of witchcraft, which I have called elsewhere "the witchcraft of the clerks and judges" and "popular witchcraft."[63] The former incorporates the "crimes" described by the witnesses but interprets them in a satanical religious context that might be straight out of the demonological treatises. The latter seems to have entirely different intellectual origins, for though it is sometimes contaminated by exposure to the judges' point of view, as in the case of the shepherd of Bazuel, it appears to be rooted chiefly in a popular mentality that is still half pagan.

I will now attempt to sort out the two strains, to transcend the language of judicial and religious repression—which was as prevalent then as it is today—in order to explore the territory of strictly popular witchcraft, as found, for example, in the village of Bazuel.

By paying much more attention to their testimony than to the witnesses themselves, historians have overlooked some fascinating sociological insights to be gained from the trials. In the Bazuel trials, which I have described in Table 5, twenty-four citizens of Bazuel, four from Landrecies, and two from Le Cateau[64] appeared as witnesses before the tribunal. But the last two trials offer only scant hints at the testimony heard there, notably in the responses of the defendant, Pasquette Barra.

This evidence indicates that as many as twenty-three households in the village were involved in the witch hunt in the years 1599, 1601, and 1621 alone (see Table 5). Indeed, there is some evidence that the judicial process was set in motion in response to popular pressure rather than by the unilateral decision of the judges of the abbey of Saint-André du Cateau, in whose territory Bazuel fell.[65] There is no evidence to this effect in the case of Reyne Percheval, in 1599, but Aldegonde de Rue, in 1601, came forward on her own to appear before a "visitor and executioner" of witches from Rocroy,[66] for, as she explained, "many persons, in lewd terms and against her honor and her good name and reputation" had been calling her a sorceress. Marie Lanechin, in 1621, brought a charge against Nicolas Deramp, who accused her of witchcraft. They both voluntarily entered the prison in Le Cateau in order to bolster their credibility, but the testimony against Marie proved so damning that the judges ordered the Bazuel aldermen to prosecute. The two final trials were the consequence of her denunciations, but Pasquette Barra, who was acquitted in 1621, was challenged a second time, in 1627, when new accusations were made against her by two inhabitants of Bazuel. Just who were these prosecution witnesses, and what motivated them to turn their hostility upon these old women?

If one calculates that two of the witnesses appeared both in 1599 and in 1627 and that, on the latter date, Pierre Wattelier was fifty-eight and Jean Parmentier (if he is indeed the alderman of 1599; see Table 5) seventy-eight, then the ages of only twelve of the thirty-two witnesses at the Bazuel trials are lacking. This gives an average age of forty-five years for the villagers: three witnesses were young (twenty-two, twenty-five, and thirty), but seven were fifty or over.

Women represented less than a third of the total: four widows aged, respectively, forty-one, thirty-eight, fifty-six, and forty, five wives, of whom one was forty, and a young girl of twenty-two. Their statuses and professions were diverse, but there is a difference apparent between the men and women: one of the widows was described as a "hostess" at Landrecies, but nothing was specified about the nine other women. The male inhabitants of Bazuel included three aldermen, one sergeant, one tenant farmer (*censier*), one weaver (*mulquinier*), one thatcher, and a series of such less distinguished occupations as day laborer, shepherd, or linen-weaving worker.

In drawing up a typical portrait of the prosecution witness based on this information, the first conclusion would have to be that he was both very like and very unlike the victims. Witnesses were generally old, especially for that era, and some were as old as or even older than the defendants. But in the case of Bazuel, the average age of the accused, at sixty, was a little bit higher than that of the accusers. The male/female ratio among the witnesses was precisely the reverse of that among the accused: 69 percent men and 31 percent women, while men represented only 19 percent of the defendants in northern France (see Table 1). As for their social backgrounds, the witnesses and defendants seem to have been drawn from different classes. Four out of five of the Bazuel suspects were widows, and not one of them appears to have belonged to the upper socioeconomic-political level in the village; several of the witnesses, however, would have to be placed there. Interesting facts are revealed in the list of mayors and aldermen of Bazuel between 1599 and 1627,[67] that is, the roster of judges who were competent to rule on witchcraft (see Table 6). Throughout the period, the Trenchant, Wyart, and Lengrand families, with the exception of the latter, which disappeared after 1621, occupied the seats of power continuously until 1627. A comparison of these names with those of the witnesses and the witches' alleged victims yields some important correlations: among the bewitched, one Pierre Wyart in 1627, the daughter of Mathieu Hennocq in 1601, the husband of Saincte Avaine, and Jean, son of Nicolas d'Avesnes, in 1621.

Many of the plaintiffs were personally related to the aldermen-judges, and many of the victims they described were also members of these families (see Tables 5 and 6). Furthermore, their spells were evidently directed, at least in part, at the most powerful and the wealthiest elements in the village, for example, Jean Lenain and Jean Parmentier,

Table 6. Bailiff, Mayors, and Aldermen of Bazuel, 1599–1627

Date	Bailiff	Mayor	Aldermen
1599	Francois Leducq		Melchior Wyart Jean Lasne Christoffle Meurant Jean Trenchant
1601		Jean Trenchant	Mathieu Hennocq Bernard Lengrand Jean Soufflet Féry Hennocq Christoffle Meurant Jean Lasne
1621		Jean Trenchant	Gaspart Denise Melchior Wyart Bernard Lengrand Andrieu Cardon Andrieu Grenier Nicolas d'Avesnes
1627		Jean Trenchant	Philippe Wyart Cornil Avaine Anthoine Lebrun Mathieu Debarlaymont

aldermen, in 1599; Nicolas d'Avesnes, an alderman, in 1621; and an anonymous tenant farmer (*censier*) cited by Nicolas Deramp in 1621. The witnesses from Landrecies, too, can hardly be said to represent the poorest segments of society! Finally, as in the case of Nicolas Deramp, the chief witness in 1621 and an employee of Mathieu Hennocq, who served as alderman in 1601, one wonders if these witnesses from more modest backgrounds were not recruited by their employers for this task. In addition to Nicolas, one Andrieu Deramp is among the witnesses, raising our suspicions of a link between their testimony and the death of Hennocq's daughter. Two other witnesses, Andrieu de Braibant and Antoine Nicaise, engaged in professions that would necessarily make them dependent upon their richer neighbors.

Finally, Pierre Wattelier and Jean Parmentier seem to have specialized in furnishing testimony against witches, in 1599 and again in 1627. (Even if the latter Jean Parmentier should have been a son or a relative of the first, a relationship clearly still exists between them.)

This relationship shows up clearly in an analysis of the accusations (Table 5): deaths cited—of chickens, cows, and horses, and of people, particularly young people and infants—alternate with anecdotes intended to incriminate the defendant as a witch. Sickness, in every form, and attacks on the personal property of those rich enough to own, for example, two horses—these are the typical charges of the accusers. These and the refrain of "explanation," which recurs like a leitmotiv in their testimony: how the witch took revenge in her spells for being refused something she wanted or for having something taken that she considered hers. For example, in Andrieu Doyen's account of a quarrel over a manure heap between Aldegonde de Rue and an inhabitant of Landrecies, Aldegonde's daughter warns that he will live to regret his claim, for it is not right "to take the property of poor people without paying for it." Grégoire Florut testifies to having seen Aldegonde go off "all in a lather" when he refused her something she wanted. And the wife of Mathieu Hennocq offers as an explanation for the death of her daughter the fact that she had refused to give some "grains of purgative" to Marie Lanechin.

In this sense, perhaps the sorceresses of Bazuel can be considered "children of want."[68] But were they really "rebels against society"?[69] It seems to me, rather, that their role was a passive one, that they formed a fixed point for all the social hostility in the village. What is significant is not whether or not they could cast spells on their more fortunate neighbors but the fact that the latter perceived them as a real and immediate threat.

The six witches of Rieux (1650–52) and the seventeen sorcerers and sorceresses from Fressies and Hem-Lenglet (1609–49),[70] as well as other isolated cases in the Cambrésis, can be considered in the same light (see Tables 7 and 8).

At Fenain, in 1611, Marie Cornu, known as "The Redhead," was brought to trial. She had been married three times and widowed three times, and she was accused, among other things, of having poisoned all her husbands, the third and last because "he was always growling at her." She also "made a girl's nose fall off," when she tried to prevent Marie from marrying her father, and she rendered a child lame who "was giving her trouble when she was doing her duty" in the house of his father. She caused the death of a cow whose owner had refused her milk.[71] In short, Marie Cornu, a domestic servant, seems to have been a child of poverty.

In 1620, at Crespin, Cécile Bérurière, a young unmarried girl, had some trouble, presumably, finding a husband. A witness, aged thirty, testified that she cast a spell on him, saying "you never told me that you were going to get engaged."[72]

In 1637, an investigation at Campeau concerning the children of Mathias Bourié, a *laboureur* (a prosperous cultivator, with his own horses), involved the testimony of eight witnesses: two *laboureurs* (aged thirty-five and forty), two widows (both sixty), the mayor (seventy-one), a former mayor (forty-three), an innkeeper and *laboureur* (thirty-four),

Table 7. *Witchcraft at Rieux, 1650–1652*

Date (beginning and end of trials)	Name	Age	Number of Witnesses	Remarks	Verdict	References (ADN)
26 August–31 October 1650	Madeleine Desnasse	78	15	Born at Rieux; mother died in prison for witchcraft; her daughter of 13, deceased, denounced her; her devil is called "do whatever you like with them"	Strangled and burned	B 1216-17615–1, 2, 3, 5, 6, 11
10 May–8 July 1652	Marie de Boubay, unmarried	28		Born at Rieux; daughter of Jaspart and Marie Hourié (see below)	Banished	B 1216-17615–13, 15
10 May 1652–?	Jenne Boubay	34		Sister of the above; says she is bewitched	Unknown	B 1216-17615 17
?–8 July 1652	Marye Hourié, widow of Jaspart de Boubay			Mother of the two preceding	Banished	B 1216-17615 14
28 May–8 July 1652	Anthoinette Lescouffe, unmarried	30	8	Born at Boursies,[b] resident of Rieux for 28 years; niece of the following	Strangled and burned	B 1216-17615–4, 8, 23, 24, 25, 27, 28
28 May–10 July 1652	Susanne Goudry, unmarried	57–58		Born at Ognain near Audenarde,[c] resident of Rieux; aunt of the above	Strangled and burned	B 1216-17615–4, 7, 25, 26, 27, 28

a. Villette, "Sorcellerie dans le Nord," p. 153, is in error concerning these trials.
b. Nord: *arrondissement* of Cambrai, *canton* of Marcoing.
c. Belgium, province of East Flanders.

Table 8. *Witchcraft at Fressies (F) and Hem-Lenglet (H.L.), 1609–1649*[a]

Date (beginning and end of trials)	Name	Age	Number of Witnesses	Remarks	Place	Verdict	References (ADN)
16 December 1609–7 January 1611	Jehanne de Monchecourt, wife of Luc Maisne		"several" mentioned in Dec. 1610 (+1 in 1609)	Gave birth in prison, which delayed the trial; tortured	F	Executed	7 G 782
?–20 November 1623	Catherine Salmon			Tortured	F	Executed by fire	7 G 783
?–20 November 1623	Barbe Salmon			Sister of the above	F	Banished	7 G 783
11 October–20 November 1623	Colette Jardet			Denounced by Catherine Salmon; tortured	F	Executed by fire	7 G 783
17 October–20 November 1623	Crespin Plazeau		17	Son of Catherine Salmon; tortured	F	Executed by fire	7 G 783
26 October–20 November 1623	Simon Dupas		20 (incl. 9 from Cambrai)	Son of Collete Jardet; tortured	F	Executed	7 G 783
7 November–13 December 1623	Péronne Desgardins		14	Tortured	F	Executed	7 G 783
13 October–14 December 1623	Catherine Leleu			Tortured	F	Executed	7 G 783

Date	Name	Age	Witnesses	Notes		Sentence	Reference
11 November–15 December 1623	Anne du Moutié, wife of Nicholas Delattre		8	Lives in the Bray woods, jurisdiction of H.L.	H.L.	Executed	7 G 783
12 October–16 December 1623	Marie Delattre		10 + others	Tortured	F	Executed by fire	7 G 783
1623 (?)	Géry de Haynin			Fugitive	F	Banished forever	7 G 783
Before 15 November 1623–1 March 1624	Jehanne Flauveau, widow of Loys Dufour	45	6	Tortured, 15 November, but will not confess; the judges consult their colleagues in Arras (?)[b]	H.L.	Banished forever	7 G 783
5 January–1 March 1624	Marie Lemaire, wife of Eloy Léger	42	8	Tortured; accused by several already executed	F	Banished forever	7 G 783
?–1 March 1624	Gilliette Clacquebert, wife of Luc de Seins	40	witnesses	Daughter of Catherine Salmon; tortured	H.L.	Strangled and burned	7 G 783
May 1645	Charles Dupas and his wife				H.L.	?	7 G 786
1649	Jeanne Lourdeau	80			F	Banished	7 G 785

a. Villette, "Sorcellerie dans le Nord," p. 151, omits Géry de Haynin and commits other errors in dating and spelling of names. In particular, we must overlook his reference to "Jehanne Flanneur," who is none other than Jehanne Flauveau, already cited by him.

b. *Chef-lieu* of the Pas-du-Calais.

and a *laboureur* (thirty-eight). Most of them were among the more privileged of the village, in terms of wealth and power.[73]

The six trials at Rieux (1650–52) were heard before the bailiff and feudal tenants of Bouchain, who sometimes submitted the matter to the high court of Mons, in Hainaut (see Table 7). But Madeleine Desnasse admitted that she was brought to trial "by the accusation" of her fellow citizens, and Marie de Boubay complained about malicious "rumors" against her. All the Rieux trials, resulting first from the denunciations of Madeleine Desnasse and later of others, who were put to torture, were in fact closely interrelated. The six suspects together represented only three different households; twenty-three prosecution witnesses appeared from the village. For example, at the Desnasse trial in 1650, the following witnesses appeared, among others: Jean Leclercq, a notary and *laboureur* (seventy-three years old), the mayor's lieutenant (sixty-four), a *laboureur* of sixty-three, three villeins (aged seventy-two, seventy-eight, and forty, respectively), and two widows, of whom one was eighty-four.[74] Unfortunately, the lack of further information makes it unnecessary to undertake a careful examination of their testimony, as in the case of Bazuel.

Seventeen trials at Fressies and Hem-Lenglet (1609–43) were heard before the bailiff and feudal tenants of the collegiate church of Saint-Géry of Cambrai, within whose jurisdiction these two adjoining villages fell (see Table 8). There are detailed records only of expenditures for these trials, along with a few verdicts. The thirteen trials in 1623–24 cost more than thirteen hundred florins, of which a part was borne by the villagers; the average cost of a trial came to one hundred florins. In this same period, eighty-three witnesses appeared, among "others" for whom the total is not given, as against three male and ten female defendants. There is no way of identifying these witnesses, but the records show that they received reimbursement amounting to six *patars* each. Should we assume that most of the villagers were called as witnesses, or that only some of them appeared but more than once, at several different trials? And did the modest sum they thus realized account in part for their willingness to come forward? What ties of family and friendship can be found among them? What were their relationships with the rich and powerful in the village, on the one hand, and with the defendants, on the other? Because the necessary records are lacking, these intriguing questions cannot be answered. And yet this single outburst of witch hunting —nine out of the thirteen tried were executed in 1623–24—is unparalleled in the rest of the Cambrésis. The violence and the speed with which the epidemic flared resulted no doubt from denunciations elicited from the suspects under torture and from the technique of confrontations arranged among the suspects or between them and other prisoners, such as Michielle and Anthoine Lengrève, whose fate is lost to history. The thirteen defendants belonged to nine family groups: four members of the Salmon family, Colette Jardet and her son, and seven other individuals. One wonders, however, if there was not some connection between Marie Delattre and Anne du Moutié, widow of Nicolas Delattre, or between Simon Dupas, accused in 1623, and Charles Dupas and his wife, defendants in 1645.

No more can be deduced from the records. It is impossible to tell what role the villagers played in initiating the trials. The most that can be said with certainty is that Jehanne de Monchecourt, in 1609, owed her trial to the denunciations of one Charles Fouveau.

If all the cases in the Cambrésis are considered together, a line of demarcation can be discerned in part along socioeconomic-political lines. Without attempting to subject them to a one-dimensional economic analysis, we can observe, as Alan Macfarlane did in the case of Essex, that "witches seem to have been poorer than their victims," who often came from rich and influential families.[75] This does not mean, however, that the witches were necessarily the poorest in the village.[76] Furthermore, as in Essex, the defendants were often old—though not significantly older than the witnesses—and were frequently the neighbors of their accusers.[77] In sum, then, we must look for clues within the village community. But first I will try to determine what part the villagers—or some of them, at least—played in the spread of the witch hunt.

The judges, inquisitors, and demonologists all shared responsibility for the witch hunt that raged like a forest fire throughout the sixteenth and seventeenth centuries. And there is no doubt that their zeal, abetted by the accusations of the defendants, played a large part in the spread of the movement. The case of Marie Lanechin is a convenient example. When the aldermen's court that was hearing her case at Bazuel obtained only a partial confession from the defendant and referred the matter to Cambrai, the higher court ordered further torture:

The reason is that in the case of this crime of witchcraft, which is completely out of the ordinary and so secret and occult, and particularly in this instance, where the aforesaid Marie confesses a pact with the devil, having danced with him, and, with powder received from him, caused the death of the daughter of Mathieu Hennocq and cast a spell over Andrieu Deramp, one can, as they say, repeat the question, for it is hardly likely that if this Marie did all that she has already admitted, she did not also make the aforesaid renunciation [of chrism and baptism], receive the abovementioned mark [of the devil], and copulate [with him].[78]

Evidently this particular witch fell short of the satanic model in the minds of her judges. Several days afterward, however, they were able to put their minds at rest, for the suspect made a full confession on all counts, including her copulation with the devil.[79] Of course, the higher court judges were not alone in their zeal; they were seconded by the judges of the aldermen's court and a good part of the village.

Pressure from the villagers is easily discernible in the trial records. For example, Jean Leclercq, a notary at Rieux, declared in 1650 that Madeleine Desnasse had been arrested earlier but released, "having not been harried further for the poverty of the village."[80] Two years later, the same source notes that the mother of Antoinette Lescouffe would have been burned "if the village had had the means," but that the funds had already been depleted in the pursuit of several other witches. The mother, he adds, married outside of Rieux, at Boursies, and "everyone was pleased, for the village no longer had to pay for it."[81]

I have already remarked that the witnesses and the defendant often came from different social strata. An extreme example is Marie de Boubay, at Rieux, who was accused in 1652 of having threatened a local bachelor in the following terms: "Worm, if you don't marry me, you'll live to regret it"; but this would have been impossible, she testifies in her defense, "since he is a *censier* [rich tenant farmer]."[82]

Was witch-hunting pressure joined in by all the inhabitants of the village? To find the answer a distinction must be made between witches from outside the village, who appear to have been the object of general opprobrium if they chanced to pass by, and witches who were natives. In the case of the outsiders, for example, at Ors in 1601, "the boys pursued a witch who had been banished from Castillon";[83] and again in 1679 near Lille, three witches were chased by the peasants as far as Seclin, where one of them was killed.[84]

But when the threat arose from within the village, the reaction tended to be less spontaneous: the authorities took charge. Thus, on 15 July 1609, the mayor, aldermen, and the community of Hem-Lenglet passed the following act:

In consideration of the losses and damage which daily affect our neighbors and coinhabitants of the said Hem, which losses in our experience derive from charms and spells and sorceries, and in the interest of cutting off such losses, and fearing even that this sort of thing might befall us, and inasmuch as there are certain persons residing in the said Hem, our village, who are tarred with the brush of witchcraft, we have agreed and consented and hereby do agree and consent, after careful discussion, that those persons should be apprehended by the proper authorities, questioned on this point, and even (if the case demands it) brought to trial, as is proper in such a case.

The community further agreed to share the expenses, "each according to our quota system." The act was then signed by twenty persons, including the mayor and aldermen.[85] Almost all were men, and the Lamandin family had four representatives among them, of whom one was an alderman. This text was drawn up during a period of intense witch hunting, three years after the reactivation of the edict against sorcery,[86] and it preceded by only a matter of months the trial of Jehanne de Monchecourt held in the adjacent commune of Fressies. In fact, it may well be this act that touched off the many trials at Fressies and Hem-Lenglet fourteen years later.

Two further cases can be cited in which village authorities played a direct role in the witch hunt. The first is documented in an act, undated but probably from the seventeenth century, addressed by the mayor, aldermen, and farming community of "Garnier"[87] to the chapter of Notre-Dame de Cambrai, under whose aegis they fell. It complained of witches in the village, who gave "reason for fear to each and every one," of the death of animals who were "spellbound and full of all sorts of venomous beasts." The community asked that the evildoers be brought to trial and offered to stand half of the costs of each case. There were forty-three signatories, mostly men, and certain families (Lempereur, Depreux, Lasselin, for example) were represented several times.[88] The final text, drawn up by the mayor, the four aldermen, and two feudal tenants of the village of Dechy,[89] is a little different from the two others. Writing to the abbey of Saint-Amand, their landlord, on 7 November 1611, they demanded prosecution of those witches, starting with Anne Monart and Catherine Tassart who had already confessed, for the village was daily experiencing the loss of men and animals. They offered to pay forty florins per banishment or execution as their share in the trial expenses.[90]

Even on a fairly simple descriptive level, the relationship of the village to its witches cannot be understood without referring to a whole complex of factors, all of which played a part in the persecution phenomenon: ties of blood, clientage, and neighborhood; economic and social tensions among the villagers; the role of the well-to-do, the nabobs, and the local political cliques—in sum, the network of relationships that made up the rural community, a community whose membership was by no means defined simply by the fact of residence in the village. The village community in turn must fit into the larger context of an outside world in full political, economic, and religious evolution. I am not attempting here to do microsociology or microanthropology, which some recent authors have touted as the most fruitful way of looking at the witchcraft phenomenon.[91] Too little is known about the rural world of the Cambrésis, or even about Bazuel, Rieux, Fressies, and Hem-Lenglet to make such an analysis. On the other hand, some partial explanations may be made by comparing the witches, the witnesses, and their own small world with the large-scale political, economic, and religious movements that were sweeping at the time across this part of Europe.

For if we can understand why and how the hatred on the part of the judges and the elites was taken up and spread—in a different but perhaps an even more violent form—through rural society, in particular among the most influential (*sanior pars*) in the village, then perhaps the witch will lose a little of her diabolical halo and appear more as she really was: not so much a satanic and vindictive magic maker as the plaything of an evolutionary process that she could not hope to understand, the focal point of tensions that were incomprehensible to her—the unconscious expiatory victim of a cultural and economic upheaval still in process.

What, in sum, motivated the rural communities and the most powerful village families to take up the witch hunt? Here lies the heart of the problem and probably also the answer to why the trials ended and why not all villages in this region were touched by them: "The men who stopped the witch trials were not the princes and the learned, but townsmen and villagers who still believed staunchly in witchcraft and the powers of the devil."[92]

The Acculturation of the Rural World in the Sixteenth and Seventeenth Centuries: The Example of the Cambrésis

Did the fear of witches shown so clearly in the witnesses' depositions and in the texts drawn up by the village communities burst suddenly upon the rural scene with the advent of the seventeenth century? On the contrary, there is reason to think that the local folk had long believed in and devised a number of protective rites against a sort of "popular witchcraft," that is, the healing or spell-casting powers of certain individuals. I have given elsewhere some examples of these rites,[93] without, however, having been able to put them into their proper context. Certain of the trials that were held at the end of the sixteenth and beginning of the seventeenth centuries contain fragmentary information about them. The testimony of Laurence Maughier, during the trial of Reyne Percheval at Bazuel in 1599, is interesting in this regard: she refers to a "Waldensian" —that is, a sorcerer—living at Saint-Souplet and also gives an account of a local exorcism. The healer involved, from the village of Bertry,[94] she characterizes as the rival and enemy of the witch of Bazuel, who is in turn allied with the Waldensian of Saint-Souplet. In the same vein, the "dean" of Bazuel, who twice exorcised Andrieu Deramp after he was put under a spell by Marie Lanechin around 1621,[95] describes himself as possessing powers equivalent to those of the witch. In Douai in 1610, at the trial of Isabeau Blary, a hundred-year-old woman born at Lewarde but resident at Douai, a neighbor relates how the mother of a sick child denounced Isabeau and swore she could obtain proof against her: "She would go to speak with the Capuchin, who would make the image [of the culprit] appear in a mirror."[96] These scraps of testimony evoke a world full of would-be spell-casters doing combat with legions of self-styled healers.

No doubt the villagers believed blindly in them all. And no doubt, also, they were, like Laurence Maughier, versed in the "geography" of sorcery in their locale and knew which exorcist to see if they thought themselves bewitched. In point of fact, healers such as these were rarely mentioned in the witch trials, especially after the first quarter of the seventeenth century. And yet one wonders why they did not, as Villette suggests in the case of the "Capuchin" of Douai,[97] run the same danger of arrest as their witch opponents. Perhaps the healers still played an important role, at the beginning of the seventeenth, as they had during the previous centuries, in establishing in the minds of the peasantry a counterpoise to the "spells" of the witches.

An intriguing text, dated Sunday, 6 February 1446 (new style), supports such a hypothesis in the case of the Cambrésis. It consists of nine separate testimonies given to the bailiff of Arleux, Rumilly, and Saint-Souplet, related to an accusation of sorcery against Péronne, widow of Gilles Pingret, resident of Saint-Martin-en-la-Rivière. Unfortunately, texts as early as this one are rare in the Cambrésis. Furthermore, there is no indication of who drew up the charges—the great witch-hunters' manuals were as yet unknown—or what the result of the trial was. In any case, five witnesses from Saint-Martin, three from Vaux-en-Arrouaise, and one from Saint-Souplet accused Péronne of being a witch: she had caused the death of several persons, including her own daughter-in-law; she was well known in the area, and inhabitants of Valenciennes, Le Cateau, and the nearby villages came to ask her to disenchant their loved ones; she could also, for a sum, "by saying masses, make runaway husbands return to their wives" and bring faithless wives back to their hearths. She was thus an ambivalent sorceress, who could both heal and destroy. And she was not alone in this ability; one of her competitors was a woman from Le Cateau who warned the wife of a villager of Saint-Martin to stay away from Péronne for nine days because she suspected Péronne of having enchanted her.[98]

Out of the pages of this text rises an image of the Cambrésis as a murky region peopled by spell-casters, whose "recipes" are readily passed along in the witnesses' testimony: herbs gathered on Midsummer Eve, holy water, and ritual signs are the chief ingredients. There are extraordinary resemblances to the seventeenth-century trials: a body of witnesses who try to disassociate themselves from the witches, professing ignorance when the judges attempt to draw them out; an almost identical geographical representation of witchcraft, in Le Cateau, Valenciennes, Saint-Souplet, even Bazuel; and finally the distinction between the witch's malevolent presence in her own village and her beneficent appearance to the outsiders who come to consult her. Her rival in Le Cateau shares this same ambivalent quality.

On the other hand, Péronne's victims all seem to have been people;

unlike her counterparts in the seventeenth century, she did no harm to crops, animals, or property. Is this distinction owing to the state of the documents that have survived, or is it one of the fundamental characteristics of the medieval rural witchcraft, about which so little is known? In the latter case, the difference would point to one of the explanations for the witch hunt: by the seventeenth century, the threat to property plays a major part in villagers' testimonies (see Table 5). Was there a breakdown in their mental equilibrium, which was founded on the possibility of using healers—who might, incidentally, act as witches in their own village—against the witches? Or were the healers no longer able to quiet the anxieties of their neighbors, in part because their fears now took a different form? Certainly fewer healers appear in the texts of the seventeenth century, but this may be only an illusion. The witnesses' instinctive caution may be the reason the healers disappear from the trial records and, consequently, seem to have lost much of their importance in village society. They did survive, however, for they reappeared in the Cambrésis and elsewhere with the end of the witch-hunting epidemic. In fact, at that time they felt the wrath of the courts. The judges, who had ceased to believe in witchcraft, condemned them in essence for their superstitious practices and their bad influence on their neighbors. Thus, on 18 September 1699, the bailiff of Cassel condemned Jean Vanacker to be thrashed and banished for six years from eastern Flanders, as a consequence "of having exorcised men and beasts, of having named the witch who he said had cast a spell over persons and animals . . . and of having done other superstitious acts."[99] On 22 April 1700, François Darche, from Furnes, was condemned to serve ten years in the galleys and to make amends before the front door of the local church of Sainte-Walburge,

and once there, bare-headed and kneeling, to say and declare, with a clear and intelligible voice, that he had said and named several persons falsely and maliciously as witches, that he had participated, among other things, in disenchanting [three women], to which end he had made use of diabolical means and dabbled in sacred matters, that he had written himself maliciously in ox blood on a half sheet of paper several names which, falsely, he had declared to have been written and signed in their own blood by would-be witches and werelocks, whom he had supposedly forced to come forth to do so.[100]

On 29 September 1740, the official of the archdiocese of Cambrai ordered the appearance of a certain "fellow" who was peddling a "brochure . . . containing a supposed miracle which happened in Marseilles and superstitions which protect against thunder, sudden death, rabies, death without confession and every evil."[101]

The curate at Viesly[102] was involved in 1752 in a suit against one Denisse, whom he refused to marry in the church until she had repented of various "scandals" in which she had been involved in the village. In particular, "she has publicly accused two local persons, a man and a woman, of having put a curse on her, she has called *shepherds to come to remove the spell* and surgeons from different areas to visit her, and the charm has finally been broken in childbirth, which has not, for all that, prevented her . . . from setting upon the so-called sorcerers as they were leaving the church."[103] Documents such as these, which occur in increasing abundance from the end of the seventeenth century, prove that the countryside, in particular, continued to produce its share of sorcerers and exorcists. This does not, however, imply a simple restoration of the situation that existed before the witch-hunting epidemic. For society was once again, in the eighteenth century, in a period of profound change, and relations among the witches, the exorcists, and the local villagers were once again undergoing a necessary transformation. Much research is needed to clarify these relationships, culminating in their role in the rural world of the twentieth century, in which spell-casters and charm-breakers are still part of the culture.[104]

A comparison, then, between the situations at the end of the sixteenth century and at the end of the seventeenth century must begin with a question: why and how did one part of rural society, in the Cambrésis, cease to look to the healers for remedies against the sorcerers' charms? Why did these villagers turn instead for protection to the judges and begin to condemn the witches mercilessly in the courts? The seer-healer as she was represented by Pieter Brueghel the Elder in the sixteenth century[105] had not really lost her powers, as far as her neighbors were concerned, but, like them, she belonged to a world that, a hundred years later, was crumbling away.

The first important series of witch trials in the Catholic Low Countries were held between 1580 and 1630 (see Figure 1). The cases at Bazuel and most of the trials at Fressies and Hem-Lenglet, in the Cambrésis, occurred at this time.

In this same era, the Counter-Reformation spread, and important economic and demographic changes occurred in the Cambrésis countryside. Were these simply parallel events or can a partial explanation of the witch hunt be found in them?

In the first place, the reign of the archdukes (1596–1633) was marked by their attempt to reorganize ecclesiastical structures and to Christianize the masses. The archbishop of Cambrai, Van der Burch, who had been promoted in 1616, wrote in 1625 to Rome that he had removed from office more than one hundred of his pastors, either by pensioning them off or by bringing them to trial on grounds of immorality or ignorance. And even though "the establishment of seminaries will have an effect only much later," the nuncio could record in 1634 that the secular clergy was now of high quality and that the ecclesiastical authorities zealously visited their districts annually.[106] Thus the Catholic hierarchy, which had been upgraded at every level, set out to raise the masses from the depths of their superstition. The public authorities supported this campaign—on 20 September 1607, one year after the edict against witchcraft—by issuing another proclamation defining "the so-called servile labors" that had hindered the "sanctification of Sundays and feast days." Specifically, this text ordered the closing of hotels and taverns and forbade dancing in public places and professional activity during the hours of sermons, parish masses, and vespers. It was designed to fill the churches once again with worshipers, and though in the beginning it seemed to have little effect and had to be renewed in 1608, 1624, 1625, and 1633, there is no doubt that this edict modified the life of the communities little by little. In effect, it channeled the population toward the churches, where now the curates had to "preach on Sundays and feast days so as to cover the whole body of religious instruction in a period of two years." A succession of jubilees, in 1597, 1605, 1606, 1608, 1617, 1621, and 1626, and the influence of the confraternities worked together to produce an "increase of devotion" among the populace.[107] In addition, the leaders of the Counter-Reformation focused upon the need to attract youth in order to supervise and mobilize them. Day schools aimed at the offspring of the "well-to-do fraction of the population" were set up under the auspices of the clergy and magistrates, who fostered in them an "atmosphere steeped in religion." Moreover, free Sunday schools were founded for the children of the poor, where they would be taught reading and writing as well as the rudiments of the faith, and where the sexes would be kept strictly separate. Parents who refused to send their children to these schools would be punished: they would be stricken from the "poor rolls" and denied public assistance. In 1586, these Sunday schools were declared obligatory throughout the province of Cambrai, where a special campaign was mounted, for example, in Valenciennes. In this archdiocese a child was to go to school from the age of seven "until he showed evidence of sufficient religious instruction."[108]

The witch trials show traces of this organized education. The recorders at the Bazuel trials in 1599 and 1601 (see Table 5) noted that the witnesses who appeared there "did not know how to write." But by 1620, at Crespin, north of Valenciennes, several individuals testifying at the trial of Cécile Bérurière were able to sign their names, notably a villein aged twenty-nine and an unmarried girl of twenty-three.[109] The same proved true during the Rieux trials, 1650–52.

The success of the Counter-Reformation in the north of France, then, explains why this area attained a higher literacy rate in the seventeenth century than did the rest of the country.[110] The introduction of written culture was accompanied by a campaign against rural "pagan-ism" and by the diffusion of Christian doctrine recently revamped by the Council of Trent. Is it not possible that the shock of the Catholic literary culture upon the rural peasant culture produced, in these conditions, a kind of mental traumatism? For educated peasants could explore the merchandise offered by itinerant book peddlers, that "escapist literature calculated to intensify the debasement of the majority in a repressive, and therefore alienated, society."[111] Such books reinforced "the magical mentalities conducive to the continued peace of mind of the dominant groups" and alienated still more those popular masses who were "con-ditioned" to know their places.[112]

The effort to strengthen this sort of control over the popular masses in the Catholic Low Countries was reinforced by the economic and demographic transformations of the seventeenth century. The course of their evolution in the Cambrésis has been documented in the works of Hugues Neveux.[113] The population of the village of Saint-Hilaire, lo-cated some fifteen kilometers east of Cambrai, doubled, at a conservative estimate, between 1450 and 1575, in a succession of "violent fits and starts," as it did elsewhere in the Cambrésis. Between 1481–82 and 1574–75, the number of births per family seems to have increased dra-matically, implying an evolution in the demographic structure, possibly, Neveux suggests, in the direction of a longer adult life span. Moreover, the sixteenth century saw an "unexpected but undeniable mobility within the population" of Saint-Hilaire while, in the next century, "a greater stability seems to have been likely."

This schema, according to Neveux, holds true for the whole of the Cambrésis. More important is a contrast in the whole area, from 1540 to 1575, between a steadily growing population and a stabilized cereal production, in most cases at a level lower than that of 1520. The Cam-brésis, which had exported part of its grain in the fifteenth century, now witnessed such a growth in local demand that its productive capabilities, in their state of "relative inertia," were hard pressed to keep up with it. The demographic upsurge "thus threatens to contribute to a transition from a relatively open economy to an economy turned in upon itself." And, in this light, the spread of the *mulquinerie* industry to the country-side can be seen as a possible response to the problem. In effect, the Cambrésis endured an economic crisis of twenty years' duration begin-ning about 1575; plague in the 1580s and the wars of the following decade "disturb the production of cereals."[114] The first important wave of witch trials began to gather force in the Cambrésis, in particular at Bazuel and Fressies, shortly after this crisis. No doubt a causal link exists between these two phenomena, in the sense that the economic stagna-tion of the end of the sixteenth century emphasized social antagonisms

258 / Robert Muchembled

precisely at a time when the villages of the Cambrésis were tending to
turn inward upon themselves: "Demographic expansion made every plot
of ground more precious and each new arrival less welcome."[115] This
closing of the village to the outside world produced a new social discom-
fort and served to exacerbate the turbulence that was affecting the floating population of that time, a population composed essentially of two
social categories: farmhands who moved about in search of employment
and a "self-conscious social group" made up of tenant farmers (*censiers*),
who rented large tracts of land—fifty to seventy-five hectares on the
average—and could thus make use of heavy machinery as well as an
abundant labor supply.[116]

These effects of demographic and economic change would have gone
unheeded by the villagers. When, under the changed conditions, their
lives became more difficult, they probably experienced only a marked
uneasiness. But they may have reacted instinctively and violently when
their property or their rented land was threatened; Neveux cites several
cases of socioeconomic antagonisms in the sixteenth century.[117] And one
study of criminality in the southern Low Countries from 1610 to 1660
has shown that 15 percent of eleven hundred "crimes" surveyed arose
out of conflicts of interest, both urban and rural. Viewed from another
perspective, 50 percent of the crimes committed by tenant farmers and
laboureurs were related to economic conflicts, as against 15 percent by
the day laborers.[118]

I have already noted that the accusations of the witnesses in the
rural witch trials of the Cambrésis revolved around the twin concepts of
threat to life and to property. Can we perhaps assume that witchcraft, for
the villagers, now connoted a form of social conflict? The judges and
witnesses at Bazuel, for the most part, did not come from the same social
stratum as the accused. On the other hand, almost all the participants
seem to have been part of the fixed populations of the villages in question. This was the case of the aldermen's court, especially, and of the
witnesses at Bazuel. The witches themselves were all natives and lifelong
inhabitants of the villages where they were brought to trial, with only
rare exceptions—such as Maxellende Vasseur, a shepherd's wife and a
resident of Bazuel for seventeen to eighteen years, and Marie Burlion,
a sixty-year-old beggar woman accused of witchcraft at Braine-le-Comte
on 19 July 1647.[119] Both were acquitted, the latter because there were no
charges that would stand up in court. Does the judges' leniency reflect the
fact that neither woman had more than superficial ties with her adopted
village and could not therefore arouse the same social anxiety as the
other suspects? In other words, this fear may have existed only within the
very core of certain villages that were threatened from the outside by
the demographic and social turbulence characteristic of the Cambrésis.

Before turning to a discussion of this social anxiety, we should note that the twenty-year-long economic crisis that afflicted the Cambrésis at the end of the sixteenth century was accompanied by the definitive ousting of the French in 1595. What effect would this new climate of peace have had upon the deep reservoir of social tensions that had accumulated in each locality? First, peace would have brought back to their villages many families or individuals who had temporarily fled during the second half of the sixteenth century. Did Rieux, for instance, where three houses out of a total of twenty-eight were empty in 1560–61, see the sudden return of some of its old inhabitants once peace was declared?[120] This may never be known, but it is certain that the external pressure from vagrants upon the Cambrésis villages rose sharply at the beginning of the seventeenth century.

Second, the church authorities, in 1592 and again in 1606, designated a whipping boy for the masses in the form of sorcerers or witches, whom they increasingly identified with evil. Little by little, the leaders of the Counter-Reformation convinced the villagers that witches might be harmful. The lessons in the Sunday or weekly schools, the curate's sermons, trial sentences read aloud in the public squares, all spoke to these countryfolk of the devil and his apostles. The endless troubles that now rained upon the southern Low Countries would reinforce their sense of doom, and the clergy would do their part by portraying these catastrophes as evidence of divine retribution. In fact, the priest's message— stressing the whole community's responsibility for the misfortunes that plagued them—had not changed since the Middle Ages. But now, of course, his parishioners were better able to accept this message because of the atmosphere of perpetual fear in which they lived. In the provinces adjoining the Cambrésis (and no doubt there, too, if they could be found), documents trace the succession of threats to human life: plague at Lille in 1606; on 27 March 1606, in Flanders, Artois, and Hainaut, "a hurricane so violent and tempestuous . . . that no one had ever seen such a great disaster"; "three suns over the city of Lille" in 1608; a "terrifying" comet in 1610; plague again at Lille in 1617, as a consequence of "God's wrath";[121] a "great fear and terror" that war would break out again in Artois early in 1625; an unspecified fear occurring in the same province in the same year, as "the wrath of God . . . roused against his people" rained war, famine, pestilence, and skin rashes upon them; a virulent plague in Artois in 1636, just as the war was starting up again.[122]

Thus the witch hunt may be seen as the end result of the process of rural acculturation, in which the guilt feelings of the masses were assuaged—and perhaps some of their economic, social, and psychological concerns as well—with the presentation of an expiatory victim. Unfortunately, this interpretation does not explain why in Artois, the neighboring province, which underwent the same acculturation but had different economic and social problems, very few witches were brought to trial. One would also especially like to know why these trials touched only a limited number of villages in the Cambrésis. My answer to this riddle lies in the interplay of three types of determinants: local or chronological differences in the acculturation and the socioeconomic evolution; the rate of decline of the old security-producing structures in the rural world; and the probable existence of other types of collective or individual expression in response to the accumulated tensions.

Before the age of the witch trials, the exorcists and healers had evidently done a good job of calming the fears of the peasantry. Their belief in the struggle between exorcist and sorcerer kept the villagers in relative security and, at the same time, supplied them with a logical—if not a rational—explanation for their countless troubles.[123] Nor did the exorcists lose all their clients between 1580 and 1680, for they reappear later in force in the documents, as we have seen. Thus, we can assume that, even during the witch hunt, most of the villagers in the Cambrésis hung onto their older, reassuring world view, their faith in the balance between good and evil, represented by the exorcists, on the one hand, and the sorcerers, on the other.

Those villagers who, at Bazuel and elsewhere, joined in the witch hunt must have been exceptions to the rule, men and women who saw the balance tilting dangerously to the side of the sorcerers. This situation suggests that the Christianization of the countryside was very uneven, touching certain villages sooner and more profoundly than others, and that in these villages it was probably diffused first among the upper classes, who had the means to buy the book peddlers' wares and the time to read them. The poor, and particularly the floating population of laborers, must have been more difficult to reach, despite the edicts of the archdukes. The curates, the key figures in the Christianization campaign on the local level, varied enormously in quality during the first quarter of the seventeenth century; the archbishop testified to this fact in 1625.

Until more work has been done on this subject, we can proceed on the hypothesis that acculturation was carried out unevenly in the countryside as a whole and selectively within each village population.

Unevenness in the provincial economy appears still more clearly in this period. For example, in Saint-Hilaire, where there were no witch trials, linen weaving (*mulquinerie*) developed as a local industry in the second half of the seventeenth century.[124] But weaving had been introduced at Bazuel as early as 1599, and one weaver was a witness in a trial in 1621 (see Table 5). The absence of detailed testimonies for Fressies during the great persecution of 1623–24 deprives us of evidence of its economic development. But the trial of 1652 at Rieux turns up one weaver, aged twenty-two, among the local population.[125]

These scattered references lend credence to the theory that "certain parts of the Cambrésis were converted to linen weaving in the sixteenth century."[126] In this light, Bazuel appears once again to be a singular locality, responding to the economic crisis by the development of rural industry long before Saint-Hilaire, for example. How does such an economic gap between two villages scarcely twenty kilometers apart fit into the overall picture of witch-hunting mania? Apparently the epidemics of persecution were closely related, on a local level, to the stage of economic and social evolution: traditional villages, in which the old ways of thought remained unchallenged, experienced fewer witch hunts, especially if their rate of acculturation was also slow.

Even though the total history of the Cambrésis cannot yet be written, the more modest attempt can be made to fit these scattered economic indices into a larger framework, starting with their effect on social structures that maintained security in the villages of this area.

John Bossy, in a brief but brilliant article, has described the impact of the Counter-Reformation upon the rural masses of Europe.[127] He has shown that, in order "to divert all streams of popular religion into a single parochial channel" and to transform something collective and popular into an individual Christianity, the reformers had to challenge existing family relationships, the notion of private warfare, and the confraternities—the most important institutions of medieval religion—and that because of their inherent opposition to the idea of the nuclear family, they could not integrate it into the new religious format. By their actions, "the bishops of the Tridentine Church . . . were laying many of the foundations of the modern state."[128] This analysis holds true in every detail for the Cambrésis and for the southern Low Countries in general. It points to the conclusion that the impact of acculturation in the more receptive villages such as Bazuel hastened the disintegration of social relations that had begun a long time before. In fact, what, in the latter stages of the witch trials, is presented as antireligion, is really the antithesis of the model Catholic life or, in other words, those sins most prevalent in rural society. Sex plays a starring role therein: for example, the judges forced each suspected witch to confess—though Villette maintains a discrete silence on this point—that she gave the devil "a hair from her shameful parts."[129] Isn't this purely and simply a denunciation of sexuality outside of Christian marriage? Similarly, in the witches' confessions we can see the implicit condemnation of many of the social practices of the pre-Tridentine period. Marriage with the devil in a purely carnal union recalls the old custom of "betrothal," a sort of trial marriage. The sabbath, a "sacrilegious feast," would seem to stand for the ritual celebrations of the Middle Ages with their guitarists and minstrels. And the communal confession, which was supposedly a feature of the sabbath, should also be considered in the context of Saint Carlo Borromeo's efforts to replace the medieval public confessions with private audiences.[130]

To sum up, then, the Counter-Reformation was attempting, in the Cambrésis and elsewhere, to promote morality in the conduct of its laymen and individualism in their religious life. But in doing so it was threatening to destroy the ties of blood and family that had held society together since the Middle Ages, and it was aided by an evolutionary process that had begun in the southern Low Countries more than a century before. The growing authority of the princes was acting to stamp out the practice of the private vendetta, which had functioned as a regulator of social tensions, helping to keep down the level of violence and to prevent warring families from exterminating each other completely. But the new theory according to which "no one is permitted to take vengeance except God and the judges appointed to punish wrongdoings"[131] was not immediately, or wholeheartedly, accepted. In the fifteenth century these new ideas had made the least inroads in the Hainaut and Namur.[132] Two centuries later there was still considerable evidence of private warfare in the southern Low Countries.[133] The old alliances were under great strain, but they continued to make themselves felt: for example, 15 percent of eleven hundred "crimes" analyzed for the period 1610–60 were attributable to clan warfare.[134] But though these family alliances continued to exist, their members no doubt vaguely sensed that their days were numbered. For, by the mid-seventeenth century, the rural family was "already in large part dismembered" in France[135] as a whole as well as in the region under study. Under these conditions, the security-producing structures in the villagers' world seemed to be crumbling. Pierre de Saint-Jacob's analysis of France during the period 1550–1650 applies to the Cambrésis: "A decisive century if there ever was one, which saw the precipitous disintegration of the old communities and the attendant rise of the propertied bourgeois, the nonresident, and the nobleman, all of whom threatened the *valuable property* and the rights of the rural population."[136] This vast expropriation that resulted essentially from the invasion of the rural world by the capitalist spirit gave rise to deep divisions within the community, where "social imbalance had grown."[137] Various studies have shown, moreover, that as a result the rural community, once open to all male inhabitants of the village, shrank further and further until, in the seventeenth century in some cases and certainly by the eighteenth century, it admitted only "those who had some means."[138] This was certainly the case in parts of the Cambrésis in the first half of the seventeenth century, based on texts from these rural communities where the witch hunt was most fierce:[139] at the very least they show the influential role played by a few powerful families within the village. The aldermen of Bazuel, for example, sat in judgment on the witches and collected testimony against them from their own relatives and friends and were thus set apart from the lower orders of the population. As a group they also formed the town council, who "oversaw every aspect of group life or at least had the legal power to do so."[140] Without going as far as Porchnev, who concluded that "the seventeenth century abounds also in intense class struggle,"[141] certainly traces of such a struggle are evident throughout the Cambrésis countryside. The disintegration of security structures, compounded by the impact of the Counter-Reformation, laid bare a network of fears beneath the surface of society. The richest and most influential villagers no doubt adhered all the more staunchly to the declining kinship structures that provided a base for their opposition to the growing number of poor, malcontents, and vagrant unemployed. They probably also tried to take over the rural community as a political and socioeconomic institution to serve their own interests. Witch hunting thus served both as a mechanism for expressing their fears of this latent social warfare and for keeping it at bay. It is perhaps no mere coincidence that their chosen victims—most often widows, young girls searching vainly for a husband, or, in some cases, children[142]—were generally poorer than their judges and almost always isolated figures within the community. The typical witch was not only very different from her judges but also from the witnesses who testified against her. Perhaps she was singled out because of her difference. She symbolized to her accusers not only a threat to their society but also the terrible helplessness of the lonely individual with no friendly or family relationships to fall back on—in short, the incarnation of their own fears for themselves. This question of the similarities and dissimilarities between the victim and her enemies bears upon the problem of the executions and their function as sacrificial rituals for the villages.

From a criminologist's point of view, the society of the southern Low Countries appears to have been steeped in violence, as a study of delinquency based on evidence of royal remissions and pardons has shown.[143] Criminal acts in this part of the country in the first half of the seventeenth century seem to have been the work essentially of young unmarried men: more than 50 percent of the criminals and more than 60 percent of their victims fall within this category, the majority of them within the age group fifteen to twenty-five. The existence of "lateral group relationships based on age" and the clear schism between married and unmarried men would suggest a group violence characteristic of youth gangs or clans.[144] But the authors of the study are at a loss to explain the abrupt decline in criminal acts by older men. Since we can hardly assume that the latter would have completely transformed their behavior, we can only suppose that they turned their aggressiveness toward other objects. Indeed, witch hunting, which was the work of the village elders, may well have functioned as the adult expression of this youthful violence, especially as it involved collective participation and tended to be organized around clans or groups who shared a mutual self-interest and who can be seen as the more mature equivalent of the adolescent gangs. Moreover, the witnesses, the witches, and their victims almost always belonged to the same community, like the criminals and their victims in 75 percent of the cases studied. Finally, among those criminal cases involving individuals who possessed some measure of property or means, 50 percent are found to be linked with quarrels over economic matters,[145] recalling the economic tensions often apparent in the witch trial testimonies. Such an explanation could never by itself justify the witch-hunting phenomenon or the general rise in violence in the seventeenth-century Cambrésis. The most that can be drawn from these similarities is the observation that the crimes that were prosecuted, like that of witchcraft, involved deviations from the dominant social norms of their time. Of these, one of the most widely accepted was the proscription of all sexual activity outside of Christian marriage.

There is no lack of evidence concerning sexual repression in the Cambrésis.[146] In the seventeenth century, the ecclesiastical court of Cambrai judged 142 morals charges involving country priests and 664 sexual offenses by laymen, both urban and rural, but especially the latter. Sexual relations between young, unmarried adults account for 38 percent of these lay crimes; adultery, sometimes accompanied by incest, constitutes 32 percent; and incest itself 11 percent.[147] Toward all those charged, clerical as well as lay persons, the church showed a marked leniency, though women were generally treated more severely than men.[148] This would indicate that the rural acculturation campaign during the seventeenth century was running into heavy local resistance: many priests, and even more villagers, remained attached to sexual mores that were much freer than we have been led to believe.[149] This seems to have been particularly true of the southern part of the archdiocese of Cambrai; the deanships of Cambrai, Beaumetz, Le Cateau, and Valenciennes account for 265 of the lay sexual offenses, or 40 percent of the total.[150] Of course, proximity to the seat of the archdiocese probably meant that the Counter-Reformation took root in the south more quickly than in the north, bringing with it an increase in the number of cases heard before the judges. In this same area, while sexual offenses were being judged lightly, the witch trials were mushrooming—and in these, sexual misdemeanors figured prominently. Could it be that the local judges, who handled the sorcery cases, were more stern than their episcopal counterparts in their application of repressive measures against sexual offenses? The hypothesis would seem to be plausible if we accept the fact that witch hunting in the Cambrésis was confined to a minority of villages, in which most influential elements of the population rallied to the Counter-Reformation earlier than their neighbors and by their zeal attempted to set themselves apart from their social environment. If the rate of change by decade in the witch trials and in the morals cases is compared, both lay and ecclesiastical, for the Cambrésis,[151] certain contrasts stand out: ecclesiastical morals charges, which are scant between 1600 and 1630, grow steadily from 1630 to 1650, return to their earlier levels in the period from 1650 to 1670, and then shoot up again to new highs from 1670 to 1700. On the other hand, the lay cases, which are very frequent between 1644 and 1664, disappear almost completely from 1664 to 1674, and then rise to unprecedented heights in the last quarter of the seventeenth century.

It is apparent that the morals cases tended to decrease between 1650 and 1664 and 1670 to 1674, in particular, just as the witch trials were multiplying; in other periods (1590–1600, 1630–40, 1670–1700), morals cases increased as witch trials diminished. Apparently, as the ecclesiastical courts grew lax, the local judges put on pressure in their turn and sought out a local witch to serve as a scapegoat. Through the mechanism of the witch hunt, they were not only working toward a goal of sexual repression, which they shared with the ecclesiastical judges, but also directing attention away from themselves and their own kind and toward a class of victims poorer and more defenseless than themselves. Might there be traces of a guilt complex in the behavior of the judges and witnesses in these witch trials? Weren't they as guilty as anyone else of the sexual sins and weaknesses the religious and political authorities were campaigning against? It must be remembered that they represented the most thoroughly acculturated elements in the village, and as such they would be most likely to apply first to themselves the guilt obsessions of that age: "sin, flesh, damnation, the sacraments and salvation."[152] In this setting of violence and social conflict, these villagers appear to have externalized through the witch hunt a destructive urge harbored deep within themselves: "Destructiveness. . . . It is not like aggression, which serves survival; but it is mediated by social and cultural factors, and for this reason it can be diminished, if not eliminated."[153] This urge can be vented not only in criminal acts but in many other ways. Unfortunately, too little is known about seventeenth-century brigandage, popular revolts, or the commonplace expressions of aggression to say more on this point. And yet the explanation for these revolts, for example, must lie in "whatever was capable of touching off in [the population] a reflex of violence."[154]

Violence, like the cemetery, was located not on the periphery but at the very heart of the village. Criminals, rebels, and "witches" were not so much social deviants as by-products of a situation controlled by a complex of sociocultural factors. In the case of the witches, the mechanism for excluding them—execution—operated in response to the will, conscious or unconscious, of the whole society.

Before attempting to measure the impact upon them of all these structural changes, an attempt must be made to establish the mood of these Cambrésis villages. Violence and aggression, together with alcoholism and a persistent sense of insecurity, were elements in the landscape against which these peasants lived out their days. Moreover, "one has the impression that these people passed their time spying on each other from behind their curtains." Sexual scandals in particular were at the heart of most of the cases that found their way into the courts. In a less serious vein, gossip-mongering and fun-poking were the daily diet of a society that was turning increasingly inward upon itself.[155] In such a world, scandal serves as a vehicle for the introduction and perpetuation of certain moral and social stereotypes. Many of these stereotypes revolved around the concept of the devil, as a semantic study of the word "honor" in the southern Low Countries between 1610 and 1660 has shown. An accusation of witchcraft, with its implication of crime against the Almighty, was considered "as the most serious threat to one's honor."[156] Thus, two plaintiffs testified in 1698 that the curate of Montigny[157] "accused [them], among other things, of belonging to a race of witches, for several weeks running, and as such a slander is extremely serious, particularly for country people, and as it could completely destroy the reputation of the plaintiffs and of their families."[158] By the end of the seventeenth century, such a charge by a curate would not have caused great concern. But the situation was different two or three generations earlier, when the priest was beginning to function as the guardian of tradition. It was his job to transmit this tradition to his parishioners; he was, in addition, the necessary mediator between them and the Almighty.[159] It is not unreasonable to imagine how some priests, motivated by a guilty knowledge of their own moral weaknesses, took an active part in the witch hunt. Thus, for example, the Cambrésis curate who, around 1626, paid a sick call on a twenty-year-old parishioner:

He took a rather strong drink, and after hearing her confession, he told the girl that she was bewitched and that if she would be willing to let him get in bed with her and to make love to her she would be cured, all of which she refused. However, he redoubled his efforts in order to gain his objective, putting his hand under the covers to touch her breasts, and even more, which modesty prevents her from mentioning.[160]

Obviously, not all the curates in the Cambrésis practiced this kind of exorcism. But this text bears out my observations concerning scandal and the notion of honor: the seventeenth-century reformers were able to superimpose an atmosphere of moral anxiety and guilt upon the substructure of very real fears and uncertainties that were troubling a society in transition. The interplay of these anxieties could touch off the witch hunting. But it was necessary first that this moral insecurity should profoundly trouble certain elements in the village, that it should, in effect, be hammered home by the local priest. He would tend to project this guilt upon his parishioners all the more strongly if he was uneasy in his conscience about his own conduct. This would explain why the majority of the villages in the Cambrésis did not take part in the witch hunt: most of the local priests conducted themselves exactly like laymen, particularly in sexual matters, which explains why the ecclesiastical courts, faced with a broad-based defiance of the rules, adopted a policy of leniency. Yet all the while the Counter-Reformation was making slow but steady progress, converting one after another, sowing its message of guilt among the priests, who in turn passed it on to their flock, and together they looked for an expiatory victim, a witch—a woman, that is, the very symbol of sexuality. The burning of witches could thus provide a means of wiping out one's own sins and of turning the attention of the authorities away from oneself. I have noted that the increase in this region in the number of witches coincides with a decline in the instances of morals cases brought against both laymen and clerics, which tends to support my hypothesis.

Following the same line of reasoning, the witch trials came to an end at the end of the seventeenth century, not only because the authorities had opted against them,[161] but also because the process of rural acculturation had ground to a halt. Henceforth the local priests—like the curate of Rumegies, near Saint-Amand[162]—stand out clearly in contrast to their lay brethren. But can one conclude that the country populace had been totally acculturated? And, if so, how can one explain "the widespread collapse of popular religion in Catholic Europe at the fall of the *ancien régime*"?[163] In any case, a very real gulf now existed between priest and layman, and curates were now, in general, distinguished by their exemplary behavior: they no longer needed to project their own guilt onto their parishioners. And thus, though the villagers continued to believe in the same superstitions, the witch-hunting mania died away, aided by a change in conditions generally. With the dawning of the eighteenth century "an ancient world was disappearing." The great demographic crises ended; the successive panics abated after 1750.[164] Though northern France remained throughout the eighteenth century, in the words of Georges Lefebvre, "a land of poor people, despite its collective strength,"[165] the rural population had now found new objects on which to vent their grudges and their violence: the representatives of the central government, in particular its tax collectors.

In every respect, an ancient world was disappearing. Henceforth the roles of layman and clergyman within society were clearly defined. The priest had become an outsider, overseeing the moral conduct of his parishioners with a high degree of detachment. The reformers had at last succeeded in cutting off the religious world from rural popular culture; they had superimposed Christian and learned culture upon a background of superstition. The witch trials were one consequence of this long battle to break down the popular culture, and they touched off a whirlwind of violence in this new world, where the boundaries of the sacred had become vague and confused. Structural changes coupled with a series of calamities had heightened a sense of existential fear in the peasantry and had created a need to redefine what was sacred through the mechanism of ritual executions. The sudden increase in witch trials at the beginning of the seventeenth century and again between 1640 and 1680 echoed, in my view, these reflexes of terror in response to the spread of the realm of the sacred beyond the control of the priests. War was a contributing factor in this, not in itself, but because of its effects. Among these should be numbered not only an increase in fear and tension but also a tendency to fuse together what was profane and what was sacred. Upon the return of peace, the lay population and their priests were unable for a time to sort out one from the other. The numerous executions of witches in 1679, following the restoration of peace and the installation of French rule in the Cambrésis, resulted from this wild confusion in the domain of the sacred and from the legacy of wartime violence. The testimony of the curate of Merbes-le-Château[166] concerning the events of 1677 provides a remarkable illustration of this process. The priest recounts how the French camped near his village and sacked his own house. He continues:

The said church was in no state to receive a sacrificial offering, being completely in disorder, partly because of an enormous amount of furniture which had been piled there for safekeeping, covering even the altars, many of which were dirty and nasty, and partly because of an unbearable stench and filth emanating from the large group of local people and others from the surrounding area who had taken refuge there, many of whom, begging your pardon, relieved themselves right there, and among whom there was a large number of sick people suffering from diarrhea . . . so much so that it would have been entirely disrespectful and lacking in the reverence we owe to his divine majesty to offer up a spotless lamb in a place such as I have described.[167]

When calm had been restored and the sacred could once again be set apart from the profane, the reappearance of violence in, for example, the witch trials, is hardly surprising. Isn't this violence instrumental in establishing a new order in the realm of the sacred, and doesn't it represent for the rural priest a victory over his rival in this realm, the local seer-healer, to whom an anxious population had previously turned for help?

The witch hunt, then, can be understood as a ritualized projection of violence away from certain individuals and certain communities. I will now examine the changes that occurred in the mental superstructures, keeping in mind the fact that an evolution in the socioeconomic infra-structures formed a necessary basis for the evolution in mentality. Of course, neither the witch-hunting phenomenon nor its disappearance can be explained away as two successive mutations in the structure of West-ern thought or by a simple evolution of popular mentality. For such a cataclysm erupts along a whole fault line of social shifts and pressures: thus, in the fourteenth century, there were massacres of Jews and lepers, who were accused of poisoning the public fountains;[168] and during the cholera epidemic of 1832 in France, doctors were accused of poisoning the poor in order to aid the rich.[169] For, in time of epidemic, "the enemy immediately becomes the poisoner."[170] The type of scapegoat chosen says most about the tensions of work in society: before the sixteenth and after the seventeenth centuries, in the West, external victims were pre-ferred, Jews and beggars, and later tax collectors or farmers-general. During the period under consideration, however, enemies were also— indeed more often—found within the community, particularly witches, who were specifically identified by witnesses as poisoners (see Table 5). The period 1580–1680 is, in this respect, unique, even though it over-laps with a parallel development, throughout the seventeenth century, in which the poor, the mad, and the beggars[171]—all of them "external" deviants—gradually were put under lock and key. The reason why ritual victims began to be taken by preference from within the community is probably to be sought in the diffusion of violence and the sacred during this period. Prior to the witch persecutions, violence was not unknown in the villages of the Cambrésis, but it was restrained by certain traditional, regulatory mechanisms such as private warfare, ties of blood and of marriage, and the willingness of the community to hear the complaints of all its citizens. The village appeared as a coherent entity, with its murders and its crimes, but also with the means of preventing the destruction of the whole community by excessive violence. The popular religion, orga-nized around groups based on shared interests or kinship, integrated the local priest into the daily life of the village; but neither the priest nor the church constituted the special domain of the sacred. In fact, the sacred penetrated everywhere, but the coherence of the group repelled its pos-sible aberrant or destructive aspects away from the community. Fear and social unrest were dealt with by recourse to exorcists, hailing generally from outside the village, who were thought to be able to rid the peasants of any charms cast upon them by their neighbors, those witches who were the apparent source of any and all misfortunes. In sum, then, a state of equilibrium seems to have existed between the peasants' fears and the necessities of their daily lives that saved them from despair during the most trying times. Schematically, the village represented, in my view, a kind of haven, an island refuge in a sea of danger and of sacred forces.

But from 1580 to 1680 or thereabouts, violence and the sacred shifted from the outskirts of the Cambrésis village toward its center. The traditional checks on violence were removed, largely through the rise of the centralized state. Feelings of solidarity grew weaker at a time when fears were multiplying. In their effort to bring morality to the rural world, churchmen, in certain areas, broke down the old distinctions between the sacred and the profane. The acculturated curate, who now felt a sense of his own guilt, introduced a new kind of sacredness at the very center of the village, by making something hallowed of the church and his own person, by preaching a new sexual repression, by sowing seeds of guilt among his parishioners, and by tracing for them horrible images of eternal damnation.

The rising tide of the sacred could wash more easily over the community now that feelings of solidarity had grown weaker and could no longer inhibit its expansion, and now that the rich and powerful were trying to safeguard their own interests by directing its flow toward the poor, weak, and defenseless elements in the village. To put it schematically once again, the boundaries of the sacred had contracted toward the heart of the community, the village square, which was now the focal point of tensions and dangers (see Figure 2).

In a brilliant, incisive essay, whose only shortcoming is a lack of sociological and chronological perspective, René Girard has proposed a fascinating explanation of the interplay of violence and the sacred.[172] "The aim of the religious," he writes, "is always to forestall violence, to prevent it from breaking out . . . , to speak authoritatively to mankind of *what it must do and not do* to avoid the return of destructive violence."[173] In cases where "the religious disintegrates through conflict," the community looks either for a scapegoat from among its members or a

Figure 2. Boundaries of the Sacred and Village Social Tensions

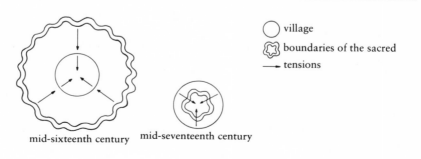

mid-sixteenth century   mid-seventeenth century

○ village
boundaries of the sacred
⟶ tensions

ritual victim chosen from outside. The internal victim represents for his
fellow citizens a kind of monster "doubling" for themselves, who is sacrificed in an effort to "keep violence outside of the community. . . . The
entire community is saved from its own violence by the act of sacrifice.
. . . The sacrifice draws to the victim like a magnet all the fragments of
dissension which are scattered about, and it then dissipates them with the
offer of partial satisfaction . . . the sacrifice is a form of violence without
the threat of vengeance."[174] This theory would certainly fit the witch
hunt in the Cambrésis, which took place at a time when the sacred
element was no longer in a state of equilibrium with other forces but was
pervading all of rural society. Perhaps a parallel may be found with the
tensions at work in Aztec society before the arrival of Cortez; the response to Cortez was an increase in ritual sacrifices, but with external
victims.[175] Regardless of the laws concerning witchcraft, was not the real
motivation of the witnesses and judges basically their feeling of terror at
the proliferation of the sacred and of the criminal forms of violence that
threatened their property, their persons, or their families? Perhaps their
aggression against the witches played a necessary part in a "rite of fixity
. . . [designed to] perpetuate and reinforce a certain order in matters of
family, religion, etc." Their merciless unanimity toward their victims
was dictated by this process of cultural stabilization and by their need
to wage all-out warfare against negativistic sentiments, which could be
"purified and excreted" only by means of the sacrificial ritual.[176] From
this point of view, the procession of witnesses, neighbors, and, occasionally, relatives of the victim, appears to have fulfilled a need to affirm their
own orthodoxy by excluding the witch from the community and heaping
on her the onus of their own guilt.[177]

A "desire for immobility, or fear of movement, which is characteristic of all societies under pressure from the sacred"[178] was clearly at work
in these witch-hunting villages. It may well be traceable to the increasing
social strains in the Cambrésis and to a new sense of guilt, especially in
sexual matters: "Sexuality is unclean because it is related to violence. . . .
Repressed sexuality opens the way to violence."[179] If this theoretical
relationship between violence and the sacred is applied to the Cambrésis,
the ritual character inherent in the executions of witches becomes clear.
The villagers were behaving very much as the French Catholics and Protestants had done a century earlier, "ridding the community of dreaded
pollution," while basing their actions upon "a store of punitive and
purificatory traditions current in sixteenth-century France."[180] The reason for emphasis during the execution upon the deviant character of the
accused becomes clear: the highly detailed sentence listed the "crimes"
committed and the solemn act of penance demanded for them,[181] and the
whole was read publicly before being put into effect. This sort of morbid

spectacle not only pleased the crowds; it also provided the spectators with a useful moral lesson in how to escape the same fate—by avoiding the same sins or, even simpler, by denouncing their "monstrous counterparts." In point of fact, this expiatory violence was linked to the moral stereotypes the church was trying to inculcate in the masses and was thus related more to the normal aspects of society than to the pathological.[182] For the witch was presented basically as a caricature of her fellow citizens, who could derive satisfaction from seeing a portion of their own sins burn with her, but who perceived themselves as being sufficiently different from her to escape the same fate. Each execution, therefore, pointed up both the differences and the resemblances between the victim and the peasants, encouraging them to still more denunciations in order to save their own skins and their own peace of mind. Thus the "conditions for a guilt-free massacre"[183] joined with the epidemic or endemic character of the witch hunt to produce a self-sustaining movement. It was not the use of torture that prompted the accused to denounce his neighbors, for, under the conditions I have described, the epidemic of witch hunting would continue indefinitely, feeding on the fears and guilt feelings of the villagers. Only a change in the mental climate at their level, for whatever reason, could account for an end to the persecution. It could not come from a change of heart, a greater rationalism, on the part of the judges, who themselves gave only the original impetus to the movement; it was up to the rural masses, once the witch hunt had been proposed to them, to respond, depending on whether or not it suited their specific needs.

One final issue remains to be raised: why were most of the Cambrésis accused, throughout this whole period, overwhelmingly drawn from the ranks of widows, young spinsters, and children? Surely the answer to this question lies in the role they played in the society of that time. But it would be a mistake to attribute it simply to the denigration of women by the ecclesiastical authorities or the judges or as a manifestation of sexual repression on the part of the judges.[184] It stemmed rather from a general debasement of human nature that, in the view of the influential and learned men of that time, applied to women and children as well as to beggars and madmen. For "the devil was ceaselessly on the prowl"[185] and preyed not on the males but on the weak and defenseless.

An anthropologist has observed: "It may be that in societies in which the majority of disadvantages accrue to women, where the status differential between the sexes is extreme, women will be portrayed as agents of destruction, particularly in the religious or mystical belief systems."[186] Yet in sixteenth-century France, urban women and young boys of ten to twelve years of age played a prominent part in acts of popular religious violence.[187] Can we then assume that they belonged to social categories that were under an excessive degree of restraint? Certainly, a century later, French men did fear women and children and protected themselves by keeping them in a state of strict subjugation: "From a legal point of view, women were at a tremendous disadvantage . . . I have the impression that these fears often had to do with the erotic aspects of marriage . . . husbands were prompted by this fear of sexual defeat."[188] We might question whether a child of about seven was really " 'cured' of the malady of infancy which had made him so incomprehensible and frightening to his elders."[189] In any case, in the Cambrésis as elsewhere, the victims were almost invariably chosen from among certain types of women and children—those who had the fewest ties and affiliations or who, as preadolescents, had not as yet attained any value in the eyes of their parents. Thus the choice fell on the weakest, on those who were least likely to elicit vengeance from their families or kin, and also on those two categories of individuals who inspired the greatest fear, because, being kept in strict subservience, they were the most likely to revolt. The theory of a socially selective fear is a good working hypothesis, at least until more is known about the history of the family in Europe. The precarious economic situation of widows and spinsters laid them open to all kinds of threats. They were also clearly exceptions to the social stereotypes then prevalent and, perhaps, disquieting examples of the unhappy fate of the isolated individual—a fate that was a little too close for the comfort of their neighbors.

Conclusion

The subject of witchcraft in the Cambrésis has been touched upon only superficially in the course of the present study: its precise role and function in the rural world is still to be defined. The fact that it has survived across the centuries and down to the present day provides a further inducement to researchers.

On the other hand, the phenomenon of the witch hunt, which took place between 1580 and 1680, is another matter entirely, and one whose characteristics I have been able to identify and discuss. The witch hunters in certain of the villages seemed to be engaged in a ritualistic purging of their own fears, in response, it would seem, to the infiltration of violence and the spread of the sacred throughout the whole area. They demanded scapegoats, chosen normally from among the common people, especially those who led a poor, or marginal, existence and who had the fewest resources of support or solidarity to fall back on. The local judges and the witnesses, who were at the same time similar to and unlike the accused, seemed to expect that by the sacrifice of these victims they would build a new cohesive social order on the ruins of the old one. On this level, the "witches" appear to be the expression of a cultural and socioeconomic situation in a state of flux.

But these deep social tensions—which may well have their roots in a class struggle as yet unexpressed, undirected, and unconscious of itself—must also be portrayed in the light of two other factors. First, the religious evolution in the Low Countries in general, and in the diocese of Cambrai in particular, accounted for the fact that certain villagers had been able to project their natural aggression onto the "witches": the religious and lay authorities had furnished the necessary frame of reference—a definition of witchcraft—and had incited these villagers to the hunt by stressing their own culpability and the omnipresence of the devil in the world. The local priests, who were a prey to the same newly inspired guilt feelings, helped to spread this philosophy through the countryside. But the work of acculturation proceeded by fits and starts, and the numerous sources of resistance it encountered explain why not all the Cambrésis villages were caught up in the witch hunt. The priest's role was crucial. Even though he might never speak out against the witches, his own disposition determined that of his parishioners. Thus, at the end of the seventeenth century, the persecution stopped, when acculturation had reached all, or almost all, of the rural priests, even though it had spread unevenly throughout the countryside (evidence is the resurgence of superstition in the rural population). The priest and his flock seemed to have reached a kind of modus vivendi. Moreover, the church and her priests had new problems to deal with, and the villagers had new and powerful enemies in the form of the king's agents, whom they now "sacrificed," both in fact and, more often, in effigy, instead of the witches. Violence and sacredness had been redefined: the church now represented an island of the sacred at the heart of the village, while much of the former power of superstition had been driven out to the margins of village life.

Second, changes occurred in the economic and demographic structures, as they did again in the eighteenth century. Their evolution from the end of the Middle Ages up to the sixteenth century had created the conditions in which the witch-hunting epidemic could break out in the Cambrésis. Their alteration had shaken the whole network of relationships of kinship and solidarity and had created in the peasantry a growing sense of insecurity in the face of a world that was, in actual fact, more dangerous and more hostile than before. The history of these groups, which reflected ties of family or mutual interest, remains to be written, for the Cambrésis as well as for the rest of France. But the witch does not seem to have been some kind of rebel from society. On the contrary, she was the passive victim of a "process of fixity," the butt of that "desire for immobility, or fear of movement, which is characteristic of all societies under pressure from the sacred."[190] Can we then see her as a point of contact in a class warfare that she herself would never have perceived or understood? Whatever the answer to that question, it is clear that the villagers who condemned and burned her felt themselves to be in danger, both economically and socially, and were testifying by this act to a profound social conservatism. The danger was, of course, quite real: criminality in seventeenth-century France posed a continual threat to property, in the north at least. Elsewhere, the appearance of popular uprisings suggests a deep social malaise. How else can we interpret the "hatred, jealousy and rivalry among men" cited by Madeleine Foisil in explanation of the revolts in Normandy in 1639, though she refuses to acknowledge the existence of a "class front"?[191]

I have tried to emphasize the character of the witch hunt as an index of the far-reaching malaise in the society of the Cambrésis. Can the same model be applied to other cultures and periods? The Peruvian Indians, for example, in the sixteenth century, underwent a very profound process of acculturation, involving cultural, political, economic, and social reorientation, and, once they had been acculturated, certain of their leaders —the *curaca*—acted against the best interests of their subjects and chose to ape their Spanish conquerors, with very serious consequences for the whole society.[192] Was the situation in Europe really very different? Was the Cambrésis any exception? Pierre Goubert quotes the example of the seventeenth-century *coqs de village*, who "went so far as to imitate . . . their lords and masters."[193] Why not trace the history of such a rural acculturation (and of urban areas as well)? A new field of research is opened up to historians, for the epidemic of witch hunting in continental Europe occurred just at the point of cleavage between two distinct rural civilizations, that of the Middle Ages and that which began with the eighteenth century. The origins of this cleavage do not lie solely in the rise to power of a new hegemonic learned culture, which repressed a popular culture that is still largely a mystery to us.[194] This phenomenon is only surface froth, hiding important underlying demographic and socio-economic changes: the intensified pursuit and seizure of wealth in Europe by a small number of men and, in their wake, the emergence, on the rural level, of many pale imitations, each of whom is trying to do the same thing in a scramble for crumbs from the banquet table. Little wonder that at the same time the modern state began to develop, for which the Counter-Reformation prepared the ground, in France and elsewhere.[195]

The witch-hunting epidemic is by no means a pathological and isolated phenomenon: rather, it is part of the process of collapse of structures (*destructuration*) that took place in the rural world during the "European crisis" of 1560–1660.[196] Like other phenomena of the same period, popular uprisings, criminality, and violence, it was a central, not a fringe, movement within society. And as such, it was symptomatic of a contagion that was not confined to the victim or even to her judges and accusers, but infected society as a whole.

These arguments can be developed in greater detail. What is needed most is a history of European popular culture before the Reformation and the Council of Trent: that popular culture which Rabelais was one of the last major writers to bring significantly into his works.

Witch Hunting and the Domino Theory

H. C. Erik Midelfort

Scholarly studies of witchcraft have been sprouting lately like mushrooms in a fairy ring. Medievalists have refined our ideas concerning witchcraft as heresy and have shown how particular heresies influenced contemporary ideas about witches.[1] These studies have shown that medieval men did not slide from some supposed early medieval skepticism down the steep ramp of scholasticism into the turbulent sewers of superstition. That idea, once popular among Protestants and rationalists, has given way to a much more judicious approach that rightly places the roots of superstition and witchcraft in the early Middle Ages.[2]

At the same time, other scholars have begun to apply the social sciences to the study of witchcraft, an enterprise that goes back at least to Kittredge in the 1920s, but is now taking hold in systematic fashion. Anthropological, sociological, and psychological accounts of witchcraft are being made. There can be little doubt that these studies have deepened our awareness of the context surrounding the witch trials.[3] Something is known, for example, about the local tensions that produced witchcraft accusations[4] and about what sorts of persons were accused of witchcraft.[5] And some scholars have begun trying out psychoanalytic theory to explain demon-possession and the hatreds that rose to the surface in any witch trial.[6] Not all of these attempts have succeeded, but on the whole they have reoriented our view of witchcraft.

In addition to this onslaught of social-scientific witchcraft literature, extraordinary insights into the nature of witchcraft itself are coming to light. Keith Thomas's wonderful book *Religion and the Decline of Magic* presents a sympathetic approach to the real problems that men tried to solve by means of magic.[7] And Carlo Ginzburg has thrown open a whole new area by showing that in at least one instance a fertility cult was

---

This essay was first presented to the Davis Seminar in 1973.

converted into witchcraft through the patient efforts of ecclesiastical officials.[8]

Amidst all of this scholarly effort, it seems odd that at least one major area has failed to attract any attention whatsoever. No one has tried to compare different kinds of witch trials, to analyze the various shapes that panic might take. We have known for over a century that English witch trials were more moderate than Scottish or continental trials, but that is about as far as our knowledge has gone. In fact, many writers are content to refer simply to the "continental" witch trial as if it were a unified and well-understood species. Quite the reverse is true. Very little is actually known about the mechanics and shape of European witch trials, and I would argue that scholars should try to develop a more rigorous morphology of witch trials. I aim to sketch one major reason why so little work has been done on the shape of witchcraft trials and to describe one major pattern that can be detected in some cases. In doing so I hope to extend and make more precise a model that was at times only implicit in my study of witchcraft trials in southwestern Germany.

The basic reason no one has troubled to develop a morphology of witch hunting is that no one has recognized it as a problem. The reason for such blindness, in turn, is that we have all been too much dominated by one picture of witch trials, a picture that I shall call the domino theory. Without knowing it, historians have accepted a model that at best can be only partially correct. In its simplest form, the domino theory works only where the judicial process used torture (or the equivalent) to obtain confessions and lists of accomplices. The theory holds that once a person stood accused of witchcraft, he had little hope of escape. Relentless torture would pry a confession from the hapless suspect or might result directly in the death of extraordinarily stubborn suspects. In addition, and almost worse, confessed witches could be required under torture to supply long lists of accomplices. These persons, too, could be interrogated, tortured, and forced to add more names to the lists of suspects. In this way a small trial could grow into a massive panic, and trials in one town might infect, through accusations, nearby towns and villages. So compelling is this model that even writers in the sixteenth and seventeenth centuries occasionally described witch trials as a chain reaction. They, too, assumed that once a witch trial began, there was no stopping it. Occasionally such assumptions found expression in the midst of panic. At Rottenburg, in the Habsburg territory of Hohenberg, in 1585, the magistrates worried that a current panic might eliminate all of the women of the town.[9] A century later the magistrates of Calw worried that a thorough campaign against all witches would exhaust the resources of the Black Forest before all the guilty were burned to death.[10] The great defender of witches, Johann Weyer, protested that torture was applied so cruelly that innocent women "would much rather die confessing to crimes they knew nothing about than suffer such long drawn-out tortures."[11] The result, in Weyer's view, was that witchcraft trials spread out of control. The only solution, he thought, was for magistrates to learn that witchcraft was really nonsense. Unfortunately, magistrates did not begin to draw that conclusion for another century or more. The same model, however, governed the thoughts of the famous Jesuit defender of witches, Friedrich von Spee. In *Cautio Criminalis* (1631) he declared: "We see again and again that a witch trial, once begun, drags on through several years, and that the number of condemned grows so that whole villages are wiped out, and nothing is concluded before the trial reports contain the names of further suspects. If this should continue, there will be no end of witch burnings before the whole country is depopulated. Thus, finally, every prince has had to stop the trials. Down to today, every trial of this sort has had to be stopped by an edict. They never find their own conclusion."[12]

Historians have rarely tried to justify their belief in an implicit domino theory, but if they tried, they could find contemporary writers who understood the trials that way. Historians have not sought these kinds of proof, however, because the domino theory of witch trials has usually been a way of escaping close scrutiny of the shape of these panics. In other words, historians have often assumed the mechanism of chain reaction so they could pay attention to supposedly more important matters. A disproportionate amount of research has gone into studying the social tensions surrounding witchcraft trials without concern for the dynamic of the trials themselves. Only by fitting the trials into the simple mold of the domino theory can scholars concentrate on other exciting questions.

One final reason exists to explain the almost universal acceptance of the domino theory. Implicit in the model is the notion that popular culture and society are irrational and that only the external forces of enlightenment and the territorial prince could still a local panic. This has enabled historians to combine legal and high intellectual history in a most gratifying manner. My own researches, of course, do not lead to a clear defense of man's rationality, but they do cast doubt upon the need for enlightenment or for external force to bring the chain-reaction panic to a halt. The domino theory does help explain the start of most large witch hunts, but even at best it does not help us understand how a series of trials ever came to an end. Must we conclude that the prince intervened in every case? Must we look for a Voltaire in every village? And what about instances in which the prince intervened only at the request of a town or village? In addition to such questions that are obscured by the domino theory, we tend in that framework to lose sight of the interesting and puzzling fact that some trials went on for years whereas others exploded but then stopped quickly. It seems obvious that the domino theory has stood too long as a substitute for clear analysis.

Once attention is called to the tacit assumption of a domino theory, it becomes instantly clear that not all trials were chain reactions. Even in the era of the largest witch hunts, many small witch trials took place with only one person accused or executed. This is true not only of England, where the lack of official torture makes it plausible, but also of France and Germany. More study will be necessary to clarify the reasons why even torture failed to produce a chain of indictments in every case. Did the chain reaction depend on the mood of prosecutors or on the specific sort of accusation? Were charges of spreading disease or causing storms more likely to trigger a series of trials than accusations of bewitching a neighbor's cow? Or was it crucial whether a given suspect had close friends? Whatever the reason, it is clear that many small trials seem to have had all the ingredients for a long series of trials but that they fizzled out. E. William Monter's recent book devotes a penetrating chapter to this form of "small panic" larger than the malefice-centered witch trials common in England, but somehow stopping short of the full-scale panic common elsewhere.[13]

Just as significant as these restrained, small panics, however, is the fact that large, even enormous, witch trials often came to an end of their own accord without outside interference. This fact forces us to examine carefully the precise pattern of each panic to try to discover what it was that pulled a large series of trials to a halt. As a preliminary hypothesis, I have proposed that in many cases witchcraft trials could continue unchecked as long as the basic stereotype of the witch remained the old, poor woman. At Rottenburg in Hohenberg this concentration on women was found from 1578 to 1602.[14] In most large trials, however, this traditional stereotype breaks down so that wealthy women, young women, even men and boys, were plausibly accused of witchcraft. At first sight, this might seem to open the floodgates to panic, and indeed this development made the largest panics possible. But it also posed the questions of who might be a witch and how witchcraft should be detected. This process of questioning seems often to have affected the judges themselves and to have made them incapable of condemning any further witches. This fact became crashingly clear to judges if any event occurred to cast serious doubt on judicial procedures. For example, if the wife of a judge or mayor was condemned and executed, it might lead to a general suspicion that the innocent were being condemned with the guilty. Or if a suspect withstood torture, and thus proved her innocence, local judges might begin to doubt the legal efficacy of torture.

In a recent study of witch hunting in southwestern Germany, I have tried to show how frequently these patterns recurred. At Rottenburg, for example, the trials continued sporadically as long as poor women were the primary suspects. As soon as members of the elite were charged, however, the trials often came to a halt. This occurred in 1595–96, again in 1599–1602, and yet again in 1605.[15] It is problematic that witch trials did not simply end in Rottenburg, but proceeded by fits and starts. And yet each minor flare-up reveals the model I have suggested: namely, that witchcraft panics came to an end when local communities perceived that the trials were not working; and that this perception was most common when obviously innocent persons were convicted of witchcraft.

The model works also for the huge witch trial at Ellwangen between 1611 and 1618. The investigators started with a single suspect and then collected denunciations of hundreds more. The domino theory seems to work well with this phase of witchcraft panic. By 1613, members of the "better families" had been executed, and still the trials went on. A Jesuit priest writing in that year commented in despair, "I do not see where this case will lead and what end it will have, for this evil has so taken over, and like the plague has infected so many, that if the magistrates continue to exercise their office, in a few years the city will be in miserable ruins."[16] The magistrates did indeed continue with the trials, and as they did, local systems of prestige and authority crumbled. In 1615 three local priests were executed as witches. When such things could happen, local society was clearly in danger of consuming itself. And yet, such events may also have shocked men into recognizing that something had gone wrong. The archives preserve the records of some protesters who denounced the trials because a close friend or relative was executed. Unfortunately, they, too, were often accused of witchcraft and executed or simply terrified into submission. The courts rarely admitted outright that they had been mistaken, but their zeal seems to have cooled, and after 1615 the panic at Ellwangen ebbed quickly.

A similar story can be told for Schwäbisch Gmünd, for Offenburg, for Mergentheim, Oberkirch, Esslingen, Reutlingen, and Calw. In each case the panic spread and executions mounted until the court recognized, for various reasons, that somewhere it had gone astray. The general breakdown of stereotype was one of the most common forces that both permitted larger witchcraft trials and ultimately called them into question. Vigorous protest was another, for even if the protester was quashed, his complaint may have planted seeds of doubt in the minds of judges and governors. We can rarely know why men change their minds, but it would be foolish to neglect these kinds of influence. In addition, I have already suggested that legal doubt could arise whenever torture failed to produce a lasting confession. According to German law, for instance, only those presumed guilty were supposed to be tortured. Therefore, a successful stand against torture could be due only to stubbornness or to innocence, and if due to innocence, it was a reproach to the whole network of denunciations derived from torture. Such an example is clear in Offenburg in 1630, where the judicial proceedings collapsed in the face of doubts like these.[17] A recent study of the witch trials in Baden-Baden shows that there, too, the first four victims were among the least socially protected class, widows. But the last suspects included disproportionate numbers of men (see Table 1).[18]

So far my examples have come from southwestern Germany, but the model developed for that region has a wider applicability. The Franconian episcopal see of Würzburg, for example, conducted a well-known and vigorous witch hunt between 1627 and 1629, in which 160 persons were executed in 29 separate burnings. An analysis by age and sex shows that the earliest trials resulted in the execution of women only.[19] But the proportion of women dropped dramatically to only 21 percent near the end of the panic. Similarly, although following the earliest trials only adults were executed, later trials concentrated on children, who comprised 61 percent of those executed in burnings numbered 16–20. The harrowing panic had clearly destroyed the traditional stereotype.[20]

In the trials at Würzburg (see Table 2) the danger of these broken stereotypes finally became clear to Bishop Adolf von Ehrenberg when both he and his chancellor were accused of witchcraft. With decisiveness, the bishop prohibited further trials and established regular memorial services for the innocent victims of justice. It would be easy to regard the bishop's belated insight with cynicism and to see only a partial truth. The bishop did indeed recognize the error of the trials only when his own life was endangered. But there was no necessity for him to establish public repentance and regular memorials. It seems likely that the breakdown of stereotypes had laid the foundation for a genuine insight into the error on which evidence given under torture rested. Instead of a domino theory, a cybernetic process of feedback would seem to explain this pattern better.

Table 1. Sex and Marital Status of Ninety-four Indicted Witches at Baden-Baden, 1627–1631

Indicted witches in order of indictment	Widows	Wives	Daughters	Spinsters	Men
Nos. 1–31	10	17	1	0	3
Nos. 32–62	3	21	6	0	1
Nos. 63–94	3	20	0	1	8
Totals	16	58	7	1	12

Table 2. *Würzburg Witchcraft Executions, 1627–1629*

Groups executed in order of execution	Adults executed			Children executed			Total executed			Percent adults in total
	Female	Male	Percent	Female	Male	Percent	Female	Male	Percent	
Groups 1–5	22	4	85	0	0	0	22	4	85	100
Groups 6–10	14	12	54	2	0	100	16	12	57	93
Groups 11–15	8	3	73	2	1	67	10	4	71	79
Groups 16–20	9	2	82	6	11	35	15	13	54	39
Groups 21–25	6	14	30	1	13	7	7	27	21	59
Groups 26–29	7	18	28	2	3	40	9	21	30	83
Subtotals	66	53	55	13	28	32	79	81	49	74
Totals	119			41			160			

At Cologne in this same period (1627–30) a large witch scare claimed the lives of between twenty-four and thirty-two persons.[21] The panic began in earnest with the spectacular trial and execution of Catharina Henot, a member of the ruling town patriciate. Her conviction seemed to sanction the conviction of other women of lesser status.[22] The turning point of the trials there came ironically with young Christina Plum (age twenty-four), who voluntarily confessed to witchcraft but went on to admit plotting with other witches to implicate innocent persons.[23] In horrified reaction to this implicit attack on the credibility of evidence given by witches, the archbishop of Cologne demanded that the documents relating to this trial be burned. Too many innocent persons were listed in her testimony. Burning the trial record was not the only result of Christina Plum's confession. After her trial no new suspects were arrested. Once again, an internal legal flaw had spoiled the chain reaction. The Cologne events show no real breakdown of stereotype, although Plum was young, but show instead a different way in which doubt might be produced.

There are certain problems with the model I am suggesting. First, not all trials produced the kind of feedback that effectively stopped the witch hunters. For example, a recent account reveals that in the Saarland between 1591 and 1594 at least sixty-five persons lost their lives as witches.[24] In the first three years about 85 percent of the victims were women. In the fourth year, however, that percentage fell to 54; with the intrusion of men, the flurry of witch trials calmed down temporarily. As in Rottenburg, however, witch trials were not over. In the early seventeenth century they flared up again, with a total of 109 executions between 1601 and 1630 throughout the Saarland. In that period a problem arose that had not previously existed: large numbers of persons were accused of witchcraft but not brought to trial. In 1603, 25 persons were named but not tried, in 1611, 30, and in 1630, 28 more. These persons may have escaped trial because of their very numbers. They may also have spread doubt on the value of denunciations. In any event, these careful records discredit the famous report that in the electorate of Trier two villages were so badly hit by witch trials that only two women survived the panic in each place. There seems to be no evidence of such a massacre.[25]

It is now clear that an unvarnished domino theory cannot explain these trials, but neither does the simple model I have suggested. Historians must try to develop other models for such trials. The Saarland trials also force us to pay close attention to the rate of acquittal in witchcraft trials. To a degree not usually recognized, acquittal was a real possibility in many areas. In a series of Finnish witch trials (1665–84), for example, 57.2 percent of the accused were released, and only 13.2 percent were executed.[26] E. William Monter has recently used the comparison between persons tried and persons executed to make the point that witch trials at Geneva were not especially severe.[27] This conclusion is interesting in itself, but we need to know more about the nature of acquittal and how it might change the morphology of witchcraft trials. Geneva executed only 17.5 percent of the 273 persons tried between 1537 and 1662 (many more were banished). The canton of Neuchatel, however, executed 67.5 percent of the 360 persons tried there between 1568 and 1677.[28] Are the differences between Geneva and Neuchatel due only to different degrees of bigotry or leniency? It seems certain that in any witch trial the rate of acquittal is correlated negatively with the degree of panic. In other words, the more intense the panic, the less likely was acquittal. At the height of some German trials, for example, no one survived, but in other cases judges might be remarkably skeptical of even voluntary confessions.[29] I suspect that in times of panic judges were not only frightened of witchcraft but anxious to set an example of decisive action. Local criticism of a rampant witchcraft panic often brought the critic before the court on charges of witchcraft. Judges saw criticism as contempt of court. And yet, it would be of interest to know what possible impact local criticism could have on the trials. As part of a tentative morphology of witchcraft trials, local criticism may well have served often as the trigger of self-doubts among the judges, doubts that might bring judicial proceedings to a halt.[30]

From this morphological point of view, fresh accounts are needed of many of the largest witchcraft trials. There is tantalizing evidence, for example, that the outburst of witch hunting in Sweden in 1669 came to an end after nearly one hundred persons were executed, in part because of the real doubts expressed by jurists about the value of evidence from the mouths of demoniac children.[31] One skeptical jurist even conducted an experiment to demonstrate that a child could be induced to change his testimony. But more information is needed before we can be sure that this hunt, too, would fit the cybernetic model that I have proposed.

Similarly, we need to know more about the only large witchcraft panic in England, the series of trials conducted by Matthew Hopkins and his fellow witch hunters in Essex, Suffolk, and Norfolk in 1645. Despite the recent and detailed account of Alan Macfarlane for Essex, there is no full account of the actual dynamics of the large trials there.[32] According to Wallace Notestein, however, Hopkins and John Stearne found great success by moving about rapidly, as if to avoid the skepticism that usually emerged in a large panic.[33] Even so, they ran into opposition as early as September of 1645 when the *Moderate Intelligencer* asked why the devil meddles "with none but poor old women" and insisted on the need for what it called "great inquisition" before executing anyone.[34] Perhaps the turning point in the notorious career of Matthew Hopkins came when the vicar of Great Stoughton, John Gaule, opposed his entry there and published in 1646 his *Select Cases of Conscience Touching Witches and Witchcraft* in which he argued for great caution even with self-confessed witches. By the spring of 1646 such opposition was becoming general, and Hopkins and Stearne turned to defensive apologies for their actions. Hopkins's *Discovery of Witches* is of special interest since he poses extremely tough and critical questions, probably revealing the severity of local criticism directed at his methods.[35] Finally, a suspect accused Stearne and forty others of witchcraft, and the trials stopped at once.[36] In Norfolk this abrupt change led to sharp questions for Hopkins, too, who was forced with Stearne into retirement. On the surface, this account also seems to display some features of the cybernetic process I have detected elsewhere, but until the inner working of these trials is studied in detail, little more can be said.

Macfarlane's book contributes little to the precise understanding of large witchcraft trials, and the recent book by Robert Mandrou on French magistrates and witchcraft ignores the problem altogether. Yet even he indicates internal reasons why the magistrates of the parlements of France changed their minds. Their *révolution mentale* came not only from pre-Enlightenment rationalism, but from legal doubts regarding the nature of some of the evidence previously accepted without question.[37]

By recognizing the limits of the domino theory and by observing that some witch trials had a clear structure, it seems to me that we can begin to integrate what is known about large and small trials and make sense of the ending of witchcraft panic across Europe. A morphology of witch hunting, by emphasizing the dynamics of accusation, torture, acquittal, and execution, can also make the witch trials of New England more understandable. Seen from a European perspective, the trials of 1692 in Salem, Massachusetts, for example, stand out not as an anomaly but as a familiar type (see Table 3).[38]

As in many trials, the first suspects at Salem were old women. But after two months of probing, that stereotype disintegrated, and many

Table 3. Witchcraft Accusations at Salem, 1692–1693

	Male	Female	Total
February–March 1692	0	7	7
April–May 1692	19	40	59
June 1692–January 1693	20	56	76
Totals	39	103	142

Table 4. *Accusations and Executions of Salem Villagers*

Date indicted	Accusations		Executions	
	Female	Male	Female	Male
29 February–8 April	8	0	3	0
11–30 April	4	4	1	3
10–28 May	7	6	0	2

men were brought into the arena of suspicion. This pattern is even clearer in Salem Village proper, where the scare had begun (see Table 4).

One can suggest on the basis of this familiar pattern that Salem Village saw its traditional stereotype of the witch break down as women of high repute (for example, Rebecca Nurse) and men fell prey to accusations.[39] Certainly it seems clear that by the end of May 1692 the villagers would no longer sanction accusations of persons from Salem. The trials continued because they were taken up in neighboring towns. From these simple tables, a second familiar fact emerges more clearly than usual. The persons finally executed in the Salem witchcraft panic (twenty in all) represent a small fraction of those actually indicted. At the time the witch trials were stopped, over a hundred suspects were lying in jail. Again it is plain that the common domino theory will not explain these results. One might respond that the Salem trials were in fact canceled by the governor, thereby satisfying the claim of Friedrich von Spee that trials, once begun, could be stopped only by the prince. Yet here it is necessary to recall that by the fall of 1692 the whole community was conscious that something had gone wrong. Obviously innocent persons were being accused, indicted, and even executed. As this realization dawned on Salem and Boston alike, it became impossible to carry on the trials. Like Catholic Würzburg before, Puritan Salem turned to public repentance.

I have suggested that many witchcraft trials followed a pattern that can be reconstructed, but this pattern cannot be found everywhere. What about trials like those in Rottenburg or in the Saarland that flared up repeatedly? What about trials that began not with old women but with men? Although a full domino reaction seems never to have occurred, the simple model I have proposed will not explain all of the various forms of panic trials.[40] Historians have not yet confronted these problems. But instead of closing on a note of confusion, I should like to suggest one important result of looking for such patterns.

A proper concern for the morphology of witch trials can lead to a far better understanding of the inner dynamics of panic. It becomes increasingly clear that most communities had theological, legal, and commonsensical resources with which to combat the panic of the witch hunt. By modifying the domino theory, historians can also drive out the condescending theory that only the superior wisdom of the prince and the enlightened, disenchanted mind of the learned could lead Europe out of darkness. As in Salem, Massachusetts, so throughout western and central Europe, the men who stopped the witch trials were not the princes and the learned, but townsmen and villagers who still believed staunchly in witchcraft and the powers of the devil.

Notes

Chapter 1

1. The one group of foreigners who provide interesting if biased insights into popular customs are the Septamanian Goths such as Agobard of Lyons, Claudius of Turin, and Theodulf of Orleans. These men, whose Spanish cultural horizons were much different from those of the Franks and Latins with whom they found refuge, were compelled by their opposition to customs in the North to attack them. Thus the writings of these men on popular beliefs, on images and relics, and on a variety of other topics are significant evidence of the nature of Carolingian society and culture as seen by outsiders.

2. "Reliquienkult und Pilgerbewegung zur Zeit der Klosterreform im Burgundisch-Aquitaniachen Gebiet," in *Vom Mittelalter zur Neuzeit. zum 65. Geburtstag von Heinrich Spoemberg*, ed. Hellmut Kretzschmar (Berlin, 1956), pp. 420–39; in more developed form in *Volk und Kirche zur Zeit der beginnenden Gottesfriedensbewegung in Frankreich* (Berlin, 1957).

3. *Gottesfriede und Treuga Dei* (Stuttgart, 1964).

4. "Stadtrömisch-Italische Märtyrerreliquien und Fränkischer Reichsadel im Mass-Moselraum," *Historisches Jahrbuch* 87 (1967): 1–25.

5. "Sinn und Art der Heiligung im frühen Mittelalter," *Mitteilungen des Institüts für österreichische Geschichtsforschung* 57 (1949): 83–122.

6. W. Holtzelt, "Translationen von Martyrreliquien aus Rom nach Bayern im 8. Jahrhundert," *Studien und Mitteilungen zur Geschichte des Benediktinordens* 53 (1935): 286–343.

7. Prinz, "Stadtrömisch-Italische Märtyrerreliquien," p. 10.

8. Mikoletzky has explained this furious activity as a reaction against the rationalist tendencies of the Carolingian renaissance and the state-dominated church of Charles the Great. As we shall see, in fact, these translations are part of a continuing tradition of interest in and support for the cult of saints of which Charles was a supporter.

9. *Das karolinische Imperium* (Zurich, 1949), pp. 178 ff.

10. *Patrologia latina (PL)* ed. J. P. Migne (Paris, 1844) 104.147.

11. Ibid., 104.158.

12. *Monumenta Germaniae Historica (MGH)*, Concilia II, 39–43.

13. On the complex role of hair as sacred object see E. R. Leach, "Magical Hair," *Journal of the Royal Anthropological Institute* 88, part 2 (July–December 1958): 144–64. On holy men see the work of Peter Brown, especially "The Rise and Function of the Holy Man in Late Antiquity," *Journal of Roman Studies* 61 (1971): 80–101.

14. *MGH Capitularia* I, c. 10, p. 25.

15. *MGH Concilia*, II, 15.

16. Ibid., pp. 581–82.

17. *MGH Concilia*, II, 282–83. Charles encouraged pilgrimages provided they were accepted from one's parish priest as a form of penitence. The capitularies of Pepin and Charles provided for the care and supervision of pilgrims to Rome and elsewhere. For example: under Pepin, *MGH Capitularia*, I, C. 13, 37; Charles on sheltering and caring for pilgrims: *Admonitio generalis* of 789, ibid., p. 60; protection from harm: *Capitulare missorum generale* of 802, ibid., pp. 93–94; on supervision of pilgrims: *Capitulare missorum* of 803, ibid., p. 115. I am grateful to Ludwig Schmugge for pointing out to me that the terms *peregrinus* and *peregrinatio* did not necessarily mean pilgrim or pilgrimage in the

ninth century. Hence one must avoid attributing all Carolingian discussion of *peregrini* to religious pilgrims. The terms still could be applied to any foreigner or voyager.

18. *MGH Capitularia*, I, 163; *Capitulare de causis cum episcopis et abbatibus tractandis*, c. 7.

19. *MGH Epistolae Karoli aevi*, III, 206.

20. I am greatly in debt to John McCulloh for allowing me to read his unpublished paper on the papal role in the Carolingian cult of Roman relics, which he delivered at the 1975 annual meeting of the American Historical Association. My essay has greatly benefited from his observations on the relationship between the rhythm of translations from Rome and papal policy on translations.

21. *MGH Concilia*, II, supplement; *Libri Carolini*, III, c. 16, p. 138.

22. Ibid., III, c. 24, pp. 153–54; c. 16, pp. 137–38.

23. Ibid., II, p. 168. See Töpfer, "Reliquienkult," p. 422. This canon is a reiteration of a capitulary of 789 (*MGH Capitularia*, I, 63), "That where bodies of saints repose there should be another oratory where brothers might pray in private," and on chapter 52 of the *Regula Sancti Benedicti*, which prescribes an oratory for private prayer.

24. *MGH Concilia*, II, 170.

25. On this complicated subject see Nicole Herrmann-Mascard, *Les reliques des saints: Formation coutumière d'un droit*(Paris, 1975), pp. 150–63.

26. *MGH Capitularia*, I, 170.

27. Ibid., p. 106.

28. *MGH Concilia*, II, 270.

29. J. D. Mansi, ed., *Sacrorum conciliorum nova et amplissima collectio*, 31 vols. (Florence and Venice, 1759–98), III, col. 971.

30. Ibid., XIV, col. 356. Arthur West Haddan and William Stubbs, *Councils and Ecclesiastical Documents Relating to Great Britain and Ireland*, 3 vols. (Oxford, 1869–78), II, 580.

31. Herrmann-Mascard, *Les reliques des saints*, p. 160.

32. On the Eucharist as relic, see Patrick Geary, *Furta Sacra: Thefts of Relics in the Central Middle Ages* (Princeton, 1978), pp. 39–40.

33. *MGH Concilia*, II, C. 51, p. 272.

34. *MGH Epist. Kar. aev.*, I, 593.

35. Herrmann-Mascard, *Les Reliques des saints*, p. 59.

36. Louis Halphen, *Charlemagne et l'empire carolingien* (Paris, 1947; reprint 1968), pp. 221–25.

37. *MGH Scriptores (SS)*, XV, 377–79.

38. Ibid., p. 386.

39. Amulo Episcopus Lugdunensis, "Epistola ad Theoboldum Episcopum Lingonensem," *MGH Epist. Kar. aev.*, III, 363.

40. Adrevaldus, *Miracula Sancti Benedicti*, ed. E. de Certain (Paris, 1858), p. 65.

41. "Les reliques romaines au IXe siècle," *Questions d'histoire et d'archéologie chrétienne* (Paris, 1906), pp. 235–57. More recently, one should consult H. Silvestre, "Commerce et vol de reliques au Moyen Age," *Revue belge de philologie et d'histoire* 30 (1952): 721–39; Heinrich Fichtenau, "Zum Reliquienwesen im früheren Mittelalter," *Mitteilungen des Instituts für Österreichische Geschichtsforschung* 60 (1952): 60–89; and Geary, *Furta Sacra*.

42. Einhard, *Translatio SS. Marcellini et Patri, MGH SS*, XV, 238–64.

43. Guiraud made this suggestion based on his position as a deacon and his familiarity with the catacombs. However, judging from the scope of his operations in collecting relics, he was not limited to any one ecclesiastical area.

44. Rudolfus, *Miracula Sanctorum in Fuldenses ecclesias translatorum, MGH SS*, XV, 332.

45. The traditional locations of the tombs of the martyrs sold by Deusdona can be determined from Usuardus's Martyrology recently edited by Jacques Dubois, *Le martyrologe d'Usuard, texte et commentaire* (Brussels, 1965), and from the early itineraries of pilgrims to Rome edited in *CCSL, Itineraria et alia geographica I & II* (Turnhout, 1965). See Geary, *Furta Sacra*, pp. 56–57, nn. 18–20.

46. Rudolfus, *Miracula*, p. 332.
47. *Liutolfi vita et translatio S. Severi, MGH SS*, XV, 292 .
48. Rudolfus, *Miracula*, p. 337.
49. Erchambertus episcopus Frisingensis, "Epistola ad suos," *PL* 116. 31–34.
50. This could be done in one of two ways: either parts of a body could be sold, as was the case of the body of Alexandrus which Deusdona divided and sold both in Switzerland and in Fulda (Rudolfus, *Miracula*, p. 332), or the merchant could simply appear with another relic although the remains of the saint had been acquired in toto by another party, as, for example, the tooth of Sebastian sold in 835 in spite of the earlier translation of the entire body to St. Médard ten years earlier.
51. *Liber Pontificalis*, ed. Louis Duchesne (Paris, 1892), II, 74.
52. *MGH SS*, II, 631.
53. *Vita Walae, PL* 120. 1608.
54. *Western Society and the Church in the Middle Ages* (Harmondsworth, 1970), p. 31.
55. *MGH Capitularia*, I, 118. In his *capitulare legi Ribuariae additum* of 803, Charles prescribed that "all oaths be made in church or on relics, and what is to be sworn in church . . . is 'may God and the saints of whom these relics are just him that he says the truth.'" This oath was used by Charles the Bald in 853 (ibid., II, 274) and Louis the Second in 860 (ibid., p. 155).
56. Keith Thomas, *Religion and the Decline of Magic* (New York and London, 1971) chap. 2, "The Magic of the Medieval Church," pp. 25–50.

Chapter 2

1. "Frömmigkeit in Deutschland um 1500," *Archiv für Reformationsgeschichte* 56 (1965): 5–30.
2. Tables giving this information form the appendices of a book in preparation to appear under the same title as this chapter. Space limitations permit only minimal documentation here. Full reference and considerable explanatory material must await the unabridged treatise. A further 69 shrines, discovered after the map for this chapter was made, are included in the figures discussed in the chapter.
3. John A. Watt, *The Theory of Papal Monarchy in the Thirteenth Century* (London, 1965), pp. 44, 103.
4. Palmer A. Throop, *Criticism of the Crusade: A Study of Public Opinion and Crusade Propaganda* (Amsterdam, 1940).
5. Harry A. Miskimin, *The Economy of Early Renaissance Europe, 1300–1460* (Englewood Cliffs, N.J., 1969), pp. 1–81.
6. See Denis Hay, *Europe: The Emergence of an Idea* (Edinburgh, 1957).
7. Herbert Moller, "The Social Causation of the Courtly Love Complex," *Comparative Studies in Society and History* 1 (1959): 148.
8. Ibid.
9. Ibid.
10. *Wallfahrten durchs deutsche Land*, ed. Christian Schreiber (Berlin, 1928), p. 114.
11. Wessobrunn (Upper Bavaria), Polling (Upper Bavaria), Kremsünster (Upper Austria), Frauenmünster (Zurich), Ebersberg (Upper Bavaria), Thierhaupten (Swabia), Metten (Lower Bavaria), Bellelay (Basel bishopric), Ebrach (Franconia), Sulzbach (Upper Palatinate), Beuron (Swabia), Ellwangen (Swabia), Kirchheim (Swabia), Retzbach (Franconia), Zöbingen (Swabia), Kirchhaslach (Swabia), Doberan (Mecklenburg), Steinhorst (Braunschweig). The information is gathered principally from M. Marx-Kruse and E. von Campe, *Chronik der deutschen Jagd. Eine Kulturgeschichte des Jagdwesens von den Anfängen bis zur Gegenwart in Dokumenten* (Munich, 1937): and Franz von Kobell, *Wildanger* (Munich, 1932), as well as *Wallfahrten*, ed. Schreiber, passim.
12. Marx-Kruse and von Campe, *Chronik*, p. 34. Could this have been a pilgrimage offering?
13. Richard W. Southern, *The Making of the Middle Ages* (New Haven, 1953), pp. 234–35.

292 / Notes to Pages 27–29

14. Walter Delius, *Geschichte der Marienverehrung* (Munich, 1963), p. 158.
15. Ibid., p. 162.
16. Indeed the tournament arena of Hassfurt (Franconia) was transformed into a holy shrine. The report, of course, like the stories referring to miracles encountered during the hunt, are part of folk legend. *Wallfahrten*, ed. Schreiber, p. 497.
17. *Lexikon für Theologie und Kirche*, 2d ed. rev. (Freiburg, 1960), s.v. "Seuse"; Delius, *Geschichte*, p. 164.
18. Delius, *Geschichte*, p. 165.
19. "In ihr ist höchster Menschenadel vereint," ibid., p. 165; Wilhelm Abel, *Handbuch der deutschen Wirtschafts- und Sozialgeschichte* ed. Hermann Aubin (Stuttgart, 1971), p. 475. See especially literature cited in note 11.
20. See *Germania Judaica von 1238 bis zur Mitte des 14. Jahrhunderts*, ed. Zvi Avneri, 3 vols., the introduction to vol. II, pt. 1, pp. xxxiv–xxxv, as well as the several maps in the last two volumes showing the areas in which Jews were annihilated. Prior to 1298 there were local massacres in: Munich (1286), Oberwesel (1280), Bacharach, near Koblenz (1283), and Mainz (1283). See Alfred Cohausz, "Vier ehemalige Sakramentswallfahrten: Gootsbüren, Hillentrup, Blomberg und Büren," *Westfälische Zeitschrift* 112 (1962): 284. For the particular virulence of German pogroms after 1298, Anton Mayer, "Die Gründung von St. Salvator in Passau—Geschichte und Legende," *Zeitschrift für Bayerische Landesgeschichte* 18 (1955): 275–76. Léon Poliakov, *The History of Anti-Semitism*, (New York, 1965), p. 100, describes these events as the "first case of Jewish genocide in Christian Europe."
21. *Reclams Kunstführer, Deutschland*, vol. 1, *Bayern*, 7th ed. rev.(Stuttgart, 1970), p. 681.
22. Wilhelm Volkert, "Die Juden in der Oberpfalz im 14. Jahrhundert," *Zeitschrift für Bayerische Landesgeschichte* 30 (1967): 161–200.
23. Several Eucharist shrines appear on sites which the maps in *Germania Judaica* show to have been places where Jews were massacred. Also we know with certainty that neighboring shrines celebrated the killing of Jews, including those in Deggendorf (1337), Würzburg (1349), Röttingen (1299), Ehingen (1320–30), Iphofen (1294), Regensburg (1519), Munich (sometime between 1315 and 1350), Ingolstadt (1384), and Lauingen (1404). Reading further the commentary and map to *Die Opfer des Paulkauer Hostienwunders, Germania Judaica*, vol. II, pt. II, pp. 665–68, describing how streams of pilgrims came to see the miracle of the bleeding Host at the shrine established to commemorate the glorious annihilation of Jews in 1338, the conclusion is inescapable that the practice was far more widespread than can be documented with statistical certitude. Although Pulkau is in Lower Austria, the zone of its attraction included Bohemia and Bavaria. Deggendorf appears to have provided a model for other shrines founded in the Passau region to celebrate the slaughter of Jews. See Mayer, "Die Gründung," especially p. 276.
24. Ernest W. McDonnell, *The Beguines and Beghards in Medieval Culture: With Special Emphasis on the Belgian Scene* (New Brunswick, N.J., 1954), pp. 311, 307–8.
25. Peter Browe, "Die Eucharistie als Zaubermittel im Mittelalter," *Archiv für Kulturgeschichte* 20 (1930): 134–54; Mayer, "Die Gründung," p. 276.
26. McDonnell, *Beguines*, p. 311; Peter Browe, *Die Verehrung der Eucharistie im Mittelalter* (Munich, 1932).
27. *Germania Judaica*, vol. II, pt. I, *Einleitung*, pp. xxxiv–xxxv.
28. Romuald Bauerreiss, *Pie Jesu. Das Schmerzensmann-Bild und sein Einfluss auf die mittelalterliche Frömmigkeit* (Munich, 1931), p. 36.
29. *Verhandlungen des Historischen Vereins für Niederbayern* 24 (1886): 289–90. The legend appears in only one English writing: the *Croxton Play at the Sacrament* (1461). But the version, not anti-Jewish, seeks only to illustrate points of doctrine. See V. J. Scattergood, *Politics and Poetry in the Fifteenth Century*, p. 259.
30. Besides the notorious Regensburg incident in 1519 (see *Probleme der Kirchenspaltung im 16. Jahrhundert*, ed. R. Kottje and J. Staber (Regensburg, 1970), pp. 11–32), killings occurred during pilgrimages at Heiligenstadt in 1373 and near Passau in 1477–78. The Landshut region of Lower Bavaria witnessed widespread killings in 1450; see Helmut Rankl, *Das vorreformatorische landesherrliche Kirchenregiment in Bayern, 1378–1526*

(Munich, 1971), p. 44. Most revealing is the "contagious" character of the massacres. For example, within six months of the Regensburg episode, the same horror was reenacted in Rothenburg. See A. Schnizlein, "Zur Geschichte der Vertreibung der Juden aus Rothenburg, 1519–1520," *Die Linde* 2 (1921): 30ff. For massacres of Jews during the great Peasants' War see Horst Gerlach, *Der englische Bauernaufstand von 1381 und der deutsche Bauernkrieg: Ein Vergleich* (Meisenheim am Glan, 1969), pp. 104–8.

31. Karl Bosl, *Die Grundlangen der modernen Gesellschaft im Mittelalter*, 2 vols. (Stuttgart, 1972), 1:200–201.

32. Karl Bosl, *Bayerische Geschichte* (Munich, 1971), pp. 119–23.

33. *Lexikon für Theologie und Kirche*, s.v. "Leonhard" and "Georg."

34. Georg von Schierghofer, "Umrittsbrauch und Rossegen. Ein Beitrag zur vergleichenden Volkskunde unter besonderer Berüchsichtigung Altbayerns," *Bayerische Hefte für Volkskunde*, 8 (1921), 39; Rudolf Hindringer, *Weihross und Rossweihe, Eine religionsgeschichtlich-volkskundliche Darstellung der Umritte, Pferdesegnungen und Leonhardifahrten im germanischen Kulturkreis* (Munich, 1932), p. 113. See Anton L. Mayer, "Die heilbringende Schau in Sitte und Kult," *Festschrift zu Ildefons Herwegen* (Münster, 1938), p. 260.

35. See the reference in Wolfgang Brückner, "Zur Phänomenologie und Nomenklatur des Wallfahrtswesens und seiner Erforschung," *Folkskultur und Geschichte, Festgabe für Joseph Dünninger* (Berlin, 1970), p. 412, n. 97.

36. Bruno Neundorfer, "Zur Entstehung von Wallfahrten und Wallfahrtspatrozinien im mittelalterlichen Bistum Bamberg," *Bericht des historischen Kreises für die Pflege der Geschichte des ehemaligen Fürstbistums Bamberg*, 99 (1963): 110. Also by the same author, "Wallfahrten zur hl. Katharina im Bistum Bamberg," ibid. 102 (1966): 233.

37. *Wallfahrten*, ed. Schreiber, p. 257.

38. *Österreichischer Volkskundeatlas*, published by the Österreichischen Akademie der Wissenschaften, ed. Ernst Burgstaller and Adolf Helbok (Linz, 1959), map, "Umritte," drawn by Helmut Fielhauer.

39. *Wallfahrten*, ed. Schreiber, p. 294.

40. Rudolf Kriss, *Die Wallfahrtsorte Europas* (Munich, 1950), pp. 55–56.

41. Gerlinde Stahl, "Die Wallfahrt zur Schönen Maria in Regensburg," *Beiträge zur Geschichte des Bistums Regensburg* 2 (1968): 1–281.

42. Moller, "The Social Causation of the Courtly Love Complex," p. 149.

43. Victor Turner, "Death and the Dead in the Pilgrimage Process" (Paper presented at the annual meeting of the American Academy for the Study of Religion, November 1973), p. 22.

44. Hanna Link, "Die geistlichen Bruderschaften des deutschen Mittelalters, insbesondere die Lubecker Antoniusbruderschaft," *Zeitschrift des Vereins für Lübeckische Geschichte und Altertumskunde* 20 (1920): 207.

45. Joachim Schiffhauer, "Unsere Liebe Frau von Reilkirch," *Archiv für Mittelrheinische Kirchengeschichte* 13 (1961); 427.

46. Link, "Die geistlichen Bruderschaften," p. 202. See also Gabriel Le Bras, *Etudes de sociologie religieuse*, 2 vols. (Paris, 1956) 2:453.

47. Joseph Duhr, "La confrérie dans la vie de l'Eglise," *Révue d'histoire ecclésiastique* 35 (1939): 267.

48. Le Bras, *Etudes*, 2:423, defines confraternities as "familles artificielles dont tous les membres son unis par une fraternité volontaire, les confréries ont pour objet de satisfaire dans un cadre étroit les plus poignants besoins du corps et de l'âme."

49. Heinrich Fichtenau, *The Carolingian Empire: The Age of Charlemagne* (New York, 1964), pp. 124–25.

50. *Western Society and the Church in the Middle Ages* (Harmondsworth, 1970), p. 30.

51. Ibid., pp. 36, 35.

52. This observation, made while compiling the table of holy shrines, receives striking confirmation from Ermelinde Erna Liebl, "Studien zum Wallfahrtswesen der Diözese Regensburg" (Ph.D. dissertation, University of Würzburg, 1951), p. 106. See also Joseph Staber, *Volksfrömmigkeit und Wallfahrtswesen des Spätmittelalters im Bistum Freising* (Munich, 1955), p. 42.

53. Heinrich Schiffers, *Aachener Heiligtumsfahrt: Reliquien—Geschichte—Brauchtum* (Aachen, 1937), pp. 133–34.

54. Liebl, "Studien zum Wallfahrtswesen der Diözese Regensburg," pp. 106, 116.

55. Schiffers, *Aachener Heiligtumsfahrt*, pp. 133–34.

56. Mayer, "Die heilbringende Schau," p. 255.

57. Anton L. Mayer, *Die Liturgie in der europäischen Geistesgeschichte: Gesammelte Aufsätze* (Darmstadt, 1971), p. 95.

58. Southern, *Western Society and the Church*, p. 141.

59. Ibid., pp. 226–27.

60. Ibid., p. 231.

61. Ibid., p. 259. *Conversi* appeared in lesser numbers among other reformed monasteries.

62. Nikolaus Paulus, *Geschichte des Ablasses im Mittelalter*, 3 vols. (Paderborn, 1922–23), 2: 170–71.

63. Ibid., p. 202. In addition to Christ's infinite merits the treasure contains "the superfluous merits of the Virgin and saints . . . there is an accumulation of expiation in the treasury" that cannot be diminished "because the more people there are saved by drawing on it, the more it, in its turn, is augmented by their merits" (Donald John Hall, *English Medieval Pilgrimage* [London, 1966], p. 13).

64. H. Zender, "Patrozinien und Namengebung," *Bijdragen en Mededelingen der Naankunde—Commissie von de koninklijke Nedelanske Akademie van Wetenschappen te Amsterdam* 15 (1959), p. 6.

65. M. Mollat and P. Wolff, *The Popular Revolutions of the Late Middle Ages* (London, 1973), pp. 309–10.

66. *Etudes*, 2: 432.

67. See E. Delaruelle, "La spiritualité aux XIVᵉ et XVᵉ siècles," *Cahiers d'Histoire Mondiale* 5 (1959): 66.

68. *Lexikon für Theologie und Kirche*, s.v. "Eulogie."

69. Georges de Lagarde, *La naissance de l'esprit laique au déclin du moyen âge*, 6 vols. (Saint-Paul-Trois-Chateaux, 1934–46), vol. 5, *L'Individualisme Ockhamiste* (1946), p. 4.

70. Ibid., p. 15.

71. Ibid., 2: 209.

72. Ernst Kantorowicz, *The King's Two Bodies: A Study in Medieval Political Theology* (Princeton, 1957), p. 196 (italics added).

73. Quoted in ibid., p. 478.

74. Ibid.

75. Ibid., pp. 472, 474–75.

76. "Thus the Romans, because of the great throng, in the year of Jubilee, upon the bridge have taken means to pass the people over; so that, on the one side, all have their faces towards the Castle, and go to St. Peter's; at the other ledge, they go towards the Mount" (*The Divine Comedy*, trans. J. A. Carlyle and P. H. Wicksteed [New York, 1932], Inferno, Canto XVIII, p. 98).

77. Kantorowicz, *King's Two Bodies*, p. 492.

78. Commentary on Aristotle's *Politics*, 3.3. Quoted also by Walter Ullmann, *The Individual and Society in the Middle Ages* (Baltimore, 1966), p. 126.

79. On this point see Frederick Copleston, *A History of Philosophy*, 8 vols.; 2, pt. II, (New York, 1962), p. 51.

80. *Defensor pacis*, trans. Alan Gewirth (New York, 1967), p. 16.

81. Ibid., pp. 164–65.

82. Ibid., pp. 40–41.

83. Lagarde, *La naissance*, 3:208.

84. For a clear summary of Ockham's epistemology see Copleston, *History*, 3, pt. I, 74–88.

85. *Laws of Ecclesiastical Polity*, 2 vols.(London, 1969), I, 194–95. (First appeared in 1594).

86. *Forerunners of the Reformation* (New York, 1966), p. 129.

87. Victor Turner, "The Center Out There: Pilgrim's Goal," *History of Religions* 12 (1973): 199.

88. Southern, *Western Society and the Church*, p. 136, refers to crusaders, but the reward applied equally to pilgrims.

89. Neundorfer, "Entstehung von Wallfahrten," p. 107.

90. "Death and the Dead in the Pilgrimage Process."

91. *Handwörterbuch des deutschen Aberglaubens*, ed. E. Hoffmann-Krayer and H. Bächtold-Stäubli, 10 vols. (Berlin and Leipzig, 1927), s.v. "Armeseelen."

92. Ibid.

93. "Sêlnapf: Schüssel mit Mehl und Eyern nebst einem Brodlaib als Opfer auf die Bahre gelegt." Johann Andreas Schmeller, *Bayerisches Wörterbuch*, 2 vols. (1872–77; reprint Aalen, 1961), s.v. "Armeseelen"; Max Rumpf, *Das Gemeine Volk. Ein soziologisches und volkskundliches Lebens- und Kulturgemälde*, 2 vols. (Stuttgart, 1933), 2:196: "Am rührendsten aber ist es wohl, wenn oft die Arbeiter im einsamen Wälde den Armen Seelen Brotstückchen auf die Baumstöcke hinlegen."

94. Rumpf, *Das Gemeine Volk*, 2:185.

95. Ibid., 2:217–18 (italics added).

96. "The Rites of Violence: Religious Riot in Sixteenth-Century France," *Past and Present*, no. 59 (May 1973), pp. 82–83.

97. See the extensive bibliography in Michel Vovelle, *Piété Baroque et déchristianisation en Provence au XVIIIe siècle* (Paris, 1973).

98. Karl Siegfried Bader, *Studien zur Rechtsgeschichte des mittelalterlichen Dorfes*, 2 vols., vol. 2, *Dorfgenossenschaft und Dorfgemeinde* (Weimar, 1962), 196; *Reallexikon zur deutschen Kunstgeschichte*, ed. Otto Schmidt, (Stuttgart, 1937), vol. 1, s.v. "Armeseelen."

99. *Reallexikon*, ed. Schmidt, vol. 2, s.v. "Beinhaus."

100. Ibid. For the Upper Palatinate see the brief but informative article of Erwin Herrmann, "Die Karner der Oberpfalz," *Oberpfälzer Heimat* 12 (1968): 7–28; *Reallexikon*, ed. Schmidt, vol. 1, s.v. "Armeseelen."

101. Hellmut Rosenfeld, "Der Totentanz als europäisches Phänomen," *Archiv für Kulturgeschichte* 48 (1966): 54–83. For a striking absence of concern with death among the nobility in Artois during the sixteenth century, see Robert Muchembled, "Un monde mental clos: Etude sémantique et historique du vocabulaire religieux d'un noble artesien à l'époque du Philippe II," *Tijdschrift voor Geschiedenis* 88 (1975): 169–89, especially p. 182.

102. Hans Karlinger, *Bayerische Kunstgeschichte* (Munich, 1967), p. 57.

103. Albrecht Miller, "Gotische Plastik," *Bayern—Kunst und Kultur, Ausstellungskatalog* (Munich, 1972), p. 69.

104. Bader, *Dorfgenossenschaft*, 2:196–97 (italics added).

105. For the south, Neundorfer, "Entstehung von Wallfahrten," pp. 33–34. For the north, Norbert Buske, "Die Marienkapellen auf dem Gollen, dem Revekol und dem Heiligen Berg bei Pollnow," *Baltische Studien* 55 (1969): 26.

106. See also Hermann Hörger, "Dorfreligion und bäuerliche Mentalité im Wandel ihrer ideologischen Grundlagen," *Zeitschrift für Bayerische Landesgeschichte* 38 (1975): 244–316. The 69 additional shrines found after the map was drawn further strengthen this "agglutination" pattern.

107. Otto von Simpson, *The Gothic Cathedral*, 2d ed. (New York, 1964), pp. 35–36.

108. I owe this information to Karl Ludwig Ay. See, for example, in Ay's forthcoming edition of *Dokumente zur Geschichte von Staat und Gesellschaft in Bayern*, Abteilung I, vol. II, Text no. 46, *mit Erläuterung*, which begins: "herren Ludwigen Pfallentzgraven bey Rein, hertzog in Bairn und graven zu Mortaini." The document is dated 1420.

109. On this point see, for example, Karl Bosl, *Repräsentation und Parlamentarismus* (Munich, 1974), p. 65. For more detailed discussion see Heinz Lieberich, *Landherren und Landleute. Zur politischen Führungsschicht Baierns im Spätmittelalter* (Munich, 1964), especially pp. 155–64.

110. Bosl, *Repräsentation*, p. 2.

111. Ceded to Austria by the Treaty of Teschen in 1779.

112. Anneliese Triller, "Zur Entstehung und Geschichte der ermländischen Wallfahrtsorte," *Zeitschrift für Geschichte Altertumskunde Ermlands* 87 (1957): 313–14.

113. The one notable exception appearing on the map is only apparent, for the

absence of shrines in the Catholic region between Ellwangen and the Danube is explained by the enormous numbers of sheep that far outnumbered the human population in this area after the Black Death (Abel, *Handbuch*, p. 318).

Several shrines clustered southeast of Stuttgart, in the region of Owen, Dettingen, and Nürtingen, present a more minor exception. The tiny area formed the independent Duchy of Teck until 1385, when it was sold to Württemberg. After the beginning of the fifteenth century the castle was the seat of "wechselnder Adelsfamilien" (*Historische Stätten, Baden Württemberg*, ed. Max Miller [Stuttgart, 1965], 6:522). The fact that every pilgrimage site dedicated to a saint in this region was founded also in the fifteenth century, indeed most of them after 1450 reflects this continual aristocratic turnover. And the sporadic, belated character of aristocratic efforts to foster popular pilgrimage explains why these pre-Reformation shrines, testifying to no grass-roots feeling, appear in an area that adopted the Protestant faith.

114. Martin Last, *Adel und Draf in Oldenburg während des Mittelalters* (Oldenburg, 1969), pp, 80–81.

115. Gebhard von Lenthe, "Niedersächsischer Adel zwischen Spätmittelalter und Neuzeit," in *Deutscher Adel, 1430–1555*, ed. Hellmuth Rössler (Darmstadt, 1965), p. 183.

116. Theuerkauf, "Niedere Adel in Westfalen," pp. 154–55.

117. Ibid., p. 160. For Lower Saxony see Lenthe, "Niedersächsischer Adel," p. 193.

118. Walter Lammers, *Die Schlacht bei Hemmingstedt*, (Neumünster, 1953).

119. Hermann Albert Schumacher, *Die Stedinger* (Bremen, 1865). Unfortunately, Nazi glorification of the Stedinger peasants seems to have caused postwar German scholars to shy away from the subject. One exception is L. Deike, "Die Entstehung der Grundherrschaft in den Hollerkolonien an der Niederweser," *Veröffentlichungen aus den Staatsarchiven der Freien Hansestadt Bremen* 27 (1959): 87ff., 94ff., 101ff. See also Herbert Schwarzwälder, "Die Kirchspiele Bremens im Mittelalter: Die Grosspfarre des Doms und ihr Zerfall," *Niedersächsisches Jahrbuch für Landesgeschichte* 32 (1960), especially pp. 164ff.

120. Largely summarizing the fundamental work by Karl Haff on the *Grosskirchspiel* and *genossenschaftliche Eigenkirche*, Hermann Aubin, *Grundlagen und Perspektiven Geschichtlicher Kulturraumforschung und Kulturmorphologie* (Bonn, 1965), p. 380.

121. Matthias Zender, "Entwicklung und Gestalt der Heiligenverehrung zwischen Rhein und Elbe im Mittelalter," *Ostwestfälisch-Weserländische Forschung zur geschichtlichen Landeskunde* (Münster, 1970), p. 293. Zender also points out (pp. 282–83) that north of a line running roughly from Osnabrück to Hanover parishes were larger in area, and a number of communities had no church, nor chapel, nor sacred structure of any sort. Ecclesiastical buildings, therefore, must have stood physically separated from local burial grounds, or, alternatively, people transported their dead to an oversized central cemetery administered by a chaplain, presumably too busy to have known personally all his clients. In other words, the burial grounds were either estranged from places of worship or, as seems more probable, at least from occasional hints in local histories, strangers were buried alongside strangers (for implicit factual support see scattered remarks in Schwarzwälder, "Kirchspiele Bremens"). Neither arrangement could be more contrary to the cult of purgatory or to a form of popular saint worship wherein "the true cemetery" was "the place where the church founders lay buried." See quotation from Bader, in Part One, section iv.

Also the allodial character of land ownership in these regions (Lenthe, "Niedersächsische Adel," p. 183) is significant in that no one *held* land from another in the feudal meaning of the term, a situation totally inconsistent with believing that divine favor created some kind of relationship between seigneur and saint.

122. Theuerkauf, "Niedere Adel in Westfalen," pp. 166–68.

123. For a parallel example in southwest Swabia see an anonymous report in an episcopal bimonthly journal, *Schwäbisches Diözesan Archiv*, no. 22 (15 Nov. 1891), p. 86. There is scarcely a history of local pilgrimage places, however anecdotal, that fails to refer to alleged profits reaped by monasteries and nobility who, financing the chapel, outward structures, and images at holy sites, actively encouraged popular pilgrimage. With respect to Bavaria, Robert Bauer, director of pilgrimage and custodian of the archives at Altötting, told me that the records show "without any doubt" the predominant role of

nobility in founding holy shrines in late medieval Lower Bavaria. It is impossible to generalize about the profit motive. Sometimes it is apparent; in other instances, there is no trace of such intentions.

124. For the relative absence of shrines—especially those dedicated to saints—see the appended map. Regarding aristocracy, see H. M. Decker-Hauff, "Die Geistige Führungsschicht Württembergs," *Beamtentum und Pfarrerstand 1400 bis 1800*, ed. Günther Franz (Limburg an der Lahn, 1972), pp. 56–57.

125. Some of the information in this paragraph comes from Karl-Ludwig Ay. Documents relating to the Hohenwaldeck war will appear in volume III of Ay's forthcoming edition of *Dokumente zur Geschichte von Staat und Gesellschaft in Bayern*.

126. Hellmuth Heyden, *Kirchengeschichte Pommerns*, 2 vols. (Cologne, 1957), 1:146.

127. Southern, *Western Society and the Church*, p. 253. Regarding monasteries, paragraph IX of the Cisterian rule decrees: "all our monasteries must be dedicated to the Queen of Heaven and Earth." Louis J. Lekai, *The Cistercians* (Kent, Ohio, 1977), p. 448.

128. Heyden, *Kirchengeschichte Pommerns*, 1:151.

129. Ibid.

130. Buske, "Marienkapellen auf dem Gollen," p. 17.

131. Triller, "Entstehung und Geschichte," p. 312.

132. Hellmuth Heyden, "Stralsunder Wallfahrten," *Greifswald-Stralsunder Jahrbuch* 8 (1968–69): 29–37. See also the same author's article, "Das Wallfahrtswesen in Pommern," *Blätter für Kirchengeschichte Pommerns*, nos. 22–23 (1940), pp. 7–20.

133. I thank William J. Bouwsma for sending me this information.

134. Ulrich Gäbler, "Die Kinderwallfahrten aus Deutschland und der Schweiz zum Mont-Saint-Michel, 1456–1459," *Schweizerische Kirchengeschichte* 63 (1969): 221–23. See also E. R. Labande, "Les pelerinages au Mont Saint-Michel pendant le Moyen Age," in *Millénaire monastique du Mont Saint-Michel* (1971), 3:235–50, especially p. 247. He shows that, beginning around 1450, adult pilgrimages formed a prelude to the children's processions.

135. Heinrich Schmidt, *Die deutschen Städtechroniken als Spiegel des bürgerlichen Selbstverständnisses im Spätmittelalter* (Göttingen, 1958), p. 63.

136. For Swabia see Dieter Hellstern, *Der Ritterkanton Neckar-Schwarzwald, 1560–1805* (Tübingen, 1971). The period before 1560 is discussed in the introduction, see especially p. 5. Also, Max Domarus, "Der Reichsadel in den Geistlichen Fürstentümern," in Hellmuth Rössler, ed., *Deutscher Adel*, 2 vols. (Darmstadt, 1965), 2:147–71, and Hellmuth Gensicke, "Der Adel im Mittelrheingebiet," ibid., 1:127–52.

137. Domarus, "Der Reichsadel," and Gensicke, "Der Adel," passim. See especially Domarus, p. 150.

138. Erwin Riedenauer, "Reichsritterschaft und Konfession," in Rössler, ed., *Deutscher Adel*, 2:8, n. 25.

139. Lewis W. Spitz, *The Religious Renaissance of the German Humanists* (Cambridge, Mass., 1963), p. 128.

140. *Ulrich von Hutten and the German Reformation*, trans. Roland H. Bainton (New York, 1965), p. 110.

141. Ibid., pp. 111, 178.

142. Spitz, *Religious Renaissance*, p. 104 (italics added).

143. Marx Treitzsaurwein von Ehrentreitz, "Der Weisskunig," *Jahrbuch der kunsthistorischen Sammlungen des allerhöchsten Kaiserhauses* 6 (1887–88): 234.

144. Paulus, *Geschichte des Ablasses*, 3:433–69.

145. Joseph Staber, *Volksfrömmigkeit und Wallfahrtswesen des Spätmittelalters im Bistum Freising* (Munich, 1955), pp. 57–60.

146. Albrecht Schöne, *Säkularisation als sprachbildende Kraft. Studien zur Dichtung deutscher Pfarrersöhne* (Göttingen, 1958).

147. "Quand vous demandez en Bavière, à un homme du peuple, quelle heure il est, ou une telle maison, il s'arrête, et pense, et rêve, comme si vous lui demandiez un problème" ("Il Bayarese piu stupido di Germani," *Oeuvres Complètes*, ed. Roger Caillois, 2 vols., vol. 1, *Voyages* [Paris, 1949], p. 809).

148. *Katholische Überlieferungen in den Lutherischen Kirchenordnungen des 16. Jahrhunderts* (Munich, 1959), p. 57.

149. A. Trautner, *Tausend Jahre Haager Geschichte* (Haag, 1951), p. 53.

150. Hans Schellnhuber, *Die Reformation in der Reichsgrafschaft Ortenburg* (Ortenburg, 1963), p. 11.

151. Robert Stupperich, "Die Reformation im Weserraum," in *Kunst und Kultur im Weserraum, 800–1600* (Münster, 1966), p. 261.

152. For these details see Robert Bauer, *Die Bayerische Wallfahrt Altötting* (Munich, 1969), pp. 33, 38–39.

153. Ibid., p. 17.

154. *Sämmtliche Werke*, 5 vols. (Munich, 1880), 1:50–51.

155. Quoted by Maria Angela König, *Weihgaben an U. L. Frau von Altötting vom Beginn der Wallfahrt bis zum Abschluss der Säkularisation* (Munich, 1939), p. 9.

156. Ibid., pp. 9–11.

157. *Das buchlein der zuflucht zu Maria der muter gottes in alten Oeding.*

158. Although much less scholarly than the Austrian work, Schierfhofer, "Umrittsbrauch und Rossegen," pp. 90–91, does present a map, roughly sketched, of Bavarian *Umritte* without reference to their dates of foundation. And the density around Altötting seems to be equivalent to that on the other side of the Inn River.

159. Joseph Huber, "Sechshundert Jahre Marianische Wallfahrt Kösslarn," *Der Zwiebelturm* 19 (1964): 221–24.

160. Philipp Hofmeister, *Die Christlichen Eidesformen. Eine Liturgie- und Rechtsgeschichtliche Untersuchung* (Munich, 1957), p. 33.

161. *Kings and Councillors: An Essay in the Comparative Anatomy of Human Society* (London, 1937, reprint ed., Chicago and London, 1970), p. 85.

162. *The Birth of the Gods; The Origin of Primitive Beliefs* (Ann Arbor, 1968), p. 187.

163. Ibid.

164. McDonnell, *Beguines*, pp. 141–53.

165. Max Heimbucher, *Die Orden und Kongregationen der Katholischen Kirche*, 2 vols. (Munich, 1933–34), 2: 637–42. These figures may require some correction. In the latest research on Beguine communities in Cologne, for example, F. M. Steiner calculates 1500 to be a conservative estimate of the Beguine population in fourteenth century Cologne. "The Religious Women of Cologne: 1120–1320," unpublished Ph.D. dissertation, Yale, 1977, p. 2. I thank Mr. Steiner for lending me a copy of his work.

166. Herbert Grundmann, *Religiöse Bewegungen im Mittelalter* (Darmstadt, 1961), pp. 312–18.

167. Otmar Decker, "Die Stellung des Predigerordens zu den Dominikanerinnen (1207–1267)" in *Quellen und Forschungen zur Geschichte des Dominikanerordens in Deutschland* 31 (1937): 70.

168. Southern, *Western Society and the Church*, p. 317, n. 19.

169. Albert Hauck, *Kirchengeschichte Deutschlands*, 3d and 4th eds., 5 vols. (Leipzig, 1904–20), 4:416.

170. Karl Bosl, *Die Reichsministerialität der Salier und Staufer. Eine Geschichte des hochmittelalterlichen Volkes, Staates und Reiches*, 2 vols., 2d ed. (Munich, 1968–69), see map appended to vol. 2.

171. Theodor Frings, *Grundlegung einer Geschichte der deutschen Sprache* (Halle, 1957), publishes a very convenient set of maps describing the historical shift of different language sounds.

172. Lina Eckenstein, *Women under Monasticism* (New York, 1896; reprint ed. New York, 1963), p. 138.

173. Ibid., p. 153; Thilo Vogelsang, "Consors regni: Die Frau als Herrscherin im Mittelalter" (Ph.D. dissertation, University of Munich, 1950), pp. 41, 65–66.

174. See appendices in Hauck, *Kirchengeschichte*, vol. 4.

175. Günther Peters, "Norddeutsches Beginnen- und Beghardwesen im Mittelalter," *Niedersächsisches Jahrbuch für Landesgeschichte* 41–42 (1969–70): 50–118.

176. Louis Réau, *Iconographie de l'art chrétien*, 3 vols. (Paris, 1955–59), 2:103–4.

For a church historian's view see *Lexikon der Marienkunde*, ed. Konrad Algermissen et al., 2 vols. (Regensburg, 1967), 1, s.v. "Compassio."

177. *Der seligen Margareta Ebner: Offenbarungen und Briefe*, ed. Hieronymus Wilms (Vechta, 1928), p. 60.

178. Grundmann, *Religiöse Bewegungen*, p. 315.

179. E. Delaruelle, E.-R. Labande, and Paul Ourliac, *L'Eglise au temps du Grand Schisme et de la crise conciliaire* (vol. 14, pt. 2, of A. Fliche, and V. Martin, *L'Histoire de l'Eglise*), pp. 783–84, n. 47; E. W. Zeeden, *Katholische Überlieferungen in den Lutherischen Kirchenordnungen des 16. Jahrhunderts* (Münster, 1959), p. 48.

180. Heinz Otto Burger, *Renaissance, Humanismus, Reformation. Deutsche Literatur im Europäischen Kontext* (Berlin, 1969), pp. 369–71.

181. See the words italicized in the passage from Jakob Issickemer, quoted above in the discussion of Altötting. He identifies explicitly the "Queen of Heaven" with the "immaculate" Virgin.

182. For example, the Pietà appears at only seven pilgrimage sites north of the Benrather line, all very late.

183. Wilhelm Stürmer, "König Artus als aristokratisches Leitbild während des Mittelalters," *Zeitschrift für Bayerische Landesgeschichte* 35 (1972): 946–71.

184. Wilhelm Hansen, "Fachwerkbau im Oberweserraum," in *Kunst und Kultur im Weserraum, 800–1600* (Münster, 1966), p. 296.

185. The Kaland brotherhood had about three hundred chapters extending from the Netherlands to Livland. See J. Rautenstrauch, *Die Kalandsbruderschaften* (Leipzig, 1903). The basic reference for the Elend brotherhood is Ernst von Moeller, *Die Elendenbruderschaften* (Leipzig, 1906), p. 106.

186. Hans Lentze, "Nürnbergs Gewerbeverfassung im Mittelalter," *Jahrbuch für Fränkische Landesforschung* 24 (1967): 207–81, discusses the subject, although intermittently, in some detail. See especially pp. 223–25, 236–39, and above all the section entitled "Der Kampf des Nürnberger Rates gegen Einung und zünftisches Wesen," pp. 254ff. For similar attitudes among other town governments see Gerhard Pfeiffer, "Die Bedeutung der Einung im Stadt- und Landfrieden," *Zeitschrift für Bayerische Landesgeschichte* 32 (1969), especially pp. 824–25.

187. "Verfassung und soziale Kräfte in der deutschen Stadt des späten Mittelalters, vornehmlich in Oberdeutschland," *Vierteljahrschrift für Sozial- und Wirtschaftsgeschichte* 46 (1959): 289–349.

188. Lentze, "Nürnbergs Gewerbeverfassung."

189. Ibid. Also Link, "Die geistlichen Bruderschaften," p. 217.

190. Le Bras, *Etudes*, 2:434; Link, "Die geistlichen Bruderschaften," p. 208; Moeller, "Frömmigkeit in Deutschland," p. 9, n. 4.

191. On this subject see Gerhard Oestreich, "Politischer Neustoizismus und Niederländische Bewegung in Europa und besonders in Brandenburg-Preussen," *Bijdragen en Mededelingen van het Historisch Genootschap* 79 (1964), and Herbert Schöffler, *Deutsches Geistesleben zwischen Reformation und Aufklärung. Von Martin Opitz zu Christian Wolff* (Frankfurt am Main, 1956), especially the chapter entitled "Das Studium in Leyden," pp. 47–68.

192. Grundmann, *Religiöse Bewegungen*, Introduction. For a full discussion of the literature concerning this point, however, see McDonnell, *Beguines*, pp. 125–26, n. 26.

193. Grundmann, *Religiöse Bewegungen*, pp. 13–90.

194. McDonnell, *Beguines*, pp. 246–65.

195. Quoted by Southern, *Western Society and the Church*, p. 319.

196. *Atlas zur Kirchengeschichte*, ed. Hubert Jedin (Freiburg, 1970), p. 53.

197. Ibid., map 68 B.

198. See R. W. Scribner, "Civic Unity and the Reformation in Erfurt," *Past and Present*, no. 66 (1975), p. 29, and Maschke, "Verfassung und Soziale Kräfte." The Moeller thesis is unconvincingly criticized in the recent work by Steven Ozment, *The Reformation in the Cities: The Appeal of the Reformation to Sixteenth Century Germany and Switzerland* (New Haven, 1975).

199. Kilian McDonnell, *John Calvin, the Church and the Eucharist* (Princeton, 1967), p. 65.

200. Ibid., pp. 64, 70.
201. Ibid., p. 71.
202. *Institutes,* Book IV, chap. XX, sec. 2. (ed. John T. McNeill and Ford Lewis Battles, 2 vols., Philadelphia, 1975, vol. 2, p. 1487.)
203. The phrase is Calvin's, ibid.
204. James M. Estes, "Church Order and the Christian Magistrate according to Johannes Brenz," *Archiv für Reformationsgeschichte* 59 (1968): 5–23.
205. John T. McNeill, *The History and Character of Calvinism* (New York, 1967), p. 46.
206. Quoted from the *Institutes* by McDonnell, *John Calvin,* p. 195.
207. Steven E. Ozment, *Mysticism and Dissent: Religious Ideology and Social Protest in the Sixteenth Century* (New Haven, 1973), p. 16.
208. McDonnell, *John Calvin,* p. 213, uses this phrase, slightly adapted here.
209. Ibid., p. 192.
210. Ibid., pp. 185, 197.
211. Calvin said the eucharistic sacrament gave a *general* assurance of salvation (ibid., pp. 201–2), but he thought "it was highly dangerous and rash to ask for particular assurance of salvation" (ibid., p. 197).
212. Ibid., p. 142.
213. Ibid.
214. *Institutes,* Book IV, chap. XVIII, secs. 7, 8.
215. Ibid., sec. 8.
216. Ibid., sec. 7.
217. "An Appeal to the Ruling Class of German Nationality," trans. John Dillenberger, *Martin Luther, Selections from His Writings* (New York, 1961), p. 463.
218. "The Pagan Servitude of the Church," in ibid., p. 279.
219. Ibid., p. 283.
220. McDonnell, *John Calvin,* p. 210.
221. Ibid., pp. 201–2.

Chapter 3

1. Bertolt Brecht, "Fragen eines Lesenden Arbeiters," in *Hundert Gedichte, 1918–1950* (Berlin, 1951), pp. 107–8.
2. M. de Certeau, D. Julia, and J. Revel, "La beauté du mort: Le concept de 'culture populaire,'" *Politique aujourd'hui,* December 1970, p. 21.
3. For example, Alan Macfarlane, *The Family Life of Ralph Josselin, a Seventeenth Century Clergyman: An Essay in Historical Anthropology* (Cambridge, Eng., 1970); but see also E. P. Thompson, "Anthropology and the Discipline of Historical Context," *Midland History* 1, no. 3 (1972): 41–45.
4. Archivio della Curia Arcivescovile di Udine, Sant'Uffizio, "Anno integro 1583 a n. 107 usque ad 128 incl.," proc. n. 126 (hereafter cited as ACAU, proc. n. 126), c. 15v. Montereale, today Montereale Valcellina, is a small hillside village (317 meters above sea level) not far from Pordenone. In 1584 the whole parish was composed of 650 people; see Archivio Vescovile di Pordenone, "Sacrarum Visitationum Nores ab anno 1582 usque ad annum 1584," c. 168v.
5. ACAU, "Sententiarum contra reos S. Officii liber II," c. 16v. For *livelli* in this period see G. Giorgetti, *Contadini e proprietari nell'Italia moderna: Rapporti di produzione e contratti agrari dal secolo XVI a oggi* (Turin, 1974), pp. 97ff. The two fields rented by Menocchio are mentioned in a document written in 1596 by order of the Venetian *Luogotenente,* Archivio de Stato di Pordenone, Notarile, b. 488, n. 3785, cc. 17r–22r.
6. Archivio de Stato de Pordenone, Notarile, b. 40, n. 333, c. 89v. The names of the "villas" are mentioned in *Leggi per la Patria, e Contadinanza del Friuli* (Udine, 1686), intr. c. d 2r. For *camarari,* see G. Marchetti, "I quaderni dei camerari di s. Michele a Gemona," *Ce fastu?* 38 (1962): 11–38.
7. ACAU, proc. n. 126, cc. 2r, 10r, 13v, 6v.
8. Ibid., cc. 10r, 8r, 11v, 5r.

9. Ibid., cc. 16r, 17r–v.

10. Ibid., cc. 2v–3r.

11. Michel Foucault, *Folie et déraison: Histoire de la folie à l'age classique* (Paris, 1961), pp. 121–22, 469.

12. ACAU, proc. n. 126, c. 19r.

13. See Pio Paschini, *Venezia e L'Inquisizione Romana da Giulio III a Pio IV* (Padua, 1959), pp. 51ff.; A. Stella, *Chiesa e Stato nelle relazioni dei nunzi pontifici a Venezia* (Vatican City, 1964), pp. 290–91.

14. ACAU, proc. n. 126, c. 27v.

15. Ibid., cc. 27v ff.

16. See Pio Paschini, *Storia del Friuli*, vol. 2 (Udine, 1954), for political events. For the social and political context, see the work of P. S. Leicht, "Un programma di parte democratica in Friuli nel Cinquecento," in *Studi e frammenti* (Udine, 1903), pp. 107–21; "La rappresentanza dei contadini presso il veneto Luogotenente della Patria del Friuli," ibid., pp. 125–44; "Un movimento agrario nel Cinquecento," in *Scritti vari di storia del diritto italiano* (Milan, 1943), 1: 73–91; "Il parlamento friulano nel primo secolo della dominazione veneziana," *Rivista di storia del diritto italiano* 21 (1948): 5–50; "Il contadini ed i Parlamenti dell'età intermedia," in *IXe Congrès International des Sciences Historiques . . . Etudes présentées à la Commission Internationale pour l'histoire des assemblées d'états* (Louvain, 1952), pp. 125–28. Among recent works, see above all A. Ventura, *Nobiltà e popolo nella società venta ne del '400 e '500* (Bari, 1964), pp. 187–214; see also A. Tagliaferri, *Struttura e politica sociale in una comunità veneta del '500 (Udine)* (Milan, 1959).

17. A. Battistella, "La servitù di masnada in Friuli," *Nuovo archivio veneto*, n.s. 11–15 (1906–8).

18. Gaetano Perusini, *Vita di popolo in Friuli: Patti agrari e consuetudini tradizionali* (Florence, 1961), pp. xxi–xxii.

19. See *Leggi per la Patria*, pp. 638ff., 642ff., 207ff.

20. Tagliaferri, *Struttura*, pp. 25ff. (with bibliography).

21. *Relazioni dei rettori veneti in Terraferma*, vol. 1, *La Patria del Friuli (luogotenenza di Udine)* (Milan, 1973). This edition, however, is marred by serious mistakes: see M. Berengo's review in *Rivista storica italiana* 86 (1974): 586–90.

22. See S. Ossowski, *Struttura di classe e coscienza di classe*, Italian trans. (Turin, 1966), pp. 23ff.

23. ACAU, proc. n. 126, cc. 27v–28r.

24. Archivio di Stato di Pordenone, Notarile, b. 488, n. 3785, cc. 17r ff.

25. A. Stella, "La proprietà ecclesiastica nella Repubblica di Venezia dal secolo XV al XVII," *Nuova rivista storica* 42 (1958): 50–77; A. Ventura, "Considerazioni sull'agricoltura veneta e sull'accumulazione originaria del capitale nei secoli XVI e XVII," *Studi storici* 9 (1968): 674–722; G. Chittolini, "Un problema aperto: La crisi della proprietà ecclesiastica fra Quattro e Cinquecento," *Rivista storica italiana* 85 (1973): 353–93.

26. ACAU, proc. n. 126, c. 27r.

27. ACAU, S. Uffizio, "Anno integro 1596 a n. 281 usque ad 306 incl.," proc. n. 285 (hereafter cited as ACAU, proc. n. 285), unnumbered pages.

28. See G. H. Williams, *The Radical Reformation* (Philadelphia, 1962); C.-P. Clasen, *Anabaptism, A Social History, 1525–1618: Switzerland, Austria, Moravia, South and Central Germany* (Ithaca and London, 1972). Important documents relating to Italian Anabaptism have been discovered by A. Stella, *Dall'anabattismo al socinianesimo nel Cinquecento veneto* (Padua, 1967); A. Stella, *Anabattismo e antitrinitarismo in Italia nel XVI secolo* (Padua, 1969).

29. ACAU, proc. n. 126, c. 28v.

30. Stella, *Dall'anabattismo*, pp. 87ff., and *Anabattismo e antitrinitarismo*, pp. 64ff. See also C. Ginzburg, *I costituti di don Pietro Manelfi*, Biblioteca del "Corpus Reformatorum Italicorum" (Florence and Chicago, 1970).

31. Stella, *Anabattismo e antitrinitarismo*, pp. 153–54. On the religious situation in Friuli in this period see P. Paschini, "Eresia e Riforma cattolica al confine orientale d'Italia," *Lateranum*, n.s. 17, nos. 1–4 (Rome, 1951); L. De Biasio, "L'eresia protestante in Friuli nella seconda metà del secolo XVI," *Memorie storiche Forogiuliesi* 52 (1972): 71–154.

32. See, for instance, Archivio di Stato di Venezia, S. Uffizio, b. 10, fasc. "Marco tintore." This recanted Anabaptist said: "They [anabaptists] preached that we must not have faith in pardons sent by the pope, because they say that they are rubbish."

33. ACAU, proc. n. 126, c. 29r.

34. Stella, *Anabattismo e antitrinitarismo*, p. 154.

35. ACAU, proc. n. 126, cc. 37v–38r.

36. Andrea da Bergamo (Piero Nelli), *Il primo libro delle satire alla carlona* (Venice, 1566), c. 31r; P. Tacchi Venturi, *Storia della Compagnia di Gesù in Italia*, vol. 1 (Rome, 1938), pp. 455–56; Ferderico Chabod, *Lo Stato e la vita religiosa a Milano nell'epoca di Carlo V* (Turin, 1971), pp. 335–36.

37. For a notable exception see the letter quoted by Paschini, *Venezia*, p. 42.

38. The following passage tries to put in more precise terms what I wrote in my essay "Folklore, magia, religione," in *Storia d'Italia*, vol. 1 (Turin, 1972), p. 645.

39. See W. L. Wakefield, "Some Unorthodox Popular Ideas of the Thirteenth Century," *Medievalia et Humanistica*, n.s., no. 4 (1973): 25–35.

40. See, for instance, the phenomena of "Popular rationalism" studied by Marino Berengo, *Nobili e mercanti nella Lucca del Cinquecento* (Turin, 1965), pp. 435ff. For a more detailed discussion of these problems, see Ginzburg, *Il formaggio e i vermi*, pp. 160–61.

41. ACAU, proc. n. 126, c. 21v.

42. Ibid., proc. n. 285, unnumbered pages.

43. Ibid., proc. n. 126, c. 23v.

44. Ibid., proc. n. 285, unnumbered pages.

45. Ibid., proc. n. 126, cc. 16r–v, 19r, 21v.

46. See Chabod, *Lo Stato*, pp. 299 ff.; Delio Cantimori, *Eretici italiani del Cinquecento* (Florence, 1939), pp. 10ff.; Marjorie Reeves, *The Influence of Prophecy in the Later Middle Ages: A Study in Joachimism* (Oxford, 1969); G. Tognetti, "Note sul profetismo nel Rinascimento e la letteratura relativa," *Bullettino dell'Instituto storico italiano per il Medio Evo*, no. 82 (1970), pp. 129–57. On Giorgio Siculo, see Cantimori, *Eretici*, pp. 57ff.; C. Ginzburg, "Due note sul profetismo cinquecentesco," *Rivista Storica Italiana* 78 (1966): 184ff.

47. ACAU, proc. n. 126, c. 16r.

48. Ibid., c. 14v.

49. I was unable to identify this edition.

50. See H. Suchier, *Denkmäler Provenzalischer Literatur und Sprache* (Halle, 1883), pp. 495ff.; P. Rohde, "Die Quellen der Romanische Weltchronik," in ibid., pp. 589–638; F. Zambrini, *Le opere volgari a stampa dei secoli XIII e XIV*, 4th ed. (Bologna, 1884), col. 408. This work was included in the *Index Librorum Prohibitorum*; F. H. Reusch, *Die Indices librorum prohibitorum des sechszehnten Jahrhunderts* (Tübingen, 1886), p. 333; A. Rotondò, "Nuovi documenti per la storia dell'Indice dei libri proibiti" (1572–1638)," *Rinascimento* 14 (1963): 157.

51. "I don't remember if the book's title was *Rosario* or *Lucidario*," said Menocchio (ACAU, proc. n. 126, c. 20r); perhaps he had also read *Lucidario*, largely derived from the *Lucidarium* of Honorius of Autun (see ed. Yves Le Fèvre, *L'Elucidarium et les lucidaires* (Paris, 1954). Of the *Rosario* by Alberto da Castello I know fifteen editions (more or less) printed between 1521 and 1573.

52. This work has been printed innumerable times. Menocchio could have seen, for instance, the edition printed in Venice in 1565.

53. See *La poesia religiosa: I cantari agiografici e le rime di argomento sacro*, ed. A. Cioni (Florence, 1963), pp. 253ff. I know four editions of this work: three of them are owned by the Biblioteca Trivulziana in Milan (see M. Sander, *Le Livre à figures italien depuis 1467 jusqu'à 1530*, vol. 2 [Milan, 1942], nn. 3178, 3180, 3181); the fourth is owned by Biblioteca Universitaria, Bologna (shelfmark: Aula V, Tab. I, J.I, vol. 51, 2).

54. The British Museum has twenty editions of the Italian version, printed between 1480 and 1567. M. H. I. Letts, *Sir John Mandeville: The Man and His Book* (London, 1949) and J. W. Bennett, *The Rediscovery of Sir John Mandeville* (New York, 1954), both try, unconvincingly, to demonstrate the historical reality of "Mandeville."

55. For *Caravia* see V. Rossi, "Un aneddoto della storia della Riforma a Venezia," in *Scritti di critica letteraria*, 3 vols., vol. 3, *Dal Rinascimento al Risorgimento* (Florence, 1930), pp. 191–222; on the literary theme of the clown's journey to hell, see the introduction (also by Rossi) to *Novelle dell'altro mondo: Poemetto buffonesco del 1513* (Bologna, 1929).

56. I know fifteen editions (more or less) of this translation, printed between 1488 and 1851. On its author, see E. Pianetti, "Fra' Iacopo Filippo Foresti e la sua opera nel quadro della cultura bergamasca," *Bergomum* 33 (1939): 100–109, 147–74; A. Azzoni, "I libri del Foresti e la biblioteca conventuale di S. Agostino," ibid., 53 (1959): 37–44; P. Lachat, "Une ambassade éthiopienne auprès de Clement V, à Avignon, en 1310," *Annali del pontificio museo missionario etnologico già lateranensi* 31 (1967): 9, n. 2.

57. See Sander, *Le livre à figures*, vol. 2, nn. 3936–43.

58. On these editions see F. H. Reusch, *Der Index der verbotenen Bücher*, 2 vols. (Bonn, 1883), 1:389–91; Rotondò, "Nuovi documenti," pp. 152–53; C. de Frede, "Tipografi, editori, librai italiani del Cinquecento coinvolti in processi d'eresia," *Rivista di storia della Chiesa in Italia* 23 (1969): 41; P. Brown, "Aims and Methods of the Second 'Rassettatura' of the Decameron," *Studi secenteschi* 8 (1967): 3–40. In general, see A. Rotondò, "La censura ecclesiastica e la cultura," *Storia d'Italia*, vol. 5 (Turin, 1973), pt. 2, pp. 1399–1492.

59. C. de Frede, *La prima traduzione italiana del Corano sullo sfondo dei rapporti tra Christianità e Islam nel Cinquecento* (Naples, 1967).

60. ACAU, proc. n. 126, cc. 20r.

61. Ibid., proc. n. 285, unnumbered pages.

62. Ibid., proc. n. 126, cc. 18r, 20r, 21v, 22r, 25v, 23v.

63. Ibid., proc. n. 285, unnumbered pages.

64. Ibid., proc. n. 126, unnumbered pages.

65. Tagliaferri, *Struttura*, p. 89; G. Chiuppani, "Storia di una scuola di grammatica dal Medio Evo fino al Seicento (Bassano)," *Nuovo archivio veneto* 29 (1915): 79.

66. For a significant parallel, see A. Wyczanski, "Alphabétisation et structure sociale en Pologne au XVIᵉ siècle," *Annales E.S.C.* 29 (1974): 705–13.

67. For instance, Leonardo probably had read Foresti's *Supplementum*; see Leonardo da Vinci, *Scritti letterari*, ed. A. Marinoni (Milan, 1974), p. 254. Surely he read Mandeville; see E. Solmi, *Le fonti dei manoscritti di Leonardo da Vinci* (Turin, 1908), suppl. n. 10–11 of "Giornale storico della letteratura italiana," p. 205. One of the extant copies of *Historia del Giudicio* (that owned by Biblioteca Universitaria, Bologna) has a note of ownership by the famous naturalist Ulisse Aldrovandi.

68. See U. Eco, "Il problema della ricezione," in *La critica tra Marx e Freud*, ed. A. Ceccaroni and G. Pagliano Ungari (Rimini, 1973), pp. 19–27.

69. *Il Fioretto della Bibbia* (Venice, 1517) ("per Zorzi di Rusconi milanese ad instantia de Nicolò dicto Zopino et Vincentio compagni"), c. Ovv.

70. ACAU, proc. n. 126, c. 16v.

71. Ibid., c. 11v.

72. Ibid., cc. 22v–23r.

73. *Iudizio universale overo finale* (Florence, "appresso alle scale di Badia," n.d. [but 1570–80]).

74. Stella, *Anabattismo e antitrinitarismo*, p. 75.

75. ACAU, proc. n. 126, cc. 33v–34r.

76. Ibid., c. 27r.

77. *Mandeville's Travels*, ed. M. C. Seymour (Oxford, 1967), p. 121.

78. Ibid., p. 152. On this passage as a possible source for Swift, see Bennett, *Rediscovery*, pp. 255–56.

79. S. Landucci, *I filosofi e i selvaggi, 1580–1780* (Bari, 1972), pp. 363–64 and passim.

80. *Mandeville's Travels*, ed. Seymour, pp. 146–47.

81. ACAU, proc. n. 126, cc. 21v–22r.

82. *Mandeville's Travels*, ed. Seymour, p. 121.

83. Ibid., pp. 121–22, 143, 227.

84. See C. Vivanti, *Lotta politica e pace religiosa in Francia fra Cinque e Seicento* (Turin, 1963), p. 42; V. Fischer, "La storia dei tre anelli: Del mito all'utopia," *Annali della Scuola Normale Superiore di Pisa: Classe di Lettere e Filosofia,* 3d ser. 3 (1973): 955–98.

85. ACAU, proc. n. 285, unnumbered pages.

86. See the edition corrected by Salviati (Florence, 1573), pp. 28–30 (reprinted Venice, 1582, and subsequently). In the edition "reformed" by Luigi Groto circo d'Adria (Venice, 1590), pp. 30–32, the whole story changed—even the title.

87. Delio Cantimori, "Castellioniana (et Servetiana)," *Rivista storica italiana* 67 (1955): 82.

88. ACAU, proc. n. 126, cc. 17r, 22r.

89. *Fioretto,* c. A iiii r.

90. Foresti, *Supplementum,* c. I v (quotations are from the edition printed in Venice, 1553).

91. ACAU, proc. n. 126, cc. 6r, 17r, 20r, 23r, 30r–v, 31v (italics added).

92. *Dante con l'espositioni di Christoforo Landino et d'Alessandro Vellutello* (Venice, 1578), c. 201r (italics added). See also B. Nardi, *Dante e la cultura medievale: Nuovi saggi di filosofia dantesca* (Bari, 1949), pp. 316–19.

93. U. Harva, *Les représentations religieuses des peuples altaïques,* French trans. (Paris, 1959), pp. 63ff.; G. de Santillana and H. von Dechend, *Hamlet's Mill* (London, 1970), pp. 382–83.

94. ACAU, proc. n. 126, c. 6r.

95. Hiram Haydn, *The Counter-Renaissance* (New York, 1960), p. 209.

96. On the relationship between them, see E. L. Eisenstein, "L'Avènement de l'imprimerie et la Réforme," *Annales E.S.C.* 26 (1971): 1355–82.

97. See the fundamental essay by Jack Goody and Ian Watt, "The Consequences of Literacy," *Comparative Studies in Society and History* 5 (1962–63): 304–45, which ignores, however, the implications of printing. E. L. Eisenstein, "The Advent of Printing and the Problem of the Renaissance," *Past and Present,* no. 45 (Nov. 1969), pp. 66–68, rightly stresses the possibilities printing offered to self-taught people.

98. ACAU, proc. n. 285, unnumbered pages.

99. See L. Febvre, *Le Problème de l'incroyance au 16ᵉ siècle: La religion de Rabelais* (Paris, 1968; 1st ed. 1942), pp. 328ff., which is very useful, even if unaware of class distinctions.

100. ACAU, proc. n. 126, cc. 17v, 28r, 37v, 21v.

101. These images were widespread; see, for instance, Keith Thomas, *Religion and the Decline of Magic* (London, 1971), p. 152.

102. ACAU, proc. n. 126, cc. 20r, 6r, 35v, 16v, 29r, 30v, 34r, 37r, 15v, 37r, 31v, 29r, 37r.

103. *Fioretto,* cc. B viii r, A iii v.

104. ACAU, proc. n. 126, c. 17r.

105. Ibid., cc. 29v, 28v, 29r, 35r, 32r–v, 35v.

106. *Mandeville's Travels,* ed. Seymour, p. 96.

107. ACAU, proc. n. 126, c. 38v.

108. Ibid., c. 30r.

109. Goody and Watt, "Consequences"; F. Graus, "Social Utopias in the Middle Ages," *Past and Present,* no. 38 (Dec. 1967), pp. 3–19; E. J. Hobsbawm, "The Social Function of the Past: Some Questions," ibid., no. 55 (May 1972), pp. 3–17.

110. ACAU, proc. n. 126, c. 35r. See G. Miccoli, "Ecclesiae primitivae forma," in *Chiesa gregoriana* (Florence, 1966), pp. 225ff.

111. Landucci, *I filosofi;* W. Kaegi, "Voltaire e la disgregazione della concezione cristiana della storia," in *Meditazioni storiche,* Italian trans. (Bari, 1960), pp. 216–38.

112. Foresti, *Supplementum,* cc. CCCLV r–v (pages wrongly numbered).

113. ACAU, proc. n. 132, unnumbered pages.

114. Ibid., proc. n. 126, cc. 9r, 7v, 11r.

115. Ibid., proc. n. 132, unnumbered pages.

116. Ibid., proc. n. 126, cc. 13v, 10v, 12v.

117. Ibid., proc. n. 132, unnumbered pages.

118. Ibid., proc. n. 126, cc. 23v–24r.
119. Ibid., c. 34v.
120. *Mundus novus* (n.p., n.d. [1500?]), unnumbered pages (italics added).
121. *Opus epistolarum Erasmi Roterodami*, ed. P. S. Allen (Oxford, 1928), 7: 232–33.
122. The *Capitolo* follows *Begola contra la Bizaria*, Modena s. a. I used a copy owned by Biblioteca Comunale dell'Archiginnasio, Bologna (Shelfmark: 8. Lett. it., *Poesie varie*, Caps. XVII, n. 43). I was unable to identify the printer. See, however, R. Ronchetti Bassi, *Caratte re popolare della stampa a Modena nei secoli XV–XVI–XVII* (Modena, 1950).
123. Graus, "Social Utopias," pp. 7ff., underestimates the popular echoes of this theme. See also V. Rossi, "Il paese di Cuccagna nella letteratura italiana," appendix of *Le lettere di messer Andrea Calmo* (Turin, 1888), pp. 398–410 (for Italy); E. M. Ackermann, *'Das Schlaraffenland' in German Literature and Folksong* . . . (Chicago, 1944); A. Huon, "'Le Roy Sainct Panigon' dans l'imagerie populaire du XVIe siècle," in *François Rabelais: Ouvrage publié pour le quatrième centenaire de sa mort* . . . (Geneva and Lille, 1953), pp. 210–25 (for France); above all, M. Bachtin, *L'Oeuvre de François Rabelais et la culture populaire au Moyen Age et sous la Renaissance* (Paris, 1970).
124. A hint of this connection can be found in Ackermann, *'Das Schlaraffenland,'* pp. 82, 102.
125. A. F. Doni, *Mondi celesti, terrestri et infernali de gli academici pellegrini* . . . (Venice, 1562), pp. 172–84. See also P. F. Grendler, *Critics of the Italian World, 1530–1560: Anton Francesco Doni, Nicolò Franco, and Ortensio Lando* (Madison, Wisc., 1969).
126. See Henry Kamen, "Golden Age, Iron Age: A Conflict of Concepts in the Renaissance," *Journal of Medieval and Renaissance Studies*, no. 4 (1974), pp. 135–55.
127. For this distinction, see Northrop Frye, "Varieties of Literary Utopia," in *Utopias and Utopian Thought*, ed. F. E. Manuel (Cambridge, Mass., 1966), p. 28.
128. Foresti, *Supplementum*, cc. CCCXXXIXv–CCCXLr.
129. ACAU, proc. n. 126, c. 34r.
130. Doni, *Mondi*, p. 184. For different interpretations of Doni's religious attitudes, see Alberto Tenenti, "L'utopia nel Rinascimento (1450–1550)," *Studi storici* 7 (1966): 697, and Grendler, *Critics*, p. 176 and passim.
131. ACAU, proc. n. 126, c. 35r.
132. *Lamento de uno poveretto huomo sopra la carestia, con l'universale allegrezza dell'abondantia, dolcissimo intertenimento de spiriti galanti* (n.p., n.d.). I used the copy owned by Biblioteca Comunale dell'Archiginnasio, Bologna (shelfmark: 8. Lett. it., *Poesie varie*, Caps. XVII, n. 40).
133. Bachtin, *L'Oeuvre de François Rabelais*, pp. 89–90.
134. ACAU, proc. n. 126, unnumbered pages.
135. M. Scalzini, *Il secretario* (Venice, 1587), c. 39. For documents written by don Cellina, see Archivio di Stato di Pordenone, Notarile, b. 488, n. 3785.
136. See P. Valesio, *Strutture dell'allitterazione: Grammatica, retorica e folklore verbale* (Bologna, 1967), p. 186. *Derivatio* is a rhetorical device akin to euphemism or understatement.
137. ACAU, "Sententiarum contra reos S. Officii liber II," cc. 1r–11v. For the abjuration, see cc. 23r–34r.
138. Foresti, *Supplementum*, cc. CLIIIv–CLIVr, CLVIIr.
139. ACAU, "Sententiarum contra reos S. Officii liber II," cc. 12r–17r.
140. Archivio della Curia Vescovile di Pordenone, "Visitationum personalium anni 1593 usque ad annum 1597," pp. 156–57.
141. Archivio di Stato di Pordenone, Notarile, b. 488, n. 3785, cc. 1r–3v, 6v, 17v.
142. ACAU, proc. n. 285, unnumbered pages.
143. All quotations are taken from the same trial, ACAU, proc. n. 285; pages are unnumbered.
144. Foresti, *Supplementum*, cc. 180r–v.
145. M. de Montaigne, *Essais*, ed. A. Thibaudet (Paris, 1950), p. 489.
146. ACAU, proc. n. 285, unnumbered pages.
147. Stella, *Chiesa e Stato*, pp. 290–91.

148. Ginzburg, "Folklore," p. 658.
149. Thomas, *Religion*, p. 163; and Thompson, "Anthropology," p. 43, whose criticism I follow almost literally.
150. Archivio di Stato di Modena, Inquisizione, b. 5 *b*, fasc. "Pighino Baroni."
151. See ed. Jacques Le Goff, *Hérésies et sociétés dans l'Europe préindustrielle (11ᵉ–18ᵉ siècles)* (Paris and The Hague, 1968), pp. 185–86, 278–80; Clasen, *Anabaptism*, pp. 319–20, 432–35.
152. Andrea da Bergamo (Piero Nelli), *Delle satire alla carlona libro secondo* (Venice, 1566), c. 36v.
153. Richard Bennett and John Elton, *History of Corn Milling*, 4 vols., vol. 3, *Feudal Laws and Customs* (London, 1900), pp. 107ff. and passim; see also, for instance, G. Fenwick Jones, "Chaucer and the Medieval Miller," *Modern Language Quarterly* 16 (1955): 3–15.
154. A. d'Ancona, *La poesia popolare italiana* (Livorno, 1878), p. 264.
155. Bergamo, *Delle satire*, c. 35v.
156. Archivio di Stato di Modena, "Inquisizione," b. 5 *b*, fasc. "Pighino Baroni."
157. See Le Goff, ed., *Hérésies*, pp. 278–80, 186.
158. See Bachtin, *L'Oeuvre de François Rabelais*.
159. See Jean Delumeau, *Le catholicisme entre Luther et Voltaire* (Paris, 1971), pp. 256ff.; John Bossy, "The Counter-Reformation and the People of Catholic Europe," *Past and Present*, no. 47 (May 1970), pp. 51–70. A similar approach has been proposed, independently, by G. Hennigsen, *The European Witch-Persecution* (Copenhagen, 1973), p. 19.
160. See Bossy, "Counter-Reformation."
161. ACAU, "Epistole Sac. Cong. S. Officii ab anno 1588 usque ad 1613 incl.," unnumbered pages.
162. ACAU, "Ab anno 1601 usque ad annum 1603 incl. a n. 449 usque ad 546 incl.," proc. n. 497. The only scholar who mentions Menocchio's case (without having seen any related document), A. Battistella, *Il S. Officio e la riforma religiosa in Friuli. Appunti storici documentati* (Udine, 1895), p. 65, wrongly affirms that Menocchio had not been killed.

Chapter 4

1. Gabriel Le Bras's most important articles have been collected and published as *Etudes de sociologie religieuse*, 2 vols. (Paris, 1956). The most important recent studies of the Counter-Reformation by his students are Jeanne Ferté, *La vie religieuse dans les campagnes parisiennes, 1622–1695* (Paris, 1962); and Louis Pérouas, *Le diocèse de La Rochelle de 1648 à 1724: Sociologie et pastorale* (Paris, 1964). An excellent synthesis of recent work, plus an extensive bibliography, may be found in Jean Delumeau, *Le Catholicisme entre Luther et Voltaire* (Paris, 1971), pp. 27–30, 192–330.
2. I know of only two significant exceptions to this statement. The first, and more important for my purposes, is the brief but suggestive discussion of the Catholic response to Protestantism in Richard Gascon's massive *Grand commerce et vie urbaine au XVIᵉ siècle: Lyon et ses marchands* (Paris and The Hague, 1971), pp. 511–15. A. N. Galpern, *The Religions of the People in Sixteenth-Century Champagne* (Cambridge, Mass., 1976), also contains some relevant information, but the author has chosen to organize it in a quite different framework from that used here and treats the later sixteenth century only briefly.
3. Philip Benedict, "Catholics and Huguenots in Sixteenth-Century Rouen: The Demographic Effects of the Religious Wars," *French Historical Studies* 9 (1975): 233. I am now completing a fuller, book-length study of the city in the later sixteenth century.
4. Between 1549 and 1560 more refugees arrived in Geneva from Rouen than from any other French city. Paul-F. Geisendorf, ed., *Livre des habitants de Genève*, vol. 1 (Geneva, 1957), p. xvi.
5. Bibliothèque Municipale de Rouen (henceforth BMR), MS Y 102 (1), p. 128.
6. Quoted by Henri Fouqueray, *Histoire de la Compagnie de Jésus en France des origines à la suppression, 1528–1762* (Paris, 1910), 1:546.
7. Pp. 3–4, 12. This work was subsequently incorporated into a longer pamphlet written in 1572 in the wake of the St. Bartholomew's Massacre with the gloating title, *La*

marmite renversée et fondue de laquelle nostre Dieu parle par les saincts Prophetes (Paris, 1572).

8. Archives Départementales de la Seine-Maritime (henceforth ADS-M), Rouen B, Parlement, Registres Secrets, Chambre des Vacations 1549–56, entry of 7 Nov. 1552; BMR, MS Y 214 (5), entries of 5 Aug. 1562 and 4 May 1570; Archives Communales de Rouen (henceforth ACR), A 19, entry of 3 March 1573; ADS-M, G 2178, entry of 13 May 1594; BMR, MS Y 214 (8), entry of 27 Sept. 1599.

9. Important processions are described in detail in François Farin, *Histoire de la ville de Rouen* (Rouen, 1668), 2; 29–32; and M. C. Oursel, "Notes pour servir a l'histoire de la Réforme en Normandie au temps de Francois Ier, principalement dans le diocèse de Rouen," *Mémoires de l'Académie Nationale des Sciences, Arts et Belles-Lettres de Caen* (1912): 161–62, 201–5. Important processions against heresy were held in 1528, 1531, 1534, 1535, 1539, 1542, 1551, 1559, and 1560. During the Second Civil War in 1567–68 they were held daily. Others were staged in 1569 and 1572. BMR, MS Y 102 (1), passim; ADS-M, G 2168–70; David J. Nicholls, "The Origins of Protestantism in Normandy: A Social Study" (Ph.D. dissertation, University of Birmingham, 1977), p. 146.

10. ADS-M, G 2166–71. This commemoration was suppressed in 1577 by the royal authorities as an unnecessary reminder of past confessional battles (ADS-M, G 2171, entry of 24 Oct. 1577).

11. *Histoire Universelle* (The Hague, 1740), vol. 2, bk. 23, pp. 705–6.

12. *Histoire ecclésiastique des Eglises Réformées au Royaume de France*, ed. G. Baum, E. Cunitz, and R. Reuss, 3 vols. (Paris, 1883–89), 1:353.

13. ADS-M, G 9870, contains a history of the foundation of the confraternity and a list of its members.

14. The similarities between the processions of this confraternity and of the seventeenth-century missions were pointed out to me by Madeleine Foisil.

15. A list of its members may be found in British Museum, Add. MS 19743.

16. He is accused by the *Histoire Ecclésiastique*, 1:858, of participating in a plot with seven other prominent individuals to exterminate the city's Calvinists in 1561.

17. ADS-M, G 9870, fol. 1.

18. ADS-M, G 9869. In three towns in Champagne—Langres, Nemours, and Troyes—confraternities of the Holy Sacrament were founded around this time, with the aim clearly stated in the first two cases as being to answer the "heresies and blasphemies" of the time. These, too, attracted a large membership (Galpern, *The Religions of the People of Champagne*, pp. 132–33).

19. ADS-M, G 2160–80, passim.

20. The standard biography of the archbishop is Eugène Saulnier, *Le rôle politique du Cardinal de Bourbon (Charles X), 1523–1590* (Paris, 1912), which briefly discusses his reforming activities in his archdiocese, pp. 98ff.

21. The council's decisions may be found in Claude de Sainctes, *Le concile provincial des diocèses de Normandie tenu à Rouen, l'an 1581* (Rouen, 1606).

22. The council provides a splendid text in support of H. R. Trevor-Roper's thesis that concern about witchcraft and religious intolerance were linked: "Comme quasi toutes les hérésies sont tombées en sorcelerie et souz la domination de Sathan, aussi avons nous occasion de nous condouloir de ce que nous voions en ce royaume et plusieurs autres lieux, la magie fort pulluler et multiplier, jusques à attester sur les mariages, les biens et vie des hommes, depuis qu'on y a donné la liberté de conscience, et la licence aux hérésies." (de Sainctes, *Concile provincial*, pp. 11–12). Did the council's subsequent call for tighter surveillance of witchcraft lead to a growing number of trials for the crime? One suspects not, given the reception of most of the council's decrees.

23. G. Bonnenfant, *Les séminaires normands du XVIe au XVIIIe siecle* (Paris, 1915), pp. 42–48, provides evidence about the state of the clergy as well as the failure of the seminary to open.

24. ADS-M, G 2174, entry of 30 Nov. 1582; G 2175, entry of 9 Nov. 1585; G 2176, entry of 3 April 1589.

25. Farin, *Histoire de la ville de Rouen*, 3:386; Godefroy de Paris, *Les Frères-Mineurs Capucins en France: Histoire de la Province de Paris*, 2 vols. (Paris, 1937–39), vol. 1, fasc. 1, p. 143, and fasc. 2, p. 30.

26. Histories of the Jesuits in Rouen in the sixteenth century are ADS-M, D 26; Michel Mollat, "Collège de Bourbon et Lycée Cornille: Notes de bibliographie et d'histoire," *Bulletin de la Société Libre d'Emulation du Commerce et de l'Industrie de la Seine-Inférieure* (1940–41); 267–318; Charles Robillard de Beaurepaire, *Recherches sur l'instruction publique dans le diocèse de Rouen avant 1789* (Evreux, 1872), vol. 2, chap. 1; Fouqueray, *Histoire*, 1, 543, 545–48, and 2: 314–16.

27. Fouqueray, *Histoire*, 1:543, 545; ADS-M, G 275; ADS-M, G 2176, entry of 13 Aug. 1588.

28. Fouqueray, *Histoire*, 1:543, 545–48.

29. Ibid., pp. 545–48.

30. Damours, the *avocat general au Parlement*, wrote to the cardinal of Broubon that Possevin had converted several heretics and generally heightened the love of God in the hearts of his listeners (ADS-M, D 26).

31. This account of the history of the foundation of the Jesuit college is drawn from the works cited in note 27. See also ADS-M, B, Parlement, Registres Secrets, entry of 6 April 1570.

32. Jean Lestocquoy, *La vie religieuse en France du VIIe au XXe siècle* (Paris, 1964), pp. 108–13; V. Vogler, "La réforme et son implantation dans les pays rhénans (1555–1619)," *L'Information Historique* 35 (1973): 170–76. Louis Binz, *Vie religieuse et réforme ecclésiastique dans le diocèse de Genève pendant le Grand Schisme et la crise conciliaire, 1378–1450* (Geneva, 1973), provides an excellent portrait of the clergy in a slightly earlier period. His fairly optimistic view of clerical morality probably needs to be tempered in the light of Robert Sauzet's important "Les procès-verbaux des visites pastorales du diocèse de Chartres au XVIIe siècle," *Archives de Sciences Sociales des Religions*, no. 35 (1973), pp. 45–56.

33. G. Panel, ed., *Documents concernant les pauvres de Rouen*, 3 vols. (Rouen, 1917), 1:29–30.

34. ADS-M, G 2160–80, passim.

35. Several members of the chapter were minor authors or scholars. Claude Chappuys, for example, had been a court poet under Francis I; Jean Nagerel was the author of chronicles and geographies; René de Clinchamp is revealed by his inventory after death to have had a strong interest in the sciences, occult as well as natural. See Louis P. Roche, *Claude Chappuys (?–1575): Poète de la cour de Francois Ier* (Poitiers, 1915); E. LeParquier, "Un chroniqueur rouennais à l'époque de la Réforme: Le chanoine Jean Nagerel," in *Congrès du Millénaire de la Normandie, 911–1911: Compte-Rendu des Travaux* (Rouen, 1912), pp. 223–44: ADS-M, G 3427. De Clinchamp's estate included an alabaster mortar and pestle; two astrolabes and books on their usage; a number of works on natural history, mathematics, and astronomy; and, hidden in a closed trunk, Agrippa's *De Oculta Philosophia* and a book identified only as *Magie Naturelle*.

36. Liasses G 3424 to G 3442 of the ADS-M, contains a large, although not complete, collection of wills and inventories after death of the canons from the fifteenth to the eighteenth centuries—a rarity under the Norman Custom. The inventories after death reveal the strongly humanist tone of many of the canons' libraries, most of which contained at least one copy of Erasmus. As for more suspect books, de Clinchamp hid copies of Marot, Rabelais, and some *Hymnes en Francois* in the same trunk with the Agrippa, while Pierre Lambert's huge 567-volume library (G 3433) included some 71 censured books, including works of all the leading reformers. Although possession of Protestant books by a Catholic cleric could always be a case of know your enemy, Lambert was one of the most tolerant and eirenic of the canons and was suspected of Protestant sympathies. In his case, books surely influenced their reader.

37. ADS-M, B, Parlement, Registres Secrets, entry of 5 Aug. 1562; LeParquier, "Un chroniqueur rouennais," pp. 224–28.

38. ADS-M, B, Parlement, Registres Secrets, entry of 28 Nov. 1570.

39. The decline in number of Protestants in Rouen under the pressure of popular violence and intolerance is discussed briefly in Benedict, "Catholics and Huguenots," pp. 225–28, and in greater detail in "Rouen during the Wars of Religion: Popular Disorder, Public Order, and the Confessional struggle" (Ph.D. dissertation, Princeton University, 1975), chaps. 4–5.

40. The best discussion of the significant colony of English Catholics in Rouen is to be found in John Bossy, "Elizabethan Catholicism: The Link with France" (Ph.D. dissertation, Cambridge University, 1960), pp. 78–91.

41. This view is implicit in much of the pamphlet literature of the time. See, for example, ADS-M, G 2476 (a call for moral reform by the Cathedral Chapter posted around Rouen in 1591); and the discussion in Denis Pallier, *Recherches sur l'imprimerie à Paris pendant la Ligue, 1585–1594* (Geneva, 1975), p. 173.

42. For example, the conclusion of *Les connivences de Henry de Valois avec Monsieur de Charouges, Gouverneur de la ville de Rouen* (Paris, 1589), pp. 9–10.

43. ADS-M, G 2476, expresses this view. It explains the wave of Catholic puritanism that swept Paris in these years, discussed in Marcel Poëte, *Une vie de cité: Paris de sa naissance à nos jours*, 3 vols. (Paris, 1924–31), 3:234–35.

44. Pallier, *Recherches sur l'imprimerie à Paris*, p. 173.

45. ADS-M, B, Parlement, Registres Secrets, entries of 27 Jan. and 5 Feb. 1594.

46. ACR, A 21, entry of 17 Sept. 1592; ADS-M, G 2178 entry of 24 Sept. 1592; Fouqueray, *Histoire*, 2:315.

47. ADS-M, G 2176, entry of 13 Aug. 1588.

48. Archives of the English College of Valladolid (hereafter ECV), Valladolid Serie 2, L 5, no. 13.

49. On the enrollment of the Jesuit colleges, see François de Dainville, "Collèges et fréquentation scolaire au XVIIe siècle," *Population* 12 (1957): 467; on its curriculum and noteworthy alumni, see Mollat, "Collège de Bourbon," pp. 284ff.

50. The best description I have found of this practice is in Antoine Richart, *Mémoires sur la Ligue dans le Laonnois* (Laon, 1869), p. 222. The payments made to the artisans who constructed the *oratoire* in each parish of Rouen are noted in the parish account books and make it clear that the practice was substantially the same in Rouen and Laon, the main difference being that in Laon two-man teams spent two-hour shifts praying before the *oratoire* and guarding it, while in Rouen special guards were paid to watch over it. Detailed payments for the *oratoire* are to be found in ADS-M, G 6245, G 6341, G 7167, and G 7767.

51. "Journal historique de Rouen, extrait d'un manuscrit de la bibliothèque de l'abbé De la Rue," *Revue de Rouen* (1840): 258; ECV, Serie 2, L 5, no. 13; ADS-M, G 6245, G 6341, and G 7767.

52. On the Quintanadoines' early years in Rouen, see Michel Mollat, *Le commerce maritime normand à la fin du Moyen Age* (Paris, 1952), p. 512.

53. ADS-M, E, Protestants de Quévilly, Baptêmes, 1564–66, entry of 9 Aug. 1566; Christiane Douyère, "Les marchands étrangers à Rouen au 16e siècle (vers 1520–vers 1580): Assimilation ou segrégation?" (Thesis, Ecole Nationale des Chartes, 1973), p. 242.

54. P. de Beauvais, *La vie de Monsieur de Brétigny, prestre, fondateur des Carmélites de Sainte Thérèse en France et aux Pays-Bas* (Paris, 1747), p. 11; Pierre Serouet, ed., *Quintanadueñas: Lettres de Jean de Brétigny 1556–1634* (Louvain, 1971), p. vii. Neither Serouet nor de Beauvais is aware of their hero's Protestant father, and thus they do not find Jehan's being sent to Spain unusual.

55. This is evident because he carried on the family's business correspondence with the important Spanish merchant Simon Ruiz (Archivo Historico Provincial y Universitario de Valladolid, Valladolid Archivo Simon Ruiz, cajas 2–4). See also Serouet, ed., *Quintana-dueñas*, p. 27n.

56. ADS-M, B, Parlement, Arrêts, Novembre 1562–Mars 1563, Arrêt of 27 Feb. 1563; ADS-M, G 2165, entries of 17 April to 3 June 1562.

57. Studies of elite family structure are only beginning to suggest the strength of the extended family in sixteenth-century urban society. It was not uncommon for sons of merchants and *officiers* in Rouen to live with their parents for a number of years after marriage, as did the upper strata in other French cities. ADS-M, Tabellionage, Meubles 2e série, contract of 10 March 1568; Jonathan S. Dewald, "The Magistrates of the Parlement of Rouen, 1499–1610" (Ph.D. dissertation, University of California at Berkeley, 1974), p. 165; Etienne Trocmé, "La Rochelle de 1560 à 1628: Tableau d'une société réformée au temps des Guerres de Religion" (Thèse de théologie protestante, Paris, 1950), p. 128; Natalie Zemon Davis, "Ghosts, Kin, and Progeny: Some Features of Family Life in Early

Modern France," *Daedalus* 106 (1977): 101; Pierre Goubert, "Famille et province: Contribution à la connaissance des structures familiales dans l'ancienne France" (Paper presented to the Davis Center, 22 Oct. 1976), p. 13. In Parisian robe circles, the work of Denis Richet will show, careers could be launched for a young man not by his father but by his uncle, and some exceedingly unusual family patterns could develop. The young Robert Arnauld d'Andilly spent half of each day at his father's house, half at his uncle's.

58. De Beauvais, *La vie de Monsieur de Brétigny*, pp. 36, 140; Paul Baudry, *Les religieuses carmélites à Rouen* (Rouen, 1875), p. 25. One of Quintanadoines's letters of 1580 strongly suggests that his illness of that year was psychosomatic (Serouet, ed., *Quintanadueñas*, p. 1).

59. Baudry, *Les religieuses carmélites*, pp. 29, 68–71.

60. Ibid., p. 69; Serouet, ed., *Quintanadueñas*, p. 335.

61. Accounts of this attempt may be found in de Beauvais, *La vie de Monsieur de Brétigny*, pp. 117ff.; Baudry, *Les religieuses carmélites*, pp. 16ff.; Henri Brémond, *Histoire littéraire du sentiment religieux en France depuis la fin des guerres de religion*, 11 vols. (Paris, 1932), 2:275–82; and Serouet, ed., *Quintanadueñas*, pp. 3–36.

62. Godefroy de Paris, *Les Frères-Mineurs Capucins*, v. 1, fasc. 2, pp. 107–8.

63. Monsieur Acarie earned the title "the valet of the League" for his role in the movement; his wife received her initiation into mysticism during the years of the League from the *ligueur* Bernard de Mont-Gaillard. These and other links between the league and the *dévots* are suggested by Marguerite Pecquet, "Des compagnies de Pénitents à la Compagnie du Saint-Sacrement," *XVIIᵉ Siècle*, no. 69 (1965), pp. 3–36.

64. Ibid.; Venard, "Les confréries de Pénitents au XVIᵉ siècle dans la province ecclésiastique d'Avignon," *Mémoires de l'Académie du Vaucluse*, 6th ser. 1 (1967): 55–79; Agulhon, *Pénitents et francs-maçons de l'ancienne Provence* (Paris, 1968).

65. The fact is noted by Louis Guibert in his still fundamental, if occasionally unreliable, "Les confréries de Pénitents en France et notamment dans le diocèse de Limoges," *Bulletin de la Société Archéologique et Historique du Limousin* 27 (1879): 5–193.

66. The confraternities in Abbeville and Laon are mentioned in Ernest Prarond, *La Ligue à Abbeville, 1576–1594*, 3 vols. (Paris, 1868–73), 1:188; Richart, *Mémoires sur la Ligue*, p. 266.

67. ECV, Serie 2, L 5, no. 13.

68. Bossy, "Elizabethan Catholicism," pp. 75, 89.

69. De Beauvais, *La vie de Monsieur de Brétigny*, p. 89; ADS-M, G 2178, entry of 15 April 1593. Penitent ceremonies are described by Venard, "Les confréries de Pénitents à Avignon," pp. 66–67.

70. Pecquet, "Des compagnies de Pénitents," pp. 26–27; Guibert, "Les confréries de Pénitents," pp. 30–32; Richart, *Mémoires sur la Ligue*, pp. 333–40.

71. There is evidence of its introduction in Lyon, Reims, and Laon. Pierre Richard, *La papauté et la Ligue française: Pierre d'Epinac Archevêque de Lyon, 1573–1599* (Paris and Lyon, n.d.), pp. 452–53; Jean Pussot, "Mémoires ou Journalier," ed. E. Henry, *Travaux de l'Academie Imperiale de Reims* 25 (1857): 8; Richart, *Mémoires sur la Ligue*, p. 222.

72. Richart, *Mémoires sur la Ligue*, pp. 261–68.

73. Poëte, *Une vie de cité*, 3:241–45.

74. Militant confraternities dedicated to the extermination of heresy existed in a number of French cities from the time of the early civil wars onward. Particularly important were the Confraternity of the Holy Spirit, spread over much of eastern France, and the Confraternity of St. Gunstan in Dieppe. The Confraternity of the Name of Jesus also played a highly visible role in the League of Orleans. Robert Harding of Yale University is now undertaking a study of the place of confraternities in the League that should clarify just what role these associations played.

75. ADS-M, B, Parlement, Registres Secrets, entry of 19 June 1593.

76. ADS-M, G 2178, entry of 15 April 1593.

77. Robert Parsons often stayed with de Monchy when he was in Rouen and called him "more than a most loving friend of our society" (L. Hicks, ed., *Letters and Memorials of Father Robert Parsons, S.J.*, Catholic Record Society Publications 39 [London, 1942], 1:107).

78. The phrase "popular religion" is, of course, fraught with ambiguity. Of the two different ways in which it can be understood—as connoting those forms of religious belief and expression not sanctioned by high priests or a religious establishment, the antithesis of learned or organized religion, and as referring simply to any belief or practice that is widely shared and "popular" in the sense of a popularity contest—I am using the phrase in the second sense.

79. Two particularly important recent historical works that employ quantitative tests of religious practice are Michel Vovelle, *Piété baroque et déchristianisation en Provence au XVIIIe siècle: Les attitudes devant la mort d'après les clauses des testaments* (Paris, 1973); and the same author's "Analyse spectrale d'un diocèse méridional au XVIIIe siècle: Aix-en-Provence," *Provence Historique* 22 (1972): 352–449. This latter article is especially valuable methodologically.

80. Many wills can be found in Rouen's notarial records, but it is highly doubtful that they are numerous enough to provide an adequate cross-section of the population. The absence of episcopal visitations and registers of ordination has already been noted.

81. The phrase "the great unknown" is borrowed from Nicholls, "Origins of Protestantism in Normandy," p. 40.

82. Perhaps the fullest discussions of the belief in continence during Lent and its relation to the monthly movement of conceptions are Roger Mols, *Introduction à la démographie historique des villes d'Europe du XIVe au XVIIIe siècle*, 3 vols. (Louvain, 1956), 3:298–99; and Etienne Hélin, "Opinions de quelques casuistes de la Contre-Réforme sur l'avortement, la contraception et la continence dans le mariage," in Hélène Bergues et al., *La prévention des naissances dans la famille, ses origines dans les temps modernes* (Paris, 1960), pp. 247–49. Francois Lebrun, "Démographie et mentalités: Le mouvement des conceptions sous l'ancien régime," *Annales de Démographie Historique* (1974): 45–50, expresses some reservations about the link between the March dip in conceptions and Lenten sexual abstinence, but his arguments are not thoroughly convincing.

83. Based on the figures in ACR, registres paroissiaux 11, 211, 226–28, 286–88, 566–69, and those kindly provided me by Jean-Pierre Bardet for St. Maclou and St. Vivien.

84. *Comptes de fabrique* from the sixteenth century are ADS-M, G 6245 (St. André-de-la-Ville); G 6300–6302 (St. Cande-le-Jeune); G 6341–42 (St. Cande-le-Vieil); G 6583–85 (St. Gervais); G 6616–18 (St. Godard); G 6727–29 (St. Jean); G 6800–6802 (St. Laurent); G 6885–6907 (St. Maclou); G 7166–69 (St. Michel); G 7228–33 (St. Nicaise); G 7329–30 (St. Nicolas); G 7373–74 (Notre-Dame-la-Ronde); and G 7754–75 (St. Vivien). I am indebted to David Nicholls for calling my attention to these accounts and for generously providing me with his figures for the years prior to 1562.

85. Individual curves for each basin and each parish may be found in Benedict, "Rouen during the Wars of Religion," Appendix V, pp. 427–31.

86. A fuller discussion of the movement of donations in these years prior to 1562 may be found in Nicholls, "Origins of Protestantism in Normandy," pp. 79–83. On the role of St. Nicaise's drapers in popular religious violence, see "Discours abbrégé et mémoires d'aulcunes choses advenues tant en Normandye que en France depuis le commencement de l'an 1559, et principalement en la ville de Rouen" in A. Héron, ed., *Deux chroniques de Rouen* (Rouen, 1900), p. 299; Ia. Maingoua, *La Ligue renversée, ou response à la Ligue réssuscitée* (n.p., n.d., reprinted by the Société des Bibliophiles Normands, Rouen, 1896), p. 9.

87. Micheline Baulant and Jean Meuvret, *Prix des céréales extraits de la mercuriale de Paris, 1520–1698*, 2 vols. (Paris, 1960), 1:243.

88. These comments are based on a brief examination of two seventeenth-century account books. In St. Cande-le-Vieil, gifts to the Virgin rose by 70 percent between 1595–600 and 1632–37. In St. Gervais the increase between 1599–1600 and 1654–55 was 133 percent.

89. Farin, *Histoire de la ville de Rouen*, vol. 3, contains a full list of the religious houses in the city with their dates of foundation.

90. ADS-M, G 7201.

91. Gascon, *Grand commerce et vie urbaine*, pp. 511–15.

92. The suggestion that there was a considerable degree of continuity between the

religious enthusiasms of the period of the League and those of the early seventeenth century is made briefly by several authors: Philippe Wolff, *Histoire de Toulouse* (Toulouse, 1961), pp. 258–59; Richard Gascon in André Latreille, ed., *Histoire de Lyon et du Lyonnais* (Toulouse, 1975), p. 200; and, most strongly, Marguerite Pecquet, "Des compagnies de Pénitents." As yet, however, concrete biographical links have not been traced between significant numbers of people active in both the League and the devotional activity of the early Counter-Reformation. The task is made extremely difficult by the problems involved in identifying those who participated in the League. The discredit that became attached to the movement after its fall made men eager to hide their participation in it, and the records of most of both its political organs and the confraternities founded at the time have been lost or destroyed. In Rouen less than forty men active in the league can be identified. The daughters of several of these men were among the first to join the Carmelite convent when it was finally established in Rouen in 1609, but such cases are far too few to prove there was a clear connection.

Chapter 5

1. Letter of Clough to Gresham, 21 Aug. 1566, J. W. Burgon, *The Life and Times of Thomas Gresham*, 2 vols. (London, 1839), 2:139–40.
2. Natalie Zemon Davis, "The Rites of Violence: Religious Riot in Sixteenth-Century France," *Past and Present*, no. 59 (May 1973), p. 56.
3. This study concerns only the southern provinces of the Netherlands: Brabant, Flanders, Hainaut, Liège, Artois, and Namur.
4. Marcus van Vaernewijck, *Troubles religieux en Flandre et dans les Pays-Bas au XVIe siècle*, trans. Hermann van Duyse, 2 vols. (Ghent, 1905), 1:65–66.
5. Ibid., 1:154–57.
6. This almost happened in Hasselt, where a minister and his followers were engaged in knocking down a huge crucifix in the center of the church. At midnight, without a breath of wind, all of their torches went out, as well as the bonfire they had made to burn the ornaments. The crowd panicked, thinking that God was about to punish them for their misdeeds (A. Hansay, *Le sac de l'Eglise de Saint-Quentin à Hasselt, le 20 Janvier 1567* [Hasselt, 1932], pp. 1–9).
7. Van Vaernewijck, *Troubles religieux*, 2:138.
8. J. Decavele, "De reformatorische beweging to Axel en Hulst, 1556–1566," *Bijdragen voor de geschiedenis der Nederlanden* 22 (1968–69): 17.
9. Van Vaernewijck, *Troubles religieux*, 2:117. The same phenomenon was reported in England. In Essex a famous rood with miraculous powers was removed and carried a quarter of a mile, "without any resistance of the said idol," and then burned (James E. Oxley, *The Reformation in Essex* [Manchester, 1965], pp. 89–90).
10. Van Vaernewijck, *Troubles religieux*, 1:163.
11. Frances Yates has suggested that perhaps the revival of magic in the Renaissance made the Reformers suspicious that all art and philosophy were tinged with magic and that this influenced the iconoclasts (*Giordano Bruno and the Hermetic Tradition* [Chicago, 1964], p. 167). This may well have been true for the Calvinist ministers, but to ordinary laymen who witnessed the image-breaking, the minister who successfully broke images must have assumed a magical quality of his own. Certainly many contemporaries felt that a miracle was required. Brother Cornelis, a monk of Bruges, scoffed, "Bah, I would like to ask these men, what miracles or wonders they can do to prove that they were really sent by God to preach the new belief" (*Historie van Br. Cornelis Adriaensz van Dordrecht, Minnebroeder tot Brugge*, [n.p., 1628], p. 40).
12. Burgon, *Life*, 2:138–39. On the number of image-breakers in Antwerp, Tournai, Turnhout, and Mechelen, see M. Dierickx, "Beeldenstrom in de Nederlanden in 1566," *Streven* 19 (1966): 1044–47. On Ghent, M. Delmotte, "Het Calvinisme in de verschillende bevolkingslagen te Gent, 1566–1567," *Tijdschrift voor Geschiedenis* 76 (1963): 159.
13. On Basel, see G. H. Williams, *The Radical Reformation* (Philadelphia, 1962), p. 196. On Wittenberg, see Charles Garside, *Zwingli and the Arts* (New Haven, 1966), p. 127. On France, see Davis, "Rites of Violence," in which the author refers to crowds of

image-breakers, but does not analyze the exact numbers. A Protestant account of the iconoclasm in Paris states that a crowd of about twelve to thirteen thousand participated ("Histoire véritable," in L. Cimber and F. Danjou, eds., *Archives curieuses de l'histoire de France*, 4 vols. [1834–40], 4:52–55). Another account says that three to four thousand controlled the neighboring streets while the crowd went "en grand nombre" into the church (relation of Bruslart, quoted from the *Memoires de Condé*, vol. 1 [1743], in Cimber and Danjou, eds., *Archives curieuses*, 4:57, n. 1).

14. Letter of Clough to Gresham, 11 Aug. 1566, Burgon, *Life*, 2:137.

15. John Lothrop Motley, *The Rise of the Dutch Republic*, 3 vols. (London, 1913), 1:505.

16. Claude de Sainctes wrote that the Huguenots found a priest and cut his garments, wounding several parishioners, while elsewhere the mob led an old monk naked through a town and then killed him (*Discours sur le saccagement des églises Catholiques* [Paris, 1563], pp. 371–72, 382). Davis, "Rites of Violence," notes that Catholics probably killed more people than Calvinists did, but she also cites numerous cases of Calvinists murdering Catholic priests. Commentators on the Netherlands iconoclasm, even Catholics, do not mention these atrocities.

17. Van Vaernewijck, *Troubles religieux*, 2:120.

18. Peter Geyl, *The Revolt of the Netherlands* (London, 1966), p. 128.

19. Delmotte, "Calvinisme."

20. Some looting did occur; in general, historians sympathetic to the Reformers minimize this, saying that some rabble got in with the "pure" Calvinists. Delmotte mentions occasional looting, but notes that the iconoclasts did not plunder the grain market, although there had been a riot there the day before (ibid., p. 162). M. Backhouse emphasizes that looting occurred in Flanders, but admits that in Ghent, Antwerp, Tournai, and West Flanders, goods were returned to the magistrates ("Beeldenstorm en bosgeuzen in het Westkwartier (1566–1568)," *Handelingen van de koninklijke geschied-en oudheidkundige kring van Kortrijk*, n.s. 38 [1971]: 86–88).

21. On the Reninghelst murders, see Backhouse, "Beeldenstorm," n. 23. The murders were committed by Calvinists coming from England, advised by consistories at Bruges and Armentières.

22. Van Vaernewijck, *Troubles religieux*, 1:67–68.

23. Hans Gerth and C. Wright Mills, ed., *From Max Weber: Essays in Sociology* (New York, 1971), pp. 245–47, from the essay, "The Sociology of Charismatic Authority."

24. M. van Deventer, *Het jaar 1566* (The Hague, 1856), p. 25.

25. Van Vaernewijck, *Troubles religieux*, 1:248.

26. On the activities of the ministers during the iconoclasm, see my "A Question of Authority: Reformed Preaching and Iconoclasm in the Netherlands, 1544–1570" (Ph.D. dissertation, Cornell University, 1974).

27. Witnesses of the ministers' sermons attested to their great knowledge of Scripture; individual ministers were cited as preaching on the subjects of idolatry, the nature of Communion, the corruption of the Catholic clergy, and other such topics (C. Blenk, "Hagepreek en beeldenstorm in 1566, een historische analyse," *Hagepreek en beeldenstorm. Een uitgave bij het derde lustrum van de C.S.F.R. met opstellen over wetenschap, maatschappij en kerk* [1966], p. 25).

28. Enno van Gelder, "Erasmus, schilders en rederijkers," *Tijdschrift voor geschiedenis* 71 (1958).

29. Ibid., p. 310.

30. Henri Liebrecht, *Les chambres de rhétorique des Pays-Bas* (Brussels, 1948), p. 117.

31. Performances of the chambers took place in nearly all of the cities and towns where hedgepreaching occurred in 1566. See the list of towns with chambers in Ferdinand van der Haeghen, ed., *Bibliotheca Belgica*, 7 vols. (Brussels, 1964), 1:483–538.

32. Anon., *Antwerpsch Chronykje . . .* (Leyden, 1743), reprinted in *Antwerpsch Archievenblad*, 9:144ff. A chronicler reported that the Calvinists preached more radical sermons against images than the "Martinists" (Robert von Roosbroeck, ed., *De kroniek van Godevaert van Haecht* [Antwerp, 1929], p. 97). But the effect of Lutheran preaching could be just as volatile. At Antwerp, a crowd almost attacked a priest during his debate with a Lutheran minister.

33. T. J. van Brught, *The Bloody Theater or Martyrs Mirror of the Defenseless Christians*, trans. Joseph Sohm (Scottdale, Pa., 1951), p. 948.
34. Ibid., p. 776.
35. A. L. E. Verheyden, *Anabaptism in Flanders, 1530—1650* (Scottdale, Pa., 1961), p. 59.
36. Van Vaernewijck, *Troubles religieux*, 1:80.
37. Van Gelder, "Erasmus," p. 290—91.
38. A. Beenakker, *Breda in de eerste storm van de epstand, 1545—1569* (Tilburg, 1971), pp. 42—43, 122, 167.
39. Decavele, "Reformatorische beweging," pp. 2—9.
40. On the activities of the early ministers, see Crew, "A Question of Authority," chap. 3.
41. Letter of Beza to the pastor Jean Taffin, 24 Aug. 1565, cited in E. Braekman, *Guy de Brès: Sa vie* (Brussels, 1960), pp. 198—99.
42. G. Moreau, *L'Histoire du protestantisme à Tournai jusqu'à la veille de la révolution des Pays-Bas* (Paris, 1962), pp. 162—64.
43. On the ministers' early writings, see Crew, "A Question of Authority," chap. 5. The ministers embraced the orthodox doctrines of obedience to the magistrate and the magistrate's own duty to protect the true religion. But on specific questions of religious toleration, the legality of image-breaking or of prison breaks, the ministers could reach no agreement. And nowhere did they conceive of violence outside the context of law. The ministers were particularly vehement against the Anabaptists as anarchists.
44. F. Prims, *Het wonderjaar, 1566—1567*, 2d ed. (Antwerp, 1941), pp. 99—100.
45. Peter Worsley, *The Trumpet Shall Sound*, 2d ed. (New York, 1970), p. xiv.
46. Letter of 10 July 1566, Burgon, *Life*, 2:130.
47. J. F. Petit, ed. Edward Grimeston (London, 1609), p. 394.
48. M. G. Groen van Prinsterer, ed., *Archives ou correspondence inédite de la maison d'Orange-Nassau* 15 vols. (Leiden, 1835—96), 1st ser., 2:217.
49. Van Vaernewijck, *Troubles religieux*, 2:14.
50. P. D. Lagomarsino, "Court Factions and the Formulation of Spanish Court Policy towards the Netherlands (1559—1567)" (Ph.D. dissertation, University of Cambridge, 1973), p. 293, letter of Villavicencio, 1 May 1566.
51. Peter Frarin, *An Oration against the Unlawfull Insurrections of the Protestantes of our Time, under Pretence to Refourme Religion* (Antwerp, 1566), n.p.
52. Claude Haton, *Mémoires*, ed. F. Bourquelst, 2 vols. (Paris, 1857), 1:189—92.
53. Pasquier de la Barre, *Mémoires*, ed. A. Pinchart, 2 vols. (Brussels, 1859), 1:75—76.
54. M. F. van Lennep, *Gaspar van der Heyden, 1530—1586* (Amsterdam, 1884), pp. 47—48.
55. Justification of the Magistrate, quoted in V. Fris, "Notes pour servir à l'histoire de l'iconoclasme et des Calvinistes à Gand de 1566—1568," *Annales de la société d'histoire et d'archéologie de Gand* 9 (1844).
56. Dierickx, "Beeldenstorm," p. 1044.
57. Pasquier de la Barre, *Mémoires*, 1:138, 2:203; van Vaernewijcke, quoted in V. Fris, ed., *Notes pour servir à l'histoire des iconoclastes et des Calvinistes à Gand de 1566 à 1568* (Ghent, 1909), p. 67.
58. Van Vaernewijck, *Troubles religieux*, 1:75.
59. This took place at Tournai, against a noble whose family had been particularly hated. Van Vaernewijck mentions numerous sepulchers turned over, but no mutilation of bodies (ibid., 1:132—35, 137).
60. On the atrocities in France, see de Sainctes, *Discours*, pp. 387—89, and Davis, "Rites of Violence."
61. For a complete list of the lay preachers, see Crew, "A Question of Authority," Appendix C. Sixty-five were of unknown origin, twenty-three were artisans or laborers, eighteen were middle class or professionals, forty-three belonged to the Catholic clergy.
62. Ch. Rahlenbeck, *L'Eglise de Liège et la révolution*, 2d ed. (Brussels, 1864), interrogation, pp. 277f.
63. E. de Coussemaker, *Troubles religieux du XVIe siècle dans la Flandre maritime, 1560—1570*, 2 vols. (Bruges, 1876), 2:213.

64. W. Bax, *Het Protestantisme in het bisdom Luik en vooral te Maastricht, 1557–1612* (The Hague, 1941), p. 79.

65. Van Vaernewijck, *Troubles religieux*, 1:321.

66. P. Heinderycx, *Jaerboeken van Veurne en Veurnambacht*, ed. E. Ronse, 2 vols. (Veurne, 1855), 2:30–31.

67. A. van Haemstede, *Historien der vromer martelaren* (Dordrecht, n.d.), fol. 421.

68. Bax, *Protestantisme*, p. 79.

69. The priest's testimony is printed in J. van Vloten, *Nederlands opstand tegen Spanje* (Haarlem, 1856), pp. 170–71.

70. De Coussemaker, *Troubles religieux*, 2:273.

71. M. Ryckaert, "Een beeldenstorm in de kerk van Oostwinkel op 23 Augustus 1566," *Appeltjes van het Meetjesland* 8 (1957): 109.

72. All classes attended; reports of spies at Valenciennes said that ninety-one trades were represented, as well as merchants, peasants, and others (G. Clark, "An Urban Study during the Revolt of the Netherlands: Valenciennes, 1540–1570" [Ph.D. dissertation, Columbia University, 1972], pp. 181–87).

73. Van Vaernewijck, *Troubles religieux*, 1:42.

74. H.-Q. Janssen, *De kerkhervorming te Brugge* (Rotterdam, 1856), pp. 49–50.

75. G. J. Brutel de la Rivière, *Het leven van Hermonnus Moded* (Haarlem, 1879), p. 26.

76. J. Desilve, *Le Protestantisme dans la seigneurie de St. Amand de 1562 à 1584* (Valenciennes, 1910), p. 225.

77. *Kroniek van Godevaert van Haecht*, ed. van Roosbroeck, pp. 121–22.

78. Van Vaernewijck, *Troubles religieux*, 1:67–68.

79. Clark, "Urban Study," pp. 188–89.

80. Van Vaernewijck, *Troubles religieux*, 1:27.

81. Blenk, "Hagepreek," p. 24.

82. Bax, *Protestantisme*, p. 128.

83. O. J. de Jong, *De reformatie in Culembourg* (n.p., n.d.), pp. 102–3.

84. Van Vaernewijck, *Troubles religieux*, 1:409, 42.

85. Quoted in Brutel de la Rivière, *Het leven van Hermanus Moded*.

86. Fl. Prims, "De Antwerpsche ommeganck op den vooravond van de beeldstormerij," *Mededeelingen van de koninklijke Vlaamsche academie voor wetenschappen, letteren en schoone kunsten van Belgie*, vol. 8, no. 5.

87. Van Vloten, *Nederlands opstand*, pp. 82–83.

88. Van Vaernewijck, *Troubles religieux*, 1:67–68.

89. Brother Cornelis, *Historie*, p. 53.

90. Robert van Roosbroeck, *Het wonderjaar te Antwerpen, 1566–1567* (Antwerp, 1930), pp. 211–15.

91. Decavele, "Reformatorische beweging," p. 22.

92. J. W. Pont, *Geschiedenis van het Lutheranisme in de Nederlanden tot 1618* (Haarlem, 1911), pp. 86–88.

93. *Notes pour servir à l'histoire des iconoclastes et des Calvinistes à Gand de 1566 à 1568* (Ghent, 1909), p. 67.

94. Davis, "Rites of Violence," pp. 61–70.

95. Lagomarsino, "Court Factions."

96. J. Hessels, ed., *Ecclesiae Londino-Batavae Archivum*, 3 vols. (Cambridge, 1889), 3:183.

97. Jean Taffin, *L'Etat de l'église* (Bergen-op-Zoom, 1605), p. 606.

Chapter 6

1. Recent bibliographies by H. C. Erik Midelfort, "Recent Witch Hunting Research, Or Where Do We Go from Here?" in *Papers of the Bibliographical Society of America* 62 (1968): 373–420, and E. William Monter, "The Historiography of European Witchcraft: Progress and Prospects," *Journal of Interdisciplinary History* 2 (1972): 435–51. Among the best books that have appeared in recent years (or have been recently translated into French) are: Julio Caro Baroja, *Les sorcières et leur monde* (Paris, 1972); Alan Macfarlane,

Witchcraft in Tudor and Stuart England (New York and Evanston, 1970), an excellent work on the county of Essex; H. C. Erik Midelfort, *Witch Hunting in Southwestern Germany, 1562–1684: The Social and Intellectual Foundations* (Stanford, 1972); Jeffrey B. Russell, *Witchcraft in the Middle Ages* (Ithaca, 1972); Keith Thomas, *Religion and the Decline of Magic* (New York, 1971); H. R. Trevor-Roper, "L'Epidémie de sorcellerie en Europe aux XVIᵉ et XVIIᵉ siècles," in *De la Réforme aux Lumières* (Paris, 1972), pp. 133–236.

2. Robert Mandrou, *Magistrats et sorciers en France au XVIIᵉ siècle: Une analyse de psychologie historique* (Paris, 1968), brings up to date the conclusions of Etienne Delcambre for Lorraine in "Les procès de sorcellerie en Lorraine: Psychologie des juges," *Revue d'histoire du Droit (Tijdschrift voor Rechtsgeschiedenis)* 21 (1953): 389–419.

3. Robert Muchembled, "Sorcellerie, culture populaire et christianisme au XVIᵉ siècle, principalement en Flandre et en Artois," in *Annales E.S.C.* 28 (1973): 264–84.

4. The concepts of acculturation and collapse of structures (*destructuration*) have received historical application in a first-rate, pioneering study by Nathan Wachtel, *La vision des vaincus: Les Indiens du Pérou devant la conquête espagnole, 1530–1570/80* (Paris, 1971). See my review in *Revue du Nord*, no. 217 (April–June 1973), pp. 175–78.

5. P. Villette, "La sorcellerie dans le Nord de la France du milieu du XVᵉ siècle à la fin du XVIIᵉ siècle," *Mélanges de science religieuse* 13 (1956): 39–62, 129–56, and 143; (also published in *Le Guetteur Wallon* [July–Aug.–Sept. 1958]: 96–132); and, by the same author, "La sorcellerie à Douai," *Mélanges de science religieuse* 18 (1961): 123–73. A bibliography of older works and of published source materials can be found in these two articles by Villette, as well as tables giving all the information available concerning the names, place of trial, ages, and sentences of the accused. I would be able to add only a very little additional information. However, a study of parish archives such as they exist could not fail to turn up other victims (see Villette, "Sorcellerie dans le Nord," p. 156). See also Michelle Protin, "La sorcellerie en Flandre gallicante, 1581–1708" (Master's thesis in history, University of Lille, 1963), which essentially reworks, in four hundred pages, the conclusions of Villette.

6. See the collection prepared under the direction of Louis Trénard, *Histoire de Pays-Bas français: Flandre, Artois, Hainaut, Boulonnais, Cambrésis* (Toulouse, 1972).

7. Louis Trénard, "Un siècle Héroïque," ch. 10 in ibid., p. 242 (following the conclusions of Charles Verlinden).

8. Ibid., p. 243, and Charles Verlinden, "En Flandre sous Philippe II; Durée de la crise économique," *Annales E.S.C.* 7 (1952): 28–30.

9. Louis Trénard, "De 'L'âge d'or' à la conquête française," ch. 11 in Trénard, *Histoire*, pp. 269–89; Henri Pirenne, *Histoire de Belgique*, 6 vols.; vols. 4 and 5 (Brussels, 1911 and 1920), particularly 5:32, concerning the territories ceded in 1678.

10. Henri Platelle, "La vie des hommes à la fin du Moyen Age," ch. 9 in Trénard, *Histoire*, p. 202.

11. F. Van der Wee and E. Van Cauwenberghe, "Histoire agraire et finances publiques en Flandre du XIVᵉ au XVIIᵉ siècle," *Annales E.S.C.* 29 (1973): 1059.

12. Trénard, "De 'l'age d'or,'" in Trénard, *Histoire*, p. 307.

13. René Fruit, *La croissance économique du pays de Saint-Amand (Nord), 1668–1914* (Paris, 1963), p. 31.

14. H. Neveux, "L'Expansion démographique dans un village du Cambrésis: Saint-Hilaire (1450–1575)," *Annales de démographie historique 1971* (Paris, 1972), p. 292.

15. A. Gamblin, cited by Trénard, *Histoire*, p. 7.

16. Trénard, chs. 10 and 11 in Trénard, *Histoire*, pp. 247, 255–56, 262, 274–76; Edouard de Moreau, *Histoire de l'eglise en Belgique*, 5 vols.; vol. 5, *Eglise des Pays-Bas, 1559–1633* (Brussels, 1952); Alexandre Pasture, *La restauration religieuse aux Pays-Bas Catholique sous les Archiducs Albert et Isabelle, 1596–1633* (Louvain, 1925).

17. Platelle, "La vie des hommes," in Trénard, *Histoire*, p. 215.

18. Léon E. Halkin, *La réforme en Belgique sous Charles Quint* (Brussels, 1957).

19. See Moreau, *Histoire*, 5:265ff. especially; Pasture, *Restauration*.

20. Pasture, *Restauration*, pp. 49–55; E. Brouette, "La sorcellerie dans le comté de Namur au début de l'époque moderne, 1509–1646," *Annales de la Société archéologique*

de Namur 47 (1954): 359–420; Marie-Sylvie Dupont-Bouchat, who is currently at work on a book concerning witchcraft in Luxemburg, is also the author of "La répression de l'hérésie dans le Namurois au XVIᵉ siècle," *Annales de la société archéologique de Namur*, 56 fasc. 2 (1972): 179–230.

21. See note 6.

22. It should be noted that Villette made no attempt at a statistical analysis of the results of his research. These should thus be treated as raw data, often very incomplete, and to be interpreted with caution. The author is not always accurate in his transcriptions or in the citation of his sources. For example, the entry concerning Denise and Barbe Le Jay, dated 5 June 1678 ("Sorcellerie dans le Nord," p. 155; and "Sorcellerie à Douai," p. 173), should be changed to read 5 June 1575. Note also that Marie Maughet was executed on 28 August 1660 (ibid., p. 173; "Sorcellerie dans le Nord," p. 154). Other minor errors have been found in his references, but it would be too lengthy to reproduce them all here.

23. Trevor-Roper, "Epidémie de sorcellerie," pp. 183–84 (p. 67 of the English edition, *The European Witch-Craze of the Sixteenth and Seventeenth Centuries* [Harmondsworth, 1969]).

24. Pasture, *Restauration*, p. 49.

25. Ibid., p. 52.

26. E. W. Monter, "Patterns of Witchcraft in the Jura," *Journal of Social History* 5 (1971): 13, according to papers from Bavoux in the Archives Départementales of the Doubs.

27. Ibid.; Midelfort, *Witch Hunting*; and Midelfort, "Witchcraft and Religion in Sixteenth Century Germany: The Formation and Consequences of an Orthodoxy," *Archiv für Reformationsgeschichte* 62 (1971): 266–78.

28. According to E. W. Monter, "men were less able than women to withstand torture"; he continues: "At Fribourg, where I could follow the use of torture case-by-case in the prison registers or *Thurnrodellen*, I found that about half of the fifty men tortured for witchcraft broke and confessed before the third round allowed by Imperial law, while only about a third of the hundred women who underwent the same three rounds of torture with the same instruments confessed" (personal letter dated 14 Jan. 1974). This observation has bearing on one aspect of the problem, but it cannot explain the chronological variations in the persecution of sorcerers and witches. It does, however, suggest a fascinating topic for further research on the question why women could stand up more successfully to torture than men. A historical examination of the psychological differences between the sexes could shed some light on this problem. My thanks to E. W. Monter for this letter.

29. Monter, "Patterns," pp. 15–16; Villette, "Sorcellerie dans le Nord," pp. 151–52 (the Couplet family, for example).

30. Pierre Deyon, "A propos du paupérisme au milieu du XVIIᵉ siècle: Peinture et charité chrétienne," *Annales E.S.C.* 22 (1967): 150.

31. Natalie Zemon Davis, "The Rites of Violence: Religious Riot in Sixteenth-Century France," *Past and Present*, no. 59 (May 1973), p. 90.

32. On the topic of child witches, see Villette, "Sorcellerie dans le Nord," pp. 149 and 155. Many charges were brought against them, in the Hainaut, especially: in 1612, the lord of Bouchain informed the court at Mons of the existence of numerous child witches, seven to nine years old, operating in the area under his jurisdiction, and he asked permission to put to death all those over eight years of age (Moreau, *Histoire*, 5:368–69). Bouchain: department of the Nord, *arrondissement* of Valenciennes, *chef-lieu* of the canton.

33. Macfarlane, *Witchcraft*, p. 251. In this rural area, however, only 108 out of 426 villages accounted for the 503 accusations documented by the author, or a maximum of 15 for one village over a thirty-five year period (ibid., pp. 29, 97).

34. Monter, "Patterns," pp. 7–8, which compares with Essex. Nowhere in the Swiss Jura were there more than twenty deaths during any two-year period.

35. See note 22. Witchcraft fell under the jurisdiction of the aldermen (and, after 1542, of the ecclesiastical courts, if there were also suspicion of heresy), but jurisdictional conflicts were frequent: see Moreau, *Histoire*, 5:368, and Pasture, *Restauration*, pp. 49ff. Wandignies-Hamage: Nord, *arr.* Douai, canton Marchiennes.

36. See Villette's two articles: the town of Douai registered thirty-two cases in the

period 1371–1708, and there were fifty-three others in the surrounding region of the Douaisis.

37. See Villette's two articles. The cases at Etroeugnt, in Avenois (two mentioned in 1611, one in 1676, and one in 1736) and in some of the other villages would be interesting to study in their local context. Etroeungt: Nord, *arr.* Avesnes-sur-Helpe, canton Sud.

38. For more information concerning this reorganization, see Moreau, *Histoire*, 5:21, and supplementary vol. 1, *Cartes* (Brussels, n.d. [1947]). See also Adrien Michaux, *Notice historique sur les circonscriptions ecclésistiques anciennes et modernes du diocèse de Cambrai*... (Avesnes and Valenciennes, 1867), p. 8. Also André Le Glay, *Glossaire topographique de l'ancien Cambrésis*... (Cambrai, 1849).

39. See Brouette, "Sorcellerie."

40. Bazuel—Nord, *arr.* Cambrai, canton and deanship of Le Cateau—was situated at a distance of four kilometers from the latter and twenty-eight kilometers southeast of Cambrai. It came under the jurisdiction of the *châtellenie* of Le Cateau, and its curate was appointed by the local abbey of Saint-André; see Le Glay, *Glossaire*, p. viii, which attributes to the village an area of 1,170 to 1,253 hectares in the mid-nineteenth century. It had 801 inhabitants in 1968.

41. Rieux-en-Cambrésis—Nord, *arr.* Cambrai, canton and deanship of Carnières—was thirty-six kilometers southeast of Douai and ten kilometers northeast of Cambrai. It fell within the province of Hainaut and under the jurisdiction of the *châtellenie* of Bouchain, though a small area of the village belonged to the Cambrésis (ibid., p. lii; 758 hectares, 1,955 inhabitants in the mid-nineteenth century). The village numbered 29 families in 1444, 36 in 1469, 47 in 1540–41, and 28, including three empty dwellings, in 1560–61. The fall-off in the sixteenth century is probably due to a temporary wartime dispersement or a redistribution of the population: see Neveux, "Expansion," pp. 269–70, and map on p. 268. Rieux had 1,470 inhabitants in 1968.

42. Fressies—Nord, *arr.* Cambrai, canton of Cambrai-Ouest—at a distance of eleven kilometers north of Cambrai and seventeen kilometers southeast of Douai, formed part of the Hainaut and had been split off from the neighboring parish of Hem-Lenglet in 1228. Hem-Lenglet was part of the Cambrésis (currently: Nord, *arr.* Cambrai, canton of Cambrai-Ouest). See Le Glay, *Glossaire*, pp. xxx–xxxi, xxxv. (In the mid-nineteenth century, Fressies encompassed a territory of 463 hectares and had 773 inhabitants, as against 485 hectares and 752 inhabitants for Hem-Lenglet. In 1968, these villages had 356 and 577 inhabitants, respectively.)

43. See Moreau, *Histoire*, supplementary vol. 1, *Cartes*.

44. Villette, "Sorcellerie dans le Nord," pp. 148, 150; "Sorcellerie à Douai," pp. 172–73, n. 1. He cites an author here who is himself giving secondhand information. The reference to 183 defendants at Bouchain is incomplete. See also Pasture, *Restauration*, p. 54, who cites Pirenne, *Histoire de Belgique*, 4: 345, n. 2.

45. See note 32.

46. Villette, "Sorcellerie dans le Nord," pp. 148–53. Villers-au-Bois and Campeau now form part of Somain (Nord, *arr.* Douai, canton Marchiennes). For Rieux, see note 41.

47. Ibid., p. 49.

48. Ibid., pp. 142. 129.

49. Ibid., p. 47, n. 14; p. 48, n. 1; p. 53, n. 1; p. 54, n. 1.

50. See the recent statement by the pope on this subject: "This shadowy and confusing being does in fact exist.... He who refuses to recognize the existence of that frightening and mysterious reality which is the Devil must fly in the face of all biblical and ecclesiastical teaching" (15 Feb. 1972, cited in *Le Monde*, 17 Nov. 1972); and Villette, "Sorcellerie à Douai," p. 159.

51. Villette, "Sorcellerie dans le Nord," p. 143; and Villette, "Sorcellerie à Douai," p. 169.

52. Villette, "Sorcellerie à Douai," pp. 168–69. He is still trying to assert that in judging the witches the ecclesiastical tribunals were less severe than the aldermen, for the latter dealt out harsh punishments because of a lack of "any culture or judicial training."

53. Ibid., pp. 132–34, cites the case of Isabeau Blary, in 1610, as an example for Douai. Douai: Nord, *chef-lieu d'arr.*

54. Ibid., pp. 134–35, à propos of Isabeau Blary.
55. Ibid., p. 142, for the same victim. I shall analyze these three stages in detail, later in the essay, but here simply draw attention to the evolution in Villette's thought that took place in the interval between these two articles. Yet, in 1961, he never transcends the level of description, and he continues to refer to the model developed at length in his first article (p. 123).
56. Testimony against Reyne Percheval (1599), Aldegonde de Rue (1601) from Bazuel (ADN, 8 H 312); Cécile Bérurière from Crespin in 1620 (ADN, 4 H 26, item 208); Madeleine Desnasse (1650), Anthoinette Lescouffe, and Susanne Goudry (1652) from Rieux (ADN, B 1216, 17615–16, 17623, 17625). The same is true of Jeanne Marchant (1679) from the town of Seclin (ADN, B 19817), who was "vehemently suspected of witchcraft, and because of this fear, she terrified those who came in contact with her," according to an anonymous witness. Crespin: Nord, *arr.* Valenciennes, canton Condé-sur-l'Escaut; Seclin: Nord, *arr.* Lille, *chef-lieu de canton.*
57. ADN, 8 H 312.
58. See note 40.
59. Bertry: Nord, *arr.* Cambrai, canton of Clary, southwest of Le Cateau, and four kilometers from Clary.
60. Saint-Souplet: Nord, *arr.* Cambrai, canton of Le Cateau, six kilometers south of the latter.
61. Ors: Nord, *arr.* Cambrai, canton of Le Cateau, seven kilometers east of the latter and not far from Bazuel.
62. See note 53.
63. Muchembled, "Sorcellerie," pp. 271–74.
64. A sergeant from Le Cateau, in 1599, and the five other witnesses from outside the village, in 1601, in the case of Aldegonde de Rue, who had resided in Le Cateau and in Landrecies (ADN, 8 H 312, 30 July 1601). Landrecies: Nord, *arr.* Avesnes-sur-Helpe, *chef-lieu* of the canton. Le Cateau: Nord, *arr.* Cambrai, *chef-lieu* of the canton.
65. See note 41.
66. Maître Jean Minart, who had the ability to recognize the mark of the devil—"the enemy of the human race"—which he imprints on witches "the first time he copulates with them." This specialist had already discovered the sign on 274 persons, who had been executed accordingly (ADN, 8 H 312, 18 July 1601). Rocroi: Ardennes, *arr.* Charleville-Mézières, *chef-lieu* of the canton.
67. Preserved as headings to the trials, ADN, 8 H 312.
68. This analysis of witchcraft is given by J. Michelet, *La Sorciére* ed. R. Mandrou (Paris, 1964), and by J. Palou, *La sorcellerie* (Paris, 1957). Cf. R. Muchembled, "Sorcellerie," pp. 264–65 and n. 3.
69. Ibid., p. 265.
70. See ADN, B 1216, 17615–1, no. 28 (Rieux) and FG 782, 783, 785, 786 (Fressies and Hem-Lenglet).
71. ADN, 10 H 54, item 937. Fenain: Nord, *arr.* Douai, canton Marchiennes.
72. ADN, 4 H 26, item 208. Crespin: see note 56.
73. R. H. Duthilloeul, "Sortilèges: Préjugés encore enracinés," *Archives historiques et littéraires du Nord de la France et du Midi de la Belgique*, 3d ser. 2 (1851): 82 ff. Campeau: see note 46.
74. See ADN, B 1216, 17615–6.
75. Macfarlane, *Witchcraft*, pp. 150–51.
76. Ibid., p. 155.
77. Ibid., pp. 164, 176, 196–97.
78. ADN, 8 H 312, 2 March 1621.
79. Ibid., 7 March 1621.
80. ADN, B 1216, 17615–6, 26 Aug. 1650.
81. Ibid., B 1216, 17615–25, 6 June 1652. Boursies: Nord, *arr.* Cambrai, canton of Marcoing; fifteen kilometers west of Cambrai.
82. Ibid., B 1216, 17615–15, 18 May 1652.
83. ADN, 3 G 505–9451, 1602. Ors: see note 61.

84. A Lottin, *Vie et mentalité d'un Lillois sous Louis XIV* (Lille, 1962), pp. 268–69. Seclin: see note 56.

85. ADN, 7 G 906. Note that the term "rural community" represents here only the most wealthy and influential villagers (see note 138).

86. See note 25.

87. I have been able to find no trace of a village with this name in the area. Could it be a mistake for Carnières (Nord, *arr.* Cambrai, *chef-lieu* of the canton), east of Cambrai and south of Rieux?

88. ADN, 4 G 205–3048.

89. Dechy: Nord, *arr.* Douai, canton of Douai-Sud.

90. ADN, 12 H 52. Saint-Amand: Nord, *arr.* Valenciennes, *chef-lieu* of the canton.

91. Monter, "Patterns," p. 22, and Macfarlane's highly successful *Witchcraft*, esp. pp. 94–99 and 147–207.

92. H. C. Erik Midelfort, "Witch Hunting and the Domino Theory," Chapter 7 in this volume.

93. Muchembled, "Sorcellerie," pp. 272–74.

94. See notes 59 and 60.

95. See Table 5.

96. Villette, "Sorcellerie à Douai," p. 133. Lewarde: Nord, *arr.* Douai, canton Douai-Sud.

97. Ibid.

98. ADN, 5 G 558/Pingret. Arleux: Nord, *arr.* Douai, *chef-lieu* of the canton. Rumilly-en-Cambrésis: Nord, *arr.* Cambrai, canton Marcoing. Saint-Souplet (see note 60). Saint-Martin-en-la-Rivière = Saint-Martin-Rivière: Aisne, *arr.* Vervins, canton Wassigny (part of which was included in the Cambrésis). Vaux-en-Arrouaise: Aisne, *arr.* Vervins, canton Wassigny (included in the Cambrésis). The village is now known as Vaux-Andigny. Le Cateau-Cambrésis: Nord, *arr.* Cambrai, *chef-lieu* of the canton. Valenciennes: Nord, *chef-lieu* of its *arrondissement.* Note that Saint-Souplet, Saint-Martin, and Vaux are located on the perimeter of a circle with a radius of approximately fifteen kilometers from its center point, Le Cateau. Many of the witchcraft cases of the seventeenth century originated in this area.

99. ADN, VIII B 770, 2d ser., fol. 30 r° 25 Sept. 1699. The defendant appealed the judgment of the bailiff, and the case was dismissed. Cassel: Nord, *arr.* Dunkerke, *chef-lieu* of the canton.

100. ADN, VIII B 770, 2d ser., fol. 74 r°–v°, 30 April 1700. The appeal of the conviction was rejected, but the court mitigated the sentence to fifteen years of banishment. Furnes: Belgium, Flandre-Occidentale.

101. ADN, 5 G 558.

102. Viesly: Nord, *arr.* Cambrai, canton Solesmes; eighteen kilometers east of Cambrai.

103. ADN, 5 G 558, Witchcraft at Viesly (italics added).

104. See Jeanne Favret, "Le malheur biologique et sa répétition," *Annales E.S.C.* 26 (1971), pp. 873–88 (on witchcraft in the *bocage* region in France, in the twentieth century).

105. H. A. Klein, *Graphic Worlds of Peter Bruegel the Elder* . . . (New York, 1963), p. 169.

106. Moreau, *Histoire*, 5:319, 323–24.

107. Pasture, *Restauration*, pp. 329–54.

108. Ibid., "La réorganisation de l'enseignement religieux," pp. 355–74.

109. ADN, 4 H 26, item 208, 1 July 1620 (see note 72).

110. Pierre Goubert, *L'Ancien régime*, 2 vols.; vol. 1, *La société* (Paris, 1969), p. 244.

111. Ibid., pp. 248–49.

112. Ibid., p. 250.

113. The doctoral thesis ("Les grains du Cambrésis (fin du XIVe–début du XVIIe siècle). Vie et déclin d'une structure economique.") of Hugues Neveux, which received its oral presentation in Paris, on 24 November 1973, is yet to be published (see the summary of it by the author: "Les Grains du Cambrésis," in *Revue du Nord*, no. 219 [Oct.–Dec. 1973], pp. 419–21). Until it appears, see articles by Neveux, "Cambrai et sa campagne de 1420 à

1450: Pour une utilisation sérielle des comptes ecclésiastiques," *Annales E.S.C.* 26 (1971): 114–36; "La mortalité des pauvres à Cambrai (1377–1473)," *Annales de démographie historique 1968* (Paris, 1968) 73–97; and the article "Expansion" on the village of Saint-Hilaire-le-Cambrai (Nord, *arr.* Cambrai, canton Carnières) cited in note 14.

114. Neveux, "Expansion," pp. 265–98.

115. Ibid., p. 298.

116. Ibid., pp. 297–98.

117. Ibid., pp. 293, n. 66; 297. The rivalry among tenant farmers (*censiers*) over land use seems to have been acute.

118. More than 50 percent of the motives of the latter concerned questions of honor: see J.-P. Sarazin and J.-P. Warlop, "Délinquance et mentalité populaire dans les Pays-Bas Espagnols (1610–1660), au travers des lettres de rémission" (Master's thesis in history, University of Lille, 1972), pp. 67 and 70, and tables on 94.

119. ADN, B 1216, 17615–18, 19 July 1647. Braine-le-Comte: Belgique, prov. Hainaut, canton Soignies.

120. Neveux, "Expansion," pp. 269–70, on these short-lived flights.

121. E. Leclair, " 'Faits divers' extraits d'une chronique lilloise manuscrite de 1600 à 1662," *Société d'études de la province de Cambrai, Bulletin* (henceforth cited as *SEPCB*) 3 (1901–2): 102, 103, 105, 107, 289.

122. Roger Rodière, "Deux vieux registres de catholicité du pays d'Artois," *SEPCB* 4 (1902): 155–57.

123. See the excellent book by E. E. Evans-Pritchard, *Witchcraft, Oracles, and Magic among the Azande* (London, 1937; 2d ed. 1951; French trans., Paris, 1972).

124. Neveux, "Expansion," p. 292.

125. ADN, B 1216, 17615–27, May 1652.

126. Neveux (citing C. Thelliez), "Expansion," p. 292, n. 55.

127. John Bossy, "The Counter-Reformation and the People of Catholic Europe," *Past and Present*, no. 47 (May 1970), pp. 51–70. My thanks to Carlo Ginzburg for this reference.

128. Ibid., p. 70.

129. See on this subject Villette, "Sorcellerie dans le Nord," p. 46, and compare it with ADN, 10 H 54–937 (Marie Cornu: 1611), 8 H 312 (Marie Lanechin: 1621).

130. Compare the "evil" cast to the descriptions of Villette, "Sorcellerie dans le Nord," with those of Bossy, "Counter-Reformation."

131. See C. Petit-Dutaillis, *Documents nouveaux sur les moeurs populaires et le droit de vengeance dans les Pays-Bas au XVe siècle . . .* (Paris, 1908), pp. 54, 90, 141.

132. Ibid., p. 131.

133. Sarazin and Warlop, "Délinquance," pp. 25ff.

134. Ibid., p. 78.

135. Pierre de Saint-Jacob, *Documents relatifs à la communauté villageoise en Bourgogne . . .* (Paris, 1962), p. ix.

136. Ibid., p. xxiii (italics added).

137. Ibid., p. xxiv–xxv. On the rural communities, see also Claude Brunet, *Une communauté rurale au XVIIIe siècle: Le Plessis-Gassot (Seine et Oise)* (Paris, 1964); and Janyne Gillot-Voisin, "La communauté des habitants de Givry au XVIIIe siècle," *Histoire sociale: Etudes sur la vie rurale dans la France de l'Est,* Cahiers de l'Association Interuniversitaire de l'Est, no. 11 (Dijon, 1966), pp. 20–83.

138. Gillot-Voisin, "Communauté" p. 29; Brunet, *Communauté,* pp. 34ff.; H. Babeau, *Les assemblées générales des communautés d'habitants en France, du XIIIe siècle à la Révolution* (Paris, 1893).

139. See notes 85–90.

140. Gillot-Voisin, "Communauté," p. 30.

141. Cited by Madeleine Foisil, *La révolte des Nu-Pieds et les révoltes normandes de 1639* (Paris, 1970), p. 30.

142. On the indifference to very young children, who began to inspire affection in their elders only after they had passed through the first critical years of infancy, see François Lebrun, *Les hommes et la mort en Anjou aux 17e et 18e siècles; essai de démographie et de*

psychologie historiques (Paris, 1971), pp. 423ff., which repeats the observations of Philippe Ariès, *L'Enfant et la vie familiale sous l'Ancien Régime* (Paris, 1960; 2d ed. 1973), p. 135.

143. Sarazin and Warlop, "Délinquance," esp. pp. 175ff.

144. Ibid., p. 55, tables; pp. 56–60, 78.

145. Ibid., pp. 70, 82.

146. See the very fine work by Jean-Marie Baheux and Gilles Deregnaucourt, "Affaires de moeurs laïques et ecclésiastiques et mentalittés populaires au XVIIᵉ siècle (1594–1706), d'apres les archives de l'officialité Métropolitaine de Cambrai" (Master's thesis in history, University of Lille, 1972).

147. Ibid., pp. 82, 210.

148. Ibid., pp. 204–6, and 261–63.

149. Ibid., p. 217, citing Pierre Chaunu, *La civilisation de l'Europe classique* (Paris, 1966), p. 196.

150. Ibid., p. 215, map (the archdiocese at that time included fourteen deanships).

151. Ibid., pp. 79, 212.

152. Deyon, "Paupérisme," p. 151.

153. Erich Fromm, interview published in the *New York Times*, 15 Dec. 1973, p. 33 (referring to the United States).

154. Foisil, *Révolte des Nu-Pieds*, p. 341 (on the Norman revolts of 1639).

155. This village atmosphere is briefly but brilliantly traced by Baheux and Deregnaucourt, "Affaires," pp. 297–325.

156. Sarazin and Warlop, "Délinquance," p. 236.

157. Montigny-en-Cambrésis: Nord, *arr.* Cambrai, canton Clary.

158. Baheux and Deregnaucourt, "Affaires," p. 164 (based on ADN, 5 G 517, 1698, dossier B. Hal).

159. Ibid., pp. 319–25: for example, in 1618, a Cambrésis curate mortally wounded one of his parishioners, who nevertheless "sent for the very same priest to administer the sacraments, who was so drunk that he didn't know what he was saying" (pp. 319–20).

160. Ibid., p. 107 (based on ADN, 5 G 509, 1626, dossier Jean Huart).

161. After 1678, the Cambrésis was part of France, and the analysis of Mandrou, *Magistrats et sorciers*, is therefore applicable.

162. Henri Platelle, *Journal d'un curé de campagne au XVIIᵉ siècle* (Paris, 1965). Rumegies: Nord, *arr.* Valenciennes, canton Saint-Amand-les-Eaux, Rive gauche.

163. Bossy, "Counter-Reformation," pp. 62–63.

164. Goubert, *Ancien régime*, 1:42–44.

165. Cited by Trénard, *Histoire*, p. 322.

166. Merbes-le-Château: Belgique, prov. Hainaut, *chef-lieu* of the canton.

167. Baheux and Deregnaucourt, "Affaires," p. 306 (based on ADN, 5 G 512, 1677, dossier A. Camusel).

168. J. Bourdon, "Psychosociologie de la famine," *Annales de démographie historique* 1968, p. 13.

169. René Baehrel, "La haine de classe en temps d'épidémie," *Annales E.S.C.* 7 (1952): 359.

170. Ibid., p. 360.

171. Michel Foucault, *Histoire de la folie à l'âge classique* (Paris, 1961), and recent works on pauperism (see the critical note by Roger Chartier, "Pauvreté et assistance dans la France moderne: L'exemple de la généralité de Lyon," *Annales E.S.C.* 28 [1973]: 572–82).

172. René Girard, *La violence et le sacré* (Paris, 1972).

173. Ibid., pp. 38, 359.

174. Ibid., pp. 435, 148, 378, 135, 22, and 29.

175. Jacques Soustelle, *La vie quotidienne des Aztèques à la veille de la conquête espagnole* (Paris, 1955).

176. Girard, *Violence*, pp. 389, 352.

177. Macfarlane, *Witchcraft*, pp. 197, 204, makes the same observation for Essex.

178. Girard, *Violence*, p. 391.

179. Ibid., pp. 57–58.

180. Davis, "Rites of Violence," pp. 57, 90.

181. One example among many: Madeleine Allard, from Fourmies (Nord, *arr.* Avesnes-sur-Helpe, canton Trélon), was condemned upon appeal, on 13 September 1679, to be led out in front of a church and there, "on her knees, with her feet and arms bare, clad only in a shirt, a cord around her neck, and bearing a burning torch weighing two pounds, she should say and declare that she had boldly and with malice aforethought renounced her baptism [a long list of her crimes follows], that she now repented her crimes and asked pardon of God, the king, and the courts" (ADN, VIII B 761, 2d ser., vol. 37 r°).

182. Girard, *Violence*, p. 352; Davis, "Rites of Violence," p. 90.

183. Ibid., p. 85, citing Troy Duster "Conditions for Guilt-Free Massacre," in Nevitt Sanford and Craig Comstock, eds., *Sanctions for Evil* (San Francisco, 1971), ch. 3.

184. See Muchembled, "Sorcellerie," p. 276.

185. Deyon, "Paupérisme," pp. 151-52.

186. Edward B. Harper, "Fear and the Status of Women," *Southwestern Journal of Anthropology* 25 (1969): 95. This essay is concerned with southern India.

187. Davis, "Rites of Violence," pp. 86-87.

188. David Hunt, *Parents and Children in History: The Psychology of Family Life in Early Modern France* (New York, 1972), pp. 71, 74, 75.

189. Ibid., p. 186.

190. Girard, *Violence*, p. 391.

191. Foisil, *Révolte des Nu-Pieds*, pp. 339-40. For Foisil, only the existence of a program on the part of the rebels would constitute a real "class consciousness."

192. Wachtel, *Vision des vaincus*.

193. Goubert, *Ancien régime*, 1:111.

194. Muchembled, "Sorcellerie," pp. 278ff. and especially the works of Carlo Ginzburg, particularly "Cheese and Worms," Chapter 3 in this volume.

195. See Bossy, "Counter-Reformation," p. 70.

196. Title of a book edited by Trevor Aston, *Crisis in Europe, 1560-1660* (New York, 1967).

Chapter 7

1. See, for example, Jeffrey B. Russell, *Witchcraft in the Middle Ages* (Ithaca, 1972). See also Norman Cohn, *Europe's Inner Demons: An Enquiry Inspired by the Great Witch-Hunt* (New York, 1975); and Richard Kieckhefer, *European Witch-Trials: Their Foundation in Popular and Learned Culture* (London, 1976).

2. Russell, *Witchcraft*; see also Charles E. Hopkin, *The Share of Thomas Aquinas in the Growth of the Witchcraft Delusion* (Philadelphia, 1940); and the excellent collection of articles in Sydney Anglo, ed., *The Damned Art: Essays in the Literature of Witchcraft* (London, 1977).

3. For recent surveys of some of this literature, see H. C. Erik Midelfort, "Recent Witch Hunting Research, Or Where Do We Go from Here?" *Papers of the Bibliographical Society of America* 62 (1968): 373-420; E. William Monter, "The Historiography of European Witchcraft, Progress and Prospects," *Journal of Interdisciplinary History* 2 (1972): 435-51; Lawrence Stone, "The Disenchantment of the World," *New York Review of Books*, 2 Dec. 1971, pp. 17-25; H. C. Erik Midelfort, "The Renaissance of Witchcraft Research," *Journal of the History of the Behavioral Sciences* 13 (1977): 294-97.

4. Alan D. J. Macfarlane, *Witchcraft in Tudor and Stuart England* (New York, 1970); Keith Thomas, *Religion and the Decline of Magic* (New York, 1971); Paul Boyer and Stephen Nissenbaum, *Salem Possessed: The Social Origins of Witchcraft* (Cambridge, Mass., 1974).

5. Macfarlane, *Witchcraft*; Werner Croissant, "Die Berücksichtigung geburts- und berufständischer und soziologischer Unterschiede im deutschen Hexenprozess" (Dr. jur. Dissertation, University of Mainz, 1953); E. William Monter, *Witchcraft in France and Switzerland: The Borderlands during the Reformation* (Ithaca, 1976).

6. This theme has become common in the studies of Salem witchcraft. See Ernest Caulfield, "Pediatric Aspects of the Salem Witchcraft Tragedy," *American Journal for the Diseases of Children* 65 (1943): 788-802; Marion Starkey, *The Devil in Massachusetts*

(New York, 1949); Chadwick Hanson, *Witchcraft at Salem* (New York, 1969); and John Demos, "Underlying Themes in the Witchcraft of 17th-Century New England," *American Historical Review* 75 (1970): 1311–26. For other kinds of psychological work on witchcraft, see Robert Mandrou, *Magistrats et sorciers au XVIᵉ siècle:: Une analyse de psychologie historique* (Paris, 1968), and Cecile Ernst, *Teufelaustreibungen: Die Praxis der katholischen Kirche im 16. und 17. Jahrhundert* (Bern, 1972).

7. See note 4. See also Julio Caro Baroja, *The World of the Witches* (Chicago, 1964).

8. *I benandanti: Ricerche sulla stregoneria e sui culti agrari tra cinquecento e seicento* (Turin, 1966).

9. H. C. Erik Midelfort, *Witch Hunting in Southwestern Germany, 1562–1684: The Social and Intellectual Foundations* (Stanford, 1972), pp. 91, 104.

10. Ibid., p. 162.

11. *De Praestigiis Daemonum* (n.p., 1578), folio 181 verso.

12. *Cautio Criminalis oder rechtliches Bedenken wegen der Hexenprozesse*, ed. and trans. Joachim-Friedrich Ritter (Weimar, 1967), p. 11.

13. Monter, *Witchcraft.*

14. Midelfort, *Witch Hunting*, pp. 90–94.

15. Ibid., pp. 93–94.

16. Ibid., p. 104.

17. Ibid., p. 130.

18. Wolfgang Reis, "Die Hexenprozesse in der Stadt Baden-Baden," *Freiburger Diözesan-Archiv* 91 (1971): 202–66.

19. W. G. Soldan and H. Heppe, *Geschichte der Hexenprozesse*, ed. Max Bauer, 2 vols. (Munich, 1912), 2:17–20.

20. Table 2 also reveals a partial recovery of the traditional stereotype in executions no. 26–29. It is not yet clear whether this is significant.

21. Freidrich Wilhelm Siebel, *Die Hexenverfolgung in Köln* (Bonn, 1959), pp. 152–53.

22. Ibid., p. 52.

23. Ibid., pp. 71–73.

24. K. Hoppstädter, "Die Hexenverfolgungen im saarländischen Raum," *Zeitschrift für die Geschichte der Saargegend* 9 (1959): 258–59.

25. Ibid., p. 235.

26. Antero Heikkinen, *Paholaisen Liitolaiset* (Helsinki, 1969), English summary, pp. 374–94.

27. "Witchcraft in Geneva, 1537–1662," *Journal of Modern History* 43 (1971): 187.

28. Ibid., p. 187.

29. Midelfort, *Witch Hunting*, pp. 147–150.

30. Ibid., pp. 126–31.

31. Soldan-Heppe, *Geschichte der Hexenprozesse*, 2:172–75.

32. Macfarlane, *Witchcraft.*

33. Wallace Notestein, *A History of Witchcraft in England from 1558 to 1718* (Washington, D.C., 1911), pp. 191–92.

34. C. L. Ewen, *Witchcraft and Demonianism* (London, 1933), p. 260.

35. Montague Summers, ed., *The Discovery of Witches: A Study of Master Matthew Hopkins commonly call'd Witch Finder Generall, Together with a Reprint of "The Discovery of Witches"* (London, 1928), pp. 43–45, 51–62.

36. Notestein, *History of Witchcraft*, p. 192.

37. Mandrou, *Magistrats et sorciers.*

38. Tables 3 and 4 are based on the information in Paul Boyer and Stephen Nissenbaum, *Salem-Village Witchcraft: A Documentary Record of Local Conflict in Colonial New England* (Belmont, Calif., 1972), pp. 375–78.

39. Boyer and Nissenbuam, *Salem Possessed*, pp. 19, 31–33; the accusations "spiraled back toward the accusers themselves, until finally the distinction between accuser and accused, between afflicter and afflicted threatened to vanish" (p. 211).

40. The composite results of many small witchcraft trials pose problems of another sort. See, for example, Robert Muchembled's study in this volume of a number of small witchcraft trials in the southern Netherlands; he found that while predominantly women

were tried around 1570 and around 1670, men were the primary target during the intervening period. Although interesting, this fact does not shed light directly on the morphology of large trials. See the forthcoming work of Muchembled, *Sorcières du Cambrésis: L'acculturation du monde rural aux XVIe et XVIIe siècles*. It seems clear that the Jura witch trials, recently studied by E. William Monter, must have had a mechanism that prevented "small panics" from becoming large, but little is known yet regarding such mechanisms. See Monter's *Witchcraft in France and Switzerland*.

Index

A

Abbeville, 182
Acarie, Mme, 181, 182, 310 (n. 63)
Agobard, Bishop of Lyons, 10, 12, 289
(n. 1)
Agulhon, Maurice, 182
Aix-la-Chapelle, 13
Albaching, 66
Albigensians, 23
Albrecht IV, duke of Bavaria, 60, 68
Aldebert, cult of, 10–13
Alsace, convents in, 73
Altötting, shrine in, 67–69
Alva, duke of, 191, 218, 219
America, discovery of, 135, 138
Anabaptists, 103–5, 112, 166, 197–99,
201, 216, 218–19, 224, 314 (n. 43)
Andrea da Bergamo (Pietro Nelli), 105, 164
Anglo-Saxon nuns, 72–73
Anjou, François, duke of, 178
Antwerp, Reformed movement in, 199–
204, 209, 213, 220; prêche in, 211, 212
Aquinas, Saint Thomas, 36, 40, 42–44
Aristocrats: influence in religious life,
26–27, 32; and persecution of Jews,
29–30, 32; graves of, as shrines, 35; and
pilgrimages, 51; in Bavaria, 53–54; and
shrines, 54, 55, 57–61, 296–97 (n. 121,
n. 123); reduced numbers of, 56; and
peasants, 56–57; social status of, 57–58;
and Holy Roman Empire, 62; as nuns,
73–75, 78; in Venetian state, 99, 100
Armeseelen, 51–52
Armleders, 28, 29, 30
Arras, witchcraft in, 224, 231; *statistics*,
228, 229
Arthur, King, cult of, 76
Artois, 222, 230, 259–60
Asteo, Gerolamo, 120, 121, 150, 151, 155,
157
Attigny, synod of, 34
Augsburg, 74
August the Strong, king of Saxony, 66
Augustine, Saint, 46, 49

Austria, *Umritte* in, 68
Aventine (Johannes Turmaier), 67
Averroist school, 42, 46
Avignon, popes in, 31, 42
Axel, 200, 211
Aztecs, 271

B

Baden, shrines in, 55, 73, 75
Baden-Baden, witch trials in, 282
Baden-Württemberg, witch trials in, 226
Bader, Karl, 53
Bar, Pierre, 170
Baroque style, 21, 22, 64–65
Bartholomew, Saint, relics of, 17
Basel, iconoclasm in, 194
Bavaria: massacre of Jews in, 28, 29, 31;
Umritte in, 30–32; confraternities in, 34;
pilgrimages in, 51, 53, 57; ossuaries in,
52; shrines in, 53, 55, 57, 58, 67–68, 70,
75; nobility in, 53–54, 58, 60, 61, 64;
Protestants in, 58, 66; Baroque in, 64;
culture of, 65; women in religious life,
72, 74, 75
Bazuel, witch trials in, 231, 232, 238–44,
249, 252, 253, 255, 257, 258, 260, 261,
tables, 233, 234–37, 243, 318 (n. 40)
Beaumetz, 264
Beauxamis, Thomas, 171
Beghards, 78
Beguine communities, 28, 61, 71–79, 298
(n. 165)
Benedetto d'Asolo, 114
Benedictines, 30, 31, 34; penitential ac-
tivity, 37, 38; nuns, 74
Benrather line (division of German
dialects), 72, 73, 76, 77, 79
Berlichingen, Götz von, 63, 64
Berne, 75
Bérulle, Pierre de, Cardinal, 181
Beuron, shrine, 27
Bèze (Beza), Théodore de, 201

Bible: Menocchio's use of, 97, 110, 142,
143; as only source of truth, 104; in
Protestantism, 199
Bionima, Andrea, 89–90
Black Death, 190; and massacre of Jews, 28
Blutritt, 31
Boccaccio, Giovanni, *Decameron*, 104–11,
120, 121
Bodin (demonologist), 231
Boguet (demonologist), 231
Bohemia, 66
Boniface, Saint, 10–11, 18, 67, 72
Boniface VIII, Pope, 22–25, 42; bull,
Ausculta Fili, 24; bull, *Unam Sanctam*,
24, 41
Borromeo, Saint Carlo, 262
Boso, Abbot, 16
Bossy, John, 261
Bouchain, 222; witchcraft in, 230, 231
Bourbon, Charles de, Cardinal, 173, 174,
176
Bourges, 182
Brandenburg, shrines in, 54
Brecht, Bertolt, 87
Breda, 199–200
Brenz, Johannes, 81
Brethren of the Common Life, 20, 79
Brotherhoods. *See* Confraternities
Bruegel, Pieter, the Elder, 165, 255
Bruno, Giordano, 167
Brussels, 214
Bucer (Butzer), Martin, 135

C

Calvin, John, 81–85, 201
Calvinism, 65, 79–86, 195; conversion of
Palatinate, 66; Eucharist in, 80–84; in
France, Catholic opposition to, 171,
172, 173, 177; in exile, 191, 201; and
Reformed movement in Netherlands,
197–220 passim; organizational system,
199, 201; and Lutheranism, policy, 201;
and Catholics in Netherlands, 201,
204–5
Calw, 278, 281
Cambrai, 222, 224, 264; witch trials in,
230–31, 248, 249, 274; education in,
256
Cambrésis. *See* Witchcraft in the Cambrésis
Camilo de Leonardis, 109
Campeau, witch trials in, 231, 244, 248
*Capitolo, qual narra tutto l'essere d'un
mondo nuovo*, 136–39
Capuchins, 174, 175, 182
Carmelites, 181–82
Carolingian period, 8–12, 18–19

Carpentier, Pieter, 220
Castello, Alberto da, *Il Rosario (lucidario)
della Madonna*, 108, 109
Castellione, 121
Catechism, 175
Catholic church: reconversion of Habsburg
territories, 66; reconversion of Palatinate,
66; and Protestantism in Rouen, 168–90;
and Reformed movement in Netherlands,
197, 198, 200, 204, 205, 207, 213–19;
and Calvinism in Netherlands, 201,
204–5; popular hatred of, in Nether-
lands, 205–6; and iconoclasm, 207
Catholic League, 189
Catholic Low Countries: religious revival
in, 224. *See also* Witchcraft
Catholic Reformation, 21, 60, 63. *See also*
Counter-Reformation
Celtis, Conrad, 63–64
Chambers of Rhetoric, plays of, 197, 313
(n. 31)
Chappuys, Claude, 177, 308 (n. 35)
Charlemagne (Charles the Great), 10–15,
67, 68, 289 (n. 8, n. 17)
Charles IV, Holy Roman Emperor, 28
Charles V, Holy Roman Emperor, 222, 224
Christ: Eucharist as body of, 14, 36,
80–83; Church as body of, 24–25,
40–41; shrines dedicated to, 28, 54, 57,
58, 69; blood of, and penance, 37, 294
(n. 63)
Christian names, use of, 38
Church: as mystical body of Christ, 24–25,
40–41; secular control of religious in-
stitutions, 24, 25; clerical representation
in secular government, 25; imperial
knights in, 62–63. *See also* Catholic
church
Cistercians, 28; *conversi* (lay brothers), 37,
59; monasteries dedicated to Virgin
Mary, 59; nuns, 71–72, 74
Civil War (French), First, 173
Claeyssone, Jan, 200
Clarisses, 71
Clement VI, Pope, 37
Clement VIII, Pope, 167
Clinchamp, René de, 308 (n. 35, n. 36)
Clough, Richard, 191, 194, 203–4
Collective redemption, 40
Collective responsibility, 38–40, 44–47
Cologne, witch trials in, 284
Columbus, Christopher, 135
Comer, Carlo, 100
Communion of saints, 33
Compagnie du Saint-Sacrement, 172, 190
Conciliarists, 24
Concordia, 89, 91, 146

Confraternities, 33–42, 49, 69; dead as kinship groups in, 33–34, 46, 48; in north Germany, 76–77; Lutheran and Calvinist views of, 84–85; of the Holy Sacrament (General, 1561), 172–73, 184; in France, 172–73, 183–84, 307 (n. 18), 310 (n. 74); of the Holy Sacrament (1435), 173; of the Name of Jesus, 183, 184, 310 (n. 44)
Convents and monasteries, number of, 73
Conversi, 37, 59
Corneille, Pierre, 179
Cornelis (monk), 214, 312 (n. 11)
Corporate forms of worship, 39–40; clerical opposition to, 42, 44–46
Corporations: limited liability of, 39; responsibility in, 48
Corpus christi, 41
Corpus Christi feast, 28, 29, 36, 78
Corpus mysticum, 41, 42, 43, 69
Cortes, Hernando, 271
Council of Carthage, 14
Council of Châlone-sur-Saône, 11
Council of Chelsea, 14
Council of Frankfurt, 13
Council of Mainz, 14
Council of Nicea, Second, 13
Council of Trent, 60, 167, 169, 170, 257
Council of Vienne, 28
Counter-Reformation, 63, 105, 121, 244; pilgrimages in, 64; in German culture, 65; in France, 168–69, 170, 188, 189, 190; witch hunts related to, 255, 256, 259, 261–65, 267, 275; and education of youth, 256–57
Crespin, witch trial in, 256
Crusades, 22–24, 37; aristocracy in, 32, 62
Cuccagna, land of, 137–40
Cuius regio, eius religio, 58, 65, 66
Culembourg, count of, 207, 212

D

Damian, Peter, 27
Dance of Death, 52
Dante Alighieri, 42–43, 124, 125
Dathenus, Pieter, 212
Davis, Natalie Zemon, 52, 191
Dead, the: in purgatory cult, 33, 37, 38, 40, 49; as kinship groups in confraternities, 33–34, 46, 48; indulgences for, 37, 49; as *Armeseelen*, 51–52; bones in ossuaries, 52; Dance of Death, 52; desecration of bodies, 52
del Rio (Jesuit), 226
Descartes, René, 86
Deusdona (deacon), 16–17, 18, 290 (n. 45), 291 (n. 50)

Devotio moderna, 79
Dieter III, duke of Regensburg, 67
Dietramszell, 30
Dijon, St. Benignus shrine, 15
Dingolfing, synod of, 34
Dominicans, 28, 64, 177, 192; nuns, 71–75; and Immaculate Conception, 75
Domino theory and witchcraft, 277–88
Doni, Anton Francesco, 138
Douai, 224; witch trials in, 224, 230, 231, 252, 253
Dunkerque, witch trials in, 230

E

Ebner, Margaret, 74
Eckhard, Meister, 74, 82
Egmont, Lamoral, comte d', 206
Ehrenberg, Bishop Adolf von, 282
Eichstätt, 62
Einhard, 16, 18
Eisengrein, Martinus, 67
Elender- und Kalandsbruderschaften, 76, 299 (n. 185)
Ellwagen, witch trial in, 281
Emden, 201
England: confraternities in, 34; revolts in fourteenth century, 39; Catholic refugees from, in France, 178; witch trials in, 231, 249, 278, 280, 285–86
Erasmus, Desiderius, 63, 135–36, 177
Erchembert, Bishop, 17
Ermland, shrines in, 55
Essex, witch trials in, 231, 249, 285
Esslingen, 281
Estates (assemblies), 25
Eucharist: as relic of Christ, 14, 36; in shrines, 28, 292 (n. 23); Lutheran and Calvinist views on, 80–84. *See also* Host
Eulogie, 40
Europe: food shortage, 24, 33; Christendom synonymous with, 25; popular revolts after 1280, 39
Excommunication, 24
Exorcists, 254, 255, 260, 269

F

Felix (dealer in relics), 17
Fenain, witch trial in, 244
Fermin, Saint, 12, 14
Fichtenau, Heinrich, 10, 34
Finland, witch trials in, 284–85
Fioretto della Bibbia, 104, 108–13, 122, 127, 130, 132, 142, 163
Flanders, 222, 224, 259; iconoclasm in, 194, 207; Reformed movement in, 200, 202; witchcraft in, 222, 230

Fleury-sur-Loire, 16
Foisil, Madeleine, 275
Folk piety. *See* Popular religion
Foresti, Jacopo Filippo, *Supplementum delle croniche*, 109, 122–23, 132–33, 138, 146, 156
France: revolts in fourteenth century, 39; Dance of Death in, 52; nobility in, 54; prohibition of relics in swearing oaths, 69–70; Counter-Reformation in, 168–69, 170, 188, 189, 190; Protestantism opposed in, 169, 177–78, 187, 189; witch trials in, 174, 280, 286, 307 (n. 22); iconoclasm in, 192, 193, 194, 207, 218. *See also* Huguenots; Witchcraft in the Cambrésis
Franche-Comté, witch trials in, 226
Francis, Saint, of Assisi, 61
Francis I, 69, 70
Franciscans, 61, 75, 132, 177; nuns, 71
Franconia, 28; ossuaries in, 52; nobility in, 54; knights in, 62, 63; shrines in, 55
Frederick III, Holy Roman Emperor, 64, 67
Free will, 42, 47, 49
Freising, 17
Fressies, witch trials in, 231, 244, 248–49, 251, 255, 257, 260, *table*, 246–47, 318 (n. 42)
Friesland, East, 57
Friuli, 88, 98–101; nobility in, 99; *contadinanza*, 99, 100; peasants in, 99–100, 135; inquisitors' trials in, 145
Fulda, 17

G

Gandersheim, convent, 73
Gascon, Richard, 189
Gaule, John, 286
Geberg II, Abbess, 73
Geertz, Clifford, 4
Geneva, witch trials in, 285
German dialects, line separating groups. *See* Benrather line
Germany, north, 22; religious practices and aristocratic influence, 25–26; shrines in, 54–55, 295–96 (n. 113); women in religious life, 71–73, 77–78; urban and rural life, 76; lay persons in religious life, 76–79; Reformation in, 79–86
Germany, south: pilgrimages in, 20–24, 30–37, 49–61, 64–65; knights in, 26–27; Christianization east of Elbe, 59; Baroque culture in, 64–65; culture influenced by popular religion, 65–70; women in religious life, 74–75; Reformation in, 79–86; witch trials in,

278–85. *See also* Aristocrats; Knights
Ghent, 195; iconoclasm in, 206, 207, 211; *prêche* in, 211–12
Ginzburg, Carlo, 277
Giocondo, Giuliano di Bartolomeo del, 135
Girard, René, 270–71
God: representations of, 27; omnipotence of, 45; Menocchio's ideas on, 127–31
Godfrey of Fontaines, 40–41
Gollen Heights, chapel of Virgin Mary, 59
Gothic architecture, 64
Goubert, Pierre, 275
Granvelle, Antoine Pierrenot, Cardinal de, 203
Great Schism, 42
Gregory IV, Pope, 18
Grimald, duke of Benevento, 10
Guilds, 34, 36, 39, 85
Guiraud, Jean, 16, 290 (n. 43)
Guise, duke of, Henry I de Lorraine, 179

H

Haag, 58
Habsburg family, 66
Hadrian I, Pope, 14–15
Hainaut, 224, 259, 262; witch trials in, 222, 226, 230, 232
Hamburg, confraternities in, 77
Hammerstetten, Augustin von, 64
Hanseatic League, 72, 76, 77, 78
Hartmann (nobleman), 29
Hasselt, 210, 312 (n. 6)
Hauck, Albert, 72
Hazard, Pieter, 200
Hedgepreaching. See *Prêche*
Heimbucher, Max, 71
Hem-Lenglet, witch trials in, 231, 244, 248–51, 255, *table*, 246–47
Hemmingstedt, battle of, 56
Henry IV (Henry of Navarre), 178, 183, 188
Heraclitus, 157
Herford, convent, 73
Herrmann-Mascard, Nicole, 15
Hesse, 55
Heyden, Gaspar van der, 199, 206
Hilduin, Abbot, 15, 16, 18
Historia del Giudicio, 109, 113–14, 115, 122
Hocart, A. M., 69
Hoffmann, Hartnut, 9
Hohenstaufen family, 26
Hohenwaldeck, 58
Hohenzollern family, 66
Holborn, Hajo, 63
Hollandère, Guillaume de, 209

Holtzelt, W., 12
Holy Land: pilgrimages to, 22; in crusades, 23, 37
Holy League, 178, 179, 181–83, 188, 190, 311–12 (n. 92)
Holy Roman Empire: pilgrimages in, 21, 22; aristocracy in support of, 29, 62; knights in, 62–64
Hongère, Mailgaert de, 210
Honorius of Autun, *Elucidarium*, 122
Hooker, Richard, 48
Hopkins, Matthew, 285–86
Horses: pilgrimages of (*Umritte*), 30–31, 32, 53, 54, 61, 65, 68; Franciscans forbidden to use, 61
Host: elevation of, 28–29, 36, 41; alleged desecration by Jews, 29, 30; as *corpus mysticum*, 41; in *oratoire*, 180
Hrotsvith, Abbess, 73
Hubert, Saint, 26, 27
Huguenots: reconversion of, 171; Catholic attacks on, 171, 172, 204–5; Rouen controlled by, 173, 178, 181; in Rouen, 176, 177
Hulst, 200, 206
Humanists, 22, 63–64, 71
Hunting, miracles associated with, 26–27, 61, 64
Hutten, Ulrich von, 63–64, 67

I

Iconoclasm, 171; in Netherlands, 191–97, 206–7, 215–20, 312–13 (n. 11, n. 13, n. 16, n. 20); in France, 192, 193, 194, 207, 218; magic associated with, 193, 312 (n. 11); in Flanders, 194; lower class in, 195
Images: and relics, 13; of saints, substituted for relics, 35–36, 37
Immaculate Conception, 64, 75
Indulgences, 22–24, 78; and purgatory cult, 33, 37, 38, 39, 49; and confraternities, 34; equal access to, 41; in shrines, 59; buildings financed by sale of, 64–65
Innocent III, Pope, 23, 36, 77
Innviertel, 55, 68
Inquisition, 23, 103, 205; Menocchio tried by, 88–98 passim, 106–8, 112–13, 115, 118, 120, 121, 140, 144–45, 153–62, 166–67
Interdict, 24, 38
Issickemer, Jacob, 67–68
Italy: revolts in fourteenth century, 39; religious controversies in, 105, 106, 112; books read in, 110, 126

J

Jerusalem, pilgrimages to, 22, 50
Jesuits, 105, 166, 177, 183, 189; Protestantism opposed by, 171; in Rouen, 174, 175, 184; college (Collège de Bourbon), Rouen, 175, 176, 178–79, 184
Jews: massacres of, 27–29, 31, 36, 53, 54, 78, 269, 292–93 (n. 20, n. 23, n. 30); alleged offenses against Christianity, 29, 30, 31
Joan of Arc, 62
John XXII, Pope, 25, 26, 29
John of Leyden, 211
Jon, François du, 200, 209
Joyeuse, duchess of, 182
Julien (preacher), 210, 211
Julius II, Pope, 132
Jura, witchcraft in, 228, 230
Justification, doctrine of, 104, 105

K

Kaland brotherhood, 76, 299 (n. 185)
Kantorowicz, Ernst, 41, 42, 43
Kaufbeuren, 74
Kittredge, George Lyman, 277
Knights, 26–27; in Holy Roman Empire, 62–64, 68, 70, 71
Knowledge and experience, 47–48
Konrad I, count, 30
Koran, 103, 109, 111, 153, 158
Kösslarn, 68

L

Lambert, Pierre, 308 (n. 36)
Lamento de uno poveretto huomo sopra la carestia, 141
Lancre, de (demonologist), 231
Laon, 182, 183
La Salle, Robert Cavelier, sieur de, 179–80
Lateran Council, fourth (1215), 23, 36
Lay persons in German religious life, 76–79
Le Bras, Gabriel, 39, 168
Le Cateau, 264; witchcraft in, 253
Lefebvre, Georges, 267
Lefèvre d'Étaples, Jacques, 177
Leibnitz, Gottfried Wilhelm von, 47
Lent, sexual relations forbidden during, 185, 186
Leo X, Pope, 132
Leo (nomenclator), 15
Liège, 28
Lille, 224; witch trials in, 224, 230; plagues in, 259
Limbourg, 209

Lippens, Jan, 199
Lothar (coemperor), 15
Louchard, Jean, 209
Louis I, the Pious, Holy Roman Emperor,
 10
Louis IV of Bavaria, Holy Roman Emperor,
 26, 29, 31, 54, 71
Louis XIV, King of France, 224
Louis the Bearded, duke of Bavaria, 53–54
Lübeck, confraternities in, 33, 77
Lunario al modo de Italia, 109
Lunisus, 16
Luther, Martin, 63, 79–85, 132–33; con-
 troversy with Zwingli, 79–81
Lutheranism, 65, 66, 71, 79–86; Eucharist
 in, 80–84; Menocchio's opinion of, 102,
 103, 112, 153–54; and Reformed
 movement in Netherlands, 198, 199,
 202, 208, 220; Calvinist policy on, 201
Lyon, 189

M

McCulloh, John, 12, 15
Macfarlane, Alan, 249, 285, 286
Malleus Maleficarum, 231–32
Mandeville, Sir John, *Travels,* 109, 110,
 111, 115–19, 122, 131, 132, 143
Mandrou, Robert, 286
Manicheans, 146
Marc, Louis, 173
Marcellinus, Saint, relics of, 16, 17, 18
Margaret of Parma, 203, 204, 218
Maro, Giambattista (general vicar), 88, 92,
 93
Marsilius of Padua, 21–22, 24–25, 32,
 44–46, 48, 83
Mary, Virgin: in aristocratic tradition,
 26–27, 59; as Queen of Heaven, 27, 59,
 63, 64, 67–68; Jews massacred in honor
 of, 28, 31; *Schöne Maria,* 31; pilgrimages
 honoring, 31, 54; shrines dedicated to,
 57, 58, 59, 67–68, 69, 73–74, 78;
 Cistercian monasteries dedicated to, 59;
 as *Stella Maris,* 59; Immaculate Conception, dogma of, 64, 75; suffering, 73–75,
 78; Protestant attitude toward, 171;
 adoration of, 187, 188, 189
Mary Magdalene, 19
Mary Magdalene Order, 71
Maschke, Erich, 76
Mass, Lutheran and Calvinist objections to,
 83–84
Matte, Sebastien, 206
Matthew of Paris, 78
Maximilian I, Holy Roman Emperor, 64,
 67

Mayenne, duke of, 182
Mechelen, 209
Mecklenburg, shrines in, 54
Medardus, Saint, 19
Medici, Lorenzo de' (son of Pietro), 135
Mendicant orders, 59, 61, 77
Mennonites, 198, 199, 214, 219
Menocchio (Domenico Scandella), 87–167;
 trials by Inquisition, 88, 89, 91–98,
 106–8, 112–13, 115, 118, 120, 121,
 140, 145, 153–62, 166–67; heretical
 opinions, 89–93, 95–98, 101–3, 112–
 13, 144–46, 150–51, 156–57; cosmogony, 92, 122–25, 156–57; Bible
 used by, 97, 110, 142, 143; new world
 and new life, ideas of, 98, 135, 138–40;
 as Anabaptist, 103–4, 112; books used
 by, 103, 104, 108–22, 126, 127; on God,
 127–31; letter to judges asking forgiveness, 140–42; in prison, 146–48; execution, 167
Mergentheim, 281
Micheus, Jean, 212
Mikoletzky, Leo, 9, 10
Ministeriales, 26, 27, 29, 31, 32, 53–54, 58,
 72
Minnesang, 26, 27
Miracles: hunting associated with, 26–27,
 61, 64; and pilgrimages, 50
Moded, Herman, 210, 213
Moeller, Bernd, 20, 79
Moller, Herbert, 26
Monasteries and convents, number of, 73
Monchy, Michel de, 179, 184, 310 (n. 77)
Monks: as substitutes in penitential system,
 37, 38; contemplative life, 50; mendic-
 ants, 59, 61, 77; in monasteries and
 outside, 77
Mont St. Michel, 62
Montaigne, Michel Eyquem de, 117, 158
Montefalco, Felice da (inquisitor), 91, 94
Monter, E. W., 228, 280, 285
Montereale, Giovan Francesco, count, 149,
 165
Montereale, 88–89; church property in,
 101–2, 300 (n. 4); Menocchio impris-
 oned in, 148–50
Montesquieu, Charles de Secondat, Baron
 de, 65
Moral law and responsibility, 45–46
More, Sir Thomas, 81, 138
Moslems, crusade against, 23, 24
Mulinheim, 17
Münster: shrines in, 54, 55, 57; nobility in,
 56; Anabaptists in, 166, 197, 201, 219
Murner, Thomas, 75
Mysticism, religious, 74

N

Nagerel, Jean, 308 (n. 35)
Namur, 262; witchcraft in, 231
Nelli, Pietro (Andrea da Bergamo), 105, 164
Netherlands, 75; revolts in fourteenth century, 39; women in religious life, 71, 73, 78; cultural influence of, 77; Wonder-year, 191–92; Reformed movement in, 191–93, 195–220 passim; iconoclasm in, 191–97, 206–7, 215–20; political authority in mid-sixteenth century, 203–4, 206; Dutch Revolt, 216, 219; States-General, 217
Neuchatel, witch trials in, 285
Neveux, Hugues, 257, 258
New world (utopia), 135–40
Nicola da Porcia, 106, 107, 110, 120
Nobility. See Aristocrats
Nominalism, 21
Norfolk, witch trials in, 285, 286
Notestein, Wallace, 285
Nuns. See Women: in religious orders
Nuremberg, 28, 76

O

Oaths: sworn on relics, 19, 69–70, 291 (n. 55); importance of, 69–70
Oberkirch, 281
Oberman, Heiko, 49
Ochino, Bernardino, 105
Odilo of St. Médard, 15
Offenburg, 281, 282
Oldenburg, 56
Oostwinkel, 210
Oratoire (perpetual adoration), 180, 183, 190, 309 (n. 50)
Origen, 146
Original sin, 42, 83
Ortenburg, 58, 66
Osnabrück, 56
Ossuaries, 52, 53
Ostroldus, Bishop of Laon, 15
Otgar, Archbishop, 17
Otto of Ötting, 67
Ovid, 123

P

Paderborn, 27
Palatinate: ossuaries in, 52; shrines in, 55; Protestantism in, 65, 66; Calvinist conversion of, 66; Catholic reconversion of, 66
Palestine. See Holy Land

Pallier, Denis, 178
Papacy: and popular religion, 24, 25; Pope as Vicar of Christ, 35, 41; and indulgences, 37, 41, 59
Paris: Catholic demonstrations against Huguenots, 172; Penitents in, 182–83; iconoclasm in, 191, 193
Paschasius Radbertus, Abbot, 18–19
Paul I, Pope, 12
Paul VI, Pope, 318 (n. 50)
Peace of God, 9
Peasants: and aristocrats, relationship of, 56–57; revolt, 70, 71; culture, and dominant classes, 165–66
Peasants' War, 70, 166
Pecquet, Marguerite, 182
Pelagianism, 49
Penitential system, 36–38, 40, 54, 61; substitutes in, 36–37; pilgrimages in, 50
Penitents, 182–83
Pepin the Brief (the Short), 9–12, 289 (n. 17)
Peregrin, Duke, 27
Perpetual adoration. See Oratoire
Peter, Saint, relics of, 16, 17, 18, 35
Petronilla, Saint, 10
Philip II, King of Spain and Netherlands, 203, 204, 206, 214, 217–19, 224
Philip IV, the Fair, King of France, 24, 25
Philip, landgrave of Hesse, 65
Pighino (Pellegrino Baroni), 162–64
Pilgrimages: and cult of saints, 11–12, 13, 17, 289–90 (n. 17); to Rome, 11–12, 23, 24, 36, 294 (n. 76); in Germany, 20–24, 30–37, 49–61 passim, 64–65, 67–69; in Reformation, 21, 61–62; to Holy Land, 22; and massacre of Jews, 29; for Virgin Mary, 31; and purgatory cult, 33, 38; and relics, 35–36; village sites, 53; of children, 62; in Counter-Reformation, 64; Dominican nuns' attitude toward, 74. See also Shrines
Pomerania: shrines in, 54; relic worship in, 59
Pope. See Papacy
Poperinge, 206
Popular religion, 3–7; definition of, 7, 311 (n. 78); study of, 8–9; and pilgrimages, 20–21, 49–61; and crusades, 23; and papacy, 24, 25; political and spiritual allegiance, 24–25; and purgatory cult, 32–34, 38–39; and relics, 35–36; and penitential system, 36–38; and intellectual life, 40–49; urban and rural piety, 50–51; German culture influenced by, 65–70; in Italy, and Reformation, 105–6; pre-Christian ideas in, 162; and

Catholic church in Rouen, 184–90; in Netherlands, hatred of Catholics, 205–6; and *prêche* in Dutch Reformed movement, 211–15, 217

Portogruaro, trial of Menocchio at, 89, 92, 103, 104, 115, 155

Possevino (Possevin), Antonio, 170–71, 175–76, 308 (n. 30)

Prêche (hedgepreaching), 196–205 passim, 209, 211–18, 315 (n. 72)

Predestination, 42, 47, 82–83, 105

Printing, spread of, 126, 127

Prinz, Friedrich, 9, 10, 12

Priuli, Daniele, 100

Protestantism, 71; shrines in Protestant regions, 54, 55, 56, 58; in German culture, 65–67; in France, opposed by Catholic church, 169, 177–78, 187, 189; Bible in, 199. *See also* Calvinism; Huguenots; Lutheranism

Prussia, shrines in, 54

Purgatory, souls in (*Armeseelen*), 51–52

Purgatory cult, 32–34, 38–39, 72

Q

Quedlinburg, convent, 73

Quintanadoines, Antoine de, 180–81

Quintanadoines, Fernande, seigneur de Brétigny, 180, 181

Quintanadoines, Jean de, 180–2, 184, 309 (n. 55)

R

Rabelais, François, 165

Raleigh, Sir Walter, 125–26

Ravenna, 17

Real Presence, doctrine of, 171, 172, 173, 189

Reason, 42, 47, 48

Reckheim, 212

Redi, Francesco, 125

Reformation, 71; pilgrimages in, 21, 61–62; as rejection of social and cultural system, 61; cultural background of, 65, 70; in north and south Germany, 79–86; influence in Italy, 102, 104, 105, 112, 126

Reformed Church in France, 169, 177–78

Reformed movement in Netherlands, 191–93, 195–220 passim, 312–13 (n. 11, n. 13, n. 32), 314 (n. 43, n. 59); charismatic leaders, 196, 197, 202, 205, 211; lay preachers, 208–11, 314 (n. 61). *See also Prêche*

Regensburg, 31

Reichskirche, 63

Reichsministerialen, 63

Reichsritterkantone, 64

Reichstag, 62

Reilkirch, 33, 34

Reininghelst, 195

Relics, 8–19; cult of, 9–14; in churches, 13–14; shortage of, 14–15; trade in, 15–19, 291 (n. 50); powers of, 18–19, 69, 70; oaths sworn on, 19, 69–70, 291 (n. 55); veneration of, 34–35, 37, 59, 69; desacralization of, 35, 36

Renaissance, 21, 70

Reutlingen, 281

Rhine Valley (Rhineland): shrines in, 55; knights in, 62; monasteries and convents in, 73, 75

Richebourg, 210

Rieux, witch trials in, 231, 244, 248, 250, 256, 259; *table*, 245, 318 (n. 41)

Rindfleisch (nobleman), 28–31

Roman saints, 9–14; relics of, 14–19

Rome: pagan celebrations of saints' days, 11; pilgrimages to, 11–12, 23, 24, 36, 294 (n. 76); St. Peter's, 18

Rore, Jacob de, 198

Rottenburg, witch trials in, 278, 280, 281, 287

Rouen: Catholic church activity and popular piety, 168–90; Cathedral Chapter, 170, 173–77, 179, 182, 308 (n. 35); Catholic demonstrations against Huguenots, 172; General Confraternity of the Holy Sacrament (1561), 172–73, 184; Confraternity of the Holy Sacrament (1435), 173; Capuchins in, 174, 175, 182; Huguenots in control of, 173, 178, 181; Jesuits in, 174, 175, 184; Jesuit college (Collège de Bourbon), 175, 176, 178–79, 184; Huguenots in, 176, 177; birth rate, *statistics*, 185–86; offerings collected in churches, *statistics*, 186, 187

Rousbrugge, 209

Rupert, Saint, 67

S

Saarland, witch trials in, 284, 287

Sacramentarian Controversy, 79–81

Saint-Amand, 211, 224; witchcraft in, 230, 231

Saint-André du Cateau, abbey, 241

Saint-Hilaire, 260, 261

Saint-Jacob, Pierre de, 262

St. Ouen, abbey, 176

Saint-Souplet, witchcraft in, 252, 253

Sainte-Union. *See* Holy League

Saints: cults of, 9–14; Roman, 9–14; relics
of, 9–19; pre-Christian practices transferred to, 11; in aristocratic traditions,
26–27; images of, substituted for relics,
35–36, 37; veneration of, 38, 42, 78; as
patrons, 39, 40, 50; intercession of, 49;
shrines of, 54–55, 57–58, 70, 296
(n. 113)
Salem, Mass., witch trials in, 286–88
Salzburg, monasteries and convents in, 73
Sanders, Elizabeth, 180, 182
Savorgnan, Antonio, 99
Saxony: shrines in, 54; nuns in, 73;
brotherhoods in, 77
Scandella, Domenico. *See* Menocchio
Scandella, Stefano, 149–50
Scandella, Ziannuto, 93–94, 95, 146, 150,
160
Scheyern, horse pilgrimages to, 30–31
Schleswig, shrines in, 54
Schwäbisch Gmünd, 281
Scotland, witch trials in, 278
Sebastian, Saint, 19; relics of, 15–16, 18
Sens, 204–5
Seuse (Suso), Heinrich, 27, 74
Severus, Saint, 17
Shrines, 20–86 passim; and relics of saints,
13–14; and miracles of hunting, 27; at
sites of Jewish massacres, 28, 292 (n. 23);
graves of ruling families, 35; of saints,
54–55, 57–58, 70, 296 (n. 113); in-
dulgences in, 59; after Reformation,
61–62. *See also* Pilgrimages
Sickingen, Franz von, 63, 64
Siculo, Giorgio, 107
Siger of Brabant, 42, 43
Silesia: shrines in, 54; Protestantism in, 66
Sin: original, 42, 83; Aquinas's concept of,
44; and forgiveness, 46, 47
Sisters of the Common Life, 79
Smet, Martin de, 209
Society of Jesus. *See* Jesuits
Sodalities, 33
Sogno dil Caravia, Il, 109, 110
Soissons, St. Médard, 15, 19
Sorcerers and sorceresses, 244, 252, 255,
260
Southern, Richard W., 19, 34–35
Spain, confraternities in, 34
Spee, Friedrich von, 279, 287
Stearne, John, 285, 286
Stedinger, peasants of, 56, 296 (n. 119)
Stephen II, Pope, 9
Strassoldo, Francesco di, 99
Stuttgart, 74
Styria, 66
Suffolk, witch trials in, 285

Swabia, 79; nobility in, 53, 54; shrines in,
55, 73; knights in, 62; convents in, 73, 75
Swanson, Guy E., 69
Sweden, witch trials in, 285
Switzerland: convents in, 73; Protestantism
in, 81, 82; witch trials in, 285

T

Taffin, Jean, 220
Tauler, Johannes, 74
Teutonic Knights, 59, 61
Theodore (papal notary), 15
Theodorus, 16
Theodulf of Orléans, 289 (n. 1)
Theology, confessional and pastoral, 49
Thirty Years' War, 66, 224
Tholozan, Antoine, 183
Thomas, Keith, 277
Thuringia, 71; shrines in, 55
Töpfer, Bernard, 9
Torregiani family, 99
Tournai, 199, 201, 205, 206–7; witchcraft
in, 224, 230
Tours, St. Martin, shrine of, 11–12
Transubstantiation, dogma of, 36
Trevor-Roper, H. R., 226
Trier, witch trials in, 284
Turks as threat to Europe, 61
Turner, Victor, 50–51

U

Udine, 99, 110, 150
Umritte (horse pilgrimages), 30–31, 32, 53,
54, 61, 65, 68
Universale allegrezza dell'abondantia, L',
139
Urban II, Pope, 22, 37
Utopia (new world), 135–40

V

Vaernewijk, Marcus van, 192, 198–99,
204, 207, 212, 213
Valenciennes, 199, 212, 224, 264; witch-
craft in, 230, 231, 253
Venard, Marc, 182
Venice (state), 98–101; peasant unrest in,
99–100
Verlinden, Charles, 222
Vespucci, Amerigo, 135
Vézelay, 19
Viaro, Stefano, 100–101
Victor of Rouen, 9
Villars, duke of, 184
Villers-au-Bois, witchcraft in, 231

Villette, P., 226, 231, 232, 253, 261
Vincent of Beauvais, 116
Virgin Mary. *See* Mary, Virgin
Vlameng, Jan de
Voghele, Lodewijck de, 199
Voragine, Jacopo da, *Il Lucendario de Santi (Legenda aurea)*, 109

W

Waldensians: witch trials of, 224; *statistics*, 228, 229; as sorcerers, 252
Wars of Religion, 169, 177, 186, 189; and witchcraft, 226
Watelet, Maurice, 209
Weber, Max, 196, 197, 202
Welf party, 26
Weingarten, shrine in, 31
Westphalia: shrines in, 54, 55, 57; nobility in, 56
Weyer, Johann, 278–79
Will as collective process, 48. *See also* Free will
William I, Prince of Orange, 204, 214, 220
William IV, duke of Bavaria, 65
William of Ockham, 21–22, 24–25, 32, 44–48, 83
Wimpfeling, Jacob, 64
Witchcraft, 166; in France, 174, 280, 286, 307 (n. 22); in Catholic Low countries, 222, 224, 226, 228–30, 255; in Hainaut, 222, 226, 230, 232; in Nord, 224, 226, 228; women and men as witches, 226, 228, 272–73, *tables*, 228, 229, 230, 282, 283, 317 (n. 28); in England, 231, 249, 278, 280, 285–86; as satanic religion, 231–32, 261–62; witches as scapegoats, 259, 265, 270–71, 273–74; studies of, 277–78; and domino theory, 277–88; torture in trials, 278–80, 317 (n. 28); in Germany, 278–82, 284–85, *tables*, 282, 283; children as witches, 282, *table*, 283, 317 (n. 32); in Salem, Mass., 286–88
Witchcraft in the Cambrésis, 221–76; trial procedures and testimony, 231–32,

238–44, 248–50; trials, *tables*, 233, 245, 246–47; witnesses at trials, *table*, 234–37; villagers in witch hunts, 250–52, 258, 260, 262–63, 273, 274; popular fear of witchcraft, 252–55; Counter-Reformation related to, 255, 256, 259, 261–65, 267, 275; economic and demographic changes affecting, 257–58; and rural acculturation, 257–63, 267–68; sexual offenses related to, 261, 264–66, 271; violence and aggression in, 263–66, 268–71
Wittenberg, 194
Women: in religious orders, 28, 61, 71–75; in religious life, 70–79; aristocrats as nuns, 73–75, 78; in lay religious work, 77–79; in Protestantism, 82; as witches, 226, 228, 272–73, *tables*, 228, 229, 230, 317 (n. 28)
Worsley, Peter, 202
Württemberg, shrines in, 58
Würzburg: chapel of Virgin Mary, 67; witch trials in, 282, 287, *table*, 283

X

Xhoka, Leonard, 209

Y

Year of Jubilee (1300), 23, 24, 36, 54, 78
Ypres, 200, 209, 210

Z

Zacharias, Pope, 10, 11
Zampollo (Il sogno dil Caravia), 109, 110
Zeeden, Ernst Walter, 65–66
Zurich, 192
Zwingli, Ulrich, controversy with Luther, 79–81
Zwinglianism, 61

3 5282 00058 6050